Master Microsoft® Word 2000

V I S U A L L Y™

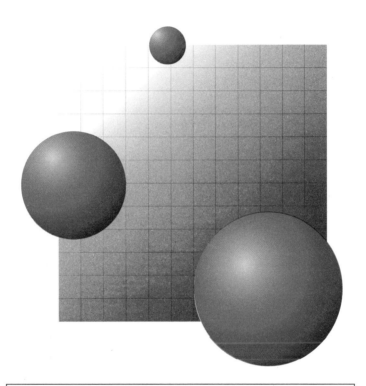

IDG's 3-D Visual Series

Shelley O'Hara

IDG BOOKS WORLDWIDE

IDG Books Worldwide, Inc.
An International Data Group Company
Foster City, CA • Indianapolis, IN • Chicago, IL • New York, NY

Master Microsoft® Word 2000 VISUALLY™

Published by
IDG Books Worldwide, Inc.
An International Data Group Company
919 E. Hillsdale Blvd., Suite 400
Foster City, CA 94404
www.idgbooks.com (IDG Books Worldwide Web site)

Library of Congress Catalog Card Number: 99-26495

ISBN: 0-7645-6046-8

Printed in the United States of America

10 9 8 7 6 5 4 3 2 1

1P/RQ/RS/ZZ/FC

Distributed in the United States by IDG Books Worldwide, Inc.

Distributed by CDG Books Canada Inc. for Canada; by Transworld Publishers Limited in the United Kingdom; by IDG Norge Books for Norway; by IDG Sweden Books for Sweden; by Woodslane Pty. Ltd. for Australia; by Woodslane (NZ) Ltd. for New Zealand; by TransQuest Publishers Pte Ltd. for Singapore, Malaysia, Thailand, Indonesia, and Hong Kong; by ICG Muse, Inc. for Japan; by Norma Comunicaciones S.A. for Colombia; by Intersoft for South Africa; by Le Monde en Tique for France; by International Thomson Publishing for Germany, Austria and Switzerland; by Distribuidora Cuspide for Argentina; by Livraria Cultura for Brazil; by Ediciones ZETA S.C.R. Ltda. for Peru; by WS Computer Publishing Corporation, Inc., for the Philippines; by Contemporanea de Ediciones for Venezuela; by Express Computer Distributors for the Caribbean and West Indies; by Micronesia Media Distributor, Inc. for Micronesia; by Grupo Editorial Norma S.A. for Guatemala; by Chips Computadoras S.A. de C.V. for Mexico; by Editorial Norma de Panama S.A. for Panama; by American Bookshops for Finland. Authorized Sales Agent: Anthony Rudkin Associates for the Middle East and North Africa.

For general information on IDG Books Worldwide's books in the U.S., please call our Consumer Customer Service department at 800-762-2974. For reseller information, including discounts and premium sales, please call our Reseller Customer Service department at 800-434-3422.

For information on where to purchase IDG Books Worldwide's books outside the U.S., please contact our International Sales department at 317-596-5530 or fax 317-596-5692.

For consumer information on foreign language translations, please contact our Customer Service department at 800-434-3422, fax 317-596-5692, or e-mail rights@idgbooks.com.

For information on licensing foreign or domestic rights, please phone +1-650-655-3109.

For sales inquiries and special prices for bulk quantities, please contact our Sales department at 650-655-3200 or write to the address above.

For information on using IDG Books Worldwide's books in the classroom or for ordering examination copies, please contact our Educational Sales department at 800-434-2086 or fax 317-596-5499.

For press review copies, author interviews, or other publicity information, please contact our Public Relations department at 650-655-3000 or fax 650-655-3299.

For authorization to photocopy items for corporate, personal, or educational use, please contact Copyright Clearance Center, 222 Rosewood Drive, Danvers, MA 01923, or fax 978-750-4470.

ABOUT IDG BOOKS WORLDWIDE

Welcome to the world of IDG Books Worldwide.

IDG Books Worldwide, Inc., is a subsidiary of International Data Group, the world's largest publisher of computer-related information and the leading global provider of information services on information technology. IDG was founded more than 30 years ago by Patrick J. McGovern and now employs more than 9,000 people worldwide. IDG publishes more than 290 computer publications in over 75 countries. More than 90 million people read one or more IDG publications each month.

Launched in 1990, IDG Books Worldwide is today the #1 publisher of best-selling computer books in the United States. We are proud to have received eight awards from the Computer Press Association in recognition of editorial excellence and three from Computer Currents' First Annual Readers' Choice Awards. Our best-selling ...For Dummies® series has more than 50 million copies in print with translations in 31 languages. IDG Books Worldwide, through a joint venture with IDG's Hi-Tech Beijing, became the first U.S. publisher to publish a computer book in the People's Republic of China. In record time, IDG Books Worldwide has become the first choice for millions of readers around the world who want to learn how to better manage their businesses.

Our mission is simple: Every one of our books is designed to bring extra value and skill-building instructions to the reader. Our books are written by experts who understand and care about our readers. The knowledge base of our editorial staff comes from years of experience in publishing, education, and journalism — experience we use to produce books to carry us into the new millennium. In short, we care about books, so we attract the best people. We devote special attention to details such as audience, interior design, use of icons, and illustrations. And because we use an efficient process of authoring, editing, and desktop publishing our books electronically, we can spend more time ensuring superior content and less time on the technicalities of making books.

You can count on our commitment to deliver high-quality books at competitive prices on topics you want to read about. At IDG Books Worldwide, we continue in the IDG tradition of delivering quality for more than 30 years. You'll find no better book on a subject than one from IDG Books Worldwide.

John Kilcullen
Chairman and CEO
IDG Books Worldwide, Inc.

Steven Berkowitz
President and Publisher
IDG Books Worldwide, Inc.

*Eighth Annual
Computer Press
Awards ≥1992*

*Ninth Annual
Computer Press
Awards ≥1993*

*Tenth Annual
Computer Press
Awards ≥1994*

*Eleventh Annual
Computer Press
Awards ≥1995*

CREDITS

Acquisitions Editor
Michael Roney

Development Editors
Steve Anderson
Katharine Dvorak

Technical Editor
David Haskins

Copy Editors
Michael D. Welch
Amanda Kaufmann
Nicole LeClerc

Book Designer
maran Graphics

Production
Publication Services, Inc.

Proofreading and Indexing
Publication Services, Inc.

To Raymond Neff Ball, my dad

ACKNOWLEDGMENTS

Thanks to Michael Roney for inviting me to do this project, to Keith Underdahl for undertaking the arduous task of reshooting all the figures, to David Haskins for his keen technical review, and to Steve Anderson, Katie Dvorak, and Michael Welch for their editing work.

MICROSOFT® WORD 2000

WHAT'S INSIDE

GETTING STARTED

TABLE OF CONTENTS

CHANGING THE LOOK OF YOUR DOCUMENT

TABLE OF CONTENTS

USING DESKTOP PUBLISHING TECHNIQUES

TABLE OF CONTENTS

TABLE OF CONTENTS

IV — CREATING SPECIAL DOCUMENTS

19 INSERTING DOCUMENT REFERENCES

20 GROUP EDITING

21 USING DATA FROM OTHER APPLICATIONS

TABLE OF CONTENTS

WORD AND THE INTERNET

MANAGING AND CUSTOMIZING WORD

24 MANAGING DOCUMENTS (Continued)

25 SETTING UP SHORTCUTS

26 CUSTOMIZING WORD

TABLE OF CONTENTS

SECTION I

1 WORD BASICS

2 CREATING A NEW DOCUMENT

GETTING STARTED

WHAT YOU CAN DO WITH WORD

Word is the most popular word-processing program for Windows. With this program, you can create just about any type of document you want — memos, letters, résumés, reports, booklets, manuscripts, form letters, and more.

A word processing program such as Word includes many features to make creating, editing, and changing the look of the document as easy as possible.

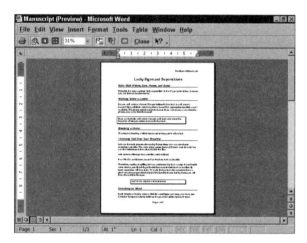

Editing Features

With Word, you can easily make changes to the text. You can move, copy, search for, and replace text. You can also easily insert or delete text.

Formatting Features

Formatting means to change the look of your document, and Word includes numerous features for formatting, from changing the look of characters to enhancing the look of the overall page.

Proofreading Tools

You can not only check spelling with Word, but also look for errors in grammar.

Desktop Publishing with Word

As you become more proficient with Word, you can explore some of the more advanced features such as creating columns, tables, and sections.

Form Letters and Labels

When you want to send the same letter to several people, but personalize each one, you can create a form letter. You can also create mailing labels to make mass mailings as easy as possible.

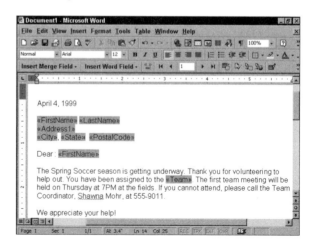

Web Pages

Word includes many features for creating, editing, and formatting documents designed for the World Wide Web. You can use the Web Publishing Wizard, and you can use any of the Web templates included with Word.

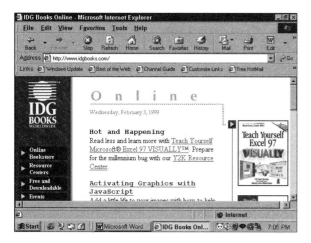

File Management Tools

Each time you save a document, you create a new file on your system. To help keep files organized, you can use Word to delete, rename, copy, and move files. You can also set up folders.

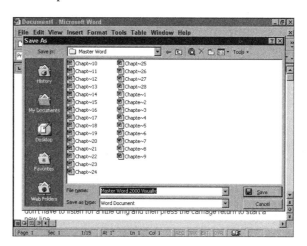

Customizing Word

You can make changes to how Word works so that the program works best in your specific job.

START AND EXIT WORD

The first step in using any program is to get it started. Starting is pretty simple: you just click a few commands. What can be confusing is that everyone's system can be set up differently. The programs on your system may be different than your neighbor's. The place you put your Word program icon may be different than your coworker's. It's like finding your car keys.

Once you find those keys — that is, the program icon — you are set.

The flip side of starting is exiting. When you finish working in Word, you can exit the program. You shouldn't just turn off your PC with Word still running because that could ruin your document and program files. Instead, be sure to save all the documents you've created. If you try to exit without saving,

Word will remind you. (You can get more information on saving in Chapter 3.) After all the documents are saved, you can exit Word.

Note: If you have not made a change since installing Word, skip this step. The program item is added to the Programs folder, and you should see the Word program icon.

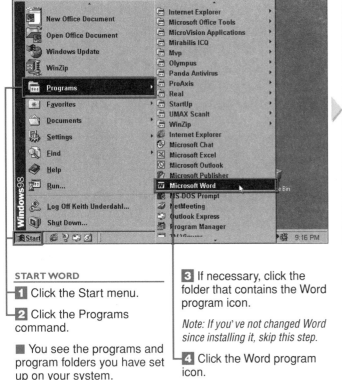

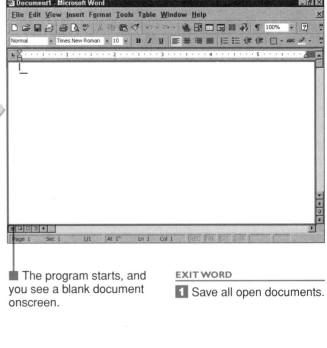

START WORD

1 Click the Start menu.

2 Click the Programs command.

■ You see the programs and program folders you have set up on your system.

3 If necessary, click the folder that contains the Word program icon.

Note: If you've not changed Word since installing it, skip this step.

4 Click the Word program icon.

■ The program starts, and you see a blank document onscreen.

EXIT WORD

1 Save all open documents.

6

What other ways can I use to start Word?

 You can also create a shortcut icon for Word and place it on the desktop. Then you can double-click this icon to start the program. For help on creating shortcut icons, see Chapter 25.

What if I can't find my program icon?

 When you (or someone else) installed Word, a program folder and icon should have been added to your Start menu. If you don't have this icon, you can start the program by finding the program icon. Double-click My Computer. Then open the folder that contains Word. (You may have to open several folders until you see the Word icon). Double-click the program icon.

How can I start Word and open a document?

 If you recently worked on a particular Word document and want to open that document and start the program, you can do so using the Windows Documents command. Click the Start button and then click Documents. Click the document you want to open.

What happens if I forget to save before exiting?

 If you forget to save before exiting, Word prompts you to save. You can click Yes to save the document, No to close without saving, or Cancel to go back to the document.

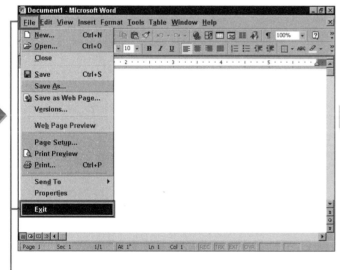

2 Click File.

3 Click the Exit command.

■ You return to the Windows desktop.

UNDERSTAND PARTS OF THE WORD SCREEN

When you start Word, you see a blank document onscreen. You can probably figure out what the big blank area of the screen is. It's like a blank piece of paper. This is where you type the text of your document.

In addition to the "writing area," notice the various tools along the top, bottom, and sides of the window. You can use these items to select commands, move around the document, change how the document is displayed, and more. The screen also

displays information about the current document, such as the page number and document name. Before you get started, take some time to familiarize yourself with the onscreen tools.

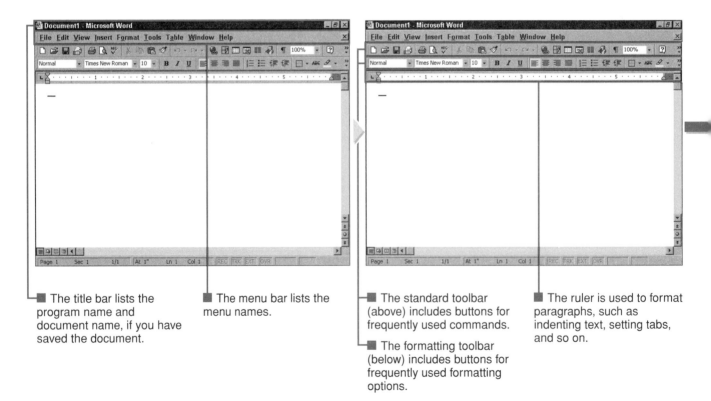

■ The title bar lists the program name and document name, if you have saved the document.

■ The menu bar lists the menu names.

■ The standard toolbar (above) includes buttons for frequently used commands.

■ The formatting toolbar (below) includes buttons for frequently used formatting options.

■ The ruler is used to format paragraphs, such as indenting text, setting tabs, and so on.

How do a I select a command from the menu bar?

 For help on using the menu bar to select a command, see the section "Select Menu Commands" later in this chapter.

Do I have to keep all these bars displayed?

You can turn off the display of most onscreen elements. To do so, open the View menu and select the Full Screen command. You see a plain white background and the Full Screen toolbar. To turn the menu bar, title bar, status bar, and toolbars back on, click the Close Full Screen button.

What does the ruler show?

The ruler shows the current margins as well as any tabs you have set manually. Use the ruler to make paragraph formatting changes. Chapter 8 covers these changes in more detail.

How do I use a toolbar button?

To use a toolbar button, click the button. For a table of what each tool does, see the task "Word 2000 Toolbars" later in this chapter.

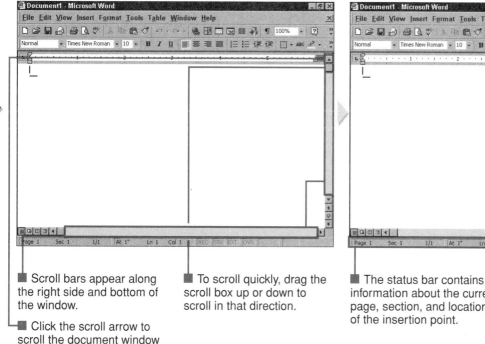

■ Scroll bars appear along the right side and bottom of the window.

■ Click the scroll arrow to scroll the document window in that direction.

■ To scroll quickly, drag the scroll box up or down to scroll in that direction.

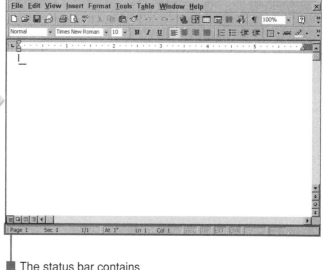

■ The status bar contains information about the current page, section, and location of the insertion point.

WORK WITH THE WORD WINDOW

If you've used Windows before, you should be familiar with how to manipulate windows. When you are working in Word, keep in mind that you have two windows open: the program window and the document window(s). Each window has its own set of controls.

You can move, resize, maximize, minimize, and close the program window. You can do the same for the document window. You might want to do this so you can see other program or document windows.

Keep in mind that when you close a document window, you simply close that document. But when you close the Word window, you are really exiting the program.

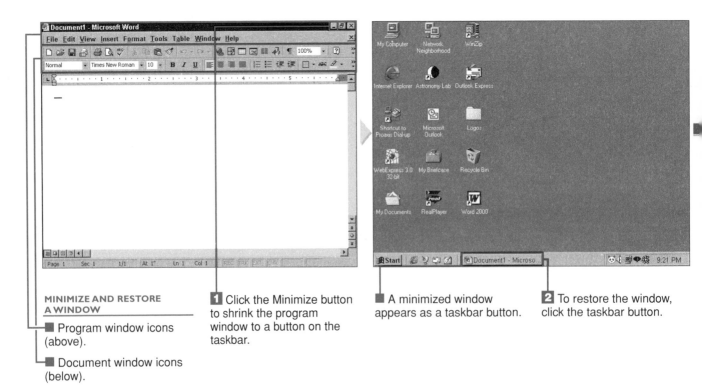

MINIMIZE AND RESTORE A WINDOW

■ Program window icons (above).

■ Document window icons (below).

1 Click the Minimize button to shrink the program window to a button on the taskbar.

■ A minimized window appears as a taskbar button.

2 To restore the window, click the taskbar button.

TIPS

How do I drag to resize a window?

 You can resize a window by dragging any of its borders. If you don't see a border it's because the window is maximized (as big as it can get). You can restore the window and then resize.

How do I move a window?

To move a window, point to the title bar and then drag (click and hold the mouse button down) the window to the location you want. Keep in mind that you cannot move a window that is maximized.

How do a I scroll a window?

 To scroll a window, click the scroll arrows to scroll in that direction, or drag the scroll box. You can scroll both vertically and horizontally in the window.

What about the Control menu icon?

 You can use the little icon in the upper-left corner to access Window commands for moving, resizing, and controlling the window size. Click this icon and then select the command you want.

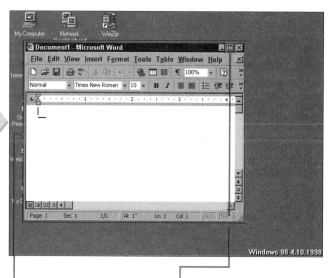

RESIZE AND MAXIMIZE A WINDOW

1 To make a window smaller than the entire screen, click the Restore button.

■ The window now has borders and does not fill the entire screen. The Restore button changes to a Maximize button.

2 To maximize the window, click the Maximize button.

SELECT MENU COMMANDS

When you want Word to do something, you have to select the command you want. Word organizes its many commands into different menu categories, which appear in the menu bar. The easiest way to select a command is to use the mouse, as covered in the how-to section.

You can also use the keyboard if you prefer to keep your hands on the keys. Press the Alt key to activate the menu. Press the key letter of the menu name. The key letter appears underlined in the menu bar. For instance, to open the File menu, press F (Alt+F). The menu drops down, and you see a list of commands. Press the key letter for the command you want. Again, the key letter is underlined.

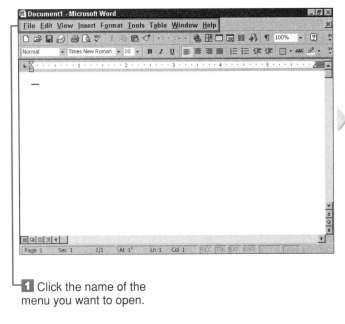

1 Click the name of the menu you want to open.

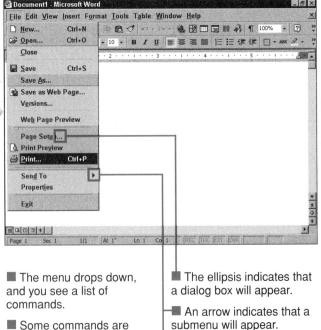

■ The menu drops down, and you see a list of commands.

■ Some commands are executed right away. Other commands display a submenu or a dialog box.

■ The ellipsis indicates that a dialog box will appear.

■ An arrow indicates that a submenu will appear.

2 Click the command you want to execute.

Why don't I see all the commands?

When you first open a menu, you see the most commonly used commands. If you keep the pointer on the menu name, the complete menu will be displayed in a second or two. You can also click the down arrow at the bottom of the menu to display all the commands. This feature is new in Word 2000.

What keyboard shortcuts can I use?

To help you learn the shortcuts, Word displays the associated keyboard shortcut and toolbar button next to each command. You can use either the keyboard shortcut or the toolbar button as a shortcut.

How do I display a shortcut menu?

To display a shortcut menu, click the right mouse button on the item you want to modify. For instance, to modify the toolbar, right-click this item. To display a shortcut menu for selected text, right-click the selected text. A shortcut menu pops up. Click the command you want.

Why are some commands gray?

If a command is gray, it means it is not available. For instance, if you try to paste text but have not first cut or copied text, the Paste command (in the Edit menu) is gray.

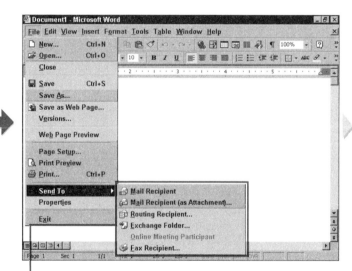

3 If you see a submenu, select the command you want from this menu.

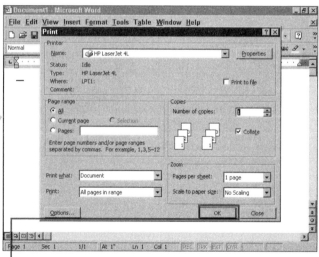

4 If you see a dialog box, select the dialog box options and then click the OK button. For more help on dialog boxes, see "Make Selections in a Dialog Box" next in this chapter.

MAKE SELECTIONS IN A DIALOG BOX

To execute some commands, Word needs additional information. For example, if you print a document, Word needs to know how many copies you want, which printer to use, and other options you may want to change. When other options for carrying out a command, Word displays a dialog box. Make your selections and then click the OK button to carry out the command.

You'll encounter dialog boxes quite a bit when using Word, and although the options differ, they all work the same way. Once you learn how to make selections for each type of item, you won't have any trouble figuring out what each option does or how to select it.

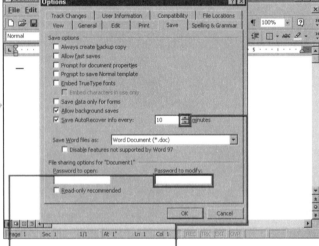

■ Some dialog boxes have tabs of options. To select the tab you want, click the tab.

■ Click a checkbox to check (turn on) or uncheck (turn off) the option. If a dialog box has more than one checkbox, you can check as many as you want.

■ Click in the text box and then type the entry. If the text box already contains an entry, drag across it to select the entry and then press Delete.

■ A spin box is a type of text box with spin arrows next to it. You can type an entry in the spin box, or you can click the spin arrows to scroll through the text box values.

What about other buttons?

Some dialog boxes also have other buttons that display other options. For instance, you might see a button that says More or Advanced. Click the button to display these options.

How do I close a dialog box without making a selection?

If you open a dialog box by mistake or if you change your mind, you can close a dialog box without carrying out the command. To do so, click the Cancel button or press the Esc key.

How can I find out what an option does?

If you don't know what a dialog box option does, you can get help with an option. Point to the item and click the right mouse button. A pop-up menu appears. Select "What's This?" In both cases, you see a pop-up explanation of the dialog box option.

What are alert boxes?

For some actions, you may see an alert box or a message box. For instance, if there's an error, you may see alert box. Read the message and then follow the appropriate directions.

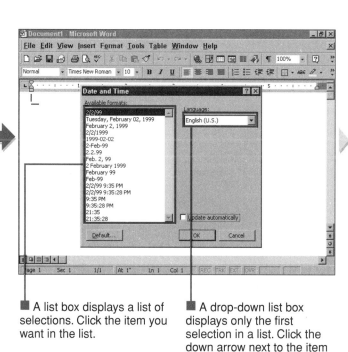

■ A list box displays a list of selections. Click the item you want in the list.

■ A drop-down list box displays only the first selection in a list. Click the down arrow next to the item to display other selections. Then click the item you want.

■ Click the option button to turn it on (appears darkened) or off (blank). You can select only one option button in each group of option buttons.

■ Click the OK command button to confirm and carry out the command. Click the Cancel command button to cancel the command.

WORD 2000 TOOLBARS

Opening a menu, finding the command you want, and clicking the command takes time. As a faster way to select the most commonly used commands, Word displays two toolbars with buttons for these commands. Rather than select a menu command, you can click the toolbar button.

The top toolbar is called the Standard toolbar and includes buttons for working with files, editing text, and inserting items such as tables and worksheets. The Formatting toolbar, as you might guess from the name, includes buttons for formatting your document. Here you find buttons for applying a style,

changing the font, making text bold, changing the alignment, and more.

To use a toolbar button, click the appropriate button. Word carries out the selected command or feature. To use a toolbar list, click the down arrow next to the button. Word displays a list. Click the option you want.

Standard Toolbar Buttons

Button	Name	Function
	New	Creates a new document.
	Save	Saves the document.
	E-mail	Creates an email message.
	Print	Prints the document onscreen.
	Print Preview	Displays a preview of the document.
	Spelling and Grammar	Checks your spelling and grammar.
	Format Painter	Copies and pastes formatting.
	Insert Hyperlink	Inserts a link to a file or Web address.
	Tables and Borders	Displays a toolbar with buttons for formatting and working with tables and paragraph borders.
	Insert Table	Inserts a table.
	Insert Microsoft Excel Worksheet	Inserts a Microsoft Excel Worksheet.
	Columns	Formats the selected section into columns.
	Drawing	Displays the Drawing toolbar.
	Document Map	Displays a separate pane with an outline of your document headings; you can use this document map to navigate through your document.
100%	Zoom	Zooms the document.
?	Microsoft Word Help	Displays help.

Formatting Toolbar Buttons

Button	Name	Function
Normal ▼	Style	Displays a style list; click the style you want.
Times New Roman ▼	Font	Displays a font list; click the font you want.
10 ▼	Font Size	Displays a size list; click the size you want.
B	Bold	Makes selected text bold, or turns on bold.
I	Italic	Makes selected text italic, or turns on italic.
U	Underline	Underlines selected text , or turns on underlining.
≣	Align Left	Left-aligns selected paragraph(s).
≣	Center	Centers selected paragraph(s).
≣	Align Right	Right-aligns selected paragraph(s).
≣	Justify	Justifies selected paragraph(s).
≣	Numbering	Creates a numbered list.
≣	Bullets	Creates a bulleted list.
镇	Decrease Indent	Decreases the indent of the selected paragraph(s).
镇	Increase Indent	Increases the indent of the selected paragraph(s).
▦ ▼	Borders	Adds a border around the current paragraph; you can select a different type of border from the drop-down list.
✐ ▼	Highlight	Highlights the selected text; the default color is yellow (you can select another color from the drop-down list).
A ▼	Font Color	Changes the color of the selected text; the default color is red (you can select another color by clicking the down-arrow next to the button and then clicking the color you want).

To find out what a button does, put the mouse pointer on the edge of the button. The button name (called a ToolTip) appears.

You can turn off the toolbars if you don't use them. Open the View menu and select the Toolbars command. You see a list of toolbars. If a checkmark appears next to a toolbar name, it is on. Select the toolbar you want to hide to uncheck it.

You can move a toolbar from its location (docked at the top of the window). Put the pointer on part of the toolbar, but not on a button. Drag the toolbar to the location you want. You can also resize a toolbar when it is not docked. To do so, drag the border.

In addition the Standard and Formatting toolbars, Word has several other toolbars. Usually these come on when appropriate.

For example, when you are creating a mail merge document, the Merge toolbar appears. You can also open the View menu, select the Toolbars command, and then select any of the toolbars you want displayed. (Follow the same procedure to turn off a toolbar.)

GET HELP WITH THE OFFICE ASSISTANT

Word is a complex program with a lot of options. For the most part, you'll quickly learn the features and commands you use day after day and won't need much help remembering how to perform common tasks. For features used less often, though, you may need a little reminder. If this book isn't handy, you can use the Office Assistant to get help.

The Office Assistant appears in a little window onscreen, and you can type questions or topics to get help. You might want to keep the Office Assistant on all the time. It displays helpful information as you perform actions. For instance, if you type *Dear John:* and press Enter, the Office Assistant asks whether you want help typing a letter. You can choose to get help or ignore the assistant.

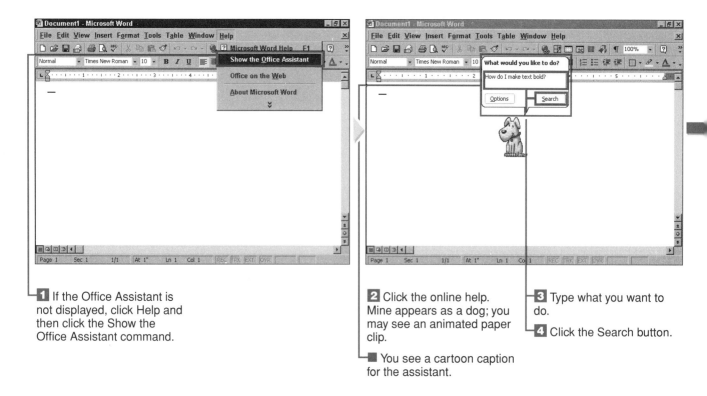

1 If the Office Assistant is not displayed, click Help and then click the Show the Office Assistant command.

2 Click the online help. Mine appears as a dog; you may see an animated paper clip.

■ You see a cartoon caption for the assistant.

3 Type what you want to do.

4 Click the Search button.

Can I customize the Office Assistant?

 Yes. You can change whatever character or icon is used in the Office Assistant. Click the Options button and then click the Gallery tab. Use the Next and Back buttons to select the character you want to use. Then click OK.

How do I close the help window?

 To close the window, click the Close (X) button.

What other kind of help is available?

You can also look up help in a table of contents or index, which is covered in the next in this chapter.

How do I turn off the Office Assistant?

If you don't use the Office Assistant, you can turn it off. To do so, select Help⇨Hide the Office Assistant.

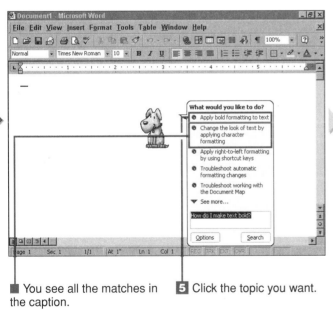

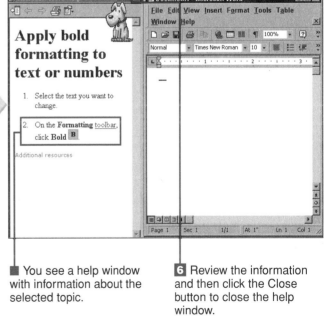

■ You see all the matches in the caption.

5 Click the topic you want.

■ You see a help window with information about the selected topic.

6 Review the information and then click the Close button to close the help window.

LOOK UP A HELP TOPIC

I f you aren't partial to animated cartoon characters, you can use the more traditional method to get help. This help system works a lot like a book. You can look up topics in the table of contents, or in the index. Unlike a book, however, you can also use the help system to search for a topic. You can also use the Answer Wizard, which is similiar to using the Office Assistant, to type a question. This task covers using the table

of contents. See the next task for help with using the index and searching.

In the Help window, you can use the references to get additional information. Any topics that appear in a different color and are underlined are links to other pages of information. Click this link to view the related information. If you see other topics indicated with a chevron, you can display these topics by clicking the reference. If you see a

dotted line under a word or phrase, it means that you can display a pop-up definition for the term. Point to the term and click the mouse button. Finally, if you want Word to show you how to perform a task, click the Show Me icon.

Note: To get the traditional help window to appear, you must turn off the assistant. Click the assistant and then click Options. Uncheck the Use the Office Assistant checkbox and then click OK.

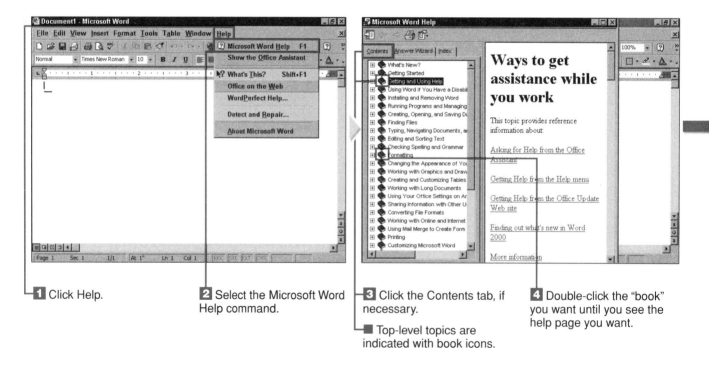

1 Click Help.

2 Select the Microsoft Word Help command.

3 Click the Contents tab, if necessary.

■ Top-level topics are indicated with book icons.

4 Double-click the "book" you want until you see the help page you want.

TIPS

What is the keyboard shortcut?

You can press F1 to get help. If the Office Assistant is on, you see this tool. If you have not turned on the Assistant, you see the help window.

What's the Hide button used for?

If you want to hide the half of the dialog box with the tabs and just display the help information, click the Hide button. To redisplay the tabs, click the Show button.

How do clear a search?

To clear a search, click the Clear button.

Can I scroll through the index?

If you want, you can scroll through the list of keywords. Simply click the scroll arrows in Step 2 of the dialog box area. You can also type a few characters to scroll to keywords that start with those letters.

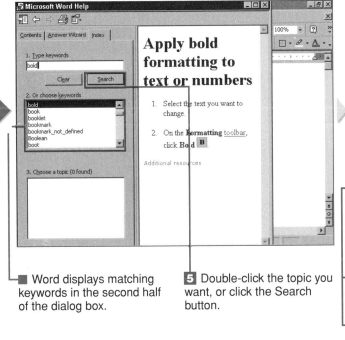

■ Word displays matching keywords in the second half of the dialog box.

5 Double-click the topic you want, or click the Search button.

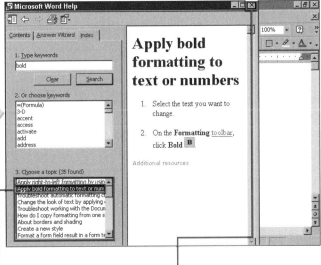

■ Word displays matching topics in the bottom half of the dialog box.

6 Double-click the topic you want.

7 Review the help information and then click the Close (X) button to close the help window.

HOW TO CREATE A NEW DOCUMENT

You can use Word to create any type of document, from the simple to the complex. You can create a short one-page memo or a 28-chapter technical book. The process of creating the document is basically the same: you type the text.

Type Text

Typing text is probably the easiest thing to do in Word (unless you have writer's block!). You simply press the keys on the keyboard, and the characters appear in your document. If you make a mistake, you can delete the characters and retype.

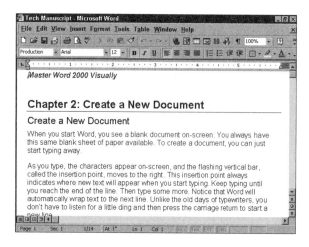

Move Around the Document

You need a way to move around the document to review what you've typed and make changes if needed. You can use the mouse or the keyboard to move around. Plus, Word includes some shortcuts for navigating around:

▸ Use the Go To command to go to a particular page.

▸ Use the Document Map feature to view the overall document structure in one pane and the document in the other.

▸ Set up bookmarks to quickly go to a particular section.

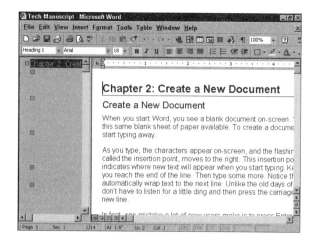

Insert Returns, Page Breaks, Tabs

You can use the characters on the keyboard to insert numbers and letters. Press Enter to insert a paragraph break. Press Tab to insert a tab. What else can you insert? You can also insert the date and time, page breaks, symbols, and special characters.

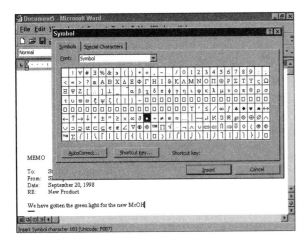

Use Shortcuts for Typing

Word tries to take as much of the hassle out of typing as possible. One of Word's handiest features is AutoText. You can find common document entries (like a signature line for a letter) already set up as AutoText entries. Plus, you can create your own. You can quickly insert this text without typing the whole word or phrase.

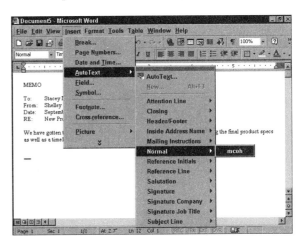

CREATE A NEW DOCUMENT

When you start Word, you see a blank document onscreen. You always have this same blank sheet of paper available. To create a document, you can just start typing.

As you type, the characters appear onscreen, and the flashing vertical bar, called the insertion point, moves to the right. This insertion point always indicates where new text will appear when you start typing. Keep typing until you reach the end of the line. Then type some more. Notice that Word automatically wraps text to the next line. Unlike the old days of typewriters, you don't have to listen for a little ding and then press the carriage return to start a new line.

In fact, one mistake a lot of new users make is to press Enter at the end of each line. You shouldn't do this because if you have to add or delete text, your lines won't automatically readjust. You should press Enter only at the end of a paragraph or when you want to insert a blank line.

When you want to start another document, you open a new blank document. You can base documents on different templates. For information on other templates, see Chapter 17.

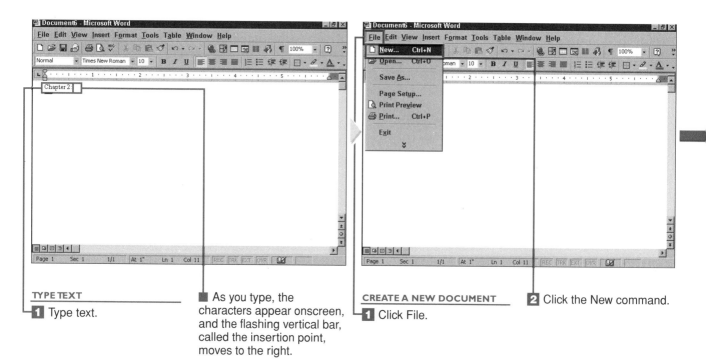

TYPE TEXT

1 Type text.

■ As you type, the characters appear onscreen, and the flashing vertical bar, called the insertion point, moves to the right.

CREATE A NEW DOCUMENT

1 Click File.

2 Click the New command.

TIPS

What happens when I press Enter?

 Word inserts a hidden paragraph mark when you press Enter. If you want to see where the breaks occur, click the Show/Hide ¶ button in the Standard toolbar.

How do I delete a hard return?

Move the insertion point before the return and press Delete. Or place the insertion point after the return and press Backspace.

What is a template?

 A template is a predesigned document that can include text and formatting. For more information on templates, see Chapter 17.

What shortcut can I use to create a new document?

 To create a document based on the default template, click the New button.

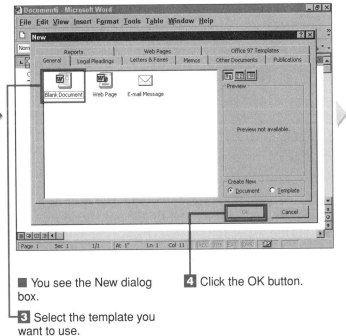

■ You see the New dialog box.

3 Select the template you want to use.

4 Click the OK button.

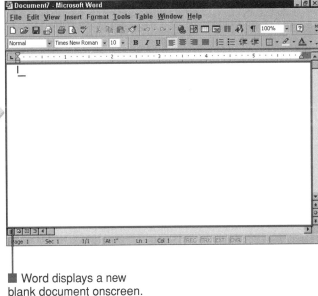

■ Word displays a new blank document onscreen.

MOVE AROUND THE DOCUMENT

The insertion point is the "You Are Here" arrow. When you want to add or delete text, start by moving the insertion point to where you want to make the change. When you want to select text, move the insertion point to the start of the text. You can use either the mouse or the keyboard to move the insertion point.

To use the mouse, point to where you want to move the pointer and click. Remember that the insertion point (the vertical flashing line) and the mouse

pointer (the I-beam) are two separate items. You can't just point to the spot you want. You have to point and click to place the insertion point.

In a long document, you may simply want to scroll through the text without moving the insertion point.

The vertical line in the page area indicates the end of the document. You cannot move the insertion point past this indicator. If you click beyond this line, nothing happens. Word doesn't permit the insertion

point to move where nothing exists. Only after you enter text or spaces onscreen can you move the insertion point.

If you prefer to keep your hands on the keyboard, use the arrow keys and other key combinations to move the insertion point. Table 2-1 lists the common movement keys. Note that if the key combination is joined with a plus sign, you must press and hold the first key, and then press the second key.

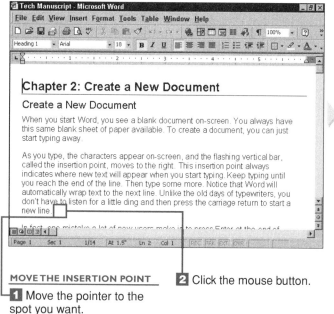

MOVE THE INSERTION POINT

1 Move the pointer to the spot you want.

2 Click the mouse button.

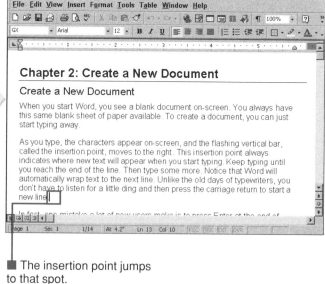

■ The insertion point jumps to that spot.

Keyboard Movement Keys

To move	Press
One character right	→
One character left	←
One line up	↑
One line down	↓
To the beginning of the line	Home
To the end of the line	End
To the beginning of the document	Ctrl+Home
To the end of the document	Ctrl+End

To move	Press
One word left	Ctrl+←
One word right	Ctrl+→
One paragraph down	Ctrl+↓
One paragraph up	Ctrl+↑
One screen up	PgUp
One screen down	PgDn
Bottom of the screen	Ctrl+PgDn
Top of the screen	Ctrl+PgUp

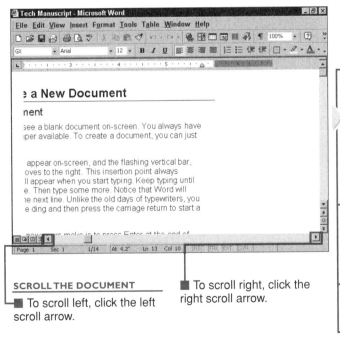

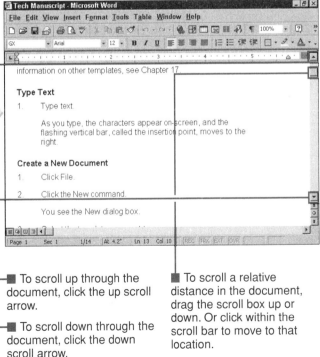

SCROLL THE DOCUMENT

■ To scroll left, click the left scroll arrow.

■ To scroll right, click the right scroll arrow.

■ To scroll up through the document, click the up scroll arrow.

■ To scroll down through the document, click the down scroll arrow.

■ To scroll a relative distance in the document, drag the scroll box up or down. Or click within the scroll bar to move to that location.

GO TO A PARTICULAR PAGE

Moving around a short document is simple. You may be able to see the entire text of a short document in one window. To move, all you have to do is point and click. For longer documents, though,

moving around isn't as easy.

You may try scrolling to the location you want. If you have tried scrolling through a document, you know it's not an exact science. The scroll box gives you some idea of where you

are in the overall document. When you drag, the page numbers do appear, but scrolling may not be the best method in a really long document. Instead, you can go directly to a page using the Go To command.

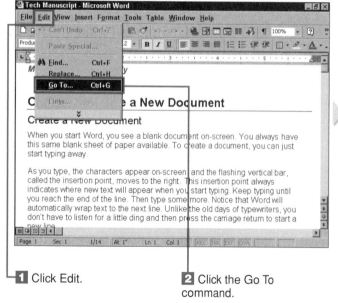

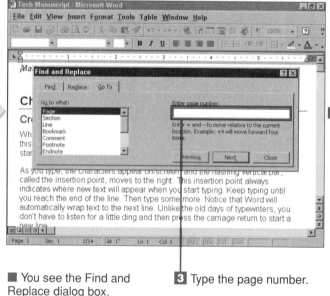

1 Click Edit.

2 Click the Go To command.

■ You see the Find and Replace dialog box.

3 Type the page number.

How can I go back to the last spot I worked on in the document?

When you open a document, press Shift+F5. Word moves to the spot where the insertion point was when you last saved the document.

What are Find and Replace?

You can use the Find and Replace tabs to search for and replace text, formatting, and other special characters in your document. For information on using Find and Replace, see Chapter 4.

What is the shortcut key?

You can also press Ctrl+G to display the Go To tab of the Find and Replace dialog box.

What else can I go to?

You can go to a page, section, line, footnote, bookmark, and other items. To go to another item, select it from the *Go to what* list.

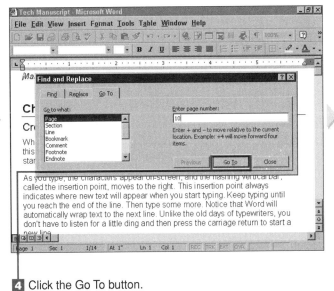

4 Click the Go To button.

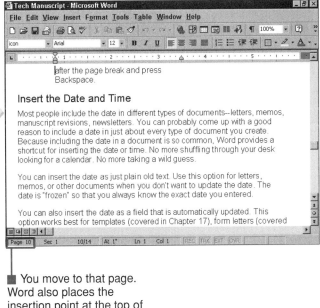

■ You move to that page. Word also places the insertion point at the top of the page.

SET UP AND GO TO BOOKMARKS

A Word bookmark is similar to a bookmark that you insert in a "regular" book. It helps you turn to a particular page or section quickly. You can set up bookmarks for sections in your document and then go to these sections quickly. You

might, for instance, bookmark places where you have to check facts or rework the text. Then you can easily find and go to these sections.

As another example, you might want to bookmark each major section in your document.

You can then quickly go to any of these sections.

Create a bookmark by assigning a name to a particular location in a document. Using this name, you can then jump quickly to the named bookmark.

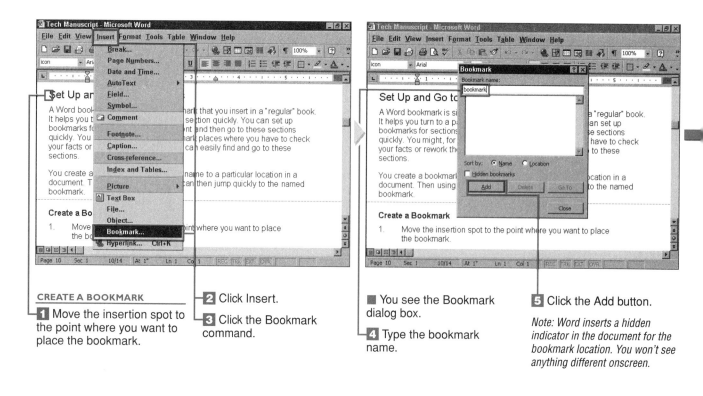

CREATE A BOOKMARK

1 Move the insertion spot to the point where you want to place the bookmark.

2 Click Insert.

3 Click the Bookmark command.

■ You see the Bookmark dialog box.

4 Type the bookmark name.

5 Click the Add button.

Note: Word inserts a hidden indicator in the document for the bookmark location. You won't see anything different onscreen.

TIPS

What other command can I use to go to a bookmark?

You can also use the Insert ⇨ Bookmark command to go to a bookmark. Select the command and then select the bookmark from the list. Click the Go To button.

How can I view bookmarks?

Select the Tools ⇨ Options command and then click the View tab. Check the Bookmarks checkbox and click OK. You see an I-beam where the bookmarks appear.

What other ways can I use to navigate?

If you use heading styles in your document, you can navigate from section to section using the Document Map. See the next section in this chapter.

How do I delete a bookmark?

Select the Insert ⇨ Bookmark command. You see a list of bookmarks. Select the one you want to delete and then click the Delete button.

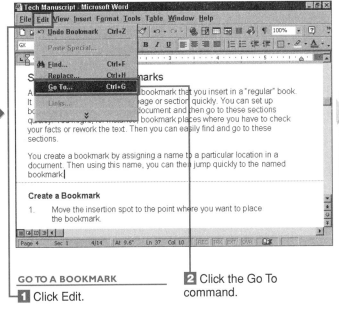

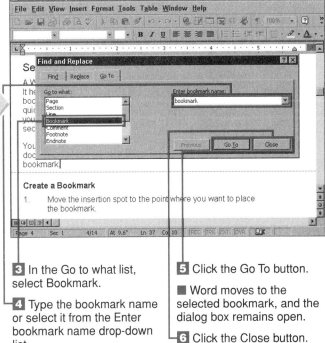

GO TO A BOOKMARK

1 Click Edit.

2 Click the Go To command.

3 In the Go to what list, select Bookmark.

4 Type the bookmark name or select it from the Enter bookmark name drop-down list.

5 Click the Go To button.

■ Word moves to the selected bookmark, and the dialog box remains open.

6 Click the Close button.

NAVIGATE USING THE DOCUMENT MAP

If you have assigned heading styles in your document, you can use the Document Map to navigate through your document. (For information on using heading styles, see Chapter 10.)

You can view a list of the headings in your document in one pane, and the contents of the selected heading in another pane. Navigate from section to section using the headings in the Document Map.

The Document Map is not only a good way to navigate, it's also a good way to see an overview of your document, and keep the document organization in mind as you write and edit.

The headings appear in outline style, and you can collapse and expand the listing.

Click the minus (–) next to a heading to hide the subheadings. Click the plus (+) next to a heading to display the subheadings.

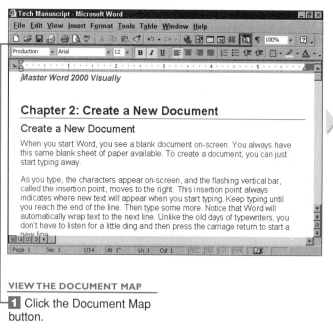

VIEW THE DOCUMENT MAP

1 Click the Document Map button.

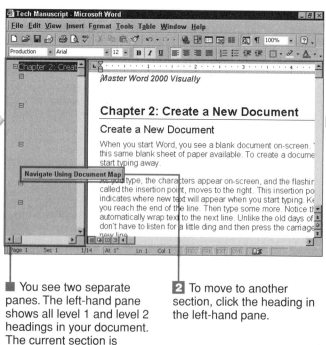

■ You see two separate panes. The left-hand pane shows all level 1 and level 2 headings in your document. The current section is highlighted. The right-hand pane shows the text of the document.

2 To move to another section, click the heading in the left-hand pane.

TIPS

Will all documents now appear with the Document Map on?

The Document Map button remains depressed (on) until you turn it off. All documents you open will display the Document Map until you turn it off.

How do I turn off the Document Map?

Click the Document Map button again to close the pane with the document headings.

What if I don't use heading styles?

 If you don't use heading styles, you will see what Word thinks are the key points in your document. Word looks for clues like the top line in a file or a short line in all capitals.

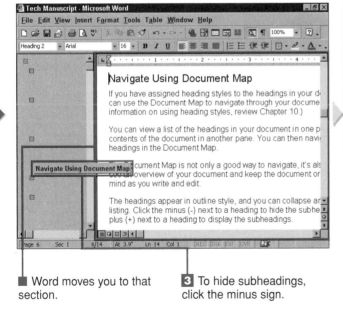

■ Word moves you to that section.

3 To hide subheadings, click the minus sign.

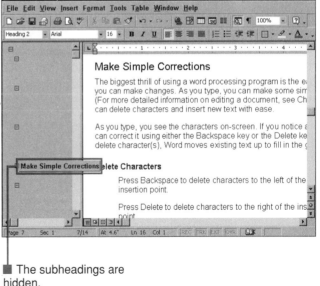

■ The subheadings are hidden.

MAKE SIMPLE CORRECTIONS

The biggest thrill of using a word processing program is the ease with which you can make changes. As you are typing, you see the characters onscreen. If you notice a mistake, you can easily correct it.

Press Backspace to delete characters to the left of the insertion point. You can backspace to delete a word or sentence and then retype it. You can also press Delete to delete characters to the right of the

insertion point. When you delete characters, Word moves existing text up to fill in the gap.

For more detailed information on editing a document, see Chapter 4.

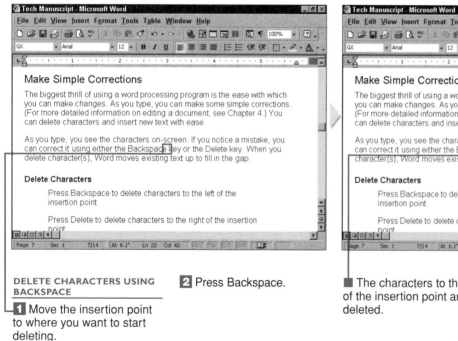

DELETE CHARACTERS USING BACKSPACE

1 Move the insertion point to where you want to start deleting.

2 Press Backspace.

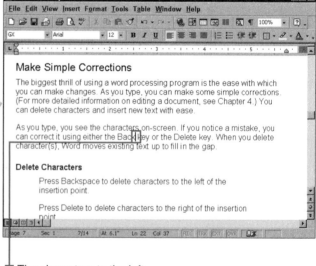

■ The characters to the left of the insertion point are deleted.

Why does text disappear when I type?

 If you ever start typing and text disappears, you are in Overtype mode (rather than Insert mode). You can use Overtype mode to type over text, although I can't think of a good reason why you would. You usually want to stay in Insert mode, where new text is inserted in the document. Check the status bar at the bottom of the window. If OVR is highlighted, you are in Overtype mode.

How do I switch from Insert to Overtype mode and vice versa?

 You toggle between Overtype and Insert mode using the Insert key. Press the Insert key to switch from one to the other.

How do I undo a mistake?

 If you delete something by accident, you can undo the deletion using the Undo button or the Edit ➪ Undo command.

What if I want to delete a lot of text?

If you have a lot of text to delete, don't delete it one character at a time. Instead, select the text and press Delete. For more information on selecting text and deleting a block of text, see Chapter 4.

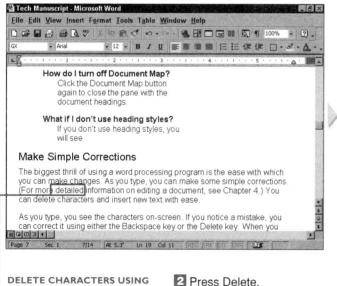

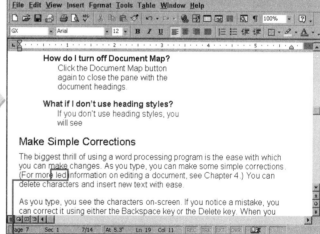

DELETE CHARACTERS USING DELETE

1 Move the insertion point to where you want to start deleting.

2 Press Delete.

■ The characters to the right of the insertion point are deleted.

INSERT TABS AND PAGE BREAKS

By default, Word has tab settings set up every half inch. (You can change the tab stops, as covered in Chapter 8.) You can insert a tab by pressing the Tab key. Word inserts the tab and moves the insertion point over. You can then type your text.

A common mistake for beginners is to use the space bar to tab over in a document. That's a typing no-no. Spaces don't always align entries exactly, so be sure to use the Tab key instead.

Word automatically inserts page breaks, as necessary. When a page fills up, Word inserts a break and creates a new page. If you add or delete text, Word adjusts the page breaks. This means that you don't have to worry about text running off the page.

In some cases, you may want to force a page break. For instance, you may want to create a title page. You might just force a page break by inserting a lot of blank returns until Word inserts a page, but you shouldn't. (Another no-no.) This method will confuse you if you add or delete text later. Instead, insert a hard page break.

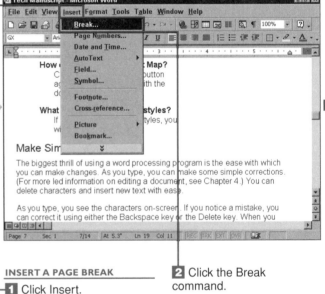

INSERT A TAB

1 Press the Tab key.

■ The insertion point moves to the first tab stop.

2 Type your text.

■ The text appears aligned at the first tab stop.

INSERT A PAGE BREAK

1 Click Insert.

2 Click the Break command.

TIPS

When should I use tabs?

 Tabs are great for a simple alignment set-up such as memo headings. For something more complex, though, use a different feature. For instance, if you want to indent paragraphs, don't use tabs. Instead, use the paragraph indent features, covered in Chapter 8. If you want to set up a list, use a table, covered in Chapter 11.

What's the keyboard shortcut for a page break?

 The easiest way to insert a hard page break is using the keyboard shortcut: press Ctrl+Enter.

How do I delete a tab or page break?

 To delete a tab, move the insertion point right after the tab and press Backspace. To delete a hard page break, move the insertion point right after the page break and press Backspace.

Can I display tab characters?

 Yes. You can click the Show/Hide ¶ button in the toolbar to display characters for returns, tabs, and spaces.

How do I get an idea of how the page breaks will fall?

 Before you print, preview your document and make sure it has no "bad" page breaks (such as right after a section heading). Click the Print Preview button to preview. See Chapter 6 for more information on printing and previewing.

GETTING STARTED

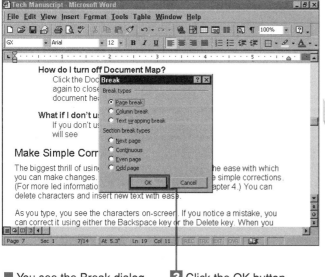

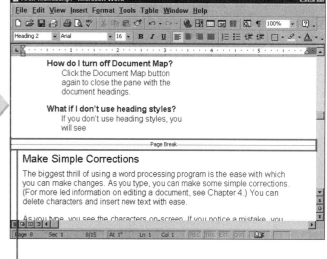

■ You see the Break dialog box.

3 Click the OK button.

■ Word inserts a manual page break. This page break will not be adjusted when you add or delete text.

39

INSERT THE DATE AND TIME

Most people include the date in different types of documents — letters, memos, manuscript revisions, and newsletters. You can probably come up with a good reason to include a date in just about every type of document you create. Because including the date in a document is so common, Word provides a shortcut for inserting the date or time. No more shuffling through your desk

looking for a calendar. No more taking a wild guess.

You can insert the date as just plain text. Use this option for letters, memos, or other documents when you don't want to update the date. The date is "frozen" so that you always know the exact date you entered.

You can also insert the date as a field that is automatically updated. This option works best for templates (covered in Chapter 17),

form letters (covered in Chapter 16), and documents that you may work on for several days (or weeks or months or years — those great American novels take *time*). For instance, suppose you are creating a report that will probably take you all week. You can insert the date as a field when you first create the document. When you finally finish and print the document, Word updates the field to the current date.

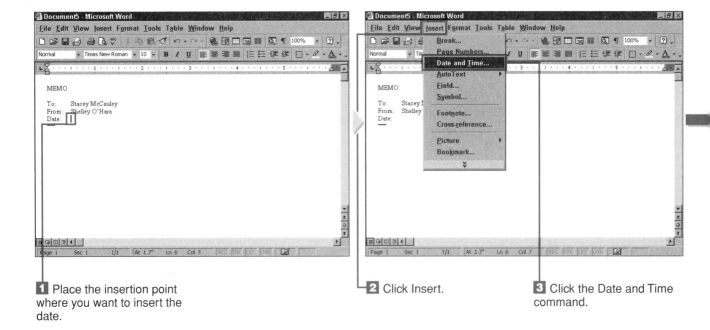

1 Place the insertion point where you want to insert the date.

2 Click Insert.

3 Click the Date and Time command.

TIPS

What's another way to enter the date quickly?

 Word recognizes certain common entries, including dates, and saves them as AutoText entries. You can simply start typing a month, and Word displays a ScreenTip with the entire month. Press Enter to have Word complete the typing for you.

Why would I change the language?

If you work in an international setting or in another country, you may prefer a different format for the dates. You can select the language (for instance, British English), from the Language drop-down list in the Date and Time dialog box to use date and time formats consistent with that language or location.

How do I delete the date?

 To delete the date, use the Edit ⇨ Undo command immediately after you insert the date. Or just select the date or time and press Delete.

How do I correct the date and time?

 If the date and time are incorrect, you can correct them using Windows. In the Windows taskbar, you should see the time in the lower right corner. Right-click this area and select the Adjust Date/Time command. You see the Date/Time Properties dialog box with the Date & Time tab selected. Select the correct date using the calendar or drop-down list boxes. Select the correct time using the clock or the spin arrows. Click the OK button.

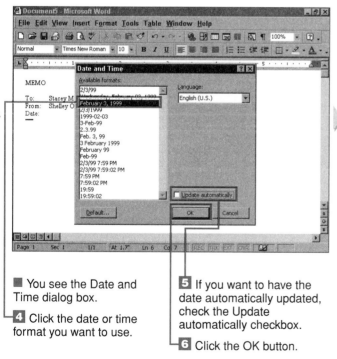

■ You see the Date and Time dialog box.

4 Click the date or time format you want to use.

5 If you want to have the date automatically updated, check the Update automatically checkbox.

6 Click the OK button.

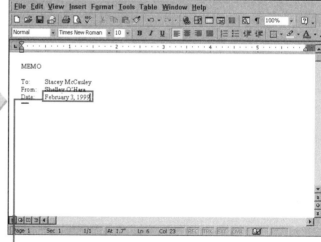

■ Word inserts the date or time in the format you selected.

INSERT A SPECIAL CHARACTER

You can insert any of the characters from the keyboard including all the letters, numbers, and most common symbols such as the dollar sign ($), percent sign (%), and so on. But what about other characters that aren't available from the keyboard?

You can insert these special characters by selecting Insert ⇨

Special Character. You can insert typographical symbols such as an em dash (—), and you can insert fun characters such as a smiley face (☺).

Word puts the most common symbols on the Special Characters tab. You can also select from many different characters on the Symbol tab. You can select different fonts that

contain nothing but symbols to choose from a variety of symbols. Some common symbol fonts include Symbol and Wingdings. Depending on what fonts you have, you may have even more symbols available.

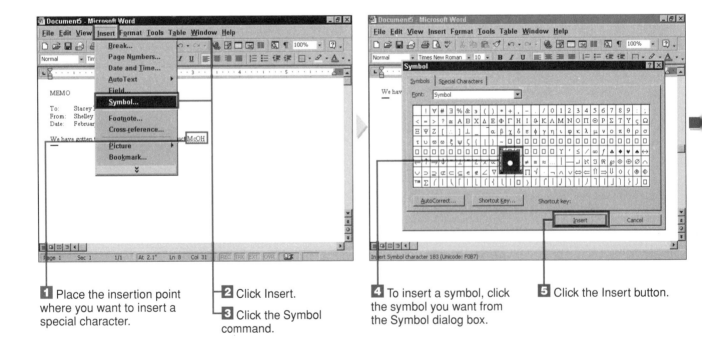

1 Place the insertion point where you want to insert a special character.

2 Click Insert.

3 Click the Symbol command.

4 To insert a symbol, click the symbol you want from the Symbol dialog box.

5 Click the Insert button.

How do I select from other symbols?

The selected font determines what symbols are available on the Symbols tab. To view other symbols, display the Font drop-down list and select another symbol font.

I can't see the symbol!

If you can't get a good idea of the symbol and want to see an enlarged view, click the symbol. You see a pop-up button with the symbol.

What shortcut keys can I use?

Many of the special characters have shortcut keys associated with them. You can press these key combinations to insert the character. You can view the keys on the Special Characters tab.

A special character appeared, and I'm not sure how. What happened?

Word has a feature called AutoCorrect that automatically replaces certain typos, misspellings, and characters. For instance, if you type "(c)," Word replaces it with the copyright symbol. For more information on AutoCorrect, see Chapter 5.

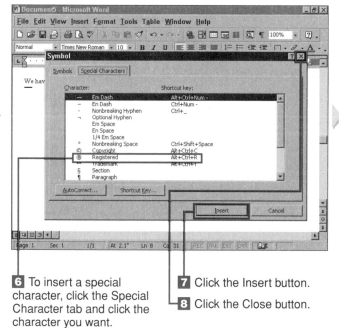

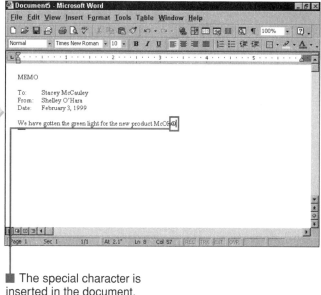

6 To insert a special character, click the Special Character tab and click the character you want.

7 Click the Insert button.

8 Click the Close button.

■ The special character is inserted in the document.

CREATE AND INSERT AN AUTOTEXT ENTRY

If you find yourself typing the same word or phrase over and over, you can save time by setting up an AutoText entry. An AutoText Entry is a piece of text — a word, sentence, even several paragraphs — that you save. You can then insert this text with a shortcut.

Word includes some AutoText entries commonly used in memos and letters. You can select an attention line, closing, header or footer, mailing instructions, reference initials, reference line, salutation, signature company, or subject line. Some entry types have several different versions.

For instance, for the attention line, you can select Attention: or ATTN:.

Word's AutoText entries are handy for memo and letters, but you'll find yourself typing certain text again and again. To save time, create AutoText entries of your own.

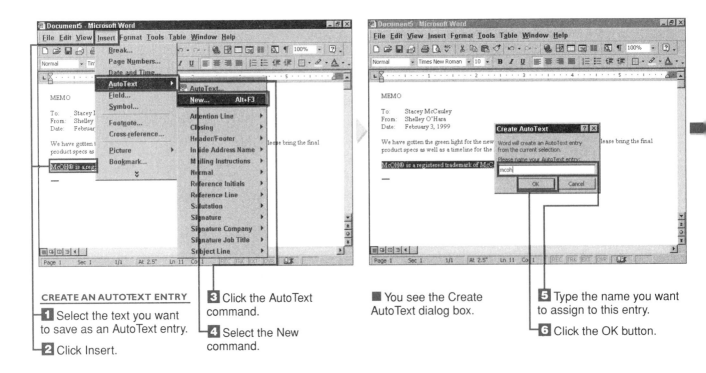

CREATE AN AUTOTEXT ENTRY

■1 Select the text you want to save as an AutoText entry.

■2 Click Insert.

■3 Click the AutoText command.

■4 Select the New command.

■ You see the Create AutoText dialog box.

■5 Type the name you want to assign to this entry.

■6 Click the OK button.

What's the fastest way to insert an entry?

To insert an AutoText entry using the keyboard, move to where you want to insert the entry. Type the name you assigned to the entry. Press F3. Word inserts the entire entry.

How can I make the AutoText entries easier to access?

If you use a lot of AutoText entries, you can turn on the AutoText toolbar. From this toolbar, you can then insert and create AutoText entries. Click View ➪ Toolbars ➪ AutoText. (Follow the same procedure to turn off the toolbar.)

What should I name the entry?

The best names are the shortest. You can even use just one character for the name. Use a name that is easy to remember.

How do I delete an AutoText entry?

To delete the text, simply select it and press Delete. To delete the entry so that it is no longer available, select Insert ➪ AutoText ➪ AutoText. In the dialog box that appears, select the entry you want to delete. Click the Delete button. Click the Close button.

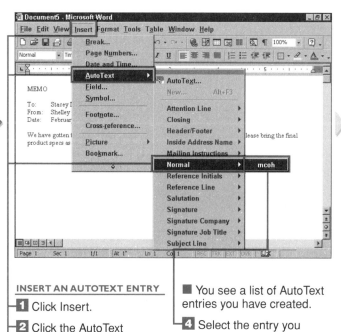

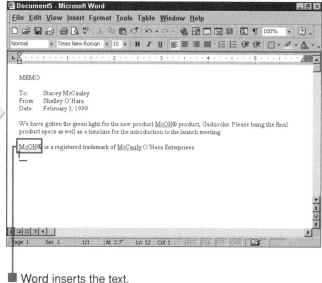

INSERT AN AUTOTEXT ENTRY

-1 Click Insert.

-2 Click the AutoText command.

-3 Select the Normal command.

■ You see a list of AutoText entries you have created.

-4 Select the entry you want.

■ Word inserts the text.

HOW TO SAVE DOCUMENTS

All your work will be lost unless you save and save often. Saving enables you to open the same document to work on again. This chapter covers the basics of saving, showing you the differences between saving a document the first time and at later times, and also covers folder creation so you can store your saved files in an organized fashion.

Save Often!

The first time you save a document, you assign a name, a folder, and drive. You can place the document anywhere on your hard drive, or on a floppy drive. After you save, the document name appears in the title bar.

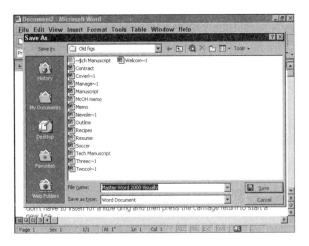

After you save once, you don't have to enter a name or folder again. Simply select File ⇨ Save to save the document with the same name and to the same location. You may want to save a copy or save the document as another file type, both covered here.

Shortcuts for Opening a Document

The reason you save is so you can go back and open the same document again. To open a document, use the File ⇨ Open command and then change to the drive and folder where you saved the document.

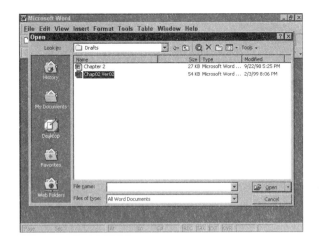

In addition to this method, you can use several shortcuts for opening a document:

- ▶ The File menu lists the last four documents on which you worked. Click File and then click the document to quickly open that document.

▸ To open a document and start Word, use the Documents command from Windows. Click Start and then click Documents. Click the document you want to open.

Working with More than One Document

With Word, you aren't limited to working on, or even viewing one document. You can open and work on several documents. You might need to consult one file while working on another, or need to copy information from one document to another. You can use the Window menu to switch among documents, and you can also choose to arrange all the documents so you can see part of each of them.

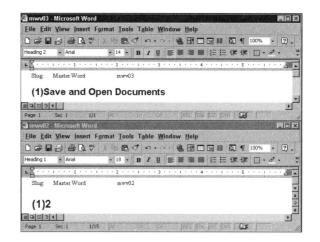

SAVE A DOCUMENT FOR THE FIRST TIME

The words you type onscreen are saved only temporarily in the computer's memory. To make a permanent copy, you need to save the onscreen version to your hard disk.

You shouldn't wait until you finish the document to save, and don't think that saving just once is enough. There's nothing more frustrating than spending several hours getting the content just perfect and then losing all that hard work because you forgot to save. If you wait until you finish the document, you run the risk of losing all your work if something happens (such as losing power) before you finish and save. You should save periodically as you work on the document.

The first time you save a document, you are prompted for a name. You also select the drive and folder where the file will be stored. Word adds the extension .doc to the file.

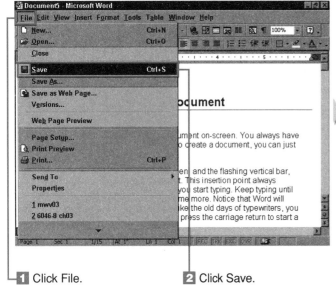

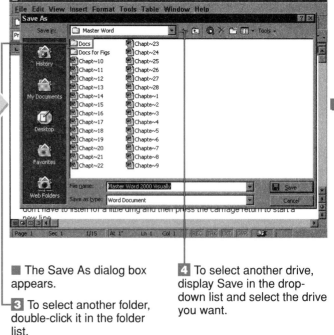

■1 Click File.

■2 Click Save.

■ The Save As dialog box appears.

■3 To select another folder, double-click it in the folder list.

■4 To select another drive, display Save in the drop-down list and select the drive you want.

Where should I keep my documents?

It's a good idea to put all your documents in a separate folder, possibly several folders. In fact, you should spend some time thinking about how you want to organize your documents. See a later task in this section for information on creating a new folder.

What are the buttons for on the left and top edge of the dialog box?

Use the buttons along the left to switch to different folders, including My Documents. Use the buttons at the top of the dialog box to navigate through the drive structure, change how the files are displayed, and create new folders.

What shortcuts can I use?

You can press Ctrl+S or click the Save button to save a document.

What can I name the file?

You used to be limited to eight characters before Windows 95. Now you can type up to 255 characters and include spaces in the file name. You cannot use the following characters:

/ \ : * ? < > |

It's best to use a descriptive name that reminds you of the contents.

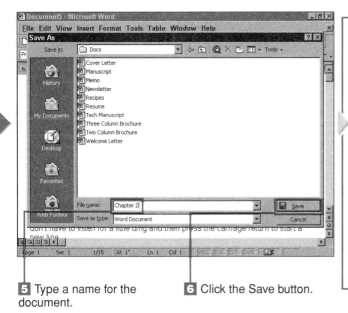

5 Type a name for the document.

6 Click the Save button.

■ Word saves the document. The file name appears in the title bar.

SAVE AND CLOSE A DOCUMENT

As you continue to work and make changes, you should update the disk file. Your changes are not saved to the disk until you give the command to do so.

Once you save the first time, you don't have to select the drive and folder. You can simply select the command to save the file with the same name and in the same folder.

After you save a document, it is not closed. It remains open so you can continue working. When you finish, you should save and then close the document. You can have several documents onscreen at once, but closing documents you are no longer working with saves memory.

When all documents are closed, you see a blank, gray area. You can create a new document or open a document you have created before.

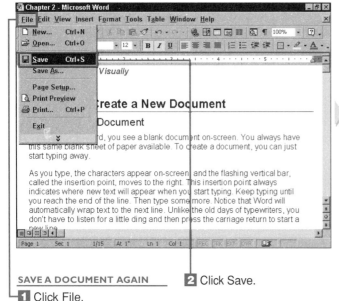

SAVE A DOCUMENT AGAIN

1 Click File.

2 Click Save.

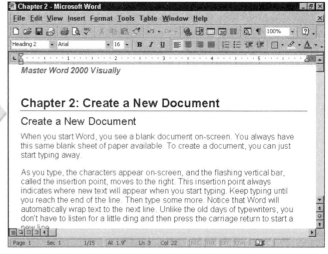

■ The document is saved to the same location with the same file name. You won't notice anything different onscreen.

TIPS

How else can I close a document?

You can also click the Close (X) button for the document window to close the document.

How do I close several documents?

If you have several documents open and want to close them all at once, hold down the Shift key and click the File menu. The Close command changes to Close All; you can select this command to close all open documents.

What if I forget to save?

If you exit Word or close a document without saving, Word prompts you to save. You can click Yes to save, No to close without saving, and Cancel to return to the document.

What if I don't want to save?

If you make changes and don't want to save them, click File ↔ Close. When prompted to save, click the No button.

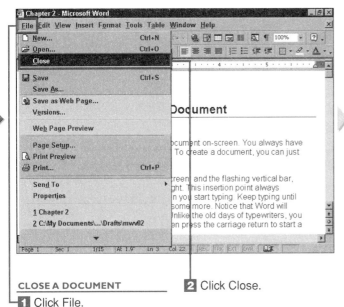

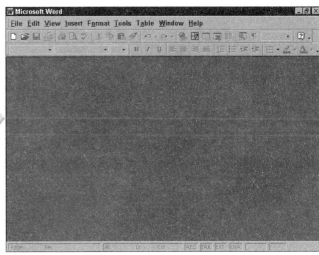

CLOSE A DOCUMENT

1 Click File.

2 Click Close.

■ The document is closed. At this point, you can open an existing document or create a new document.

CREATE A NEW FOLDER

To keep your documents organized, you should consider creating folders to store similar documents together. You might set up folders for each type of document you create. For instance, you can create a folder for memos, a folder for reports, and so on. Or,

you might set up folders for each project on which you are working.

You can use Windows to create folders, but often you don't realize you need a new folder until you save a document. Instead of switching to the Windows desktop, you can create

a new folder right from the Word Save As dialog box.

For folder names, use something descriptive. You can type up to 255 characters, including spaces.

Once you have created the folder, you can then save documents to the new folder.

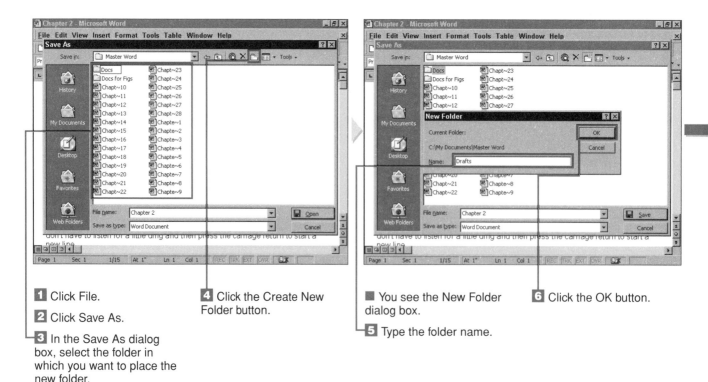

1 Click File.

2 Click Save As.

3 In the Save As dialog box, select the folder in which you want to place the new folder.

4 Click the Create New Folder button.

■ You see the New Folder dialog box.

5 Type the folder name.

6 Click the OK button.

What is the My Documents folder?

The My Documents folder is a special folder set up by Windows. In addition to the folder itself, Windows sets up shortcuts to this folder so that it is easy to select. You may consider creating all your document folders as subfolders of My Documents.

What is the Favorites list?

You can add folders (and documents) you often use to the Favorites list. Then you can click the Favorites button to quickly select a folder or file in this list. To add a folder to the Favorites list, select that folder and then click the Tools button and select Add to Favorites.

Can I move existing documents to the new folder?

Yes. You can move documents from one folder to another using Windows Explorer or Word. For information on using the file management features of Word, see Chapter 24.

How do I delete a folder?

To delete a folder, right-click the folder and select Delete. Confirm the deletion by clicking the Yes button. For information on using the file management features of Word, see Chapter 24.

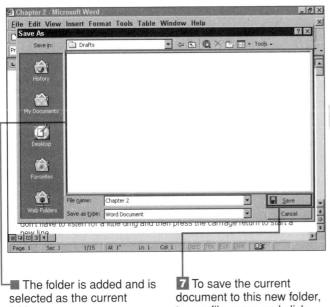

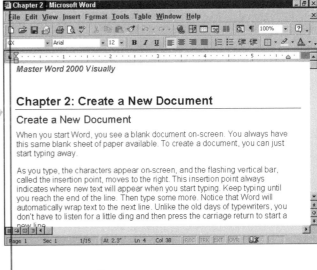

■ The folder is added and is selected as the current folder.

7 To save the current document to this new folder, type a file name and click Save.

Note: To close the dialog box without saving, click Cancel.

■ If you save the file, you see the file name in the title bar. The file is saved to the new folder.

SAVE A DOCUMENT WITH A NEW NAME

You can use Windows for file management tasks such as copying, renaming, or moving a document. You can also accomplish the same tasks using the Save As command. For instance, suppose you want to keep track of each version of a document on which you are

working. You can save the first version as VERSION01. When you edit this document, you can save it as VERSION02 so you have the original (VERSION01) as well as the new document.

Another reason to use Save As is to change the folder where you placed the document. You can

select a different drive or folder for the document. Remember that the original file remains in the same spot with the same name, so you are in effect creating another copy of the file.

As another example, you can even save the file as a different file type.

1 Click File.

2 Click Save As.

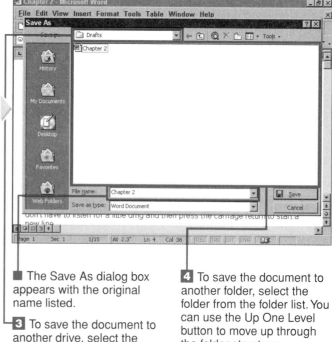

■ The Save As dialog box appears with the original name listed.

3 To save the document to another drive, select the drive from the Save in drop-down list.

4 To save the document to another folder, select the folder from the folder list. You can use the Up One Level button to move up through the folder structure.

What about automatic saves and other options?

 You can set up Word to automatically save a backup copy of your document at specific intervals. You can also save summary information and add a password. See Chapter 24 for information on other save options.

How do I save a document to a new folder?

You can create a new folder in which to save a document. To do so, click the New Folder button in the Save As dialog box. Then type the folder name. Then save the document. For more information on organizing your Word documents, see Chapter 24.

How do I save a document as another file type?

 You can also use the File ⇨ Save As command to save a document in another format. For instance, suppose a coworker has an earlier version of Word or uses a different word processing program. To save a Word document as another file type, select File ⇨ Save As. Display the Save as type drop-down list and select the format. Click the OK button.

5 Type a new file name.

6 Click Save.

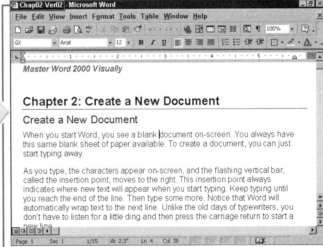

■ Word saves the onscreen document with the new name or to the new location. This document remains onscreen. The original file is closed and is kept intact on disk.

OPEN A DOCUMENT

The reason you save a document is so that the document is available when you want to view it again. You can open a document to review the text, make changes to the text or formatting, print the document, and so on.

Word has made some changes to the Open dialog box in this new version. You can use the toolbar buttons to navigate through your drive structure. You can also use the buttons along

the left edge of the dialog box to select what folder is displayed:

► Click the History button to view a list of recently opened files.

► Click My Documents to open the My Documents folder.

► Click Desktop to view files stored on the desktop.

► Click Favorites to view a list of favorite folders and

files. (For more information on adding a file or folder to your Favorites list, see Chapter 24.)

► Click Web Folders to view a list of Internet sites to which you can save your files. These must be set up for you in advance by a network administrator.

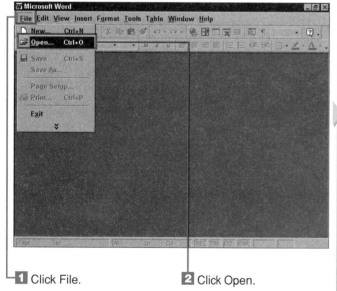

1 Click File.

2 Click Open.

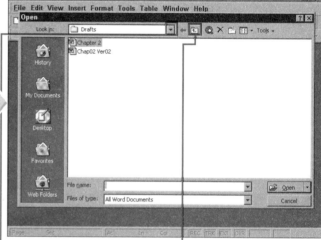

■ You see the Open dialog box with the last folder you used selected.

3 If the file is stored on another drive, display the Look in drop-down list and select the drive you want.

4 If the file is stored in another folder, open that folder. If you see the folder listed, double-click it. You can also use the Up One Level button to move up through the folder structure.

TIPS

How do I open a document from the Windows desktop?

 You can use the Documents menu to open a Word document on which you have recently worked. Click the Start button and then select Documents. Windows lists the last 15 open documents (all document types, not just Word documents). Click the Word document you want. Windows starts Word and opens that document.

What if I can't find the file?

 If you can't find the file, try searching for it. See Chapter 24 for help on searching for a particular file.

What are some shortcuts for opening a document?

 To open a document you have recently worked on, open the File menu. Notice that the last files opened are listed at the bottom of the menu. Simply click the file you want to open. You can also click the Open button in the Standard toolbar, or use the keyboard shortcut (Ctrl+O).

How do I create a new document?

 To create a new document, click the New button in the toolbar.

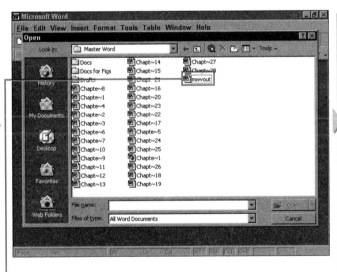

 Double-click the file name.

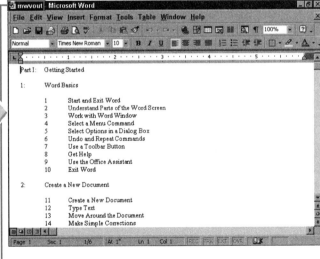

 The document is displayed onscreen.

WORK IN MORE THAN ONE DOCUMENT

In Word, you aren't limited to just one document. You can open and work with several documents. For instance, if you are writing a book, you may want to have several chapters open so you can refer to the material you have already completed.

To open more than one document, select File ⇨ Open to open each document you want.

You can open as many documents as your system memory will allow.

Keep in mind that only one document is active at a time. The active document has a darker title bar, and the insertion point appears in this document. You can switch among open documents using the Window menu.

Most often, a document opens in a maximized window, and you see just the current or active document. You can use Word to arrange all the open documents so that each one has its own pane. Then you can compare and easily switch among documents.

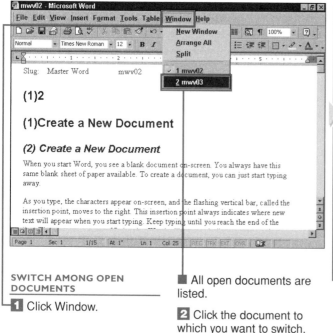

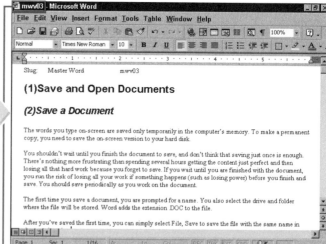

SWITCH AMONG OPEN DOCUMENTS

1 Click Window.

■ All open documents are listed.

2 Click the document to which you want to switch.

■ That document becomes the active document.

What other changes can I make to the document window?

 The controls for working with windows apply to the document windows in Word. That is, you can minimize, restore, resize, and move any of the open windows using the window control buttons.

Can I open two copies of the same document?

 Yes. To do so, open the Window menu and select the New Window command. You see a second version of the document. (The document is named the same, but has :2 after the name so that you remember you have two versions open.) You might want to do this in a really long document so that one window can display part of the document and the second window a different part.

How do I run more than one program?

 You can also use Windows to run more than one program at a time. To start another program, click the Start button, select Programs, select the appropriate folder (if necessary) and then select the program name.

How do I switch programs?

 To switch from one running program to another, use the Windows taskbar. Click the button for the program you want.

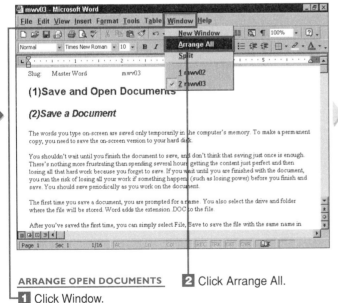

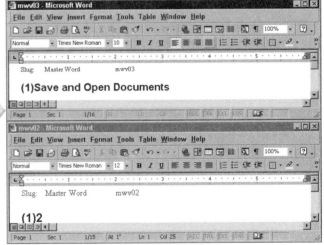

ARRANGE OPEN DOCUMENTS

1 Click Window.

2 Click Arrange All.

■ All open documents are arranged in separate panes.

CHANGE THE FILE LIST DISPLAY

B y default, the contents of the selected drive and folder are displayed in list view, which simply shows the names of the files and folders. To find the file you want to open, you may prefer a different view. You can change to another view using the Views button in either the Save As or Open dialog boxes.

You can switch to Details view to see additional file information such as the file size, type, and modification date.

Use Properties to view the properties (title, author, template, revision number, creation date, number of pages and words, and so on) of the selected file.

To view a preview of the selected file, use Preview.

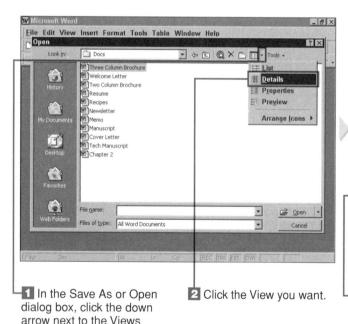

1 In the Save As or Open dialog box, click the down arrow next to the Views button.

■ You see a list of the available views.

2 Click the View you want.

■ Details view shows the file details of all the files and folders.

How do I sort files?

You can also select how files are sorted by displaying the Views menu and selecting Arrange Icons. Then select the arrangement you want (name, type, size, or date).

How do I display files in another drive?

You can display files on another drive by displaying the Save in list (Save As dialog box) or Look in list (Open dialog box). Then click the drive you want to view.

How do I display files in another folder?

You can double-click a folder to display its contents. If the folder is not listed, you may need to navigate through the drive structure to display it. Use the Up One Level button to move up through the overall drive structure.

■ Properties view shows the properties of the selected file.

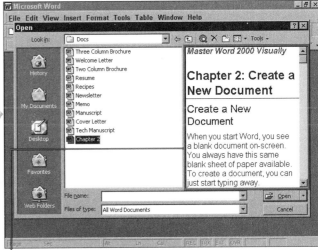

■ Preview shows a preview of the selected file.

DISPLAY OTHER FOLDERS

As mentioned, Word has revamped the Open and Save As dialog box, including buttons for navigating through your folders and for displaying special folders.

For instance, My Documents is a special folder set up in Windows. You can quickly access

this folder from the shortcut icon on the desktop. You can also view the files and folders by clicking the My Documents button (in the Place bar) in either the Open or Save As dialog box.

You can also view the History folder, which displays the last files on which you have worked.

This is handy when you know you worked on a file, but can't remember the name, or where you saved it.

As a final alternative, you can view the folders in your Favorites folder. For information on adding a folder to this list, see Chapter 24.

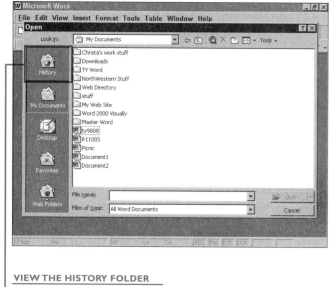

VIEW THE HISTORY FOLDER

1 In the Save As or Open dialog box, click the History button.

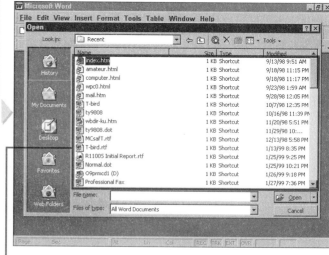

■ You see a list of the files on which you have recently worked.

How do I open a file?

 You can open any of the displayed files or folders by double-clicking it.

What is the Desktop button?

You can display the files and folders on the desktop by clicking the Desktop button. You can also select Desktop from the Save in list (Save As dialog box) or Look in list (Open dialog box).

How do I go back to a previous list?

As you navigate from one folder to another, you may need to go back a step. To do so, you can click the Back button. You see the last file and folder list you viewed. You can continue to back up until you find the list you want.

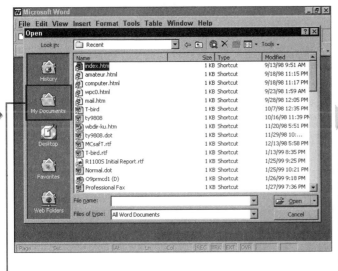

VIEW THE MY DOCUMENTS FOLDER

1 In the Save As or Open dialog box, click the My Documents button.

■ You see a list of the files and folders in this folder.

WAYS TO EDIT TEXT

After you create a document, you most likely review it and make adjustments. Maybe you fine-tune the organization or wording.

Maybe you do massive rewriting. It doesn't matter. Word provides several editing tools to help you to accomplish what you need to do.

Select Text

When you want to work with a block of text, start by selecting it. Select text for editing and formatting tasks. For instance, select text when you want to copy it. To delete text, select it. To move text, select it.

Selecting text is simple. Drag the mouse pointer over the text, or use the keyboard to select text. Once text is selected, it appears in reverse video so that you know what text you picked.

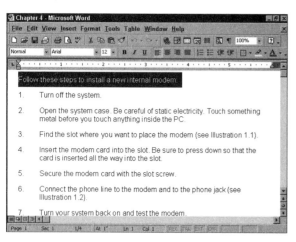

Delete, Move, and Copy Text

When you review a document, short or long, you need to consider the organization. Does it flow logically? Are there redundancies? Does it make sense? When making these editing decisions, you might want to delete text that isn't working, move it to a better position, or even copy it for use somewhere else.

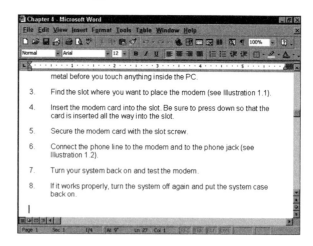

Word uses a scissors and paste analogy for moving and copying. First you cut (or copy) text and then paste it in the new location. You can copy or move text from one spot in a document to another, or from one document to another.

Note: For information on copying data from another program, see Chapter 12.

Find and Replace Text

Another handy editing feature is Find and Replace. Use the Find command to quickly locate a particular word, phrase, or section. Use the Replace command to find text (or formatting) and replace it with another entry.

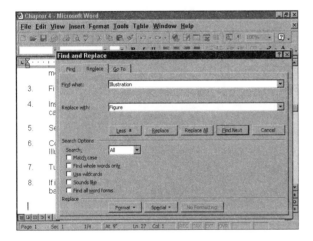

Sort Text

This chapter also covers how to sort text, which comes in handy when you want to alphabetize a list or organize a table of data.

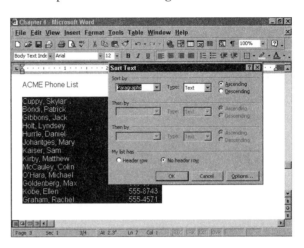

SELECT TEXT

The first thing to do when you want to change text is to select it. You select text when performing editing changes such as copying or moving. You also select text when you want to change the appearance or format of it (this is covered in the next few chapters).

Use one of several methods for selecting text. Drag the mouse over the text you want to select, or use the keyboard. There also are many shortcuts for selecting text. You can select a single word, phrase, sentence, paragraph, several paragraphs, or even the entire document.

Selected text appears in reverse video. The action you perform with selected text is carried out with that text only.

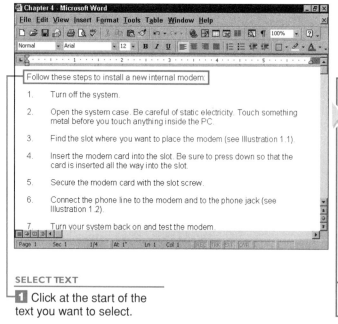

SELECT TEXT

1 Click at the start of the text you want to select.

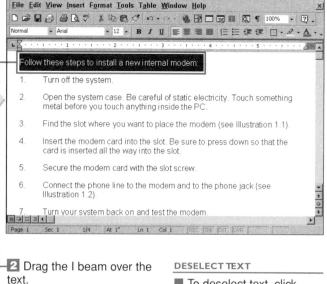

2 Drag the I beam over the text.

■ The text appears in reverse video.

DESELECT TEXT

■ To deselect text, click outside the selected text.

How do I select text with the keyboard?

Use the cursor movement keys to move to the start of the text that you want to select. Hold down the Shift key and then use the arrow keys to highlight the text.

What are the other shortcuts?

Triple-click within a paragraph to select the entire paragraph. To select the entire document, press Ctrl+A or open the Edit menu and choose the Select All command.

What is the selection bar?

The selection bar is the narrow strip along the left edge of the screen. Click once in the selection bar next to the line to select the entire line. Click twice in the selection bar next to the paragraph to select the entire paragraph. Click three times in the selection bar to select the entire document.

All of my text disappeared or moved. What happened?

Be careful when you select text. If you type something, Word thinks you want to replace the selected text with what you are typing. If this happens, choose Edit ⇨ Undo to undo the deletion.

Also, if you select text, release the mouse button, and then try to drag the selection, Word thinks you want to move it. Undo the move and select the text again.

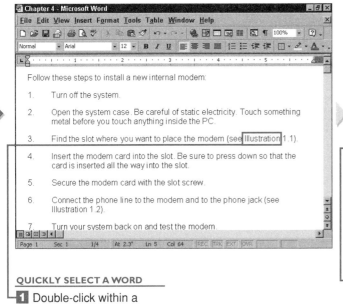

QUICKLY SELECT A WORD

1 Double-click within a word.

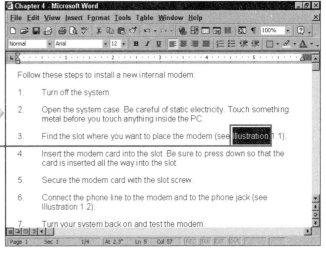

■ That word is selected.

ADD AND DELETE TEXT

As you write, you may want to add a thought or an idea. Maybe you forgot something. Or perhaps you want to add a word or two to clarify the meaning. You can add text to any spot in the document — the existing text moves to make room.

You also can easily delete text no longer needed. Chapter 2 covers how to delete text one character at a time, which is okay for simple changes, but when you want to delete a lot of text, there is a better method. When you delete text, the existing text moves up to fill the gap.

If you want to replace text with something new, simply select the text and start typing. Word replaces the selected text with what you start typing.

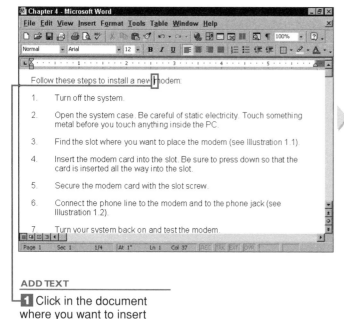

ADD TEXT

1 Click in the document where you want to insert new text.

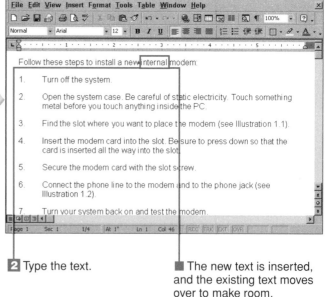

2 Type the text.

■ The new text is inserted, and the existing text moves over to make room.

How do I switch to Overtype mode?

If you *want* to type over text, press the Insert key to switch to Overtype mode. Then any text you type will overwrite what's onscreen at that point.

What keyboard shortcuts can I use?

Press Delete to delete characters to the right of the insertion point. Press Backspace to delete characters to the left of the insertion point. You can also press Ctrl+Delete to delete the next word or Ctrl+Backspace to delete the preceding word.

How do I undo a text deletion?

If you delete text by mistake, you can undo the deletion. Click the Undo button or choose Edit ➪ Undo.

Why does text disappear when I start typing?

Check the status bar. If you see OVR, you are in Overtype mode rather than Insert mode. Switch to Insert mode by pressing the Insert key.

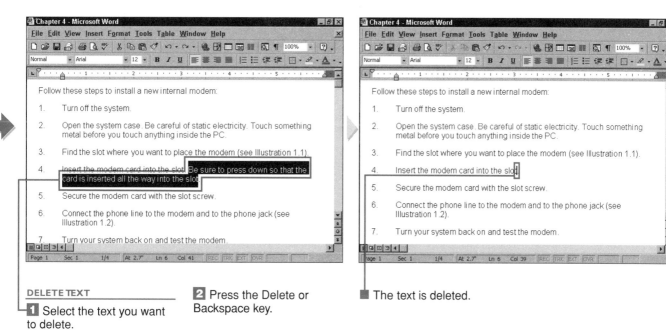

DELETE TEXT

1 Select the text you want to delete.

2 Press the Delete or Backspace key.

■ The text is deleted.

UNDO AND REPEAT A COMMAND

The command you will probably value the most in Word is Undo. Use this command to undo any action just performed. For instance, if you accidentally delete text, use the Undo command. Just choose

Edit ➪ Undo or click the Undo button.

Sometimes you may undo a command and then think, "Why did I undo that? Now I want to undo the undo!" In this case,

click the Redo button. What you just undid is restored.

If you want to execute the same command again, choose it again or simply choose Edit ➪ Repeat.

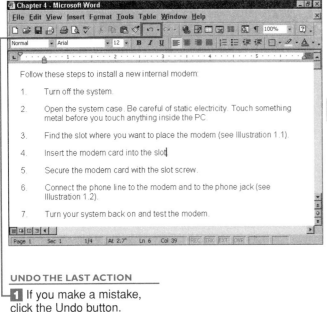

UNDO THE LAST ACTION

1 If you make a mistake, click the Undo button.

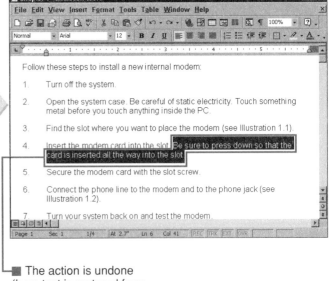

■ The action is undone (here text is restored from being deleted).

TIPS

I'm not sure what I've done! What happened?

Be careful when you choose an action to undo from the Undo list. Some of the items listed may sound similar. Be sure to choose the correct action.

How do I undo the undo?

You can undo the last undo by clicking the Redo button. To undo a previous undo, click the down arrow next to the Redo button and choose the action you want to redo.

How else can I undo something?

You can also choose Edit ➪ Undo, or press Ctrl+Z.

What's the shortcut key for repeating a command?

Press F4 to repeat a command.

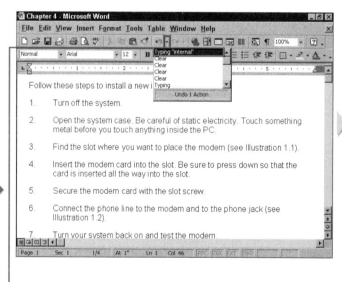

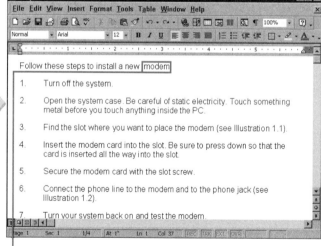

UNDO A PREVIOUS ACTION

1 Click the down arrow next to the Undo button.

2 Choose the command you want to undo.

■ That command is undone.

MOVE TEXT

W hen you edit a document, think about the flow of the content. Are the ideas in the right order? Does the document follow logically from one point to the next? If the order isn't exactly right, you can move text.

When moving text, first cut it from its current location and then paste it in the new location. The fastest way to do this is with the toolbar buttons (shown here), but you can also use the Edit ⇨ Cut and Edit ⇨ Paste commands.

Word places the cut text on the clipboard, a temporary holding spot. The text remains on the clipboard until you cut or copy something else.

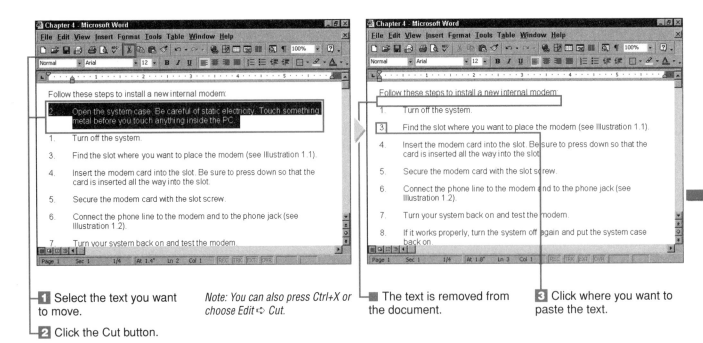

1 Select the text you want to move.

2 Click the Cut button.

Note: You can also press Ctrl+X or choose Edit ⇨ Cut.

■ The text is removed from the document.

3 Click where you want to paste the text.

Can I drag and drop text?

As another alternative for moving text, you can perform a drag and drop. Usually beginners have a hard time getting a feel for this. To drag text to a new location, select the text. Then put the pointer over the selected text, hold down the left mouse button, and drag. Release the mouse button when you have dragged the text to the desired spot.

How do I move something to another document?

To move text to another document, select the text and click the Cut button. Use the Window menu to switch to that document. Then click where you want to place the text and click the Paste button.

How do I undo a text move?

Choose Edit ⇨ Undo or click the Undo button to undo a move.

The Cut command or button or the Paste command or button is dimmed. Why?

Before you can cut text, you must select it. If the Cut command and button are dimmed, it means nothing is selected. Before you can paste text, you must cut or copy it. If the Paste command and button are dimmed, first select the text you want to cut and then paste it.

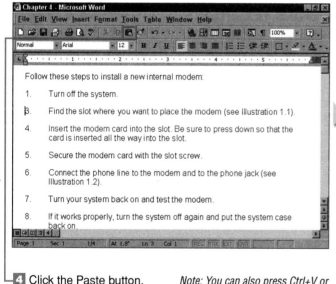

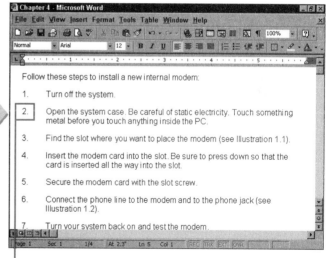

4 Click the Paste button.

Note: You can also press Ctrl+V or choose Edit ⇨ Paste.

■ The text is moved to the new location.

COPY TEXT

If you have to repeat the same information in a document, you can copy the text rather than retype it. Another reason you might copy text is when you want to say something similar. You can copy the text and then modify it. For instance, I can copy the steps for moving text and then modify them so that they pertain to copying text.

You can also copy a passage that you want to edit and then compare the original to the edited version.

Copying text is similar to moving text, but you end up with two versions of the text and use the Copy button or command. To paste the text, use the Paste button or command.

When you copy text, it is placed on the clipboard. A new feature in this version of Word is the capability to cut and paste multiple selections (this is covered in the next task).

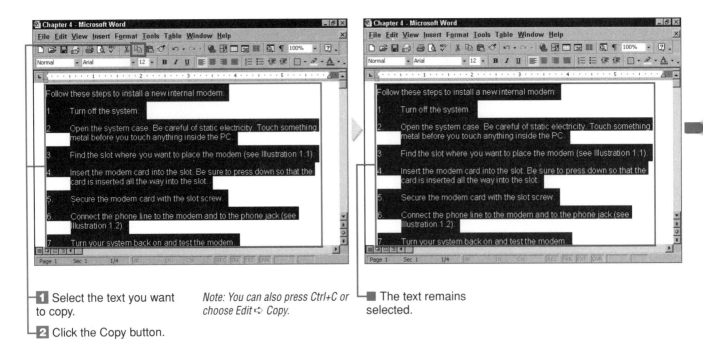

1 Select the text you want to copy.

2 Click the Copy button.

Note: You can also press Ctrl+C or choose Edit ⇨ Copy.

■ The text remains selected.

TIPS

How do I undo a copy?

If you realize right away that you want to undo a copy, choose Edit ⇨ Undo or click the Undo button. Or select the text and press Delete to remove it.

How do I drag a copy?

To drag a copy of text, start by selecting the text. Hold down the Ctrl key. Then put the pointer over the selected text and drag it to the desired location in the document.

Can I copy formatting?

To copy formatting from one section of text to another, use the Format Painter button. For more information on this feature, see Chapter 10.

How do I copy something to another program?

Use the same procedure to copy text from one program to another. For specific information on this task, see Chapter 21.

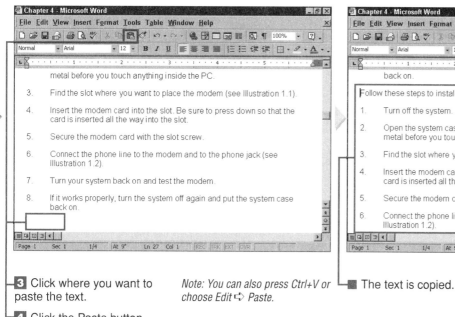

 3 Click where you want to paste the text.

4 Click the Paste button.

Note: You can also press Ctrl+V or choose Edit ⇨ Paste.

 ■ The text is copied.

COPY MULTIPLE SELECTIONS

A new feature in this version of Word is the capability to copy and paste more than one selection. In previous versions you had to copy and paste, and copy and paste again. If you copied something new to the clipboard, it overwrote the last thing you copied (or cut).

Now you can display the clipboard toolbar and use it to copy items to the clipboard or paste items from the clipboard. For example, you might want to pick up several sections of text and then paste them in one location. Or you might want to move several items to a different location in a chapter. When you need to do multiple moves or copies, use the Clipboard toolbar.

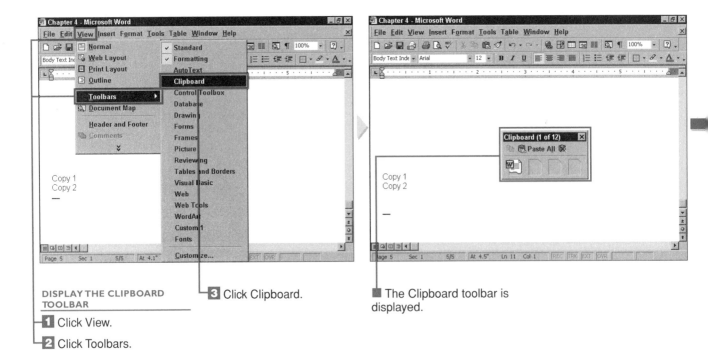

DISPLAY THE CLIPBOARD TOOLBAR

1 Click View.

2 Click Toolbars.

3 Click Clipboard.

■ The Clipboard toolbar is displayed.

How can I tell what each selection contains?

 You can view the contents of the clipboard item by putting the pointer on it. The contents (or the first part of the contents for longer entries) appear as a Screen Tip.

Can I use this toolbar to copy from one Office program to another?

Yes. You can display the Clipboard toolbar in other Office programs. The toolbar displays the last selections cut or copied to the clipboard.

How do I clear the entries?

 To clear the entries on the Clipboard toolbar, click the Clear Clipboard button.

How do I paste all the entries?

 If you want to paste all the entries at once, click the Paste All button.

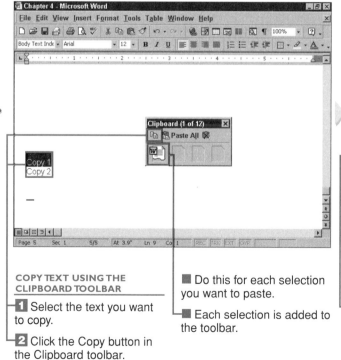

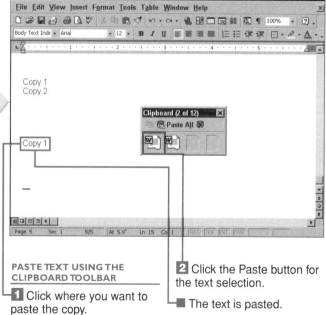

COPY TEXT USING THE CLIPBOARD TOOLBAR

1 Select the text you want to copy.

2 Click the Copy button in the Clipboard toolbar.

■ Do this for each selection you want to paste.

■ Each selection is added to the toolbar.

PASTE TEXT USING THE CLIPBOARD TOOLBAR

1 Click where you want to paste the copy.

2 Click the Paste button for the text selection.

■ The text is pasted.

FIND TEXT

In a short document, finding a particular section is easy — just scan through the text. In a longer document, finding something may not be as simple. You can scroll through and look for a particular section or word, but there's a faster method: have Word do it for you.

Finding text also is useful when you want to check a document. For instance, suppose I want to find all the places where I discuss Internet Service Providers. I can search for this phrase and then review the pertinent sections.

You can control how Word matches what you enter: choose to match the case exactly as you enter it, choose the direction of the search, choose whether whole or partial words are flagged, and so on. You can also search for special characters such as page breaks. This option is covered later in this section. (For information on finding formatting, see Chapter 10.)

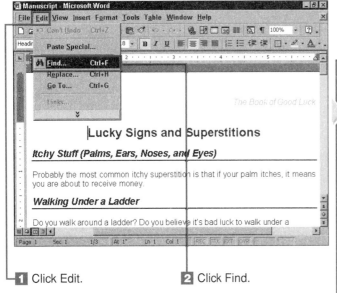

1 Click Edit.

2 Click Find.

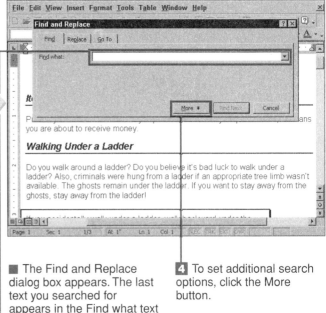

■ The Find and Replace dialog box appears. The last text you searched for appears in the Find what text box.

3 If necessary, delete any entries and then type the text you want to find.

4 To set additional search options, click the More button.

TIPS

Can I search just part of a document?

To search just part of a document, select the text you want to find. Then choose Edit ➪ Find. Word then searches the selection and prompts you to choose whether you want to search the rest of the document.

Why wasn't the word found?

If you don't find a word by searching, there are a few things to try. First, make sure no options are set that limit the search (such as Match case). Second, make sure you typed the word correctly. If you are sure that no options are set and the word was entered correctly, try searching for another word or phrase.

What keyboard shortcuts can I use?

To search again, press Shift+F4. To start a new search, press Ctrl+F.

What options are useful?

If you want to find the entry exactly as you typed it, check Match case. To find all word forms (swim, swimming, swimmer, for instance), check the Find all word forms check box.

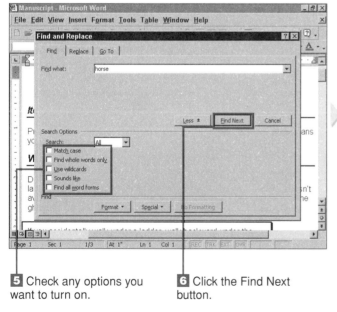

5 Check any options you want to turn on.

6 Click the Find Next button.

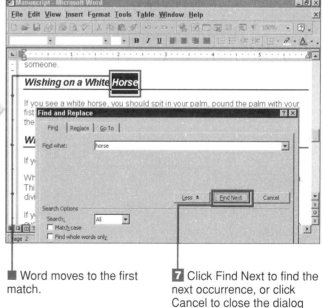

■ Word moves to the first match.

7 Click Find Next to find the next occurrence, or click Cancel to close the dialog box.

REPLACE TEXT

The companion command to Find is Replace. With this command you can find one word or phrase in your document and replace it with another. For instance, suppose you referred to all illustrations in a chapter as Illustration, but your editor wants you to use Figure. You can search for all instances of Illustration and replace them with Figure.

When Word finds a match, it displays the Find and Replace dialog box. You can choose to make the replacement, skip the replacement and find the next one, or make all replacements.

Before you choose Replace All to make all the replacements, make sure the search is working as you intended. It is easy to make replacements that you didn't intend. For example, if you

replace all instances of man with person, you can end up with words such as personager (man is replaced with person in manager). Instead, go through and confirm a few replacements one by one to make sure no weird replacements are made. You can also make changes to how the Replace is done, such as by choosing to Find whole words only.

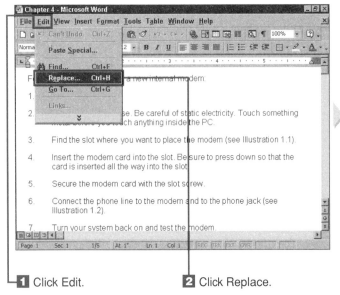

■1 Click Edit.

■2 Click Replace.

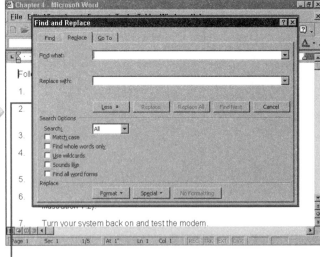

■ The Find and Replace dialog box appears. The last text searched for appears in the Find what text box.

Note: If the dialog box is expanded to show all the options, you can hide these options by clicking the Less button.

TIPS

What are the keyboard shortcuts?

To search again, press F4. To start a new search and replace, press Ctrl+G.

What else can I search and replace?

If you want to replace something with nothing, simply leave the Replace with text box empty. Then perform the Find and Replace. You can also search for and replace formatting, as covered in Chapter 10.

How do I undo a replacement?

If you make a replacement you didn't intend, choose Edit ⇨ Undo or click the Undo button to undo the change.

How can I stop a Find and Replace?

You can cancel a Find and Replace at any time. To do so, click the Cancel button in the Find and Replace dialog box.

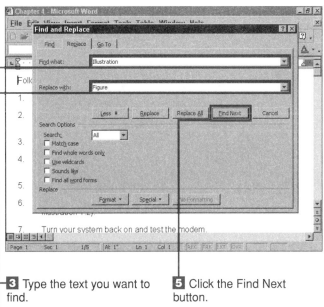

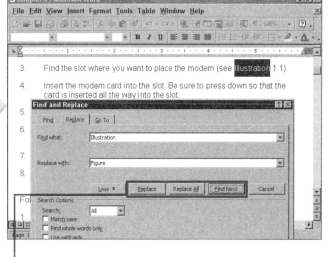

3 Type the text you want to find.

4 Type the text you want to use as the replacement.

5 Click the Find Next button.

6 When Word flags a match, your options are:

■ To skip this replacement and find the next match, click Find Next.

■ To make the replacement, click Replace.

■ To make all replacements, click Replace All.

7 Follow Step 6 for each match found. When the entire document has been searched, you receive a message. Click OK and then Cancel.

FIND AND REPLACE SPECIAL CHARACTERS

Sometimes it's not a word or a phrase you want to find, but a particular character, such as a tab or a page break. For instance, suppose you want to check all page breaks in a chapter. You can search for page breaks.

You can also search for and replace special characters. As an example, suppose you used the spacebar to indent text rather than the Tab key. You can search for the spaces and replace them with tabs. Or as another example, you can search for extra hard returns in your document.

You can search for the following special characters: paragraph mark, tab character, comment mark, caret character, column break, em dash, en dash, endnote mark, field, footnote mark, graphic, manual line break, manual page break, nonbreaking hyphen, nonbreaking space, optional hyphen, section break, and white space. You can also use the Special button to insert wildcards for any character, digit, or letter.

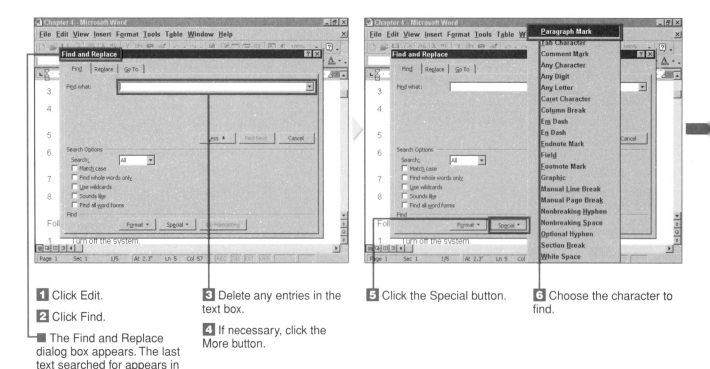

1 Click Edit.

2 Click Find.

■ The Find and Replace dialog box appears. The last text searched for appears in the Find what text box.

3 Delete any entries in the text box.

4 If necessary, click the More button.

5 Click the Special button.

6 Choose the character to find.

How do I even get these special characters to start with?

 You can insert special characters such as an em dash in your document by using keyboard shortcuts or by choosing Insert ⇨ Special Character. See Chapter 3 for information on inserting special characters.

How can I view entries such as tabs and returns?

You can display nonprinting characters such as hard returns, spaces, and tabs. To do so, click the Show/Hide ¶. To hide these characters, click the button again.

How do I search for and replace special characters?

 To search and replace, either choose Edit ⇨ Replace or, once the Find and Replace dialog box displays, click the Replace tab. Enter the character to find and replace, and then click the Find Next button.

Can I search for and replace formatting or styles?

Yes. You can also find and replace styles or formatting. For information on this topic, see Chapter 10.

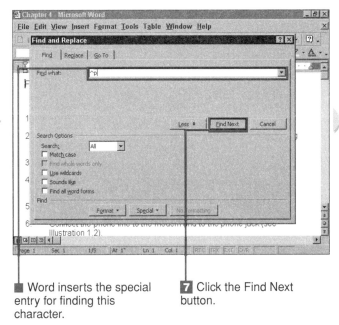

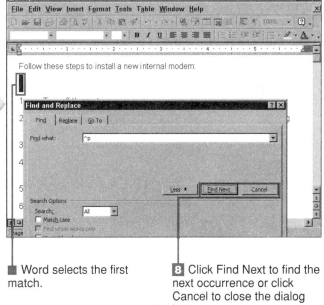

■ Word inserts the special entry for finding this character.

7 Click the Find Next button.

■ Word selects the first match.

8 Click Find Next to find the next occurrence or click Cancel to close the dialog box.

SORT TEXT

The Sort command is easy to miss because it is in the Table menu, and although you can sort table entries, you can also use this command to sort paragraphs. You might, for example, want to alphabetize a phone list or sort a to-do list based on dates. You can sort text, numbers, or dates using the Sort command. Word reorders the selected paragraphs in either ascending or descending order based on what you chose.

You can also choose to sort a tabbed list via more than one field. Select the first sort field from the Sort by drop-down list. Use the other Sort by drop-down lists to choose a second (or third) sort order. Note that this does not work with paragraphs without tabs.

For information on sorting table entries, see Chapter 11.

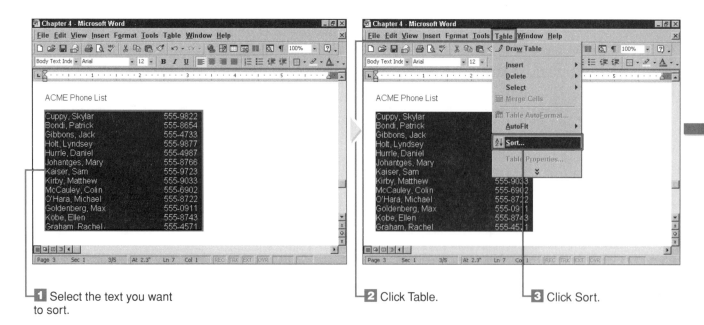

1 Select the text you want to sort.

2 Click Table.

3 Click Sort.

How do I sort numbers?

To change how Word views selected paragraphs, display the Type drop-down list and select text, numbers, or dates.

Why was the entire document sorted?

If you don't select text before choosing Table ⇨ Sort, Word thinks you want to sort the entire document. Click Cancel and then select the text you want to sort.

How do I keep the headings from being sorted?

If you are sorting a tabbed list and each column has a heading, you won't want to sort this header row. Tell Word to leave this row alone by checking the Header row option.

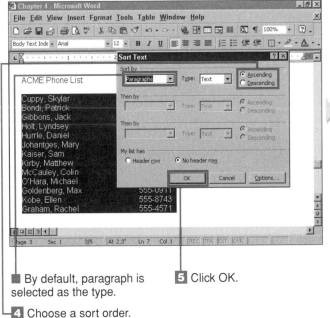

■ By default, paragraph is selected as the type.

4 Choose a sort order.

5 Click OK.

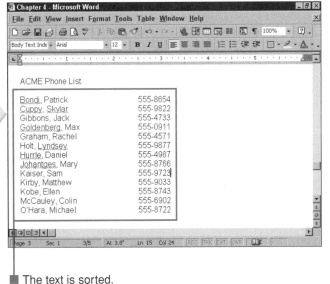

■ The text is sorted.

CHANGE THE CASE OF TEXT

One mistake that used to be easy to make is typing with the Caps Lock key on — but no longer. Word automatically checks for this and toggles it off. But if it ever happens — if you look at your screen and see something like "nOW IS THE TIME FOR ALL GOOD MEN" — there is a shortcut for changing the case.

You can choose from several different cases. Use Sentence case to capitalize the first word in a sentence and make all other text lowercase. (Any words that are capitalized remain this way.) You can also choose lowercase or uppercase. Use Title case to capitalize all words in a sentence. And finally, use Toggle case to reverse the capitalization in a selection.

Note that you can tell when the Caps Lock key is on because it switches on a light on your keyboard. This key is a toggle. Press it once to turn on Caps Lock. Press it again to turn off Caps Lock.

To view how Word handles typing with the Caps Lock key on and other automatic capitalizations, display the AutoCorrect options.

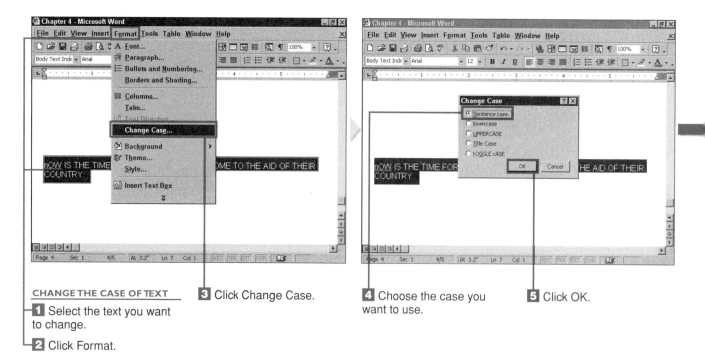

CHANGE THE CASE OF TEXT

1 Select the text you want to change.

2 Click Format.

3 Click Change Case.

4 Choose the case you want to use.

5 Click OK.

What are the keyboard shortcuts?

To toggle from one case style to another, select the text and then press Shift+F3. Word cycles through each of the available case styles.

What is another way to change the case?

You can also apply a case format to selected text. Use Small Caps to display the first letter in a regular-size capital and other letters in smaller caps. You can also use All Caps to make text all uppercase. To make these changes, select the text and then choose Format ⇨ Font. In the Effects area, choose the case style you want. Click OK.

What is AutoCorrect?

AutoCorrect is a Word feature that automatically corrects some common mistakes such as typing with the Caps Lock key on. Word also replaces common misspellings with the correct spelling. For more information on this feature, see Chapter 5.

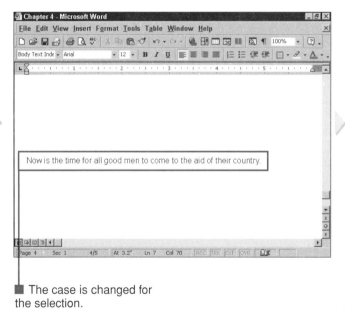

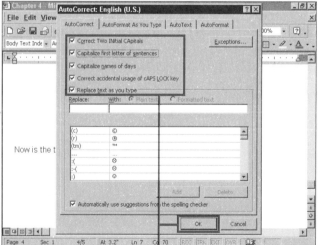

■ The case is changed for the selection.

SET CAPITALIZATION OPTIONS

1 Click Tools.

2 Click AutoCorrect.

■ You see the AutoCorrect tab of the Options dialog box.

Note: Any options with a check are turned on.

3 Check or uncheck any options.

4 Click OK.

HOW TO CHECK FOR ERRORS

A key step in editing a document is checking for errors. You can use some of the features of Word to help with this task, such as checking your spelling and grammar.

Note: Keep in mind that you still need to proofread. Word's spelling and grammar features are not foolproof. For instance, Word doesn't always know if a word is misused, only if it is misspelled. Be sure to do a final read of the document yourself.

Checking for Spelling Errors

There's nothing more unprofessional than a spelling error. You can make all the excuses in the world, but if your document contains a spelling error (even if it's a typo!) your audience will notice.

Word provides a couple ways to check and fix spelling errors:

► Word automatically corrects some common misspellings. Try typing "alot," for instance. You can't!

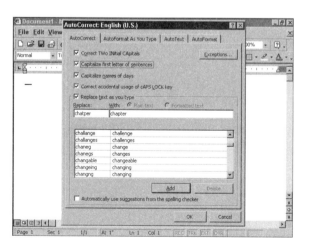

► Word flags words it thinks are misspelled with a red squiggly line. You can retype the word, display suggested spellings, or ignore the flagged word.

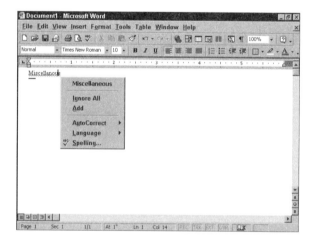

► You can run the spelling check program and go through and verify any flagged words. You have the choice of replacing the word, ignoring the word, or correcting the word manually.

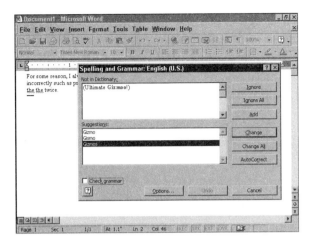 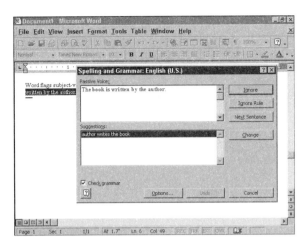

Checking Your Grammar

If your spelling is perfect, but your grammar
ain't, you are in trouble. You can also use
Word to flag possible grammatical mistakes.
You can review any automatically flagged
errors (indicated by green squiggly
underlines), or run the grammar checker and
go through and verify the document.

MAKE AUTOMATIC SPELLING CORRECTIONS

Word tries to help you create a document that is free from error. For some words, you can't type them incorrectly even if you wanted to! Word automatically corrects some mistakes. For example, try typing "teh." You can't. Word automatically replaces this common typo with the correct

word *the*. Word recognizes some common misspellings and typographical mistakes and makes the replacement automatically.

The feature that makes spelling changes automatically is AutoCorrect. You can review the AutoCorrect entries that are already set up and control what other AutoCorrect options apply.

In addition to the words that Word already "knows," you can add other words to the list. For instance, I commonly mistype chapter as *chatper*. Rather than correct this mistake in each document, I added an AutoCorrect entry so that Word makes the replacement for me.

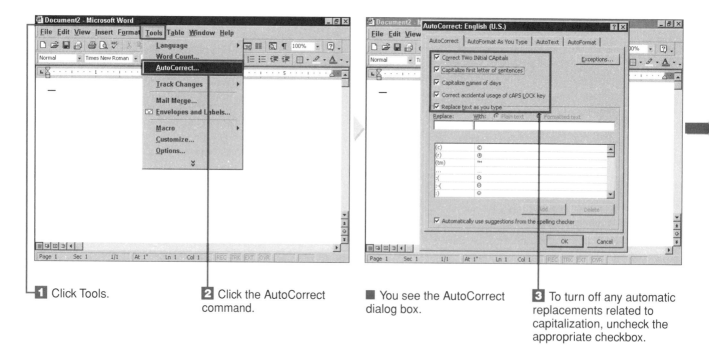

1 Click Tools.

2 Click the AutoCorrect command.

■ You see the AutoCorrect dialog box.

3 To turn off any automatic replacements related to capitalization, uncheck the appropriate checkbox.

How do I set exceptions?

You can set exceptions for capitalization for First Letter, Initial Caps, and Other Corrections. To do so, click the Exceptions button and then click the appropriate tab. Make any additions or deletions and then click OK.

Sometimes I get formatting, such as bullets. What happened?

In addition to AutoCorrect entries, Word also makes some changes to formatting. You can view and make changes to these automatic replacements on the AutoFormat As You Type tab. See Chapter 10 for more information.

What do the checkbox options do?

The checkboxes set some of the capitalization changes that are made automatically. You can turn any option off by unchecking its checkbox.

Sometimes when I start to type I see a little screen tip with a word or phrase. Why?

Word automatically saves common entries (such as the months of the year) as AutoText entries. You can start to type the entry and when Word guesses the entry, press Enter to have Word complete the rest of the entry.

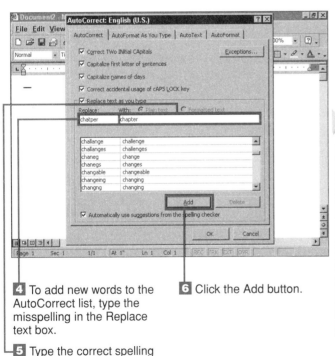

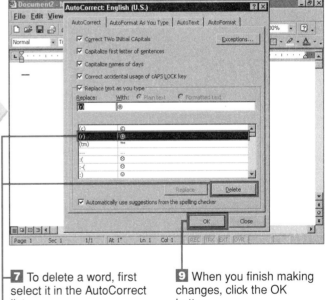

4 To add new words to the AutoCorrect list, type the misspelling in the Replace text box.

5 Type the correct spelling in the With text box.

6 Click the Add button.

7 To delete a word, first select it in the AutoCorrect list.

8 Click the Delete button.

9 When you finish making changes, click the OK button.

CHECK YOUR SPELLING AS YOU TYPE

As you type, you may notice that Word puts a squiggly red line under some words, and some sentences, words, or phrases are flagged with a green squiggly line. These squiggly lines are Word's red flags alerting to you to possible misspellings (red) or grammar mistakes (green). You can ignore these flags and continue working, or you can make corrections as you create the document.

When Word flags a spelling mistake, you can ignore it and check your spelling when you are done (covered later in this chapter). Or you can make a correction. You can do any of the following:

► If you made a typo or know the right spelling, you can press Backspace to delete the misspelled word. Then retype the word.

► If only a few characters are wrong, you don't have to retype the entire word. You can also edit the word to correct the misspelling.

► If you don't know the right spelling, you can have Word display some choices.

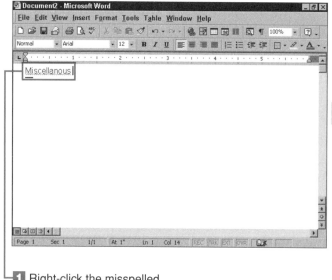

1 Right-click the misspelled word.

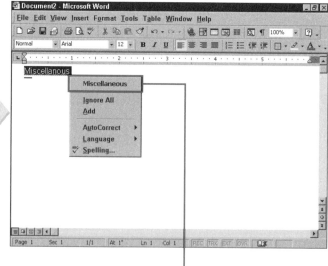

■ You see a pop-up menu.

2 If you see the correct spelling, click it.

I don't see the lines in my document? How do I turn them on?

If you don't see these squiggly lines, this feature may have been turned off. Select the Tools ⇨ Options command and click the Spelling & Grammar tab. Be sure the Check spelling as you type checkbox is checked.

My document still had spelling errors! What happened?

Remember that the spelling program does not replace a careful proofreading of your work. Word does not know the difference between *there*, *their*, or *they're*. Word doesn't know when you mean *weather* and when you mean *whether*. The program just knows when a word is misspelled. You can have perfect spelling, and still look like an ignoramus. Proofread your document!

What if I don't see any suggested spellings?

If you don't see any suggested spellings, be sure you right-clicked on a flagged word. If you right-click on a word that is not flagged, you see a shortcut menu for editing the text.

I make the same mistake all the time!

If you make the same mistake all the time, add the word to the dictionary so that it is not flagged (click Add), or add the word to the AutoCorrect list (click AutoCorrect and then select the correct spelling).

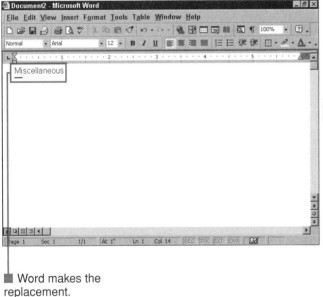

■ Word makes the replacement.

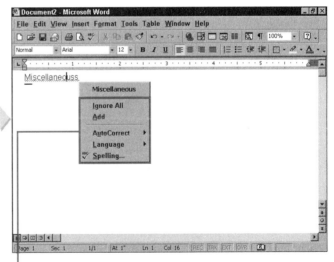

■ You can also choose to ignore the misspelling, add the misspelled word to the dictionary, or start the Spelling program by selecting the appropriate command.

CHECK YOUR GRAMMAR AS YOU TYPE

In addition to checking spelling errors, Word also flags grammatical errors. (Or at least what it thinks are grammatical errors.) Word underlines what it considers questionable phrases and sentences. You can spot these grammatical errors by the green squiggly underline. Like the on-the-fly spelling check, you can choose to ignore the errors and check your grammar later. Or you can make corrections as you go.

You can do any of the following: select a replacement from the suggested list, display an explanation of the flagged error, choose to ignore the error, or start a complete grammar check.

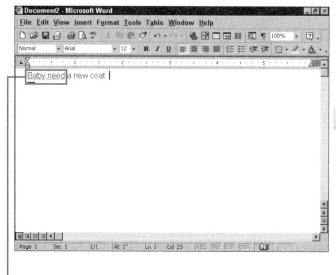

1 Right-click the green underlined word(s).

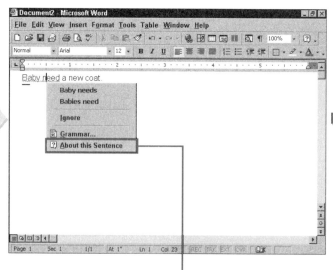

■ You see a pop-up menu that lists suggestions.

2 To get an explanation, click the About this Sentence command.

TIPS

I don't see the lines in my document. How do I turn them on?

If you don't see the squiggly lines, this feature may have been turned off. Select Tools ➪ Options and click the Spelling & Grammar tab. Be sure the Check grammar as you type checkbox is checked.

I don't want to see the lines in my document. How do I turn them off?

You can turn off the grammar checker by unchecking the Check grammar as you type checkbox on the Spelling & Grammar tab. You can also hide the grammar errors (hide the flags) by checking the Hide grammatical errors option in this dialog box.

My document still had grammatical errors! What happened?

Just because you got an A+ according to the grammar checker doesn't mean your document doesn't include errors. You still must proofread. You'd be surprised at how many problems Word doesn't flag.

I don't see a menu with grammar options. What happened?

Word may flag a single word or phrase in the document. Be sure to right-click a flagged item. Otherwise, you see a shortcut menu for editing the text.

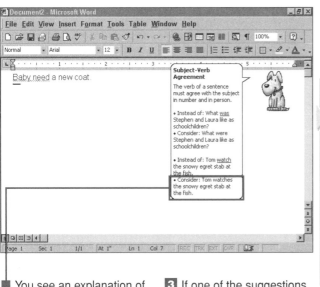

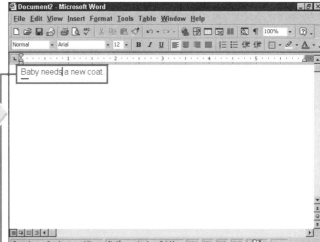

■ You see an explanation of the error. Click outside the help balloon.

3 If one of the suggestions is correct, click it to replace your original text with the new suggested revision.

■ Word makes the replacement and moves to the next error.

CHECK YOUR SPELLING

When you are trying to concentrate on your writing, you may not want to be bothered with spelling. You might want to keep your train of thought going and worry about corrections later. If so, you can run the spelling check program to check the words in your document.

The spelling check program works by comparing words in the document to words in its dictionary. When the speller cannot find a word, it flags it as misspelled and displays a dialog box. Keep in mind that just because a word is flagged doesn't necessarily mean it is misspelled. It just means Word cannot find the word in its dictionary. Proper names and some terminology, for instance, may be flagged although they are spelled correctly.

When Word flags a word and displays the dialog box, you have the option of replacing the word with a suggested spelling, correcting the word yourself, skipping the word, creating an AutoCorrect entry, or adding the word to a custom dictionary. After you select an option, Word moves to the next word and checks all words in the document.

Word also flags double words such as "the the." You can choose to delete the second occurrence or skip it. Word may also flag grammar errors. For more information on making corrections to these errors, see the next task.

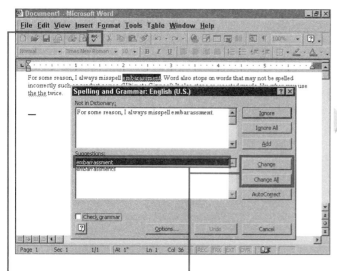

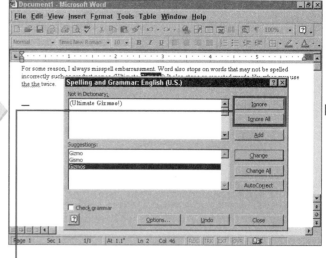

1 Click the Spelling and Grammar button.

■ For spelling errors, Word highlights the word and displays the Spelling and Grammar dialog box.

2 To replace the word with one of the suggested spellings, click the spelling in the Suggestions list. Click Change to change this occurrence. Click Change All to replace all occurrences of the word.

3 To skip this occurrence and go to the next one, click Ignore. To skip all occurrences of this word, click Ignore All. Use this option for names or terms that are spelled correctly but not included in Word s dictionary.

What if Word flags a word all the time that is not misspelled?

If you want Word to stop flagging a word, add it to your dictionary. To do so, click the Add button. Do this for words, such as common names or terms, that you don't want to continually have to check.

What's the keyboard shortcut for starting a spelling check?

You can also press F7 to select the Spelling and Grammar command.

I make the same mistake all the time!

If you want to add the error and its correction to the AutoCorrect list, click the AutoCorrect button. When you make this same mistake, Word automatically replaces the misspelled word with the correct spelling.

Do I have to check the entire document?

No. To check just part of the document, select the part you want to check. Then select the Spelling and Grammar command.

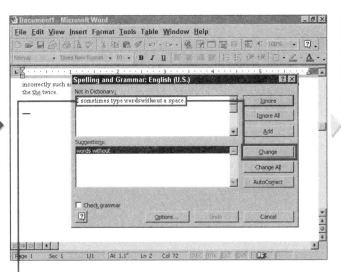

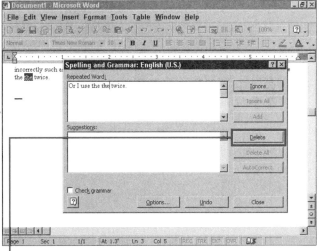

4 If none of the replacements are correct, you can correct the error manually. Edit or type the word and click the Change button.

5 If Word flags a repeated word, click the Ignore button to ignore and keep the repeated word. Or click the Delete button to delete one of the words.

6 Continue making corrections until you go through the entire document. When you see the message that the spelling and grammar check is complete, click the OK button.

CHECK YOUR GRAMMAR

By default, Word also checks grammar when you do a spelling check. The grammar checker knows and checks for certain grammatical rules such as subject-verb agreement. When the grammar checker finds a word, phrase, or sentence that breaks one of these rules, it flags the error and often makes suggestions on how to correct the problem.

For some problems, a suggested correction will be listed. You can choose to change the text to the suggestion. Sometimes a correction will not be listed (or will be incorrect).

As another alternative, you may intend the grammatical mistake. You can ignore the flag. If you don't understand why a sentence was flagged, use the Office Assistant to display help on the grammatical problem.

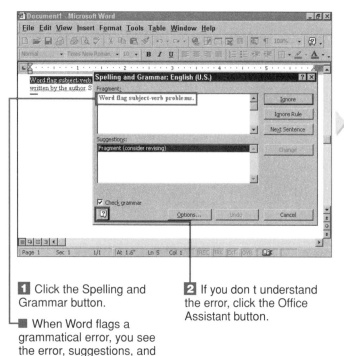

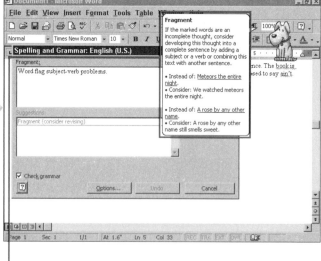

1 Click the Spelling and Grammar button.

■ When Word flags a grammatical error, you see the error, suggestions, and options for fixing the problem.

2 If you don t understand the error, click the Office Assistant button.

■ You see a pop-up explanation of the problem as well as some examples.

TIPS

I don't want to deal with grammar checking. How do I turn it off?

If you don't use the grammar checker, you can tell Word not to check grammar. To do so, uncheck the Check grammar checkbox in the Spelling and Grammar dialog box.

What controls what is flagged and what is not?

The writing style and rules for that style control what is flagged. You can select a different writing style and also customize the rules. See the next task in this chapter.

What if I don't like a particular rule?

You can tell Word to ignore a rule by clicking the Ignore Rule button during a spelling and grammar check. You can also customize the rules, as covered in the next task.

How do I get rid of the explanation?

If you click the Office Assistant button in the dialog box, it will display an explanation for each flagged sentence. To turn these explanations off, click the Office Assistant button again.

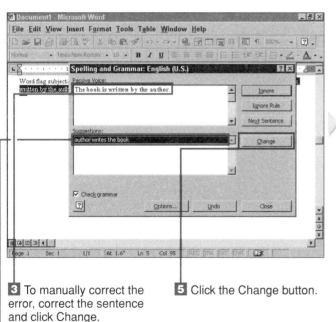

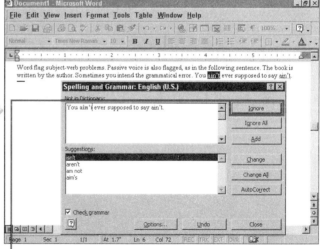

3 To manually correct the error, correct the sentence and click Change.

4 To use one of the suggested changes, click the one you want in the Suggestions list.

5 Click the Change button.

6 To ignore the flagged sentence and move to the next one, click the Ignore button. To skip to the next sentence and leave this sentence flagged, click the Next Sentence button (not shown when checking a spelling error).

■ Continue making corrections until you go through the entire document. When you see the message that the spelling and grammar check is complete, click the OK button.

CHANGE HOW THE CHECKS ARE PERFORMED

As with most of Word's features, you have a great deal of control over how the Spelling and Grammar features work. For instance, you may prefer to just check the spelling and not the grammar. As another example, Word always displays suggested alternative spellings. If you don't want these displayed, turn off this option. You can also select to ignore certain words.

Word uses business writing rules when it does its grammar check. You may want to use a more formal writing style or a less formal writing style. You can also select whether readability statistics are displayed.

Finally, you can view the specific rules for a particular writing style.

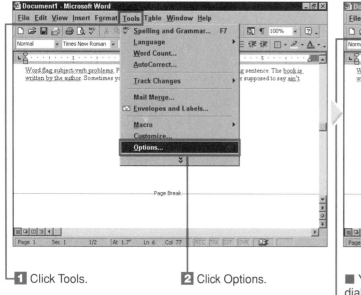

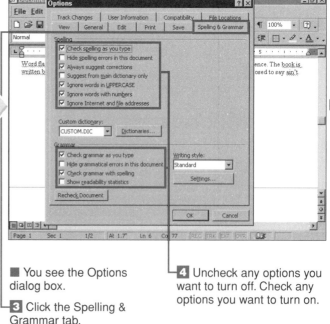

1 Click Tools.

2 Click Options.

■ You see the Options dialog box.

3 Click the Spelling & Grammar tab.

4 Uncheck any options you want to turn off. Check any options you want to turn on.

I made a hodgepodge of the rules. How do I go back to the original rules?re

To go back to the original rules, click the Reset All button in the Grammar Settings dialog box.

What is the custom dictionary?

All words you add to the dictionary are saved to the custom dictionary named custom.dic. If you want, you can create more than one dictionary and then switch among them using the Dictionaries button. For instance, you might want to create a custom dictionary if you are a technical writer and have a highly specialized vocabulary pertinent to your writing.

How else can I access the Spelling and Grammar options?

You can also click the Options button in the dialog box that appears during a spelling check to display the Spelling and Grammar tab. Make any changes and click OK.

What rules can I select for a writing style?

You can select what is required (commas, punctuation, or spaces). You can also check certain grammar and style rules.

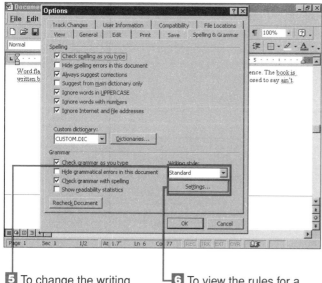

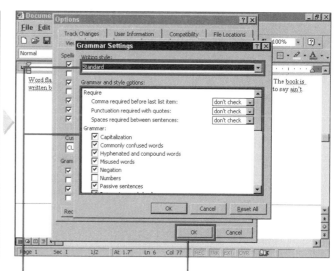

5 To change the writing style used for the grammar check, display the Writing style list and select the style you want.

6 To view the rules for a style, click the Settings button.

7 Check any options to include in the rules. Uncheck rules that you don t want included.

8 Click the OK button.

LOOK UP A SYNONYM

Finding the right word can make the difference between a mediocre writer and one with true talent. As Mark Twain once said, there's a world of difference between lightning and a lightning bug. As you write, you may want to tinker carefully with your word selection. There's nothing more frustrating than having a word right on the tip of your tongue. It means fabulous, but it's not *that* word. What is it?

Rather than go insane (crazy, mad, bonkers, and so on), you can have Word display a list of synonyms. If you find the word in this list, you can replace the word you looked up with the new, *improved* word. If you find a word that's close, you can look up that word, and continue looking until you find the word you want.

With Word, you can look up words and see not only several meanings and synonyms for each of those meanings, but for some words, you can view antonyms or related words.

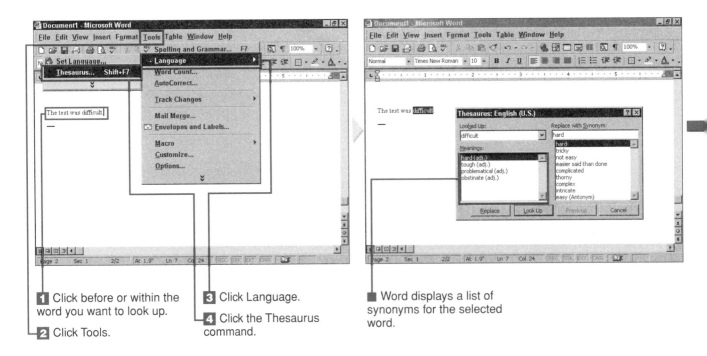

1 Click before or within the word you want to look up.

2 Click Tools.

3 Click Language.

4 Click the Thesaurus command.

■ Word displays a list of synonyms for the selected word.

TIPS

I want to look up one of the words listed in the dialog box.

You can look up any of the words in the dialog box. Click the word for which you want to display synonyms, and then click the Look Up button.

I think I liked an earlier word. How do I go back to a previous list?

If you look up other words and want to go back to a word you previously looked up, click the down arrow next to Looked Up drop-down list. Then click the word you want. Word returns to that list of synonyms.

What if the word is not found?

If Word cannot find the word you are looking up, the dialog box displays the phrase "Not Found" and the selected word. An alphabetical list appears in the dialog box. If you see the word you want in this list, click it, and then click the Look Up button.

What other references can I look up?

If you have other reference products such as Microsoft Bookshelf, you can look up information in these works. Insert the appropriate CD-ROM and then select Tools ➪ Look Up Reference.

GETTING STARTED

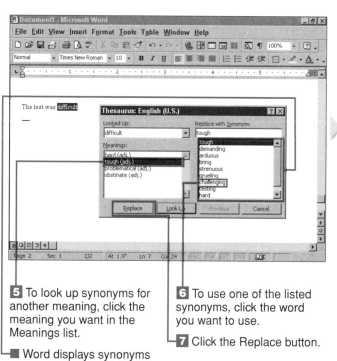

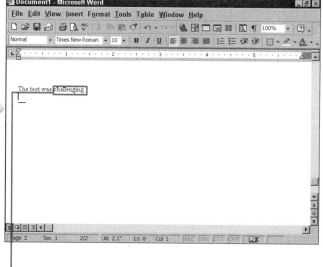

5 To look up synonyms for another meaning, click the meaning you want in the Meanings list.

■ Word displays synonyms for the selected meaning.

6 To use one of the listed synonyms, click the word you want to use.

7 Click the Replace button.

■ Word uses the new word.

103

COUNT THE WORDS IN YOUR DOCUMENT

Many times a writer needs to know the number of words in a document. For instance, magazine and newspaper writers may have to stay within a certain word count. Or a writer may even get paid by the word.

If you want to review the word count and other statistics (number of pages, number of lines, and so on) for your document, you can do so.

You can get additional information about the document by displaying the Properties

dialog box. You can view the same statistics, but also information about modification, print, and creation dates for the document. You can also see the revision number and total editing time for the document.

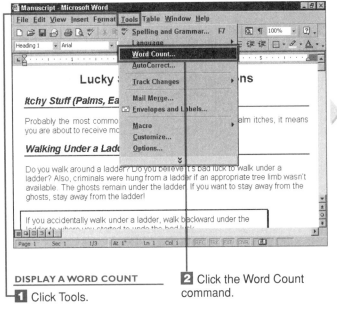

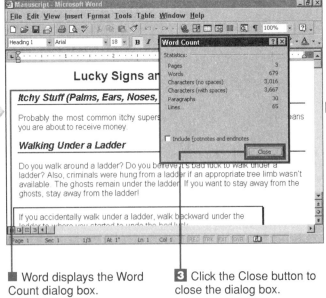

DISPLAY A WORD COUNT

■1 Click Tools.

■2 Click the Word Count command.

■ Word displays the Word Count dialog box.

■3 Click the Close button to close the dialog box.

TIPS

What about the other Properties tabs?

You can click any of the other tabs in the Properties dialog box to review that information. Click the Summary tab, for instance, to view summary information such as the title, subject, author, and keywords for the file.

Do I have to be in Word to view file properties?

No. You can also view file properties from any file window. Right-click the file and select the Properties command.

Are footnotes and endnotes included in the word count?

No. If you want to include them, check the Include footnotes and endnotes checkbox in the Word Count dialog box.

Can I edit the file properties?

You cannot edit some of the file properties such as the file name, file dates, and statistics. You can edit the entries on the Summary tab.

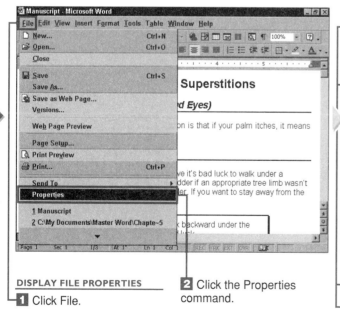

DISPLAY FILE PROPERTIES

1 Click File.

2 Click the Properties command.

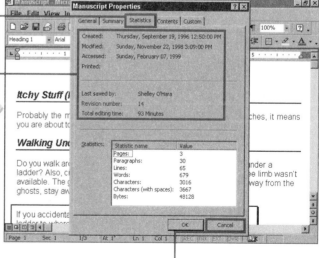

3 Click the Statistics tab.

4 Review document statistics as well as create, modify, access, and print dates for the document.

5 Click the Cancel button to close the dialog box.

WAYS TO VIEW AND PRINT

Depending on what you are working on in a document, you have different ways to view the document. Working on the text? Then Normal view works well. Adding page layout features such as headers or footers? Try Print Layout view. Want to see how the page will appear when printed? Preview the document. Want to proofread (or distribute) a document? Print it. This chapter covers these tasks.

Views of a Document

As mentioned, Word provides several ways to view a document. You can use each of these views, as appropriate to the task at hand:

- To get an overall view of a document, including headers, footers, margins, and other page layout features, preview it.

- To work with some page layout features such as graphics or headers and footers, use Print Layout view.

- To take a closer look (or a step back), zoom the document.

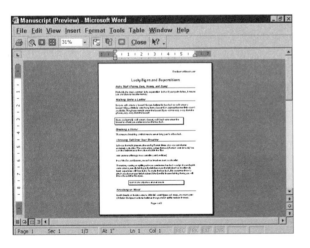

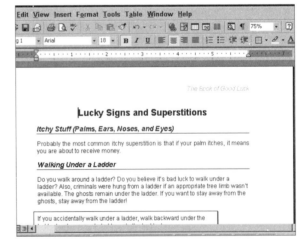

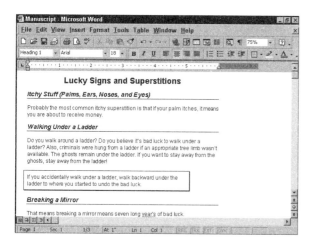

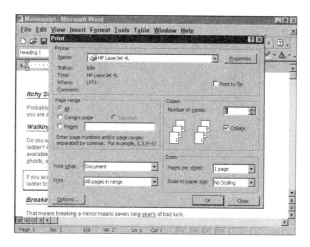

Printing Your Work

When the view looks good, print. You have several options for printing. You can select the number of copies to print, what pages are printed, the printer that is used, and more. You make most of these selections in the Print dialog box.

You can also view the print queue and make any changes to the print jobs, including pausing the printer, canceling a print job, and so on.

PREVIEW A DOCUMENT

Your screen shows only a part of the document, and it doesn't really give you a sense of how the document will look on the page. When you want to see how the document will look when printed, preview it. You can see whether the document is balanced, and whether the margins are right, and whether the headers and footers look okay. (These formatting features are covered in the next part.) If the preview looks good, you can print right from the preview window.

The preview window includes a toolbar with buttons for changing the view, displaying a ruler, and printing. You can even change the margins in print preview.

It's always a good idea to preview the document before printing. Then you can make any changes, if necessary, without wasting paper.

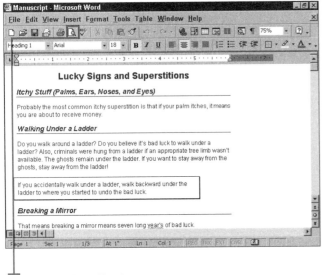

1 Click the Print Preview button.

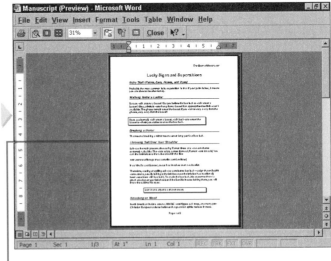

■ You see a full-page preview.

How do I zoom to a different percentage?

 You can use the Zoom control to display other zoom percentages. Zoom in or out on the document, or select other page views (Whole Page, Two Pages, Page Width). Click the down arrow and then select the zoom percentage from the drop-down list.

How do I change the margins in Print Preview?

 One handy feature of preview is that you can change margins. If the ruler isn't visible, click the View Ruler button. Then you can use the rulers to change the margins. See Chapter 9 for more information on changing page margins.

What other views are available?

 You can also click the Shrink to Fit button to shrink the document to fit on one page. Click Toggle Full Screen View to hide the menu bar and toolbars.

Can I print from preview?

 Yes. To do so, click the Print button.

What about formatting a document?

 Before printing your text, you may want to tinker with the appearance of the document — make text bold, center the page, change the margins, indent lines, and so on. Part II of this book covers formatting.

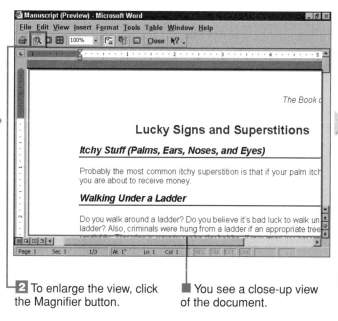

2 To enlarge the view, click the Magnifier button.

■ You see a close-up view of the document.

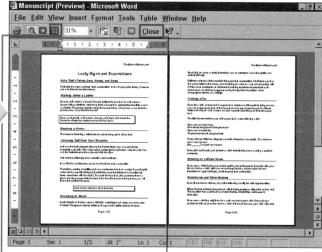

3 To view multiple pages, click the Multiple Pages button and then select the number of pages you want to view from the drop-down palette.

■ You can view two pages side-by-side.

4 When you are done previewing the document, click the Close button.

DISPLAY A PRINT LAYOUT VIEW

When you create a new document, you see the text in Normal view. This view works best most of the time because you can easily see the text and most formatting changes. When you make more complex formatting changes, such as using multiple columns

or adding a picture, you can change to Print Layout view. (For some formatting tasks, you must be in this view.)

Print Layout view shows you the margin areas of the page as well as any headers or footers you have added. You get a sense of where the text falls on the

page. You also see the effects of columns and page breaks as they will appear when you print the document. Rather than seeing a continuous document with dotted lines for page breaks, you see the document page by page.

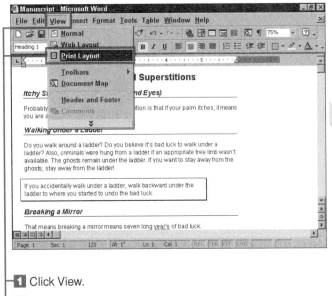

1 Click View.

2 Click Print Layout.

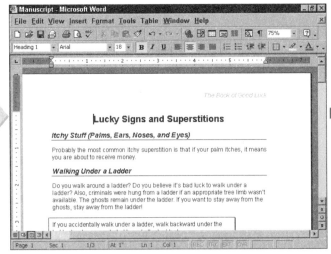

■ You see the document in Print Layout view.

What are the other views listed on the View menu?

If you work with outlines or create Web pages using Word, you can also change to and work with views appropriate for these types of documents.

What are the shortcuts?

You can use the view buttons in the lower-left corner of the screen to switch views. Click the view button you want. If you aren't sure which button does what, put your pointer on the button to display the ToolTip name.

I am in Print Layout view. How did I get there?

For some tasks, Word switches you automatically to Print Layout view. For instance, Word does this if you are adding a graphic such as a clip art image.

I selected the Print Layout command to turn it off, but I am still in Print Layout. How do I get back to the regular view?

The Print Layout command is not a toggle. To turn off Print Layout view, you must select another view.

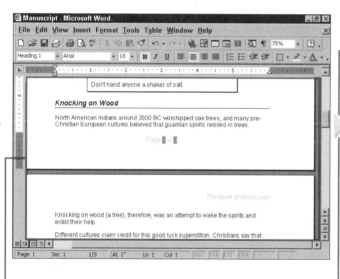

◼ You can scroll through the document to see how the pages break. You can also view headers and footers.

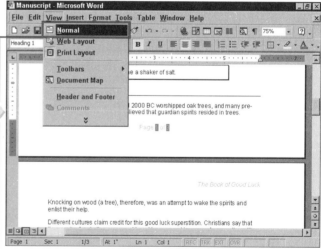

3 To return to Normal view, select the Normal command from the View menu.

ZOOM A DOCUMENT

As you work in a document, you may also want to zoom in or out. If the document is wide, you may want to shrink the view so you can see an entire line without scrolling. If the document uses a small font, you may want to enlarge it so that you can easily read the text.

The default view of a document is 100 percent. You can select a different percentage. Keep in mind that the larger zoom percentage you select, the larger your document will appear. The smaller the percentage, the smaller the document's appearance.

You can also select other views that automatically scale the document to fit.

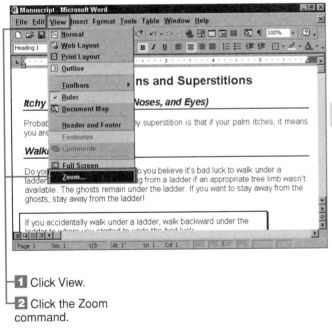

1 Click View.

2 Click the Zoom command.

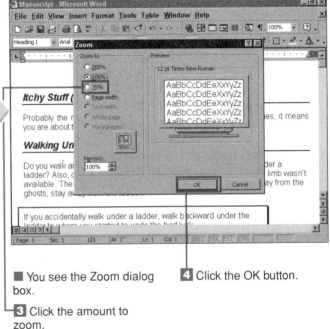

■ You see the Zoom dialog box.

3 Click the amount to zoom.

4 Click the OK button.

GETTING STARTED

What if I want to zoom to a different percentage?

To select a different percentage, type it in the Percent text box or use the spin arrows to set the zoom percentage.

What if I don't know the right percentage to use?

To reduce the document so it fits within the left and right margin, click the Page width option. To reduce the document so the entire page fits within the document window, click the Whole page option.

How do I view multiple pages?

To display multiple pages, click the Many pages option and then click the number of pages you want to view. (You must be in Print Layout mode to access this option.)

What's a shortcut?

You can also use the Zoom Control button in the toolbar to select a zoom percentage. Click the down arrow next to the button and then select the zoom level you want.

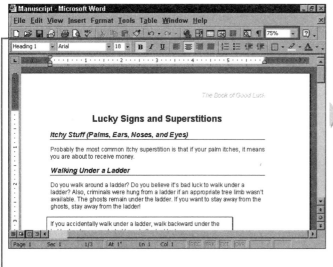

■ The document is zoomed to the selected percentage (here it s 75 percent)

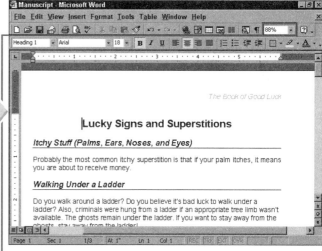

■ You can also select options such as Page width to zoom the text to fill the entire screen (in this case, the page width equals 88 percent).

113

PRINT A DOCUMENT

You will most likely print a copy of your document to proof it and print again when the document is finally complete. Printing is the payoff for all of your hard work.

Most of the time you will print one copy of all pages of the document on the current printer. In this case, you don't need to make any changes to the Print dialog box. Just click OK and the document is printed. In some special cases, you may want to make a change. For instance, you

may not want to print the entire document. Or you may have several printers installed and want to switch among them.

Here are some of the changes you can make:

▸ If you have more than one printer installed, you can switch to a different printer.

▸ If you want to print just the current page, or a range of pages, select what you want to print in the Print range area.

▸ You can print more than one copy of the document. If you print more than one copy, you can also select whether the pages are collated or not by checking (or unchecking) the Collate checkbox.

▸ You can print other information about a document such as comments, styles, and properties.

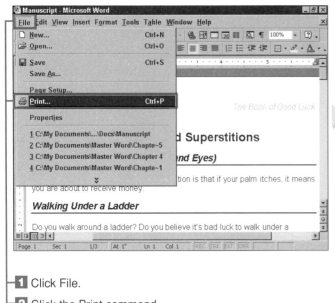

1 Click File.

2 Click the Print command.

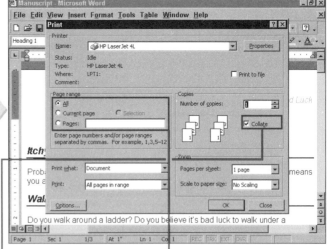

■ You see the Print dialog box, listing the current printer.

3 To print more than one copy, enter the number of copies.

4 To print a different page range, select the range here.

What's the fastest way to print?

If you don't want to make any changes to the Print dialog box, you can simply click the Print button in the toolbar. The shortcut key for the Print command is Ctrl+P.

How do I cancel a print job?

When Word is printing, you see a little printer icon in the taskbar. You can cancel a print job by double-clicking this icon. You see a list of all the current print jobs. Right-click the job you want to cancel and then select the Cancel Printing command. You have to be quick because Word sends the document to the printer pretty quickly.

How do I print just odd or even pages?

You can select to print odd or even pages by displaying the Print drop-down list and then selecting Odd pages or Even pages.

How do I set printer options?

To display additional print settings, click the Options button. Check the options you want to turn on. Uncheck options you want to turn off.

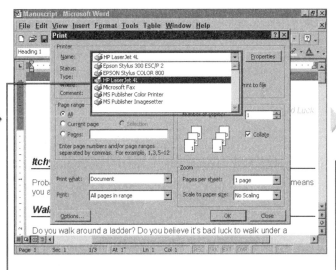

5 To print to a different printer, select it from this list.

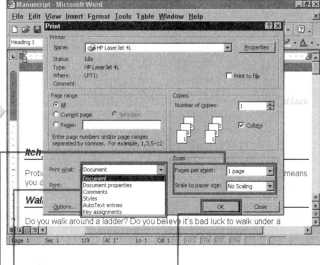

6 To select what is printed, select it from this drop-down list.

7 Select any zoom or scaling options.

8 Click the OK button.

PRINT AN ENVELOPE

A few years ago, it was truly a pain to print an envelope using a word processing program and a printer. You had to set up the margins for the envelope and hope the address somehow got on the envelope. You had to have special trays or feeders for envelopes. Most people simply kept a typewriter and did the envelopes manually. Not so anymore. New printers have simplified handling envelopes, and word processing programs, such as Word, have simplified setting up the envelope layout.

If the document includes an address, you don't even have to type it. Word can find and use the address from a letter. If the document doesn't include an address, you can type it manually. Word takes care of setting up the appropriate settings for printing the envelope. You don't have to worry about complicated indents and margins.

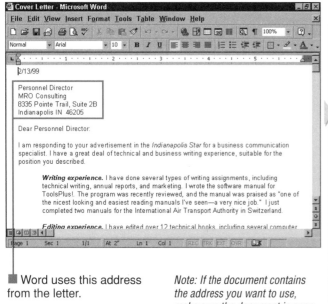

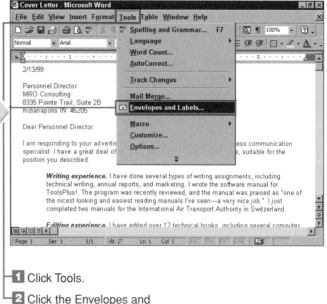

■ Word uses this address from the letter.

Note: If the document contains the address you want to use, make sure the document is open. If the document doesn't include the address, the document does not have to be open.

1 Click Tools.

2 Click the Envelopes and Labels command.

What if I have preprinted envelopes?

If you already have your return address printed on the envelopes, check the Omit checkbox to leave off the return address.

Do I have to enter my return address each time?

After you type your return address once and print an envelope, Word asks whether you want to use this address as the default. If you choose Yes, you won't have to type the address again.

How do I feed the envelope into the printer?

If you aren't sure how to feed the envelope, check out the Feed picture on your printer and in the dialog box.

How do I print mailing labels?

For help on printing mailing labels, see Chapter 16.

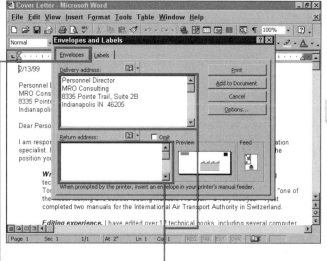

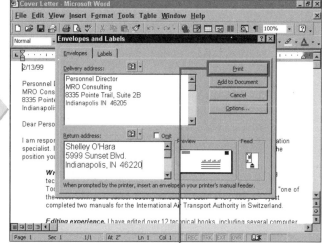

■ You see the Envelopes and Labels dialog box. If your document contains an address, Word displays it in the Delivery address area.

3 If necessary, click the Envelopes tab.

■ The Return Address appears if you have used this feature before.

4 Type or make changes to the Delivery address.

5 Type or edit your return address if needed.

6 Insert the envelope in the manual feed for your printer.

7 Click the Print button.

■ Word prints the envelope.

117

VIEW THE PRINT QUEUE

I f you are printing several documents, or if you share a printer, you may want to view the status of a print job. For instance, you may want to view the number and order of documents in the print queue.

You can also make changes, such as canceling a particular job or pausing a print job.

When you issue the Print command, Word sends the document to the print queue. If the document is short, you may

not even have time to view the print queue. If the document is long, or if other documents are printing, then you can view the print queue. From this queue, you can then make any changes.

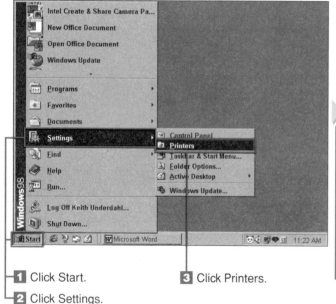

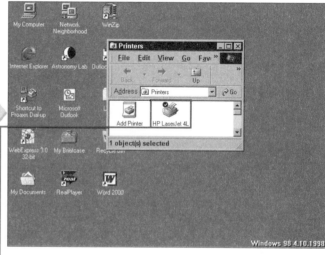

■1 Click Start.

■2 Click Settings.

■3 Click Printers.

■4 Double-click the printer whose queue you want to view.

There's nothing in the print queue. Why?

Documents are sent to the printer pretty quickly. If you don't see anything, all the data has been sent from the print queue to the printer. You cannot cancel or pause the print job.

I get a printer error message!

If the paper runs out or gets jammed, you will see an error message. Correct the problem and then resume printing. For more help on printing problems, see Appendix A.

How do I pause a print job?

If you need to pause a print job, you can open the Printer menu and select the Pause Printing command. To resume printing again, click Printer and then select Pause Printing again.

How do I cancel all print jobs?

To cancel all print jobs, select all the jobs in the print queue. Then open the Document menu and select Cancel Printing.

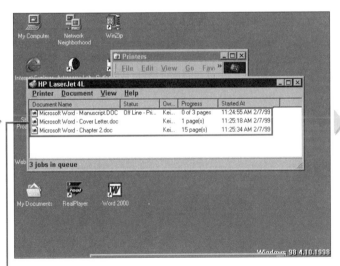

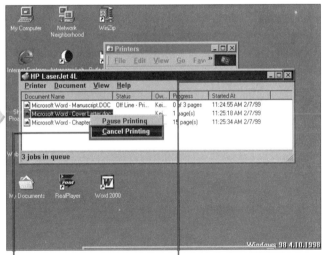

■ You see the jobs in the print queue.

5 To cancel a print job, right-click the job and then select Cancel.

6 To close the printer window, click the Close button.

SET UP A NEW PRINTER

If you purchase a new printer, you need to install it and then set it up in Windows. After the printer is installed, you can use it to print using any applications, including Word.

Windows makes it easy to set up a new printer by including an Add Printer Wizard. You can

follow the steps to install a new printer.

If you have more than one printer connected, you can set up each one. Then you can select which printer is used when printing a document. You can also select one printer as the

default (one that is used unless you make a change).

To set up a new printer, you need your printer disk (if it came with one), or your Windows CD-ROM. You also need to know to which port you connected the printer (usually LPT1).

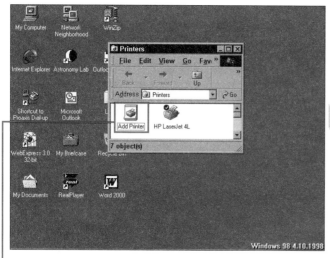

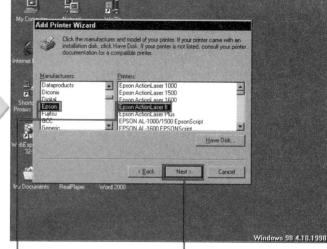

1 Click Start.

2 Click Settings.

3 Click Printers.

4 Double-click the Add Printer icon.

■ You see the first step of the wizard.

5 Click Next.

6 Select the manufacturer and printer.

7 Click Next.

How do I delete an old printer?

If a printer is no longer connected to your PC and you want to delete the printer icon, click Start ➪ Settings ➪ Printers. Right-click the printer you want to remove and then select the Delete command. When prompted, click the Yes button to confirm the deletion.

How do I switch to a different printer?

The Print dialog box lists the default printer. To select another printer, display the Name drop-down list and then select the printer you want to use.

How do I change the default printer?

If you want, you can select a different printer as the default. Select the printer that you use most often. Open the Printers folder and then select the printer you want to set as the default. Open the File menu and select the Set as Default command.

I want to change printer options, such as the paper type. How do I do so?

You can use the Properties tab of the printer to make changes. See the next task.

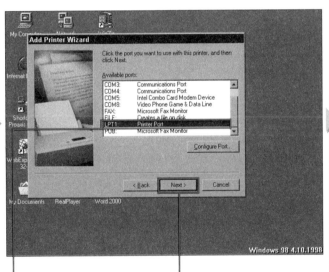

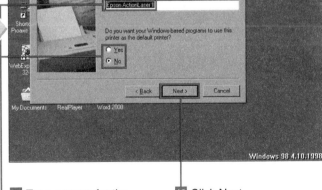

8 Select the port to which your printer is connected (usually LPT1).

9 Click Next.

10 Type a name for the printer.

11 Select whether this printer should be the default printer.

12 Click Next.

` If you want to print a test page, click Yes.

" Select Finish.

15 If prompted, insert the Windows CD-ROM and click OK.

SET PRINTER OPTIONS

I f your printouts are acceptable, you may not even need to alter the printer options. If you aren't satisfied, you can tinker with the settings. Most of these are high-level, nit-picky types of changes. If you want to make a change, you need to have some idea of concepts such as timeout settings and dithering. Also, keep in mind that these settings are always in effect — unless

you change them for a specific print job.

Probably the most common change is to the Paper settings. You might make a change if you use a different paper size all the time. You can select the size you use.

If you share a printer, you might want to make some changes to the General options. Here you can select to print a separator page after each print job, for instance.

If you are having problems with the port, make changes to the Details tab. Don't like how the graphics are printing? Adjust the settings on the Graphics tab. You can also adjust device options such as print density on the Device Options tab.

Depending on your printer, you may see different options listed.

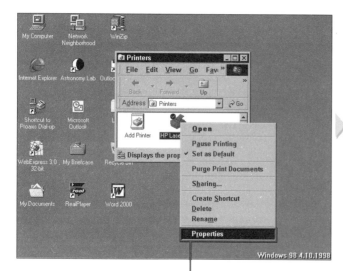

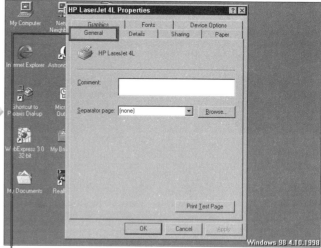

1 Open the printer window by clicking Start ⇨ Settings ⇨ Printers.

2 Right-click the printer you want to modify and select Properties.

3 Select the General tab of the printer Properties dialog box (if it is not already selected) and make any changes.

What is a timeout setting?

If you have a printing problem (for instance, the printer runs out of paper), the program will display an error message. You can select how long before this error message is reported by changing the timeout setting.

How do I select Graphics options?

Graphics options include selecting the resolution, dithering, and intensity of an image. Most of the options are pretty obscure, and you may never need to change them. You can, if needed, experiment with the settings. Or check with your printer manual regarding which options you should try.

What options are available on the Device Options tab?

The Device Options tab includes options for print density, quality, image control, and printer memory. Not sure what an option does? You can get help on any option in a dialog box by right-clicking the option and selecting What's This. You see an explanation of the option.

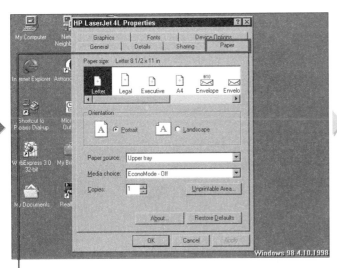

4 To select different paper, click the Paper tab and make any changes.

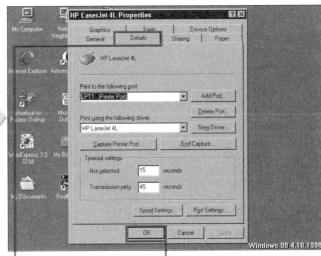

5 To adjust the port settings, click the Details tab and make any changes.

6 Make any changes to the other tabs.

7 Click the OK button.

7 FORMATTING TEXT

8 FORMATTING PARAGRAPHS

THE LOOK OF YOUR DOCUMENT

9 FORMATTING PAGES

7

HOW TO FORMAT TEXT

O ne of the easiest ways to change the look of a document is to change the look of the text. You can make text red or use a fancy font, make the text big or little, or even add animations to make your text dance. You have lots of choices, all covered in this chapter.

Font Styles: Bold, Italic, Underline

The simplest way to make a change to the text is to change the font style. The three most common font styles are bold, italic, and underline. Use these styles to add emphasis to words or headings in a document. Use them for special words such as foreign phrases or references to a source.

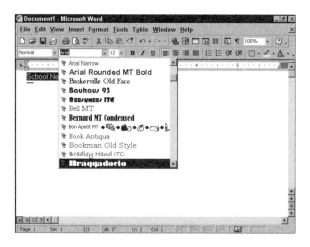

Fonts and Font Sizes

A font is a set of characters (letters and numbers) with a particular look. One font may say party! Another font may say sophisticated. One font may work for a professional report, another for a map to a hoe-down. You can use any of the fonts on your system.

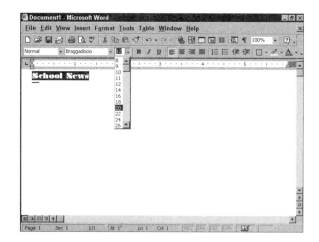

In addition to the look, you can also change the size of the text. You can make the headings bigger, and the fine print smaller. The easiest way to make a change is to use the Font and Font Size drop-down lists in the Formatting toolbar.

Font Special Effects

You have still more choices for the look of the text. You can do any of the following:

▶ Change the color

▶ Highlight text

▶ Use special underline styles

▶ Animate text

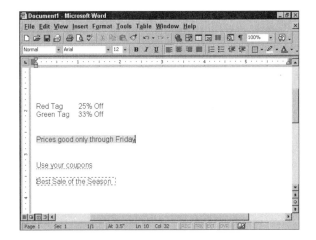

MAKE TEXT BOLD, ITALIC, OR UNDERLINE

One of the easiest changes you can make to your text is to apply some type of emphasis — bold, italic, or underline. These changes are called font styles, and you can use them for any section of text in a document.

You might, for example, want to make the headings bold so they stand out, or use italic to add a particular *emphasis* to a word or phrase. You can also underline text to draw extra attention to it.

To make text bold, italic, or underline, use the Font dialog box or the toolbar. The toolbar is the fastest method. Use this method when you want to make one change quickly. The dialog box method works best when you are making several changes at once (changing the font, style, and size, for example), and when you want to use special features such as selecting an underline style. See the "Change the Font and Font Size" and "Select an Underline Style and Color" tasks later in this chapter for information on using the dialog box.

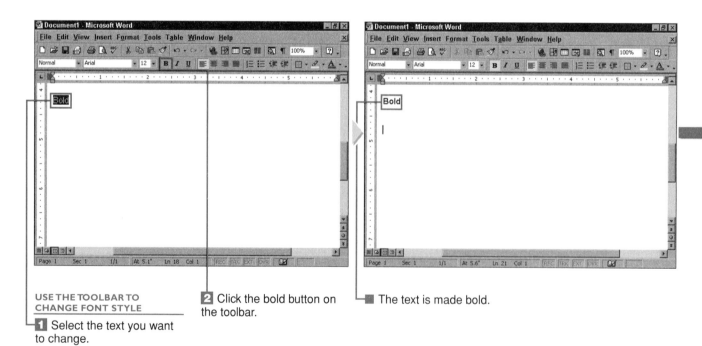

USE THE TOOLBAR TO CHANGE FONT STYLE

1 Select the text you want to change.

2 Click the bold button on the toolbar.

■ The text is made bold.

Can I combine styles?

You can combine styles. For example, click the Bold button and then the Italic button to make text both bold and italic. You can also add underline.

Can I apply formatting as I type?

If you want to turn on a style, you can click the appropriate button, type the text, and then click the button again to turn off the style.

What are the keyboard shortcuts?

If you are a fast typist, you may prefer to use keyboard shortcuts for making changes. If so, you can use these keyboard shortcuts: Ctrl+B for bold, Ctrl+I for italic, and Ctrl+U for underline.

How do I undo a change?

To undo a font style change, select the text again and click the button to turn off the style.

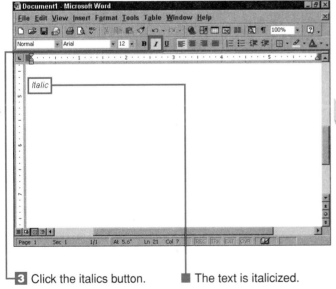

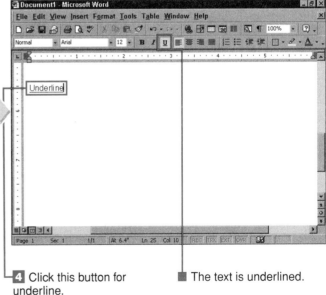

3 Click the italics button. ■ The text is italicized.

4 Click this button for underline. ■ The text is underlined.

CHANGE THE FONT OR FONT SIZE

A font is a set of characters and numbers with a certain look. By changing the font, you can change the look of a document. You can select a font that is appropriate to the type of document. For instance, for a business report, you most likely will use a professional font such as Arial or Rotis Serif. For a party invitation, you might use something fancy such as *Perpetua Italic* or something fun like **Poplar**.

The fonts that are available on your system depend on the type of printer you have and the type of

fonts installed. Your printer has certain built-in fonts that you can use; these fonts are indicated with a printer icon in the Font list. You can also install TrueType fonts, fonts that are actually files stored on your system. Windows includes a lot of TrueType fonts. Some programs also include TrueType fonts, which are installed when you install the program. Plus you can purchase packages of TrueType fonts. This type of font is indicated with a TT in the Font list.

Fonts are measured in points, and there are 72 points to an

inch. The bigger the point size, the bigger the font. You can select from very small fonts such as 8-point type to very large fonts such as 24-point — or larger.

The fastest way to make a change is to use the toolbar. To make several changes at once, use the dialog box.

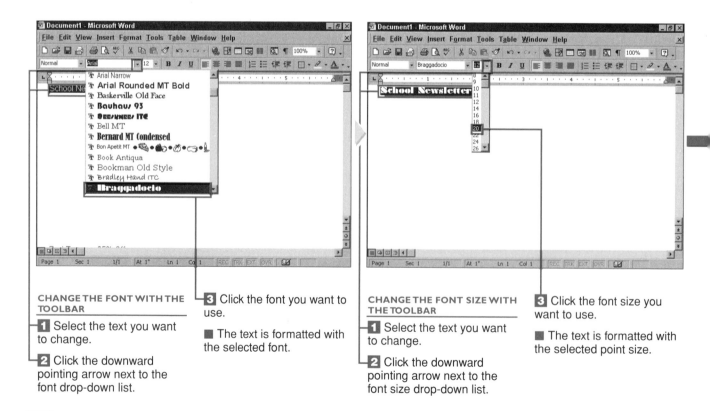

CHANGE THE FONT WITH THE TOOLBAR

◼1 Select the text you want to change.

◼2 Click the downward pointing arrow next to the font drop-down list.

◼3 Click the font you want to use.

■ The text is formatted with the selected font.

CHANGE THE FONT SIZE WITH THE TOOLBAR

◼1 Select the text you want to change.

◼2 Click the downward pointing arrow next to the font size drop-down list.

◼3 Click the font size you want to use.

■ The text is formatted with the selected point size.

Why do I have different fonts than someone else?

 You may have different fonts because you have a different printer and because different fonts have been installed on your system.

How do I install new fonts?

You can purchase font packages to add new TrueType fonts to your system. Click Start ➪ Settings ➪ Control Panel. Double-click the Fonts folder. In the Fonts window, select File ➪ Install New Font. Insert the font disk and then select the appropriate disk and folder from the dialog box. Click OK.

How do I undo a font change?

You can immediately undo a font change by selecting Edit ➪ Undo or by clicking the Undo button. Or you can select the text again, display the Font list, and select another font.

How do I change the default font?

Word uses a certain font and font size for all new documents. If you don't like this font, you can select a different font. To do so, select Format ➪ Font. Select the font and font size you want to use. Click the Default button. When prompted to confirm this change, click the Yes button.

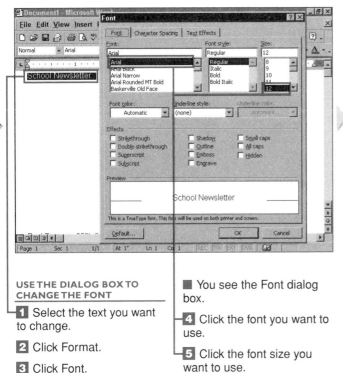

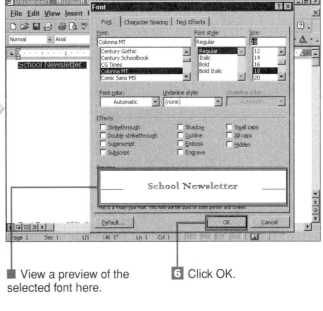

USE THE DIALOG BOX TO CHANGE THE FONT

1 Select the text you want to change.

2 Click Format.

3 Click Font.

■ You see the Font dialog box.

4 Click the font you want to use.

5 Click the font size you want to use.

■ View a preview of the selected font here.

6 Click OK.

CHANGE THE TEXT COLOR

If you have a color printer, or if your document will be displayed rather than printed, you can change the color of text.

You can use color to make certain headings or sections stand out in an office memo sent via e-mail. Because the document will be reviewed onscreen, it won't matter if you don't have a color printer. If you create Web documents (covered in Chapter 23), you can use color to create a more visually appealing document. You can use color to liven up an invitation, flyer, or other document printed on a color printer.

You can select from several different colors. The default color for all text is black.

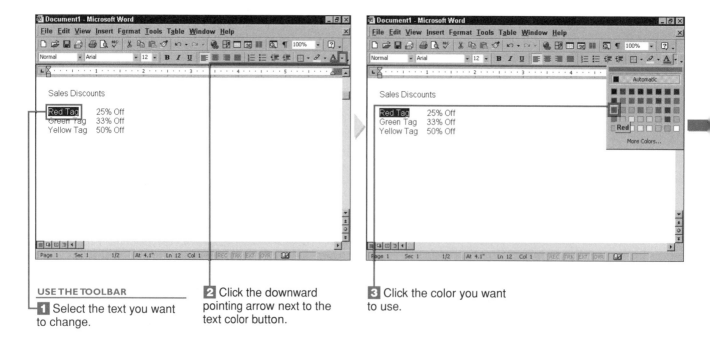

USE THE TOOLBAR

1 Select the text you want to change.

2 Click the downward pointing arrow next to the text color button.

3 Click the color you want to use.

CHANGING THE LOOK OF YOUR DOCUMENT

What if I want to use the same color again on another section of text?

If you are formatting several text sections in the same color, you don't have to display the drop-down list each time and select the color. Instead, you can select the text and click the Font Color button. Word applies the last color you used, which is displayed on the button.

How do colors print on a black and white printer?

If you print a color document on a black and white printer, the colors will be printed in shades of gray.

Why did my text disappear?

If you selected white as the font color, you won't see the text on the white background of the Word screen. You can add a shaded background to make the text stand out, or select another text color.

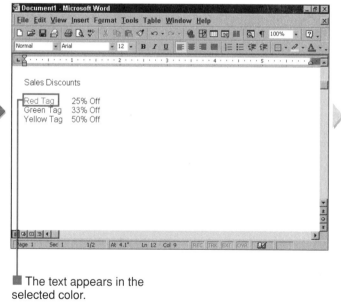

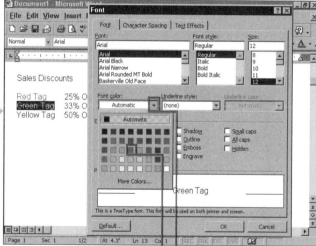

 ■ The text appears in the selected color.

USE THE FONT DIALOG BOX

1 Select the text you want to change.

2 Click Format ➪ Font to see the Font dialog box.

3 Display the Font color drop-down list.

4 Click the color you want to use.

5 Click OK.

133

7

HIGHLIGHT TEXT

When you read a document, you may highlight certain words, sentences, or passages to call attention to the main ideas. Then you can easily skim the document to pick up the main points. It's easy to highlight text in Word.

You might want to highlight the key points in an agenda or meeting summary or to call attention to the most important facts in a report. You might make the section headings in a document stand out by highlighting them.

You can highlight any amount of text you choose. If you have just a little highlighting, you can select the text first. If you want to highlight several passages in a document, use the highlighting pen.

You can select one of several colors for the highlighting. The default color is yellow.

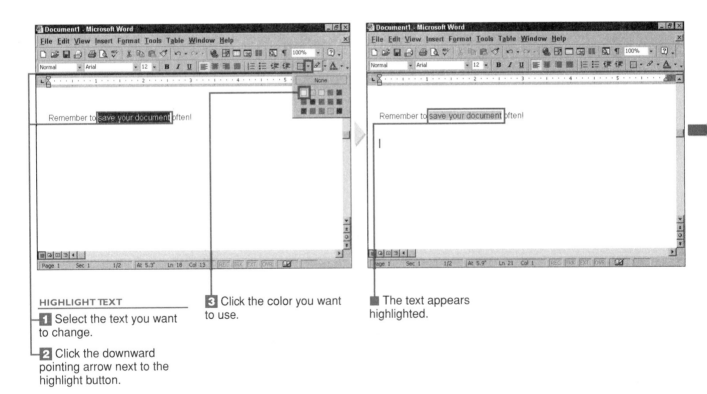

HIGHLIGHT TEXT

1 Select the text you want to change.

2 Click the downward pointing arrow next to the highlight button.

3 Click the color you want to use.

■ The text appears highlighted.

TIPS

How does highlighting print?

If you have a color printer, the highlighting prints in the color you selected. If you have a black-and-white printer, the highlighting is printed as a shade of gray.

Why is my text highlighted when I didn't select highlighting?

When you insert a comment into the text using Insert ➪ Comment, the text is automatically highlighted. You can delete the comment to undo the highlighting.

How do I undo highlighting?

To undo highlighting, select the text with the highlighting and then click the downward pointing arrow next to the Highlight button. Select None. You can also click the arrow next to the Highlight button, select None, and then drag the highlighter pen across all of the text you want to remove highlighting from.

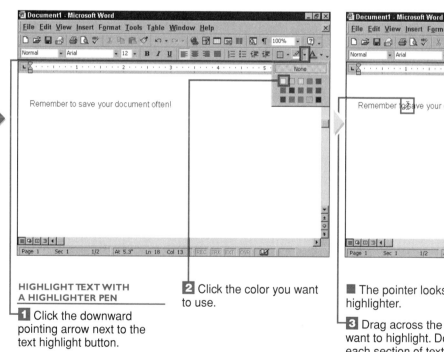

HIGHLIGHT TEXT WITH A HIGHLIGHTER PEN

■1 Click the downward pointing arrow next to the text highlight button.

■2 Click the color you want to use.

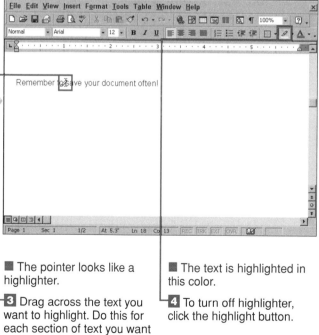

■ The pointer looks like a highlighter.

■3 Drag across the text you want to highlight. Do this for each section of text you want to highlight.

■ The text is highlighted in this color.

■4 To turn off highlighter, click the highlight button.

SELECT AN UNDERLINE STYLE AND COLOR

You can use a simple underline by clicking the Underline button in the toolbar. But if you want something fancier, you can select an underline style and color using the Font dialog box.

You can select from several underline styles including double, dotted, thick, dash, wave, and others. You can also select a color for the underline (new with this version of Word).

Keep in mind that underlining adds a line under the text. You can also add a border to a paragraph, as covered in the next chapter.

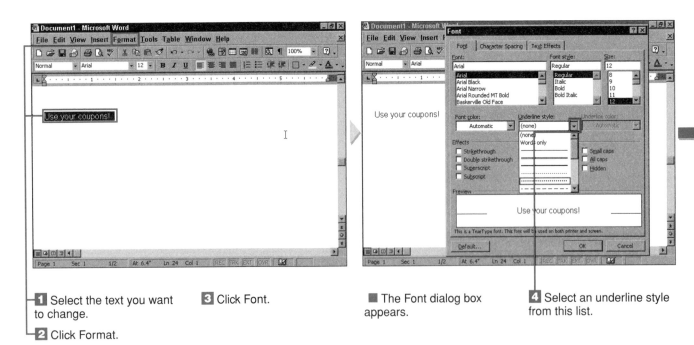

1 Select the text you want to change.

2 Click Format.

3 Click Font.

■ The Font dialog box appears.

4 Select an underline style from this list.

TIPS

How do I undo underlining?

To undo a special underline effect, select the text. Then select Format ⇨ Font. Display the Underline style drop-down list and select None.

Why can't I select a color?

To select a color for the underline, you must first select a style. Then the Underline color option becomes available.

What if I want just words underlined, not blank spaces?

To underline just words, select Words only from the Underline style.

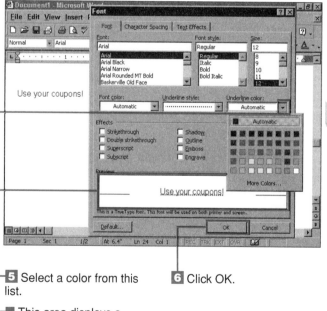

5 Select a color from this list.

■ This area displays a preview of the selected effects.

6 Click OK.

■ The text is underlined in the manner you specified.

ADD TEXT SPECIAL EFFECTS

In addition to the most common text formatting changes, you can also use some special effects for special situations. For instance, use strikethrough to indicate text that should be deleted in an edited document. To create formulas, you may need to use superscript or subscript to raise text above or below the baseline.

If you want to create unique text, try some of the other effects including shadow, outline, emboss, engrave, small caps, and all caps. (Hidden text is covered next in this chapter.) With these features, you have a great deal of control over the look of your text.

To make these changes, you must use the Font dialog box. You can check any of the available effects, including more than one. The dialog box displays a preview of the selections.

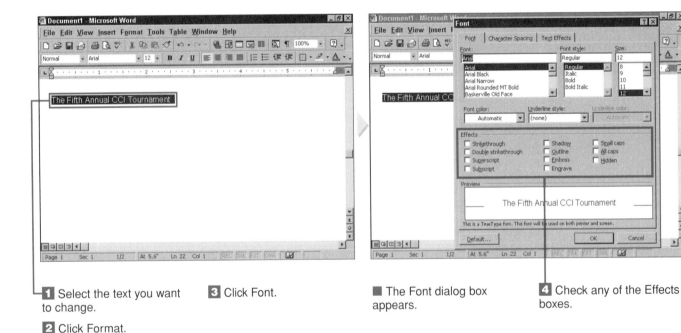

1 Select the text you want to change.

2 Click Format.

3 Click Font.

■ The Font dialog box appears.

4 Check any of the Effects boxes.

TIPS

How do I undo a special effect?

To undo a special effect, select the text. Then select Format ➪ Font. Uncheck the options you want to turn off. Then click OK.

Is there a better way to indicate editing changes than formatting the text as strikethrough?

Rather than manually format text you want to delete with strikethrough, you can use the revision marking features of Word. For more information on this topic, see Chapter 20.

What's the difference between superscript and subscript?

For superscript, the text is formatted in a smaller font and then raised above the baseline. For subscript, the text is in a smaller font and then lowered below the baseline of the text.

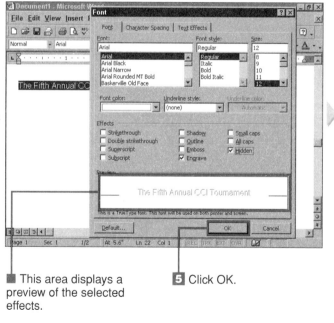

■ This area displays a preview of the selected effects.

5 Click OK.

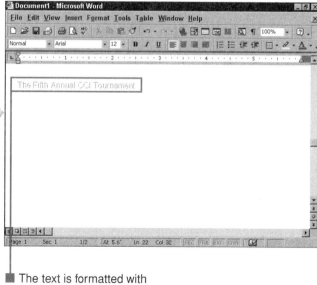

■ The text is formatted with the selected effects.

HIDE TEXT

If you need to make notes to yourself about a particular paragraph or section in a document, you can type notes and then hide them. You might remind yourself to check a figure, or you might cite the source in your notes. You can format text as hidden. Hidden text, by default, is not displayed or printed in the document.

When you do want to view your hidden text, you can easily display it. Hidden text is displayed with a dotted underline. You can also select to print hidden text. You can then handle any notes to yourself and delete the hidden text. (If you use hidden text, you may want to check the document for notes before you send the file to anyone else.)

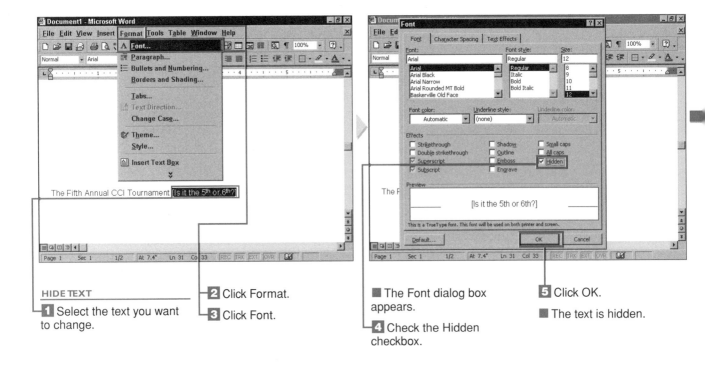

HIDE TEXT

1 Select the text you want to change.

2 Click Format.

3 Click Font.

■ The Font dialog box appears.

4 Check the Hidden checkbox.

5 Click OK.

■ The text is hidden.

TIPS

Is there another way to insert comments into a document?

Rather than format text as hidden, you can also select Insert ⇨ Comment. Type your comment in the pane that appears and then click Close. Note that the text is automatically highlighted. To display the comment, put the pointer on the comment.

What's the keyboard shortcut?

You can also use a keyboard shortcut for hiding text. Select the text and then press Ctrl+Shift+H.

How do I print hidden text?

Hidden text will print when you have selected to display or print hidden text. You don't have to unhide the text and then print. You can also view hidden text in Print Preview if you have selected to print hidden text.

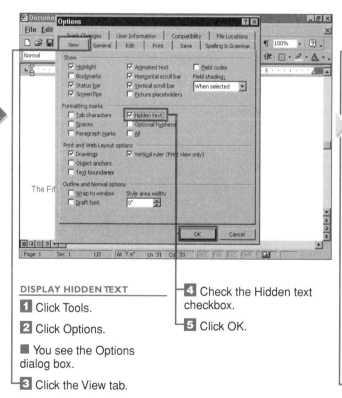

DISPLAY HIDDEN TEXT

1 Click Tools.

2 Click Options.

■ You see the Options dialog box.

3 Click the View tab.

4 Check the Hidden text checkbox.

5 Click OK.

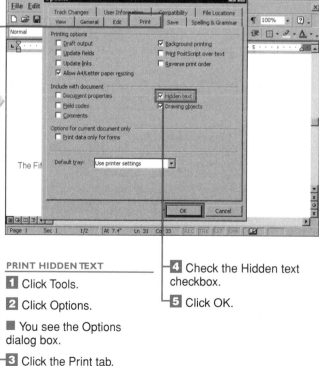

PRINT HIDDEN TEXT

1 Click Tools.

2 Click Options.

■ You see the Options dialog box.

3 Click the Print tab.

4 Check the Hidden text checkbox.

5 Click OK.

ANIMATE TEXT

One of the fun features of Word is text animation. Although this may not be all that useful for printed documents, you can create some special effects for documents that will be displayed rather than printed. You can also use text animations in Web documents.

You can select from one of several text animations including Blinking Background, Las Vegas Lights, Marching Black Ants, Marching Red Ants, Shimmer, and Sparkle Text. The dialog box displays a preview of each of the animations.

When you are formatting your document, be sure not to go overboard. Too much busyness will detract from your message. Be sure the content is what your audience notices!

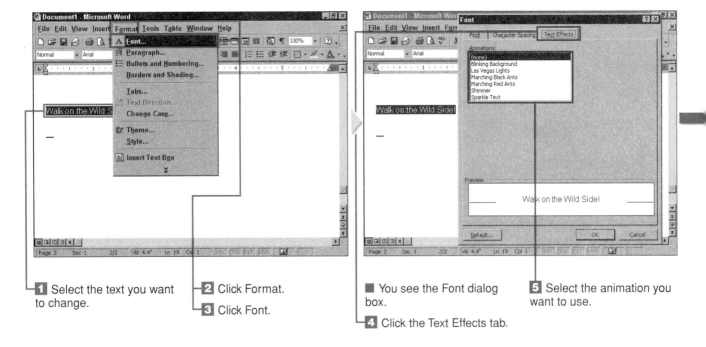

1 Select the text you want to change.

2 Click Format.

3 Click Font.

■ You see the Font dialog box.

4 Click the Text Effects tab.

5 Select the animation you want to use.

TIPS

How do I undo an animation?

You can select Edit ➪ Undo or click the Undo button immediately after you make the change. Or select Format ➪ Font and click the Animation tab. Select None and then click OK.

What other text special effects can I use?

As other ways to add fancy text, you can insert WordArt or use a text box. See Chapter 13 for more information on these topics.

Can I add space between the text and the animation?

The animation surrounds the text, and in this version of Word, you do not have any control over how closely together the text and the animation border appear.

Do animations print?

Animations are not printed when you print the document. They are only displayed.

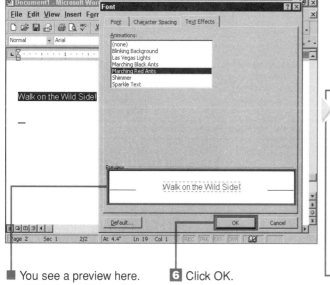

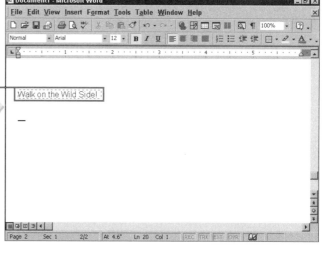

■ You see a preview here.   **6** Click OK.

■ The text is animated.

SET CHARACTER SPACING

Word spaces the characters to 100 percent scale and places them right on the baseline of the line. If you do a lot of electronic publishing, you may want to tinker with the character spacing.

You can, for instance, select to scale the text to a larger percentage to make it bigger.

You can also expand or condense the space between the text using the spacing option. Select the exact amount of points you want between the characters. (The higher the number of points, the more space between characters.) Check the preview to see the results of your spacing.

For another special effect, you can place the text above or below

the baseline by a certain number of points. A positive entry raises the text that many points above the baseline. A negative entry places the text that many points below the baseline.

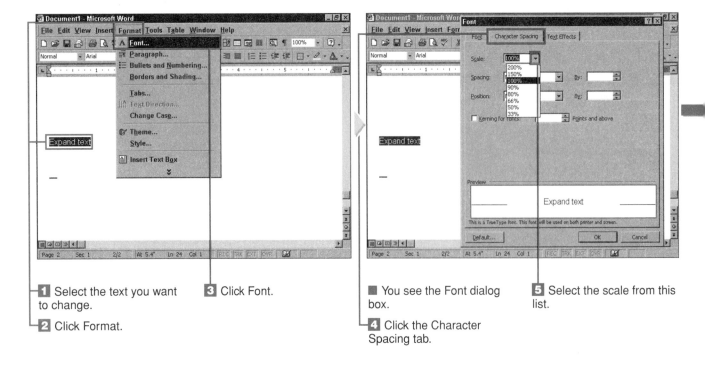

-■1 Select the text you want to change.

-■2 Click Format.

■3 Click Font.

■ You see the Font dialog box.

-■4 Click the Character Spacing tab.

■5 Select the scale from this list.

TIPS

How do I return to the default settings?

Follow the same procedure to return to the normal settings. Select 100% for the scale, Normal for the Spacing, and Normal for the Position.

What is kerning?

Kerning is the amount of space between certain combinations of characters, such as WA. You can adjust the spacing so it looks more even. Use the Kerning for fonts option to make this adjustment.

What if I don't understand the option?

If you don't understand the option, right-click the option and select What's This? to view a pop-up explanation. You can also experiment and check the preview in the dialog box to see how your choices affect the text.

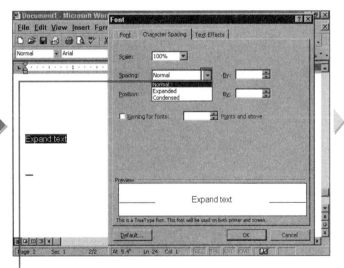

6 Select the spacing and number of points for expanded or condensed text.

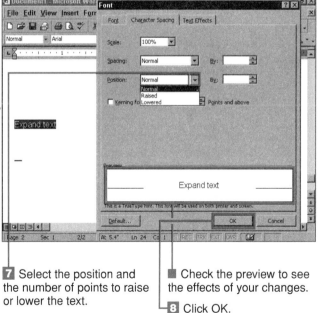

7 Select the position and the number of points to raise or lower the text.

■ Check the preview to see the effects of your changes.

8 Click OK.

HOW TO FORMAT PARAGRAPHS

Words go together to make sentences, and sentences combine to make paragraphs. In addition to changing the look of text itself, you can enhance the paragraphs in your document.

Alignment Changes

One of the most common formatting changes is to change the alignment. For instance, you may want to center the title of a document, justify (make the left and right margins even) the paragraphs in a newsletter, or right-align the date in a letter.

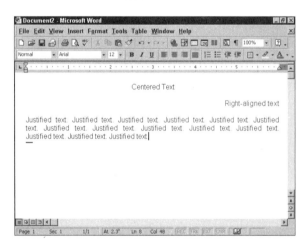

Indents

Something else you may want to do is indent paragraphs. Create a first-line indent so your reader can easily see where each new paragraph starts. Indent a paragraph from the left and right margins to set it off from other text. You have several choices.

Spacing

You can also change paragraph spacing . As one option, change the amount of spacing between each line in a paragraph (double space, for instance). As another example, add space above or below a paragraph to give it extra room.

Borders, Bullets, and More

You can try decorative changes, such as adding a border or shading to a paragraph. Choose from several border styles (different thicknesses, colors, and so on).

Add bullets to paragraphs, choosing from different bullet characters. If the paragraphs are in some type of sequence, such as a series of steps, you can number the paragraphs.

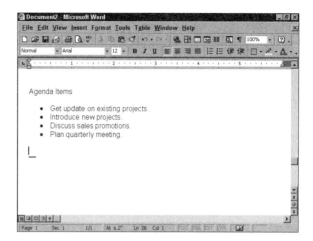

UNDERSTAND AND DISPLAY PARAGRAPH MARKS

A paragraph is any text followed by a hard return. A single line, for instance, can be a paragraph.

Each paragraph can have different settings or styles. Each paragraph, for example, can have different tab settings or be in a different font or type size.

You can apply the formatting options covered in this chapter to a single paragraph or several paragraphs. To apply formatting to one paragraph, simply click

within the paragraph. To apply formatting to several paragraphs, select the ones you want to change.

Each time you press Enter, the paragraph options are carried to the next paragraph. If you delete the paragraph mark, the paragraph takes on the formatting of the following paragraph. For example, if you type a line, center it, and press Enter, the next line is centered as well. This is confusing to

beginners who wonder how a paragraph became formatted without them making a change. Think of the paragraph mark as the holder of all formatting options for that paragraph.

If something bizarre happens, try undoing the change using Edit ➪ Undo. If you have trouble visualizing where the paragraph marks appear, you can display them.

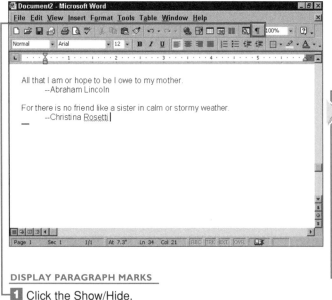

DISPLAY PARAGRAPH MARKS

1 Click the Show/Hide.

■ The paragraph marks are displayed.

What are all the other marks?

 When you choose to display paragraph marks, you also see indicators for tabs and spaces.

What if I want to apply the paragraph formatting to the entire document?

If you want to format all the text in a document, select the entire document by pressing Ctrl+A, or opening the Edit menu and choosing the Select All command.

What other special characters can I view?

 As an alternative, choose Tools ⇨ Options and click the View tab. In the Formatting marks area, check the characters you want displayed. You can choose to display tabs, spaces, paragraph marks, hidden text, or optional hyphens.

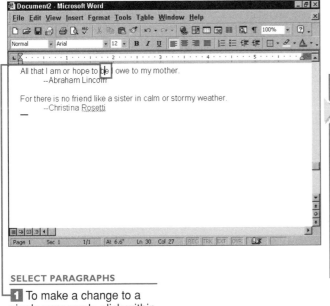

SELECT PARAGRAPHS

1 To make a change to a single paragraph, click within the paragraph.

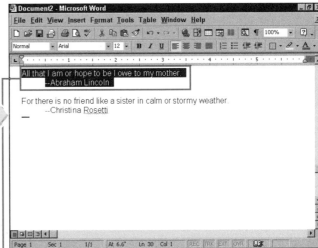

2 To make a change to several paragraphs, select the ones you want to change.

ALIGN A PARAGRAPH

When you type in Word, the text is left-aligned, and the right margin is ragged or uneven. For most text, this alignment works well. For other paragraphs, you may want to make a change. For instance, you can center the document title. Or you may want to right-align text like a newspaper banner. You can justify the text in the paragraphs to keep the right margin even.

There are four types of alignment, and the best way to make a change is to use the Formatting toolbar.

You can also use the Paragraph dialog box to change alignment. This method involves more steps and offers no advantages over the toolbar method, unless you want to make several paragraph formatting changes at once. To use this method, display the dialog box by choosing Format ⇨ Paragraph and clicking the Indents and Spacing tab. Display the Alignment list box and choose the alignment you want. Click the OK button to close the dialog box.

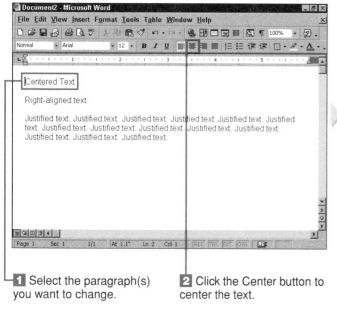

1 Select the paragraph(s) you want to change.

2 Click the Center button to center the text.

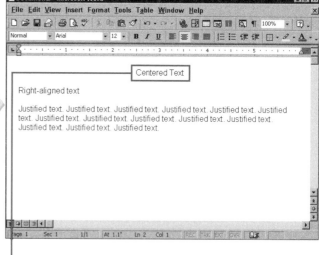

■ The text is centered.

How do I undo a change?

To undo the change, click the Undo button or choose Edit ➪ Undo. If you realize later that you want to use a different alignment, select the paragraph(s) and then click another alignment button. To go back to the default alignment, click the Align Left button.

What are the keyboard shortcuts?

Use these keyboard shortcuts to change the alignment: Ctrl+E for Center, Ctrl+L for Left, Ctrl+R for Right, and Ctrl+J for Justify.

Do I need to hyphenate the text when it is justified?

When you justify text, you may find that there are big gaps of white space. You can fix this problem by making changes to the hyphenation. See the task "Hyphenate Text" later in this chapter.

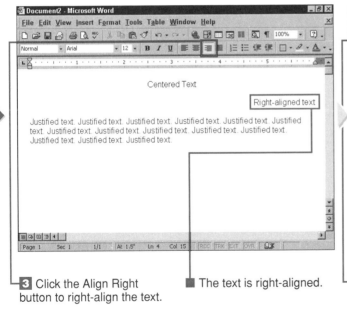

3 Click the Align Right button to right-align the text.

■ The text is right-aligned.

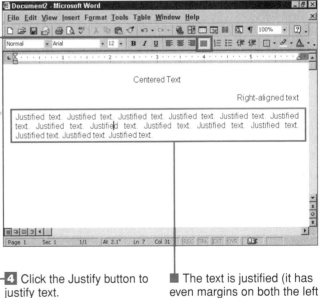

4 Click the Justify button to justify text.

■ The text is justified (it has even margins on both the left and right sides).

INDENT TEXT

Alignment changes are most appropriate for headings or other special paragraphs in a document. But what about the body of a document?

Another common way to change how text aligns on a page is to use indents. You can, for instance, indent the first line of each paragraph, providing a visual clue to help your reader

see how the document is divided into paragraphs. You can also indent paragraphs, such as quotations, that you want to set apart from the main document text. As another option, you may want to use a special kind of indent, called a hanging indent, for numbered lists.

Indent text the amount you want, and use the Formatting

toolbar or the Paragraph dialog box to make a change.

If you use the toolbar button, the paragraph is indented $\frac{1}{2}$ inch from the left margin. If you want to indent from the left and right, or create a special kind of indent, you need to use the Paragraph dialog box.

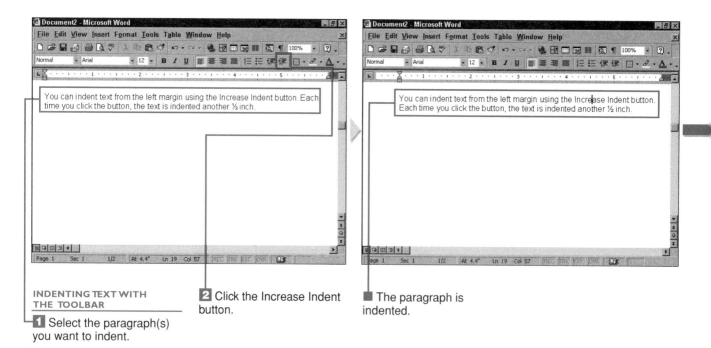

INDENTING TEXT WITH THE TOOLBAR

1 Select the paragraph(s) you want to indent.

2 Click the Increase Indent button.

■ The paragraph is indented.

How do I use the Ruler to indent text?

Another way to set indents is to use the Ruler. To do so, drag the appropriate indent marker to where you want the indent. To indent the text from the left, drag the left indent marker (the rectangle). When you drag this marker, the other markers move as well. To indent text from the right, drag the right indent marker. To indent the first line of the paragraph, drag the first-line indent marker (the top triangle); the bottom marker stays in place. To create a hanging indent, drag the left indent marker (the bottom triangle); the first line indent remains in the same spot.

What are the keyboard shortcuts?

Press Ctrl+M to indent the paragraph to the left. Press Ctrl+Shift+M to unindent or decrease an indent. Press Ctrl+T to create a hanging indent. Press Ctrl+Shift+T to undo a hanging indent.

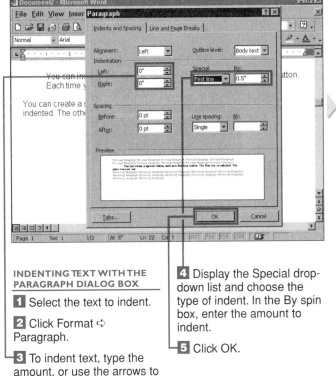

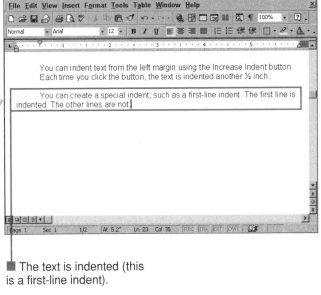

INDENTING TEXT WITH THE PARAGRAPH DIALOG BOX

1 Select the text to indent.

2 Click Format ➪ Paragraph.

3 To indent text, type the amount, or use the arrows to choose a value.

4 Display the Special drop-down list and choose the type of indent. In the By spin box, enter the amount to indent.

5 Click OK.

■ The text is indented (this is a first-line indent).

CHANGE LINE SPACING

By default, Word single spaces text. This spacing works well for short documents such as letters and memos, but in longer documents, such as a manuscript, you may want to use a different spacing increment. For instance, you can double space a document to make it more readable.

To single space a document, choose Single. Word adjusts the lines to accommodate the largest font and adds a small amount of space (the amount depends on the font size in the selected paragraph).

To add 1½ lines of spacing, choose 1.5 Lines. To double space the document, choose Double.

To specify the minimum amount of spacing, choose At Least and then enter the desired spacing in the At box.

To specify an exact amount of spacing, choose Exactly and then enter the spacing value you want. If characters are chopped off, enter a larger value.

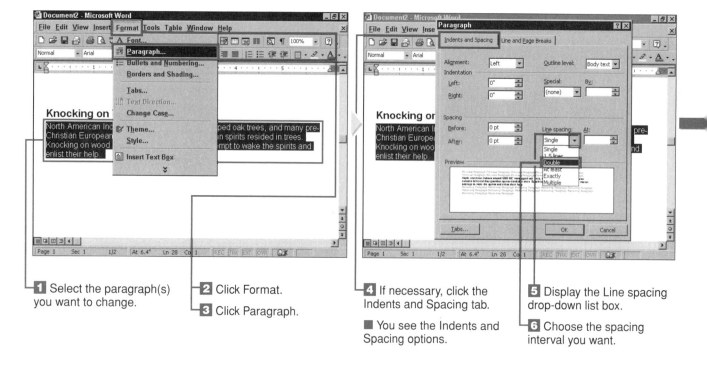

1 Select the paragraph(s) you want to change.

2 Click Format.

3 Click Paragraph.

4 If necessary, click the Indents and Spacing tab.

■ You see the Indents and Spacing options.

5 Display the Line spacing drop-down list box.

6 Choose the spacing interval you want.

What are the keyboard shortcuts?

Press Ctrl+1 for single spacing, Ctrl+5 for 1.5 spacing, or Ctrl+2 for double spacing.

I want to fit more (or less) on the page. Besides adjusting the line spacing, what other changes can I make?

If you are trying to fit more (or less) on a page, one possibility is to adjust the line spacing. Another possibility is to change the page margins. See the next chapter for information on how to do this.

What is another way to add spacing?

You can add space above or below a paragraph, rather than to each line. See the next task for more information.

How do I enter a percentage to increase spacing?

To specify a multiple amount, choose Multiple and enter the value you want. For instance, the value 1 is single spacing; 1.2 increases the spacing 20 percent. The value 2 double spaces the paragraph.

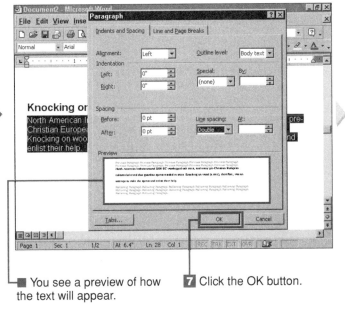

■ You see a preview of how the text will appear.

7 Click the OK button.

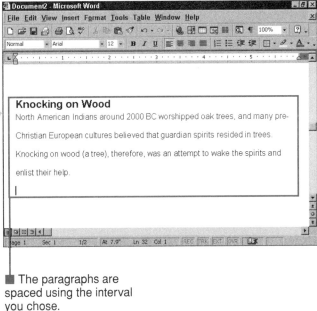

■ The paragraphs are spaced using the interval you chose.

155

ADD SPACE ABOVE OR BELOW A PARAGRAPH

Line spacing affects each line in a paragraph. Sometimes you may want to add space above or below a paragraph, but not within it. For example, you may want to add buffer space after document headings.

You can press Enter to insert a blank line, but this isn't the best method for a couple of reasons. First, you may want less space than a whole line. Second, when you insert a blank line, you can't use the break features to keep text together. (See "Keep Lines

Together," which follows.) Instead, set the paragraph spacing.

You can choose a number of points to add before and/or after a paragraph.

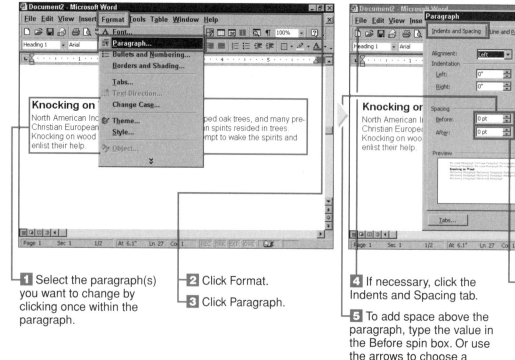

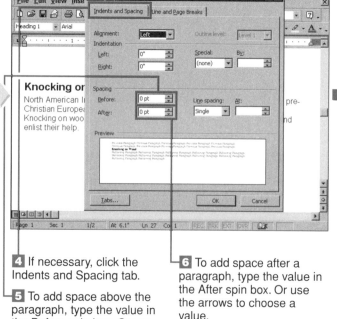

1 Select the paragraph(s) you want to change by clicking once within the paragraph.

2 Click Format.

3 Click Paragraph.

4 If necessary, click the Indents and Spacing tab.

5 To add space above the paragraph, type the value in the Before spin box. Or use the arrows to choose a value.

6 To add space after a paragraph, type the value in the After spin box. Or use the arrows to choose a value.

TIPS

How do I use a different measurement unit?

The default measurement unit for most changes is inches. (For some options such as paragraph spacing, Word uses points.) You can use a different measurement by entering the value and appropriate abbreviation (in for inches, pt for points, cm for centimeters, and pi for picas).

How do I keep a section heading with the section text?

You can control where page breaks occur using the Line and Page Breaks tab. See "Keep Lines Together" in this chapter for information on these options.

How do I control spacing between characters?

Word automatically adjusts the spacing between characters, depending on the font you choose. You can also make manual adjustments. See the task on kerning in the previous chapter.

CHANGING THE LOOK OF YOUR DOCUMENT

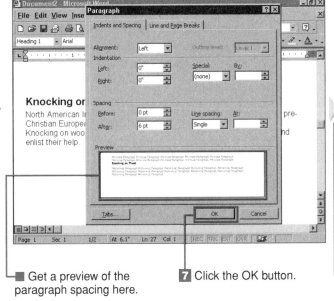

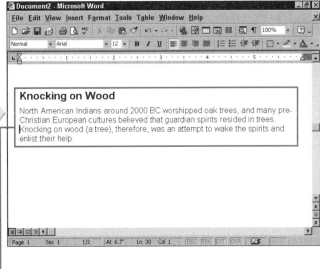

■ Get a preview of the paragraph spacing here.

7 Click the OK button.

■ The paragraph is formatted with the chosen spacing amount.

157

KEEP LINES TOGETHER

A bad line or page break can make a perfect document seem like a careless work. Visually check each page and line break in your document, or use Word to set up page and line break limits.

One option is to turn on Widow/Orphan control. This ensures that the last line of a page isn't a single line (the first line of a paragraph) and that the first line of a new page isn't a single line (the last line of a paragraph).

You can select text (such as a tabbed list or table) to make sure that it remains one unit.

You may want to make sure a heading stays with the text that follows it. (You don't want a new section heading at the end of a page!) If all headings start on a new page, have Word insert a page break before each heading.

All of these options are on the Line and Page Breaks tab of the Paragraph dialog box.

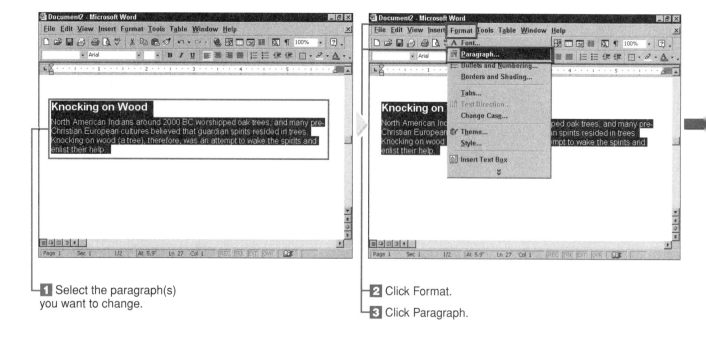

1 Select the paragraph(s) you want to change.

2 Click Format.

3 Click Paragraph.

TIPS

What are the other options used for?

You can use the Line and Page Breaks tab to turn off line numbers for the selected text. For information on using line numbers, see Chapter 19. You can also turn off hyphenation. For more information on hyphenation, see "Hyphenate Text" later in this chapter.

How do I insert a page break?

Word automatically inserts page breaks as needed. Insert manual page breaks by choosing Insert ➪ Break. Choose Page break and click OK.

How do I insert a line break?

When you want text within the same paragraph to have the same settings, but have the lines break, insert a line break. Press Shift+Enter, or choose Insert ➪ Break and then choose Text wrapping break and click OK.

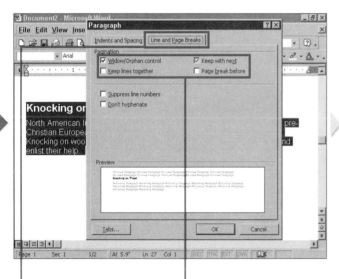

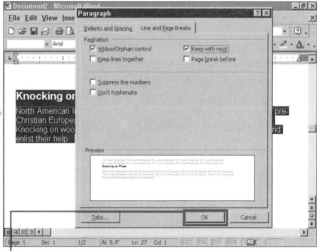

■4 If necessary, click the Line and Page Breaks tab.

■5 Check or uncheck the pagination options you want to turn on or off.

■6 Click the OK button.

SET TABS

In some documents you may want to include a list of columnar data, such as a price list. Or maybe you want to create a list of names and phone numbers, with one column for the name and one for the phone number. The best way to set up this type of data is to create a

table, as covered in Chapter 10. Tables are much easier to work with than tabbed lists, and Word includes several features for changing the look of a table.

Even though tables have pretty much replaced tabs, you may find that you want to set tabs for some types of lists —

for instance, when you want to align a column of numbers, use dot leaders, or just create a simple tabbed list.

Use the Ruler or the Tab dialog box to set tabs, selecting from four tab types: left, right, center, and decimal.

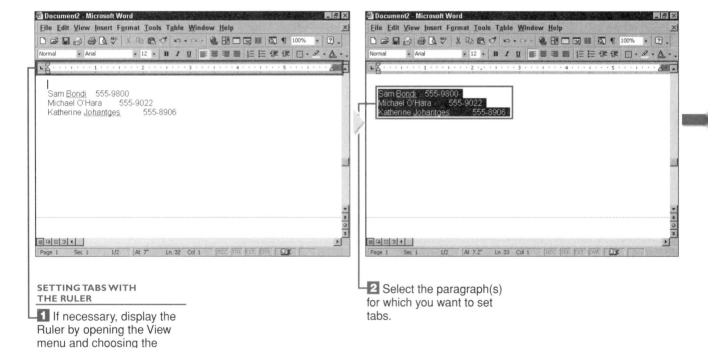

SETTING TABS WITH THE RULER

1 If necessary, display the Ruler by opening the View menu and choosing the Ruler command.

2 Select the paragraph(s) for which you want to set tabs.

Tab Types

Tab	Name	What it Does
L	Left tab	Text starts on the marker and moves left.
⌟	Right tab	Text starts on the marker and moves right.
⊥	Center tab	Text is centered on the marker.
⊥∙	Decimal tab	Text is aligned on the decimal point.

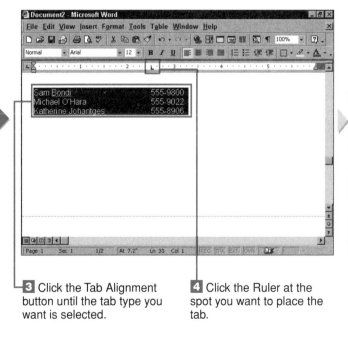

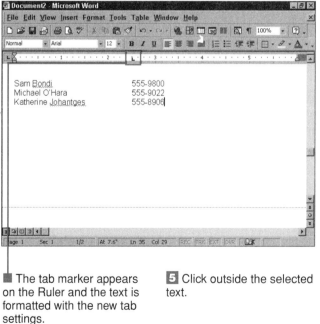

-3 Click the Tab Alignment button until the tab type you want is selected.

4 Click the Ruler at the spot you want to place the tab.

■ The tab marker appears on the Ruler and the text is formatted with the new tab settings.

5 Click outside the selected text.

CONTINUED

SET TABS CONTINUED

The Ruler is easy to use because it is visual, but if you can't remember which tab button to use, or want to set a tab with a precise measurement, use the Tabs dialog box.

When you create tabs, remember that you are setting them only for the selected paragraphs. Tab stops are not permanent, that is, they apply only to selected paragraphs. If

you create another document, or want to use the same tab settings elsewhere, you must set the tabs again.

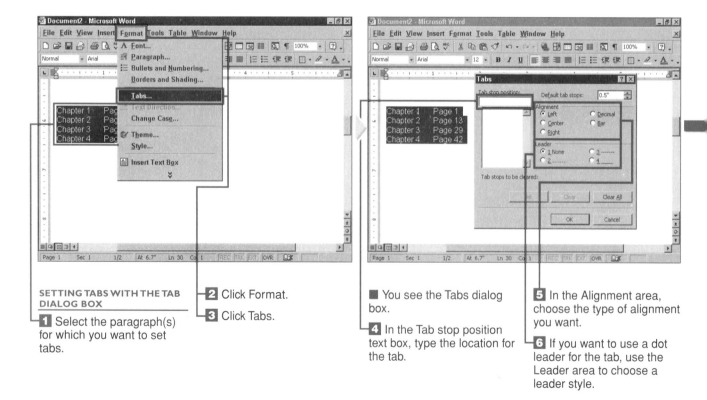

SETTING TABS WITH THE TAB DIALOG BOX

1 Select the paragraph(s) for which you want to set tabs.

2 Click Format.

3 Click Tabs.

■ You see the Tabs dialog box.

4 In the Tab stop position text box, type the location for the tab.

5 In the Alignment area, choose the type of alignment you want.

6 If you want to use a dot leader for the tab, use the Leader area to choose a leader style.

TIPS

Why weren't all the paragraphs formatted?

Remember that each paragraph can have individual tab settings. If you don't select all the paragraphs, the changes apply only to the current paragraph (the one with the insertion point). Be sure to select all the paragraphs you want to format.

What are the default tab stops?

Word sets up default tab stops every 1/2 inch. Simply press Tab to use these tabs.

How do I view tab characters?

If you have a hard time figuring out where tabs are inserted, display a character (an arrow) for the tabs. Click the Hide/Show ¶ to show characters for the tabs.

How do I delete or change a tab?

To delete a tab from the Ruler, click it and drag it off the Ruler. To change the tab position, click it and drag it to a new location on the Ruler.

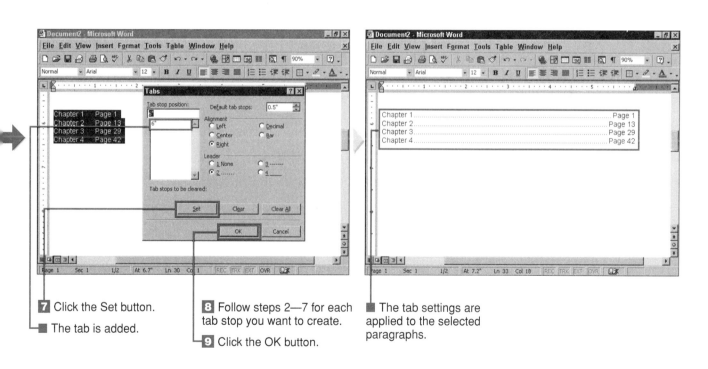

7 Click the Set button.

■ The tab is added.

8 Follow steps 2—7 for each tab stop you want to create.

9 Click the OK button.

■ The tab settings are applied to the selected paragraphs.

CHANGING THE LOOK OF YOUR DOCUMENT

ADD BORDERS

Remember when you wanted to try something fancy with a typewriter? Maybe you went back over a line and typed an underscore to create an underline. Or maybe you created borders by typing dashes or asterisks. These style flourishes are way out of date.

Now you can easily add a border. For example, maybe you want to add borders to document headings to make them easy to scan. You can add borders to the top, sides, or bottom of a single paragraph or a group of paragraphs. You can specify the thickness and style of a border.

For a quick border, use the toolbar. Choose different border placements using the Border button on the Formatting toolbar. You can choose to place a line above a paragraph, on all sides, on the bottom, in between two paragraphs, and so on.

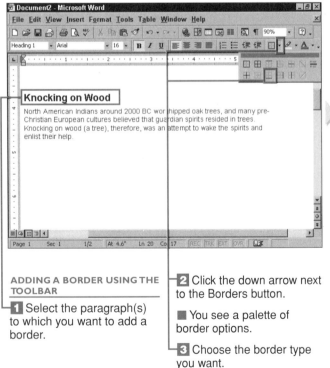

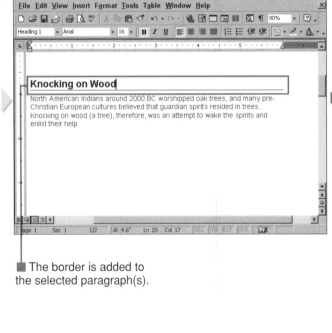

ADDING A BORDER USING THE TOOLBAR

1 Select the paragraph(s) to which you want to add a border.

2 Click the down arrow next to the Borders button.

■ You see a palette of border options.

3 Choose the border type you want.

■ The border is added to the selected paragraph(s).

How do I remove a border?

Remove a border by selecting the paragraph, clicking the down arrow next to the Borders button, and then clicking the button without a border.

How do I insert a different type of border for each side of a paragraph?

If you want to use a different border for each side of a paragraph, choose Custom. Then choose the style, color, and width of the line. In the Preview area, click the side of the paragraph where you want to place the border.

How do I set the amount of space between the border and the text?

Control the amount of space between the border and the text by clicking the Options button. Then choose the amount of points from the top, left, bottom, and right. Click OK.

How do I add a horizontal line?

You can insert a graphical horizontal line (a line that is a graphical image). To do so, click the Horizontal line button. Choose a line style and click the Insert clip button.

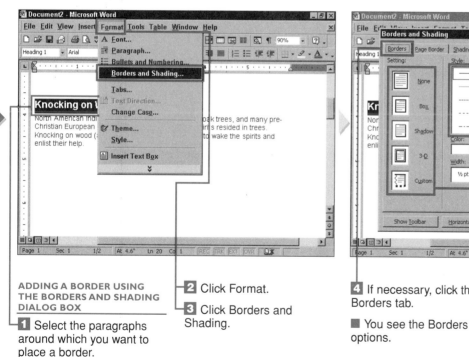

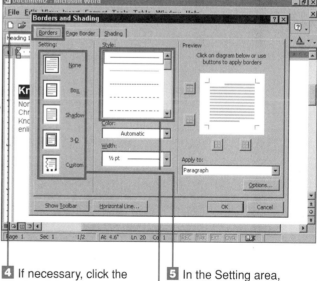

ADDING A BORDER USING THE BORDERS AND SHADING DIALOG BOX

■1 Select the paragraphs around which you want to place a border.

■2 Click Format.

■3 Click Borders and Shading.

■4 If necessary, click the Borders tab.

■ You see the Borders options.

■5 In the Setting area, choose the type of border you want.

■6 In the Style list, choose the line style you want.

CONTINUED ▶

ADD BORDERS CONTINUED

For more control over the line style and placement of a border, use the dialog box. Using the dialog box, you can choose special border effects such as box, shadow, and 3D, plus you can choose different line styles, colors, and widths. (The width is measured in points. Remember that there are 72 points in 1 inch.)

In addition, you can add a horizontal line and set options for the space between a line and paragraph text. You can even choose to use a different line for each side of a paragraph. To do this, go to Custom in the Setting area.

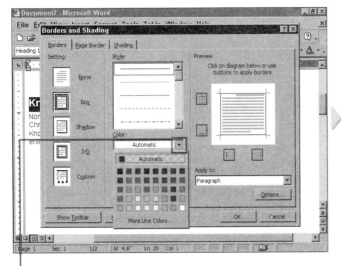

7 To change the border color, display the Color drop-down list and then choose the color you want.

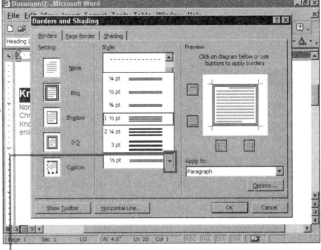

8 To change the thickness of the line, display the Width drop-down list and choose the width you want.

TIPS

How do I add a page border?

Use the Page Border tab to add a border to a page. For information on this feature, see Chapter 9.

What about shortcuts?

If you like to work with toolbars, click the Toolbar button to display the Tables and Borders toolbar, which includes buttons for adding borders. Use the toolbar to choose a line style, width, and placement.

What else can I use borders with?

You can use the Borders and Shading command to add (or remove) borders from a text box, table, or frame. Use this command to add a border to any text (not just a paragraph).

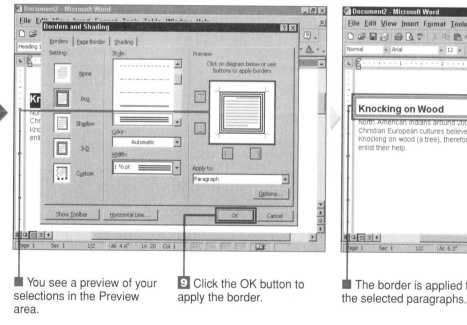

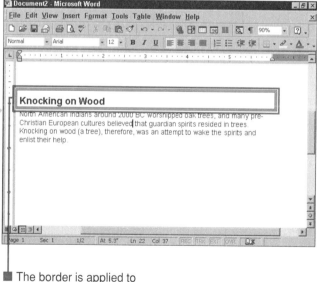

■ You see a preview of your selections in the Preview area.

9 Click the OK button to apply the border.

■ The border is applied to the selected paragraphs.

ADD SHADING

Another way to add some flash to your paragraphs is to apply shading. You may want to combine a border with shading (although you don't have to add a border to use shading). Choose from several levels of gray shading, from 100 percent (solid) to 5 percent (light). You can also choose different patterns.

If you have a color printer, you can use a color for the shading or pattern. You may want to use colors if the document is intended for onscreen viewing. If you don't see a color you like in the initial palette, click the More Colors button and choose one from the color wheel.

Keep in mind that if you don't have a color printer and select colors anyway, the colors print in shades of gray.

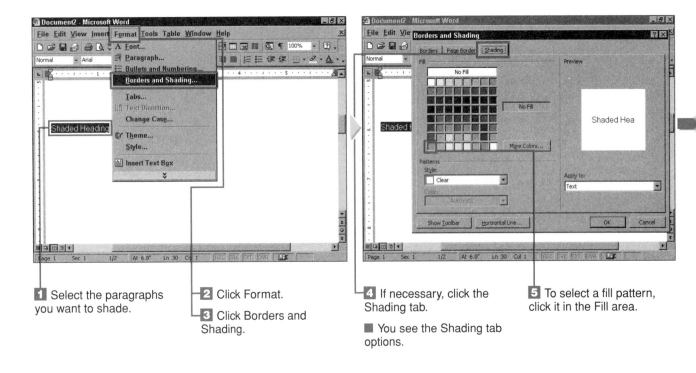

1 Select the paragraphs you want to shade.

2 Click Format.

3 Click Borders and Shading.

4 If necessary, click the Shading tab.

■ You see the Shading tab options.

5 To select a fill pattern, click it in the Fill area.

How do I remove shading?

 Remove shading by selecting the paragraph and then choosing Format ⇨ Borders and Shading. Choose No Fill and click OK.

How do the fills and colors work together?

To use a color and a fill, choose the color you want in the Fill area. Then display the Style drop-down list and choose the pattern you want. Understanding how the fills and colors work together can take some time. Experiment in the dialog box and check the Preview, which shows you what your selection looks like.

What special effects can I create with shading?

 You can combine text color changes with shading to create white text on a black background. To do so, change the font color to white. Then apply a solid color or black shading to the paragraph.

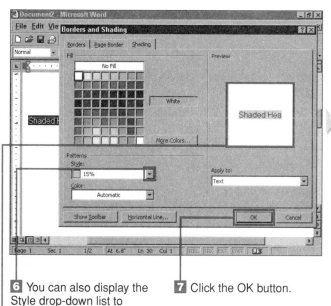

6 You can also display the Style drop-down list to choose the pattern you want.

■ See a preview here.

7 Click the OK button.

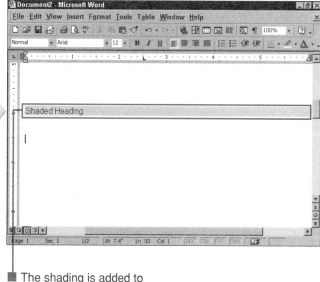

■ The shading is added to the selected paragraph(s).

CREATE A BULLETED LIST

In the information age, you are constantly bombarded with messages from different media. You may have an office mailbox, an e-mail mailbox, and a mailbox at home, all of which may be crammed with some type of message. How can you tell what's important and what's not?

You don't want your reader to struggle with finding your document's main message. Highlight key points to make the document easy to scan and assimilate. A well-organized document is more likely to be noticed than one that is a mishmash of ideas.

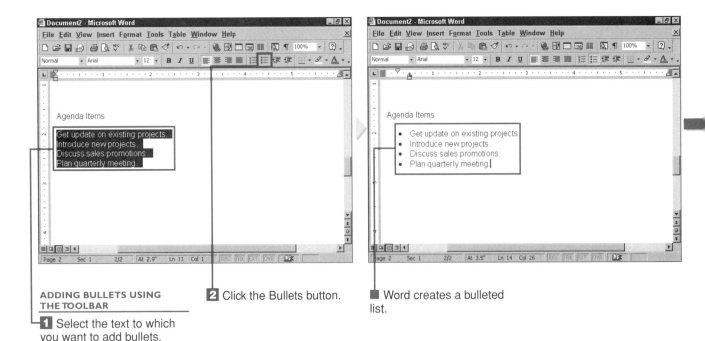

ADDING BULLETS USING THE TOOLBAR

1 Select the text to which you want to add bullets.

Note: Word does not add bullets to blank lines within a selection.

2 Click the Bullets button.

■ Word creates a bulleted list.

TIPS

Bullets appeared automatically. What happened?

Word may make automatic formatting changes as you type. For instance, if you type an asterisk and press Tab, Word may replace this with a bullet. To review and make changes to these AutoFormat options, open the Tools menu and choose the AutoCorrect command. Click the AutoFormat As You Type tab. Make any changes and click OK.

Also, if you turn on bullets, type text, and then press Enter, the next paragraph will be bulleted.

How do I remove bullets?

To remove bullets, select the list. Then click the Bullets button.

What if I want to use a different symbol for the bullet?

You aren't limited to the bullets listed. You can choose any character or symbol to use for a bullet. In the Customize Bulleted List dialog box, click the Bullet button. Then use the Symbol dialog box to choose the symbol you want to use. (Change the font with the Font drop-down list.)

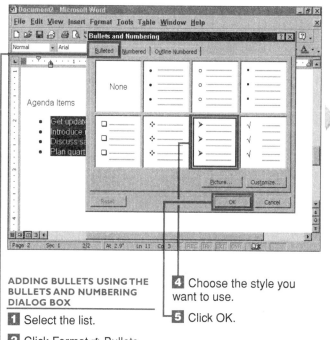

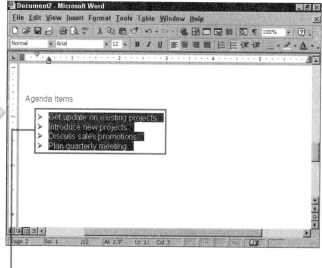

ADDING BULLETS USING THE BULLETS AND NUMBERING DIALOG BOX

1 Select the list.

2 Click Format ⇨ Bullets and Numbering.

3 If necessary, click the Bulleted tab.

4 Choose the style you want to use.

5 Click OK.

■ The bullets are added.

CONTINUED ▶

CREATE A BULLETED LIST CONTINUED

One way to set off a list of points or topics in a document is to create a bulleted list. A bullet precedes each item in the list, and the text is indented.

The fastest way to create a bulleted list is to use the Bullets button on the Formatting toolbar. When you use this method, you get a round bullet and a $1/5$-inch indent.

You can jazz up a bulleted list by choosing a different bullet. Choose from one of several bullet characters, including check boxes, diamonds, check marks, and so on. You can also set the amount to indent the bullet and text.

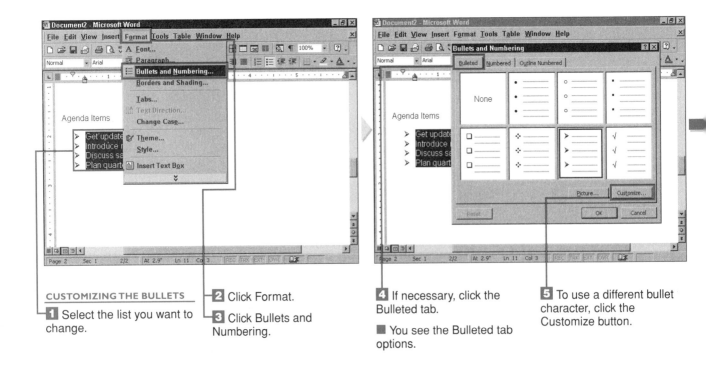

CUSTOMIZING THE BULLETS

1 Select the list you want to change.

2 Click Format.

3 Click Bullets and Numbering.

4 If necessary, click the Bulleted tab.

■ You see the Bulleted tab options.

5 To use a different bullet character, click the Customize button.

TIPS

How do I make the bullet bigger (or smaller)?

Change the font size to change the bullet size. In the Customize Bulleted List dialog box, click the Font button. Then choose the size you want and click OK.

Can I use a picture for the bullet?

New with this version of Word is the capability to insert a picture as a bullet. In the Bullets and Numbering dialog box, click the Picture button. Then choose the image you want to use. Click the Insert image button.

How do I go back to the original bullets?

Word has room to display only eight bullet styles. When you make a change, you replace one of these styles with the new setting. To go back to an original bullet, click the bullet you changed and then click the Reset button.

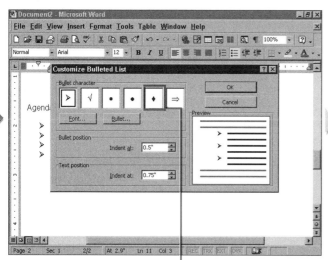

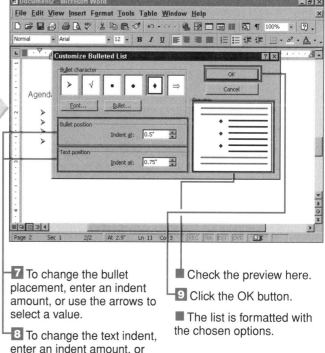

■ You see the Customize Bulleted List dialog box.

6 Choose the symbol you want to use.

7 To change the bullet placement, enter an indent amount, or use the arrows to select a value.

8 To change the text indent, enter an indent amount, or use the arrows to select a value.

■ Check the preview here.

9 Click the OK button.

■ The list is formatted with the chosen options.

CREATE A NUMBERED LIST

For items that appear in a specific order, such as a series of steps, you can create a numbered list. Word automatically adds the numbers and indents the paragraphs so that the text is properly aligned.

All you have to do is click the button.

Another great thing about a numbered list is if you add or delete an item within a list, Word automatically renumbers it.

Just as you can change a bullet character, you can change the numbering style. Choose from one of six predefined styles, or create your own.

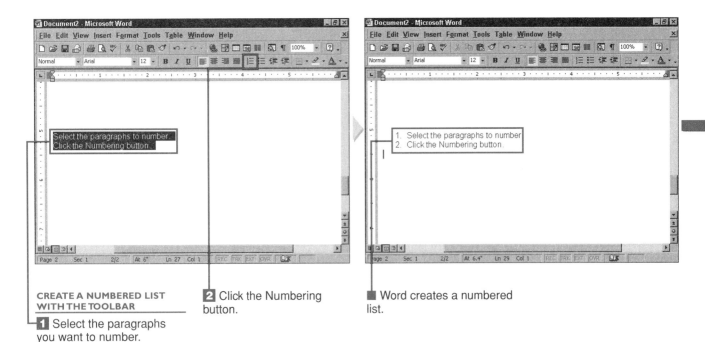

CREATE A NUMBERED LIST WITH THE TOOLBAR

1 Select the paragraphs you want to number.

■ Word numbers each paragraph. Blank lines within the selection are not numbered.

2 Click the Numbering button.

■ Word creates a numbered list.

TIPS

How do I remove the numbers?

Choose Edit ⇨ Undo or click the Undo button to remove numbers from a list. Or select the list and then click the Numbering button.

How do I restart numbering (or continue numbering)?

If you have other text with the numbered list, you can choose to continue the numbering. To do so, choose Continue previous list from the Numbered tab.

How do I customize the numbers?

If none of the selections meets your needs, you can create a customized list. Click the Customize button. Then choose the Number format, style, and position. You can also choose the font and starting number. Click OK.

What about outlines?

You can use Word to create outlines. For information on this topic, see Chapter 18.

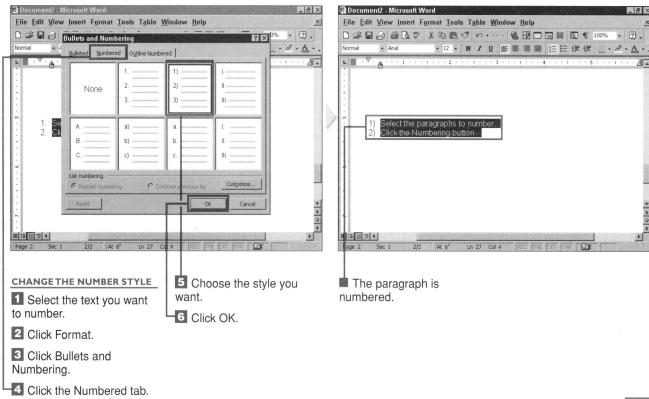

CHANGE THE NUMBER STYLE

1 Select the text you want to number.

2 Click Format.

3 Click Bullets and Numbering.

4 Click the Numbered tab.

5 Choose the style you want.

6 Click OK.

■ The paragraph is numbered.

HYPHENATE TEXT

Some formatting options may cause a problem known as a river of white space. If you use columns and/or justify text, you may find white gaps running through your document. You can fix this problem by hyphenating the text.

You can hyphenate text automatically. When you choose to do so, set the hyphenation

zone and the number of consecutive hyphens. (According to Word's online help, the hyphenation zone is defined as "the amount of space to leave between the end of the last word in a line and the right margin.") The smaller the hyphenation zone, the closer to the right margin the text must be before hyphenation occurs.

You can go through and manually hyphenate text, confirming each optional hyphen that is inserted.

You also can manually insert optional hyphens and nonbreaking hyphens using the Insert ⇨ Special Character command.

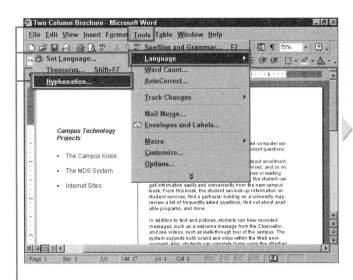

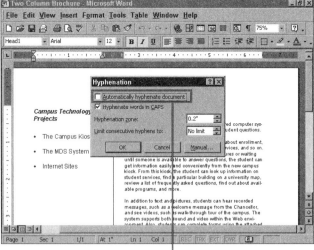

-1 Click Tools.

-2 Click Language.

-3 Click Hyphenation.

■ You see the Hyphenation dialog box.

-4 Check the Automatically hyphenate document option.

TIPS

What is a nonbreaking hyphen?

A nonbreaking hyphen is a hyphen that occurs in the spelling of the word. When you insert a nonbreaking hyphen, Word does not break this word (hyphenate it) if it falls at the end of a line.

What are the keyboard shortcuts for inserting hyphens?

Press Ctrl+Shift+Hyphen to insert a nonbreaking hyphen. Press Ctrl+Hyphen to insert an optional hyphen.

What happens when I manually hyphenate text?

When you manually hyphenate text by clicking the Manual button, Word prompts you to confirm each hyphen that is inserted. If you choose this method, be sure to do it when you are completely done with editing and formatting. If you make changes, Word does not adjust the hyphenation.

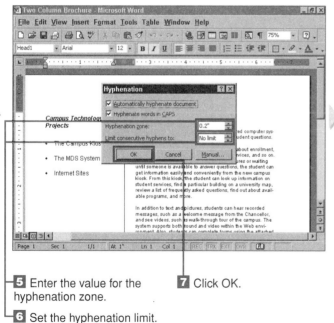

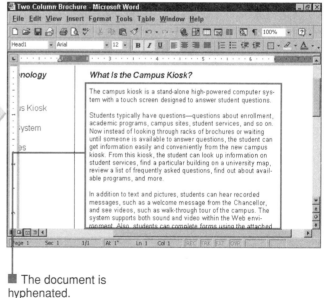

5 Enter the value for the hyphenation zone.

6 Set the hyphenation limit.

7 Click OK.

■ The document is hyphenated.

FORMATTING PAGES

In the first stage of creating a document, you most likely concentrate on the content. Then you may think about how the text looks and how the paragraphs flow on the page. Finally, you may take another step back and think about how the document is positioned on the page. Then you can make any changes. This chapter covers page formatting changes.

Margins

When you look at the page, does the text look balanced? If you have a short document, all the text may be crammed at the top, and the page will look out of balance. Maybe you need to change the margins. That's a common page-formatting change.

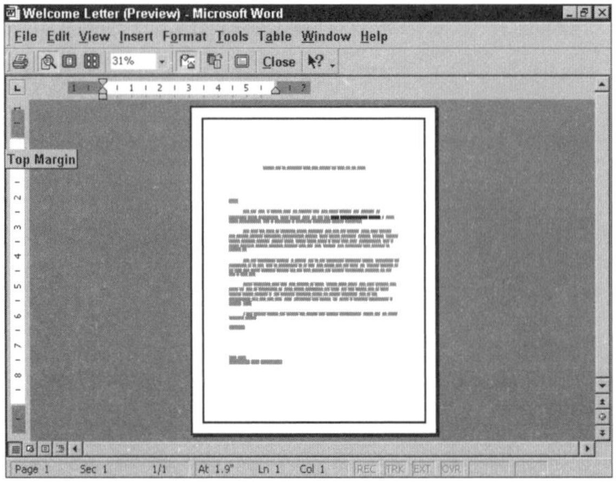

Paper Orientation, Source, and Layout

If you have a wide document, if you use different paper, or if you want to center the page, you can check out the options on the Layout and Paper Source tabs of the Page Setup dialog box. You might, for instance, use landscape orientation.

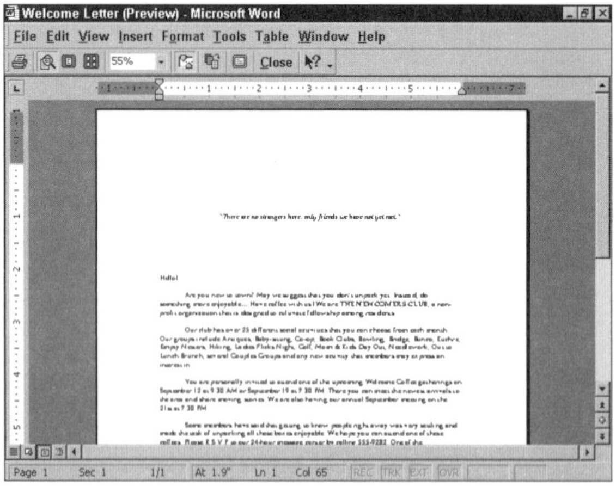

Headers and Footers

As another consideration, think about how the pages flow. Are the pages organized? If the document has several pages, you may want to add page numbers. You can also include headers or footers to identify the document. You can include information such as the date or file name in the header or footer.

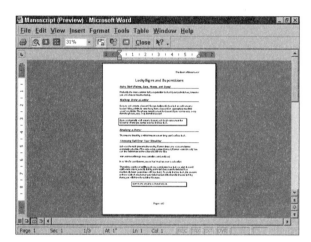

Decorative Options

You may also want to dress up a document by adding a page border. If you will be displaying the document, you can add a background color or pattern. You have lots of options for making your page look just perfect.

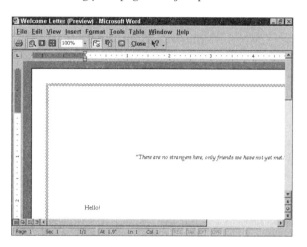

SET MARGINS

Margin settings control how close Word prints to the edge of the page. If you have a big top margin, for instance, Word leaves white space at the top of the document. If you have a small top margin, Word prints closer to the top of the page.

The default margins are 1-inch top and bottom margins and

1.25-inch left and right margins. These settings — like most of Word's defaults — work fine for a lot of documents. If necessary, you can change the margins to add more or less space around any edges of the page (top, bottom, left, or right).

For example, if you print on letterhead, you may need to make the top margin larger and

move the text down. As another example, you may want a bigger top margin for a short document so that the text is not crammed at the top of the page.

You can change margins using either of two methods. Use the dialog box to enter a precise measurement, or drag the margin guides in Print Preview.

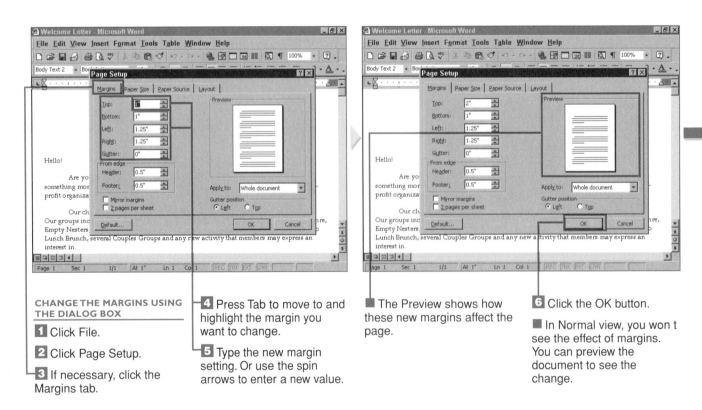

CHANGE THE MARGINS USING THE DIALOG BOX

■1 Click File.

■2 Click Page Setup.

■3 If necessary, click the Margins tab.

■4 Press Tab to move to and highlight the margin you want to change.

■5 Type the new margin setting. Or use the spin arrows to enter a new value.

■ The Preview shows how these new margins affect the page.

■6 Click the OK button.

■ In Normal view, you won t see the effect of margins. You can preview the document to see the change.

TIPS

What is mirroring the margins?

 Mirroring margins is appropriate when you print on both sides of the paper. The left and right margins are adjusted so that the inside and outside margins are the same width.

How do I change the default margins?

If you always use a certain margin, you can change the default. To do so, set the margins with the values you want and then click the Default button. When prompted to confirm the change, click the Yes button.

What is the gutter?

 The gutter is the space that is added to the margin for binding. You can select the gutter width as well as placement (top or side) on the Margins tab.

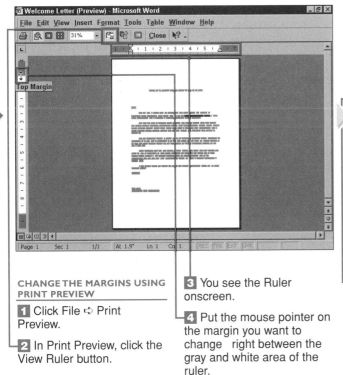

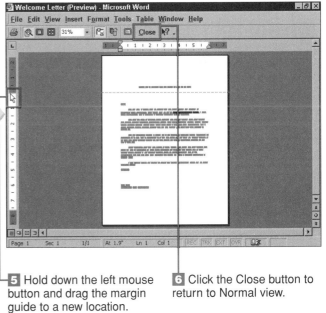

CHANGE THE MARGINS USING PRINT PREVIEW

1 Click File ⇨ Print Preview.

2 In Print Preview, click the View Ruler button.

3 You see the Ruler onscreen.

4 Put the mouse pointer on the margin you want to change — right between the gray and white area of the ruler.

5 Hold down the left mouse button and drag the margin guide to a new location.

6 Click the Close button to return to Normal view.

SELECT THE PAPER SOURCE AND LAYOUT

When you don't have a lot of text on the page, the page may look imbalanced. You can try tinkering with the margins to align the text better on the page, or you can simply center the page. For instance, centering a page works well for title pages. To make this change, use the Layout tab in the Page Setup dialog box.

You can also use the Paper Source tab to select a paper source for the first and following pages in a document. This feature is handy if you print the first page on letterhead and the following pages on regular paper. You can select a particular printer tray or manual feed for the first and following pages.

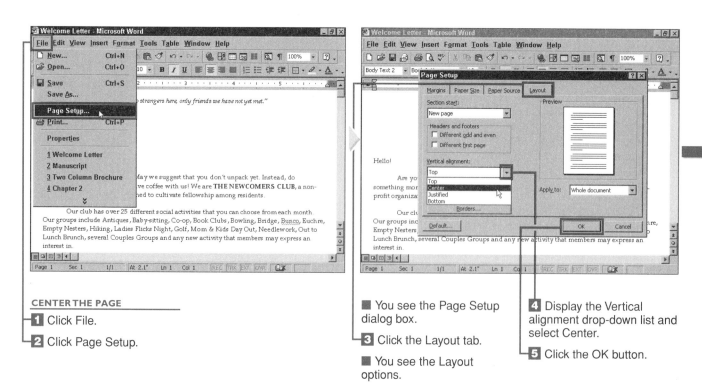

CENTER THE PAGE

1 Click File.

2 Click Page Setup.

■ You see the Page Setup dialog box.

3 Click the Layout tab.

■ You see the Layout options.

4 Display the Vertical alignment drop-down list and select Center.

5 Click the OK button.

TIPS

What if I want to print on two different types of paper?

If you print several pages on different sheets of paper (the first sheet on letterhead, for example), select which printer tray is used for the first page, and which is used for following pages. Make this change on the Paper Source tab.

How do I print on both sides of the paper?

Some network printers support double-sided printing. To select this option, use the Print dialog box.

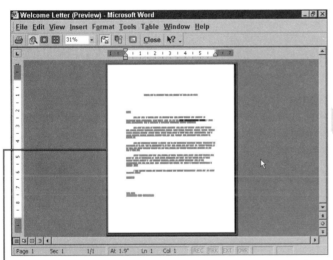

■ Word centers the page. In Normal view, you won t see this change. Preview or change to Print Layout mode to see the page.

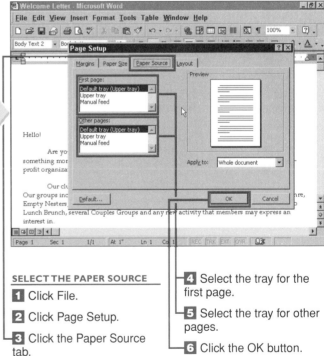

SELECT THE PAPER SOURCE

1 Click File.

2 Click Page Setup.

3 Click the Paper Source tab.

4 Select the tray for the first page.

5 Select the tray for other pages.

6 Click the OK button.

CHANGE THE PAGE ORIENTATION AND PAPER SIZE

Think of a portrait. What dimensions do you think of? Usually the portrait is taller than it is wide, right? Now think of a landscape picture. What are the dimensions? Wider than it is tall? These two terms carry over to Word's page orientation. You can print left to right across the short side (8½")

and down the long edge (11"). This orientation is called portrait. Or you can print left to right across the long side (11") and down the short side (8½"). This orientation is called landscape. If your document is wider than it is long—for instance, you have a table with many columns—print in landscape mode.

Most documents in North America are printed on 8½" × 11" paper. You can also select other paper sizes. For instance, you may have a printer with a bin for legal paper. You can then select and print on this paper size.

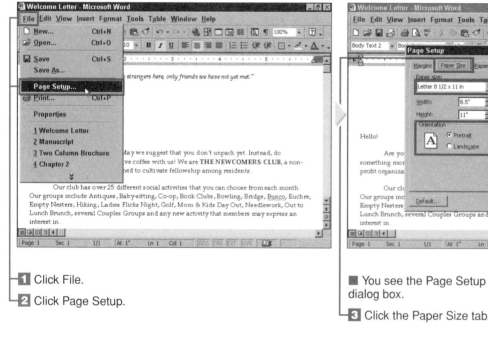

1 Click File.

2 Click Page Setup.

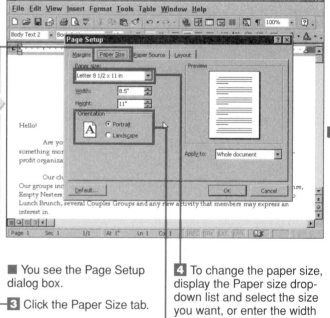

■ You see the Page Setup dialog box.

3 Click the Paper Size tab.

4 To change the paper size, display the Paper size drop-down list and select the size you want, or enter the width and height in the spin boxes.

5 In the Orientation area, click Portrait or Landscape.

TIPS

How do I format just some pages in a certain orientation?

 You can divide a document into sections and format each with different orientations. Use the Apply to drop-down list to apply the change from this point forward. For more information on sections, see Chapter 12.

How do I print an envelope?

You can select envelope from the Paper size drop-down list, but you don't have to manually format the page. Instead, you can use the Tools ⇨ Envelopes and Labels command. See Chapter 6 for more information on printing an envelope.

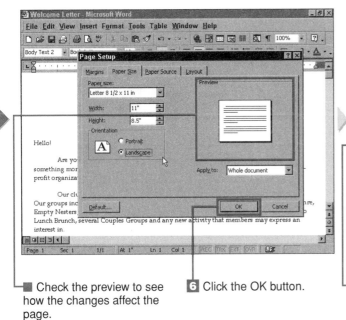

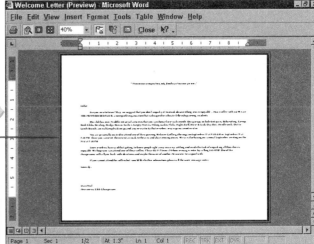

■ Check the preview to see how the changes affect the page.

6 Click the OK button.

■ Word formats the pages in the document. To see the effects of the change, preview the document.

NUMBER PAGES

Imagine a 20-page document without page numbers. How would you keep the pages in order? Even if the pages were stapled or bound, how would you refer to a particular page? In a long document page numbers are a necessity.

Word makes it easy to insert page numbers. When you use Word to number the pages, you don't have to worry about renumbering when you add or delete a page. The page numbers are updated automatically.

If all you want to do is insert a page number, do so using the Insert ➪ Page Numbers command. This command automatically creates a footer or header, depending on where you choose to place the page numbers. If you want to include additional information in the header or footer, such as the date or document name, you can set up the headers and footers. See the task on this topic.

When you insert page numbers, you can select whether they appear at the top or bottom of the page. Choose to align the page number right, center, left, inside, or outside.

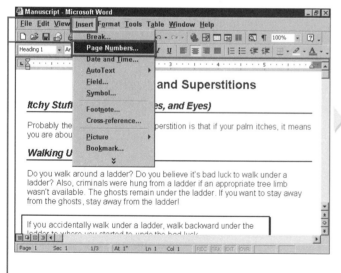

1 Click Insert.

2 Click Page Numbers.

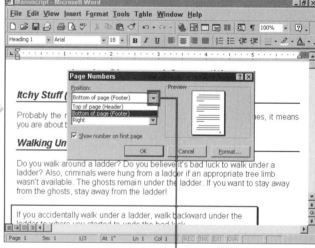

■ You see the Page Numbers dialog box.

3 Display the Position drop-down list box and select Top of Page (Header) or Bottom of Page (Footer).

How do I turn off page numbers for the first page?

To skip a page number on the first page, uncheck the Show number on first page checkbox. For instance, you may not want to include a page number on a title page.

How do I delete a page number?

You can delete the page number by viewing the header or footer (View ⇨ Header and Footer); then click the page number text box to select it and press Delete.

What if I want to use a different numbering style?

You can select a different numbering style as well as other options for printing the page numbers using the Format button. See the next task for information on these features.

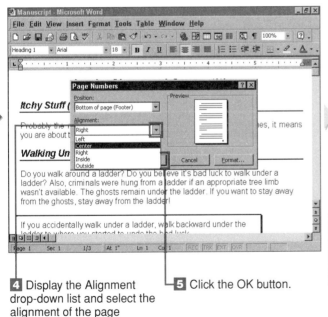

4 Display the Alignment drop-down list and select the alignment of the page number.

5 Click the OK button.

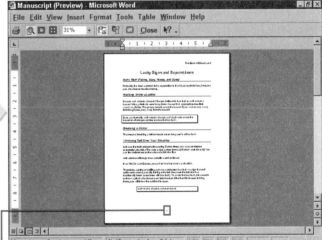

■ Word creates a header or footer and inserts the page number. In Normal view, you don t see the page numbers. Switch to Print Layout view or preview the document.

FORMAT PAGE NUMBERS

If plain old Arabic numbers aren't fancy enough for you, you can select another number style. You can choose Arabic numbers, lowercase letters, uppercase letters, lowercase Roman numerals, or uppercase Roman numerals.

You can even include additional numbering

information, such as the chapter number. To use this feature, you must assign a style to the chapter heading so Word knows the chapter number. See Chapter 10 for more information on styles.

If you have a long document that is broken into several files, you may need to start numbering with a different number other

than 1. For instance, suppose that you write an epic novel with one file for each of the chapters. When you print out this tome, you want continuous page numbering. You can also select a different starting page for each section.

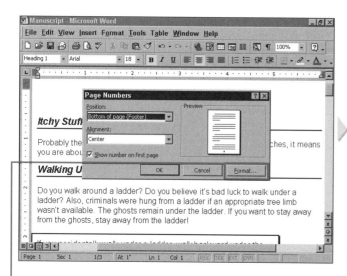

■1 In the Page Numbers dialog box, click the Format button.

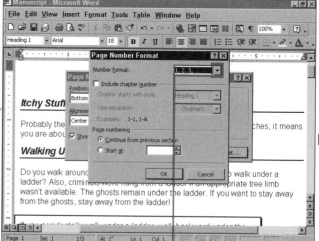

■ You see the Page Number Format dialog box.

■2 To change the numbering style, display the Number format drop-down list and click the style you want.

How do I number page numbers within sections?

 If you've broken up the document into sections and want to number each section separately, click the Continue from previous section option button to turn off this option. Chapter 12 covers sections in more detail.

How do I include the number of pages as well?

You can include the page number as well as the number of pages ("Page 1 of 42," for instance). To do so, use the buttons on the Header and Footer toolbar. See the next task.

What are styles?

 You can assign heading styles to your document headings. Use these styles to not only insert the chapter information, but also to generate a table of contents. If you use the chapter numbering option, you must apply the styles consist-ently to all chapter headings. For more information on styles, see Chapter 10.

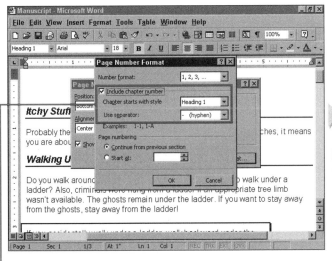

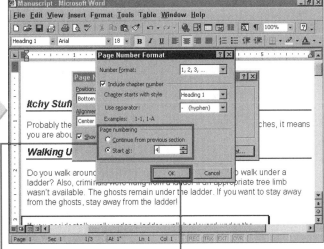

3 To include the chapter number and the page number, check the Include chapter number checkbox. Then display the Chapter starts with style drop-down list and select the style assigned to the chapter

head. Display the Use separator drop-down list and select which character you want to use to separate the chapter and page number (hyphen, period, em dash, and so on).

4 To change the starting page number, click the Start at option button and then enter the number to use in the spin box.

5 Click the OK button twice.

■ Word uses the selected numbering style to number the pages.

ADD HEADERS

When you start creating documents that are longer than one page, you will most likely want to include some type of reference number on the page. For instance, page numbers are practically a must. In addition, you may want to include other text that helps the reader identify the document. For example, you can include the document title or a date or your last name. You might include the section name to help the reader navigate through a long document. Rather than type this information on each page, create a header and footer. Word then inserts the text on each page automatically.

By default, the header includes a centered tab and a right-aligned tab. You can include text at the left and then at the center or the right side of the header by pressing Tab and then typing the text you want to include.

You can use the buttons on the Header and Footer toolbar to insert special information in the header or footer (see the table on the following page).

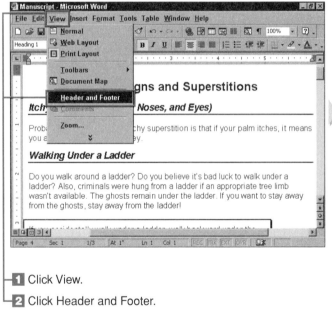

1 Click View.

2 Click Header and Footer.

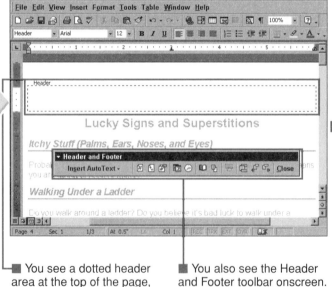

■ You see a dotted header area at the top of the page, with the insertion point.

■ You also see the Header and Footer toolbar onscreen.

Header and Footer Toolbar Icons

Button	Name	Function
Insert AutoText ▾	AutoText	Word sets up some AutoText entries that are commonly used in headers and footers. Some examples include Author, Created by, Last printed, Page X of Y, and so on. To use one of these predefined headers/footers, display the list and select the one you want.
(icon)	Insert Page Number	Inserts a page number that is updated automatically.
(icon)	Insert Number of Pages	Inserts the number of pages. You can combine the Insert Page Number button and this button to create a header or footer that says something like "Page 5 of 10."
(icon)	Format Page Number	Use to select a format for the page numbers. See the section on page numbers for information on using this dialog box.
(icon)	Insert Date	Inserts a date field that is automatically updated.
(icon)	Insert Time	Inserts a time field that is automatically updated.

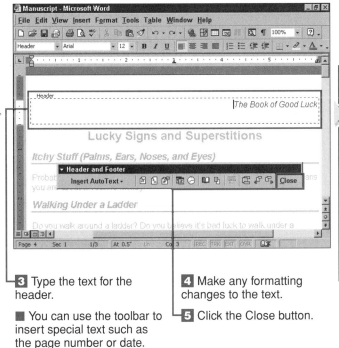

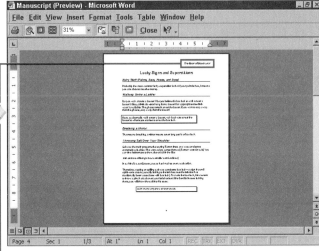

3 Type the text for the header.

■ You can use the toolbar to insert special text such as the page number or date.

4 Make any formatting changes to the text.

5 Click the Close button.

■ Word adds the header to the document, which you won't see in Normal view. To see the header, switch to Print Layout view or Print Preview.

ADD FOOTERS

A footer is printed at the bottom of each page. You create a footer in just about the same way as a header. You just need to use a toolbar button to move to the footer area.

Which one — a header or footer — is preferable?

Whichever one you prefer. You can even include both a header and a footer.

Like the header, the footer includes a centered tab and a right-aligned tab. You can include text at the left and then at the center or the right side of the

footer by pressing Tab and then typing the text you want to include, as well as use the toolbar buttons to insert special text. You can also make any formatting changes to the text. For instance, you can make text bold or italic, or change the font.

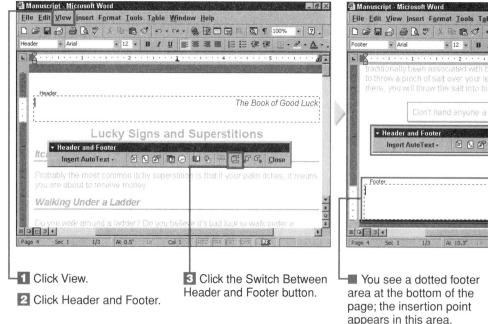

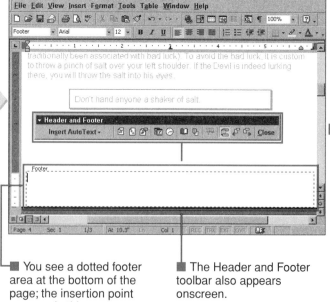

1 Click View.

2 Click Header and Footer.

3 Click the Switch Between Header and Footer button.

■ You see a dotted footer area at the bottom of the page; the insertion point appears in this area.

■ The Header and Footer toolbar also appears onscreen.

TIPS

Can I change the appearance of the text?

You can make text italic, change the font, use a different font size, add a border — just about everything you learned in Chapters 7 and 8.

What are the other toolbar buttons used for?

You can click the Page Setup to display the Page Setup dialog box so you can change the margins, paper size, and other options. Click Show/Hide Document Text to hide (or show) the document text.

In a document with different headers and footers, use the Show Previous and Show Next buttons to switch to the other headers or footers.

How do I delete a header or footer?

To get rid of a header or footer, all you need to do is display the header or footer and then delete the text.

Can I change the margins?

Word prints the headers and footers half an inch from the top and bottom of the page. If you want to use different margins, select File ➪ Page Setup. Click the Margins tab. In the Header spin box, enter the amount of margin you want for the top of the page. In the Footer spin box, enter the amount of margin you want for the bottom of the page. Click the OK button.

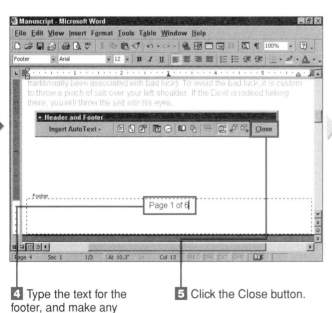

4 Type the text for the footer, and make any formatting changes to the text.

5 Click the Close button.

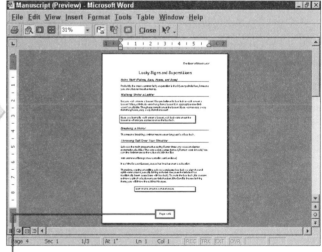

■ Word adds the footer to the document. To see the footer, preview the document or change to Print Layout view.

ADD A PAGE BORDER

Want to add something fancy to your document? Perhaps you are creating an invitation, or just want to liven up an otherwise dull memo. One way to add something interesting to the page is to add a border. The steps you follow are similar to those for adding a border to a paragraph (covered in Chapter 8).

To make these changes, use the Page Border tab. You can select from some predefined settings such as a box, shadow, or 3-D. With these options, you can select the style, thickness, and color of the line. The preview area gives you an idea of how the selection will appear on the page.

If you don't like the predefined settings, you can create a custom border. You can even add a fancy art border.

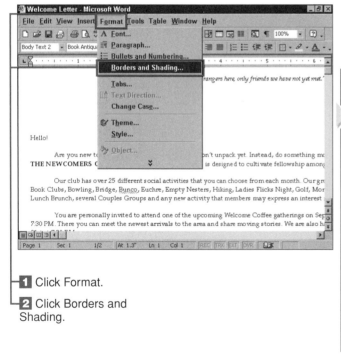

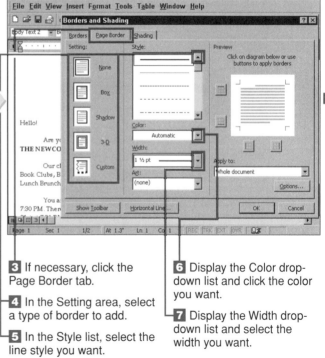

1 Click Format.

2 Click Borders and Shading.

3 If necessary, click the Page Border tab.

4 In the Setting area, select a type of border to add.

5 In the Style list, select the line style you want.

6 Display the Color drop-down list and click the color you want.

7 Display the Width drop-down list and select the width you want.

How do I use borders for just a particular page in the document?

If you have multiple sections (covered in Chapter 12), you can control where the page border is placed. Display the Apply to drop-down list and select to add the border to all pages (Whole Document), the pages in the current section (This section), the first page in this section (This section - First page only), or all pages in this section except the first one (This section - All except first page).

What about adding art?

New with this version of Word is the capability to select an image to use as the page border. To do so, click the Art button and then select the image you want to use.

Can I use a different border for each side?

Yes. To do so, select Custom. When you have the style, color, and width selected, click in the preview area on the side where you want to place the border. For example, click the top of the diagram to add the border to the top. Word adds the selected border to that side. Do this for each border you want to add.

How do I add more (or less) space between the border and the text?

You can use the Options button to select the distance of the border. You can also select where the this measurement is measured from.

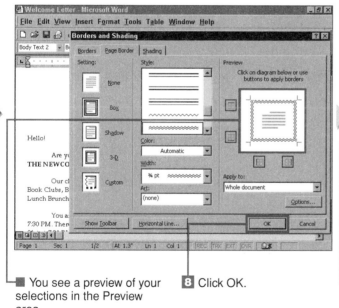

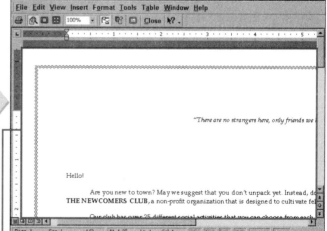

■ You see a preview of your selections in the Preview area.

8 Click OK.

■ Word adds the page border. To see the change, preview the document.

USE A BACKGROUND FILL OR COLOR

Many documents are sent via e-mail and read onscreen. If your document will be displayed onscreen rather than printed, you may want to add a colored background. Colored backgrounds also work for documents created for the World Wide Web. (This topic is covered in Chapter 23.)

On a color printer, the color you select will be printed. On a black-and-white printer, colors will be printed as shades of gray.

In addition to a color, you can select Fill Effects such as a gradient, texture, pattern, or picture. For a gradient, for instance, you can select several variants of shading styles. For a texture, you can select from

several marble-like designs. The available patterns include stripes, dots, checks, and others. For a picture, you can select any picture graphic file. You can use these images to add a watermark to the page.

When you add these elements, be careful not to get carried away. You don't want to distract from your message.

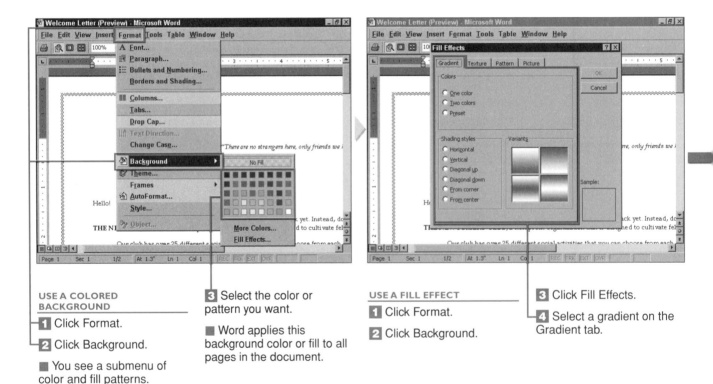

USE A COLORED BACKGROUND

1 Click Format.

2 Click Background.

■ You see a submenu of color and fill patterns.

3 Select the color or pattern you want.

■ Word applies this background color or fill to all pages in the document.

USE A FILL EFFECT

1 Click Format.

2 Click Background.

3 Click Fill Effects.

4 Select a gradient on the Gradient tab.

TIPS

How do I use a picture for the background?

To use a picture, click the Picture tab in the Fill Effects dialog box. Then click the Select Picture button. Select the file you want to use and click Insert.

Can I use a colored pattern?

Yes. To do so, select the pattern and then select the colors for the foreground and background from the drop-down lists on the Pattern tab.

How do I customize the gradient?

For the gradient, you can select colors as well as shading styles. You can select horizontal, vertical, or diagonal, for instance. You can also select the variant of the gradient.

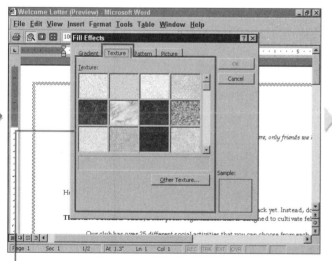

5 Select a texture from the Texture tab.

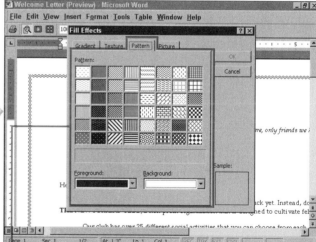

6 Select a pattern from the Pattern tab.

7 Click OK.

USING

DESKTOP PUBLISHING TECHNIQUES

FORMATTING SHORTCUTS

When you format a document, you may find yourself selecting the same commands over and over. For example, for your section headings, you may change the font and make them boldface. You may also add a border. If your document had ten heads, you'd select 30 commands (three commands, ten times).

Are you thinking there's got to be a better way? There is. You can use some of the formatting shortcuts in this chapter.

Copy Formatting

For one or two changes, you may simply want to copy the formatting. You can pick up the formatting from one section of text and apply the same set of formatting to another selection.

Use Word Styles

Another timesaver is styles. Styles offer a lot of benefits:

► Styles save time. Rather than select the same set of commands to make the formatting changes over and over, you can create a style and then apply that style with one command.

► If you use styles, you are assured that your document is consistently formatted. You don't have to worry about which font size or border to use for the headings. Simply select the style heading, and Word applies all the formatting options for you.

► If you decide to modify a style, Word automatically updates all of the paragraphs tagged with that style. For example, suppose you decide that the Woodstock font is a little much for the headings in your business report. If you formatted the document manually, you'd have to go through and modify each heading. If you used a style for the headings, you modify the style once, and Word updates all paragraphs formatted with that style.

You can use any of the styles in the templates provided with Word. You can even copy styles from one template to another.

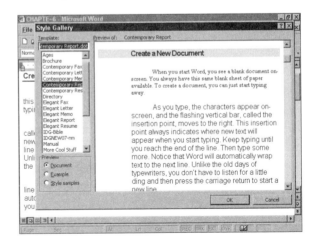

You can apply a theme, a set of visual elements with a unified design.

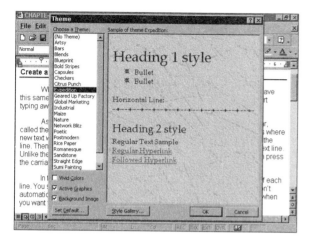

You can create your own styles and save them as part of the template. You can select any set of formatting you want.

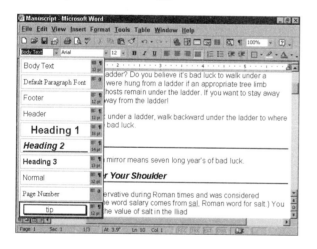

Use AutoFormat

Word's AutoFormat feature automatically makes some style changes as you type. For instance, if you type an asterisk, press Tab, and type some text, Word automatically creates a bulleted list. If you manually format a heading in a document, Word creates a style based on the formatting you applied. You may wonder how these changes happened. It's magic! It's AutoFormat As You Type.

You can also have Word go through a particular document and make suggested formatting changes. This feature is also called AutoFormat.

COPY FORMATTING

Usually you tinker with one text selection (a word, sentence, paragraph, line, whatever). You may try an option, view the results, and make some additional changes until the text looks just the way you want. Now what do you do when you want to use that same set of formatting options on another

line or paragraph? Start over?

If you want to use the same set of formatting options in one or two other places in the document, you can copy the formatting. To do so, use the Format Painter button in the toolbar.

If you plan on using this same set of formatting options more than once or twice, create a style,

as covered in the next section. Styles offer several advantages over simply copying the formatting.

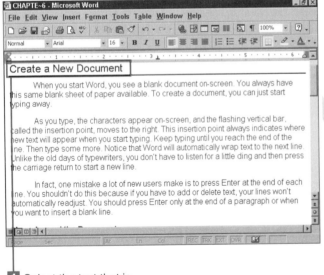

1 Select the text that is formatted as you want it.

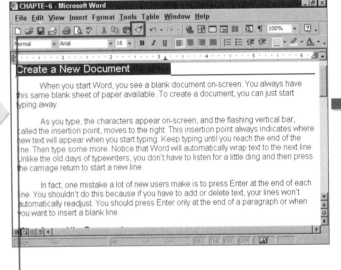

2 Click the Format Painter button.

Can I apply the formatting more than once?

Yes, but you must select the text, click the Format Painter button, and then select the text for each section you want to format.

How do I undo a formatting copy?

Click the Undo button or select Edit ➪ Undo.

When should I create a style?

If you find that you do want to use the same set of formatting over and over, instead of copying the formatting, create a style, as covered in this chapter.

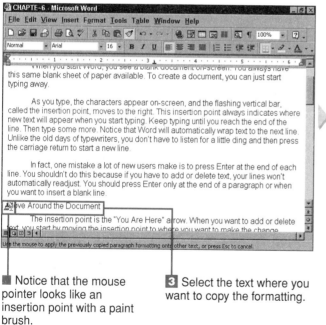

■ Notice that the mouse pointer looks like an insertion point with a paint brush.

3 Select the text where you want to copy the formatting.

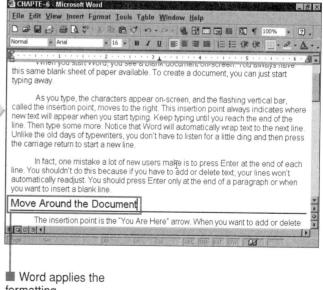

■ Word applies the formatting.

USE WORD STYLES

If you want to use the same set of formatting options more than once or twice, you're better off creating a style. A style is a collection of character formatting (font, size, style, color, and so on) and paragraph formatting (alignment, indents, borders, and so on). You can apply the style to other text, and Word applies all the associated formatting options.

Word provides some predefined styles that you can use without going to the trouble of creating your own. Trying these styles is a good way to see how styles work. You can practice applying styles and see what types of formatting options a style can include.

The styles that are available depend on the *template* you are using. You select the template when you choose the File ⇨ New command. For the most part, you will use the Normal template. (Templates are covered in more detail in Chapter 17.)

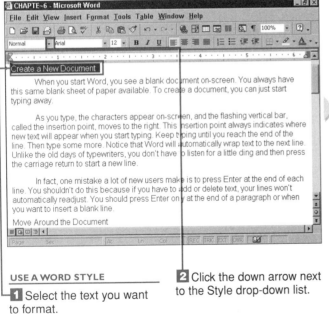

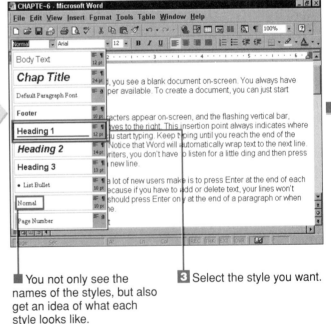

USE A WORD STYLE

■1 Select the text you want to format.

■2 Click the down arrow next to the Style drop-down list.

■ You not only see the names of the styles, but also get an idea of what each style looks like.

■3 Select the style you want.

What are the shortcut keys for applying Word styles?

 You can use the following shortcut keys to apply Word's styles: Ctrl+Shift+N for Normal style, Alt+Ctrl+1 for Heading 1, Alt+Ctrl+2 for Heading 2, and Alt+Ctrl+3 for Heading 3.

What if I don't want to use the styles?

To close the dialog box without copying the styles, click the Cancel button.

How do I use a different template?

When you use the Style Gallery command to add styles to the document, you do not change the template that is attached. The styles are simply added to the document. If you want to use a different template, see Chapter 17.

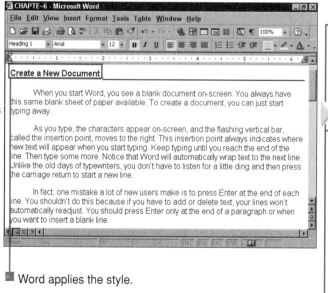

Word applies the style.

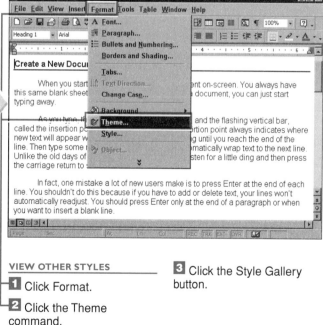

VIEW OTHER STYLES

■1 Click Format.

■2 Click the Theme command.

■3 Click the Style Gallery button.

CONTINUED ▶

USE WORD STYLES CONTINUED

You can view and try the styles from other templates without actually starting with that template. Each template has its own set of styles, and each style can vary from template to template. For instance, the heading 1 style in one template may look different than the heading 1 style in another template.

You can use the Style Gallery to view the styles in other templates. Then if you want to use a template, you can copy the styles from the template to your document.

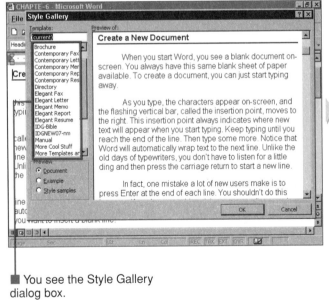

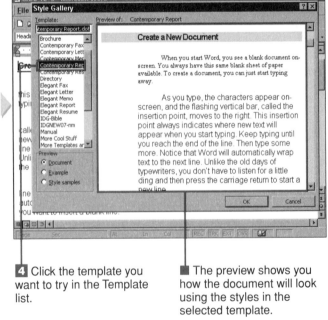

■ You see the Style Gallery dialog box.

4 Click the template you want to try in the Template list.

■ The preview shows you how the document will look using the styles in the selected template.

What is a theme?

A theme consists of a style for headings 1 and 2, bullets, text, and hyperlinks. See the next task for information on themes. For more information on using themes to create a Web page, see Chapter 23.

Can I create my own templates and styles?

Yes. Creating your own templates is covered in Chapter 17. This chapter covers creating your own styles.

What if the templates have not been installed?

Depending on how you installed Word, not all of the templates may be installed. If so, you will see a prompt when you select a template. You can choose to install the template then. Follow the onscreen directions.

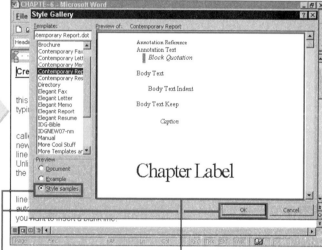

5 To see an example of this template, click the Example option button.

■ The preview shows an example document.

6 To see samples of the various styles, click the Style samples button.

■ The preview shows each style.

7 To copy these styles (make them available in your document) click the OK button.

■ Word copies the new styles from this template to the onscreen document and template. You can then use any of these styles to format your text.

USE A WORD THEME

In addition to styles, Word includes some themes. These include a design for headings, background images, bullets, fonts, horizontal lines, and other elements. You can select a theme to pick one of these preset designs.

Themes are useful for Web pages (covered in Chapter 23), e-mail messages, and any other type of Word document where you want to use a consistent visual element throughout.

You can select from several styles including artsy, blends, expedition, industrial, checkers, and so on. You can view a preview of the background, line, and styles from the Theme dialog box.

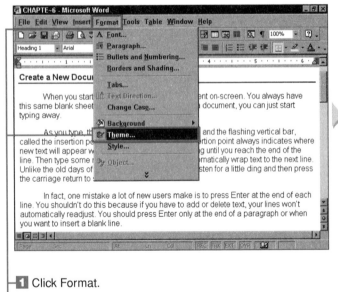

1 Click Format.

2 Click the Theme command.

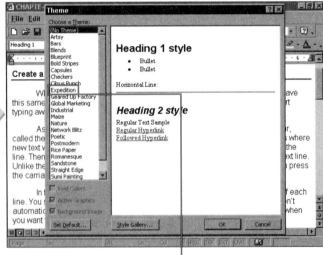

■ You see the Theme dialog box.

3 Select the theme you want to use.

TIPS

How is a theme different from a template?

 A theme includes visual elements, but does not include customization features such as AutoText entries, predefined text, macros, custom toolbars, or commands. A template may include these elements.

How do I undo a theme?

You can go back to the default — that is, no theme — by selecting (No Theme) from the Theme dialog box.

Where can I find additional themes?

 You can also use themes from FrontPage 4.0 or later (a Web publishing program). Or download themes from Microsoft's Word page.

What if the themes have not been installed?

 If you select a theme that has not been installed, you will be prompted to install it. Follow the onscreen directions.

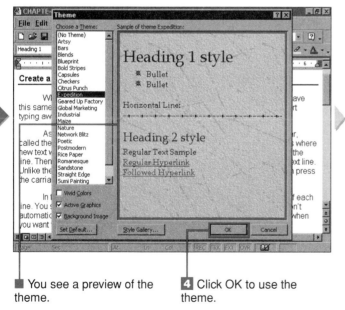

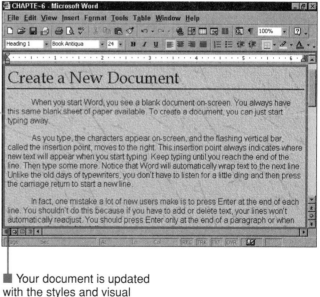

■ You see a preview of the theme.

4 Click OK to use the theme.

■ Your document is updated with the styles and visual elements from the theme.

209

CREATE A NEW STYLE BY EXAMPLE

You aren't limited to the predefined styles. You can also create your own styles with the formatting options that you want to use. You can use any formatting features on the toolbar or within the Format menu. And you can create styles for any type of document element you include — for headings, subheadings, notes, captions, headers, footers, sidebars, and so on.

If you find yourself using the same formatting options over and over in a document, you should create a style.

The easiest way to create a style is to format a paragraph with the formats you want and base the new style on this paragraph. That's the method covered here. You can also build a style from scratch, as covered in the next section of this chapter.

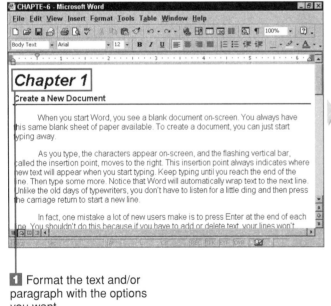

1 Format the text and/or paragraph with the options you want.

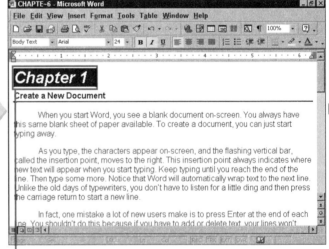

2 Select the text with the formatting.

TIPS

What formatting is saved with the style?

All of the formatting within the selected paragraph becomes part of the style.

What if I want to make a change?

You can change a style and then have all of the text **formatted** with that style **updated** automatically. To do so, see the task "Modifying a Style" later in this chapter.

What happens to the paragraph formatting?

When you use this method to create a style, that style is applied to the paragraph. You see the style name listed in the Style drop-down list box.

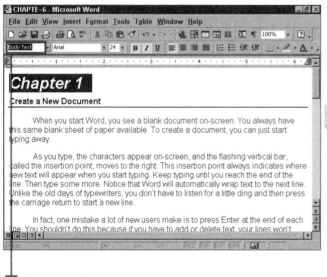

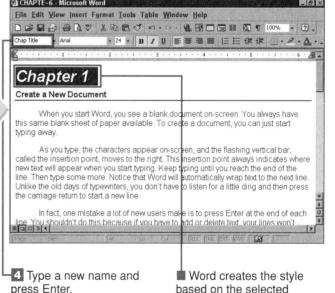

3 Click in the Style list box and highlight the current name.

4 Type a new name and press Enter.

■ Word creates the style based on the selected paragraph and applies this style to that paragraph.

CREATE A NEW STYLE FROM SCRATCH

The benefits of creating a style by example is that you can see the results of the commands. Check to see if the style is the way you want it before creating the style. You can also create a new style from scratch by entering a name and then selecting the formatting features you want.

To make the changes, use the Format button, and then select

the command you want. You can select multiple formatting options. For example, you can use the Font command to select a font, size, and style. Then you can add a border using the Border command. To add space below the paragraph, use the Paragraph command.

You can get an idea of how your selections affect the text by looking at the Paragraph and

Character previews in the dialog box.

When you use this method, you can set other style options, such as what style follows the selected one.

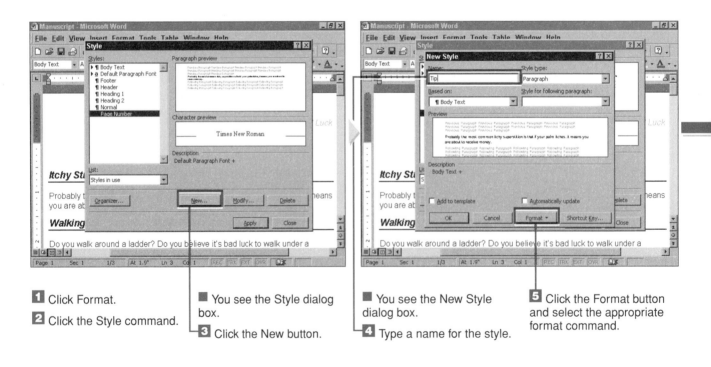

■ **1** Click Format.

■ **2** Click the Style command.

■ You see the Style dialog box.

3 Click the New button.

■ You see the New Style dialog box.

4 Type a name for the style.

■ **5** Click the Format button and select the appropriate format command.

TIPS

What should I name the style?

 Use a name that reminds you of the style's purpose.

What are some shortcuts?

When you know that a certain style will follow another style, you can select the style for the following paragraph. For instance, you may have a Heading 1 style. That style is always followed by a Body Text style.

What is the Based On option used for?

 You can base one style on another. Then when you change one style, styles based on that style are updated as well.

What are the style types?

 In the New Style dialog box, you can create a paragraph style, which is applied to the entire paragraph, or a character style, which is applied to just text.

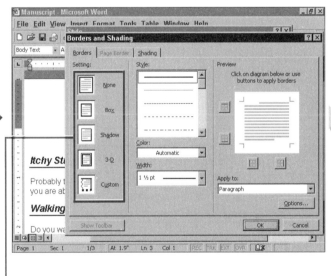

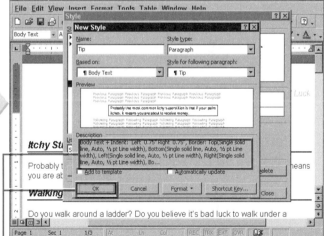

■ You see the appropriate dialog box.

6 Make the appropriate choices from the dialog boxes that appear.

7 Follow Steps 5 and 6 for each formatting option you want to add to the style.

8 When you have selected all the formats you want, click the OK button.

■ You see the Style dialog box again, with a preview of the style. You can also read the Description for a list of formatting options in effect.

9 To apply the new style to the selected paragraph, click the Apply button. To close the dialog box without applying the style, click the Close button.

APPLY A STYLE

Y ou only have to create a style once. Then you can apply it to any text in the document. The styles will also be available in other documents you create that are based on the same template.

The fastest way to apply a style is to use the Style drop-down list. In earlier versions of

Word, you only saw the name in the Style drop-down list, so it was hard to tell how the paragraph would look when formatted. Word 97 and later versions do show text using the listed style, so you get some idea of how the text will appear when formatted. However, you don't get an exact sense of how the

paragraph is aligned (for instance, centered, right-aligned, indented, and so on).

If you want a more detailed description, and want to see both a paragraph and character preview, use the dialog box.

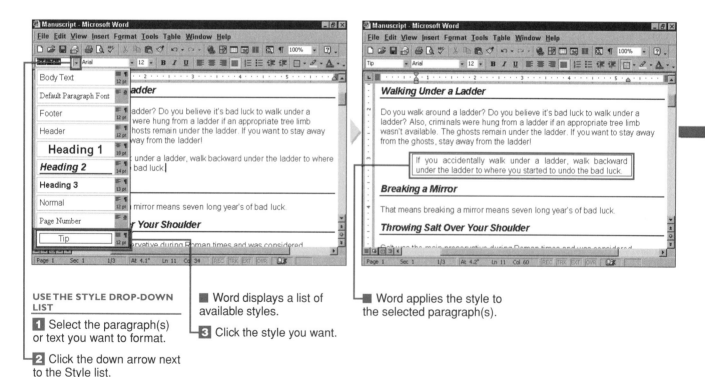

USE THE STYLE DROP-DOWN LIST

1 Select the paragraph(s) or text you want to format.

2 Click the down arrow next to the Style list.

■ Word displays a list of available styles.

3 Click the style you want.

■ Word applies the style to the selected paragraph(s).

TIPS

What text do I need to select?

If you are formatting a single paragraph, you can just place the insertion point within the paragraph. To format several paragraphs, select them. If you are applying a character style, select the text you want to format.

What if the style is not listed in the dialog box?

If the style is not listed, click the down arrow next to the List drop-down list. Then select which styles you want listed: all styles, styles in use, or user-defined styles.

How do I use styles from another document?

You can copy styles from one document to another using the Organizer. Click this button and then use the Organizer dialog box to copy files. See the chapter on templates (Chapter 17) for more information on using this feature.

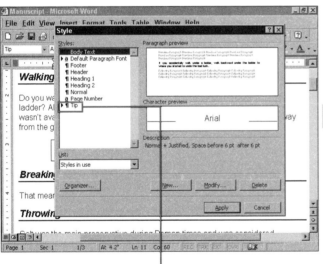

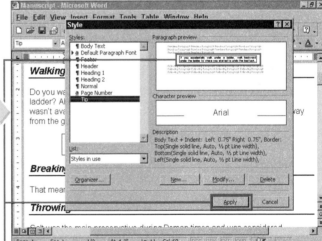

USE THE STYLE COMMAND

■1 Select the paragraph(s) you want to format.

■2 Click Format.

■3 Click the Style command.

■ You see the Style dialog box.

■4 Click the style you want in the Styles list.

■ You see a preview in the Paragraph and Character previews. Check this area to see whether you like the style.

■5 Click the Apply button.

■ Word applies the style and closes the dialog box.

MODIFY A STYLE

One of the benefits of using a style is that it is simple to make a change and update all the paragraphs formatted with a style. Maybe you decide you don't want a paragraph border for your headings. Or maybe your boss decides that all report headings should be in italic. Whatever the reason, simply update the style, and Word updates the document.

When you make a change, you use the Modify Style dialog box, which is similar to the New Style dialog box. The name is different, and some options are not available. You cannot change the Based On style or the style type.

You can, though, change some of the other style options, such as what style follows another, and the style on which the current style is based.

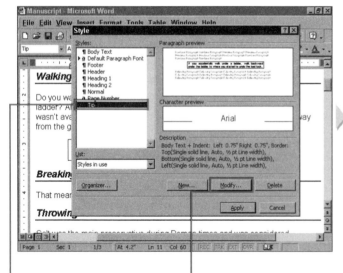

1 Open the Format menu and select the Style command.

■ You see the Style dialog box.

2 Select the style you want to change.

3 Click the Modify button.

■ You see the Modify Style dialog box.

4 Click the Format button and select the formatting you want to change.

■ Word displays the appropriate dialog box.

5 Make the selections you want and click OK.

6 Follow Steps 3 and 4 for each change you want to make.

How do I delete a style?

If you have styles that you don't use, you can delete them. All paragraphs formatted with the deleted style will be reformatted with the Normal style. From the Style dialog box, select the style you want to delete. Click the Delete button. When prompted to confirm the deletion, click the Yes button.

What if I don't want to apply the style?

To close the dialog box without applying the style, click the Close button.

How do I assign a style to a shortcut key?

You can assign a style to a shortcut key. Then you can apply this style using the key combination. Click the Shortcut Key button. Then press the shortcut key combination and click Assign. For more information on shortcut keys, see Chapter 25.

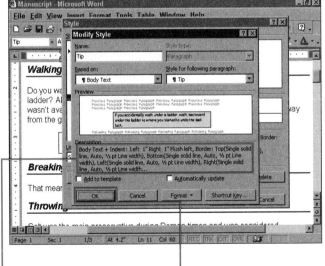

■ You see an updated preview as well as a description.

7 When you finish making changes, click OK to return to the Style dialog box.

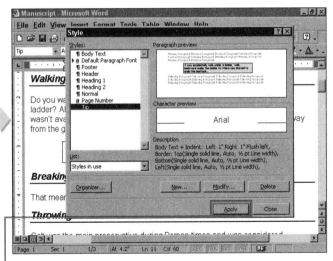

8 To apply the new style to the selected paragraph, click the Apply button.

10

USE AUTOFORMAT

Another timesaving formatting feature is AutoFormat. Some AutoFormat options occur as you type. For instance, if you type an asterisk, press Tab, type some text, and press Enter, Word formats the item as a bulleted list. To get an idea of what types of changes are made, check out the AutoFormat As You Type tab in the AutoCorrect dialog box. You can turn off

features you don't want to use (and turn on additional features).

You can also go through and use AutoFormat to format the entire document. AutoFormat searches the document and makes style recommendations based on the document type (general, letter, fax). For instance, if Word finds what it thinks is a title, it suggests adding the title style.

The same is true for headings, bulleted lists, and numbered lists in your document. Word also replaces certain characters — 1st with 1st, 1/2 with $^1/_2$, and so on.

For each change, you can choose to accept all suggestions, go through each change and accept or reject it, or reject all suggestions. You can also select which options are in effect.

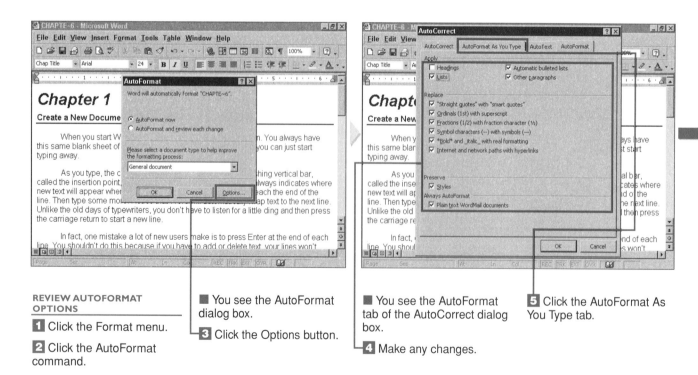

REVIEW AUTOFORMAT OPTIONS

1 Click the Format menu.

2 Click the AutoFormat command.

■ You see the AutoFormat dialog box.

3 Click the Options button.

■ You see the AutoFormat tab of the AutoCorrect dialog box.

4 Make any changes.

5 Click the AutoFormat As You Type tab.

TIPS

How do I confirm each change?

If you want Word to go through each change and prompt you, select AutoFormat and review each change. You can also review changes by clicking the Review Changes button in the AutoFormat dialog box.

What styles are applied to the text during an AutoFormat?

In the Apply area, select which types of styles you want to apply: Headings, Lists, Automatic bulleted lists, and Other paragraphs.

What replacements are made when I use AutoFormat?

In the Replace area, select which options you want automatically replaced. To retain styles you've applied, keep the Styles checkbox checked. If you don't want to retain the styles, uncheck this checkbox. Click the OK button. The next time you use AutoFormat, Word makes only the suggestions and replacements you selected.

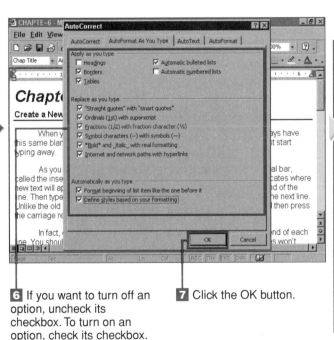

6 If you want to turn off an option, uncheck its checkbox. To turn on an option, check its checkbox.

7 Click the OK button.

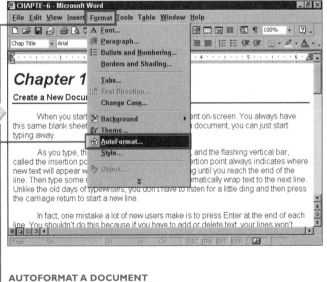

AUTOFORMAT A DOCUMENT

1 Click the Format menu.

2 Click the AutoFormat command.

CONTINUED ▶

USE AUTOFORMAT CONTINUED

If you accept all the changes, the dialog box is closed, and your document is reformatted with the selected formats.

If you reject the changes, the dialog box is closed, and your document is unchanged.

If you selected to review the changes, you see the Review AutoFormat Changes dialog box.

Word displays all text recommended for deletion in red and strikethrough. New text appears in blue and is underlined. Paragraph marks may appear in blue when a new format is suggested for that paragraph. You also see a description of the change.

Move to each change using the Find Next or Find Previous buttons. For each change, accept or reject it. To accept the change, just move on to the next change. To reject the change, click the Reject button. To undo the last change, click the Undo button.

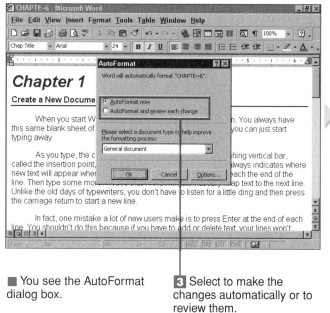

■ You see the AutoFormat dialog box.

3 Select to make the changes automatically or to review them.

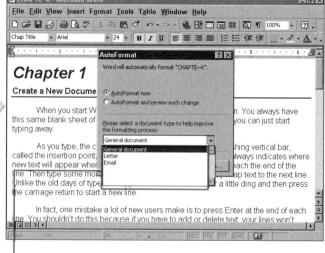

4 Select the document type from the drop-down list.

5 Click the OK button.

TIPS

What document types can I select?

You can select letter or e-mail from the drop-down list. Doing so will help Word select formatting most appropriate for that document type.

What is AutoCorrect?

AutoCorrect is Word's automatic spelling feature. Certain misspelled words and typos are corrected automatically. You can find more about AutoCorrect in Chapter 5.

What is AutoText?

AutoText is a feature for quickly typing common words and phrases (such as the closing of a letter). You can find information on AutoText in Chapter 2.

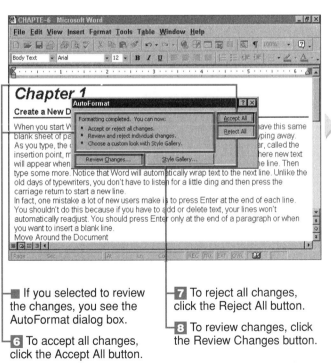

■ If you selected to review the changes, you see the AutoFormat dialog box.

6 To accept all changes, click the Accept All button.

7 To reject all changes, click the Reject All button.

8 To review changes, click the Review Changes button.

9 If you reviewed the changes, click the lower Find button to select the first change.

10 Confirm or reject this change. Do this for each change.

SEARCH FOR AND REPLACE FORMATTING

Sometimes you may need to update the formatting by searching and replacing. For instance, you may want to search for each place you used a particular style or formatting feature. You can then quickly go to each selection formatted with these options. You can search for just the formatting or for

particular text formatted with the options.

If needed, you can also search for and replace formatting. For instance, you can change all instances of italic in a document to bold. Or you can search for text formatted with one style and replace it with another style.

You can select to skip the replacement and find the next match by clicking Find Next. Or you can make the replacement by clicking Replace. To make all replacements, click Replace All.

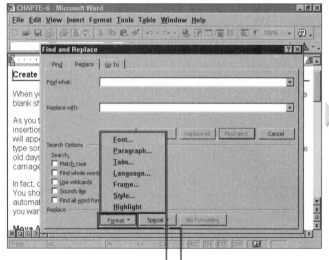

1 Click Edit.

2 Click Replace.

■ The Find and Replace dialog box appears.

3 Click the More button to see a more detailed version of the dialog box.

4 Click the Format button.

5 Select the appropriate command. For instance, to search for a style, select Style.

6 Select the option you want to find. For instance, select the style you want to find.

TIPS

How do I simply search for formatting?

To search for formatting, select the Edit ➪ Find command. Then select the formatting to find.

What if I want to find text and formatting?

You can find a particular word or phrase formatted with the selected options by typing the word or phrase in the Find What text box. To replace the text, type the replacement in the Replace with text box.

How do I undo a replacement?

If you make a replacement you didn't intend, you can use Edit ➪ Undo or click the Undo button to undo the change.

How do I clear formatting?

Word remembers the last item for which you searched. If you see formatting options listed in the dialog box, you can clear them by clicking the No Formatting button.

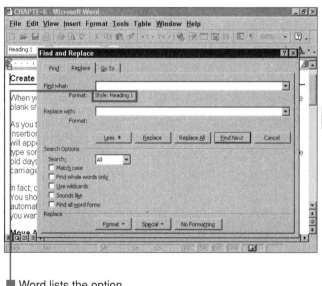

■ Word lists the option under the text box.

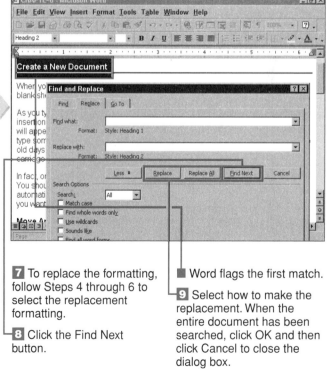

7 To replace the formatting, follow Steps 4 through 6 to select the replacement formatting.

8 Click the Find Next button.

■ Word flags the first match.

9 Select how to make the replacement. When the entire document has been searched, click OK and then click Cancel to close the dialog box.

223

CREATING AND FORMATTING TABLES

Forget the old-fashioned method of creating a table: set up tabs, type a few words, press Enter, type the next line, and hope that, when you get to the end, the table is somewhat aligned (just don't add or delete anything, because the alignment will go out the window). Instead, Word provides two convenient methods for creating a table, plus several features for formatting and editing it.

Creating a Table

Word makes creating a table much easier. You can use the Insert Tables button and simply select the number of columns and rows you want and Word creates the table.

You also can draw a table, drawing the outside border and then each column and row. Use this method to set up a table with different row and column sizes.

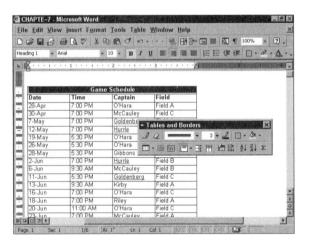

Once you've set up the table, type an entry within each cubbyhole (called a *cell*) in the table. You can enter a single word, a line, a paragraph, or several paragraphs and Word keeps the text aligned.

Formatting a Table

You have a lot of control over how the table looks. You can change the column width, add borders, shade cells, and more. For quick formatting, use one of Word's preset AutoFormats for tables. If one of these doesn't work, format the table manually.

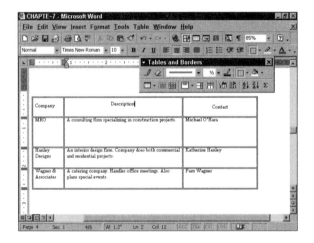

Special Table Features

In addition to formatting, you also can do some special things with tables. Insert a formula into a table to perform a mathematical operation with the entries, or sort a table based on any of the columns. You can create fancy tables using Word's Table menu.

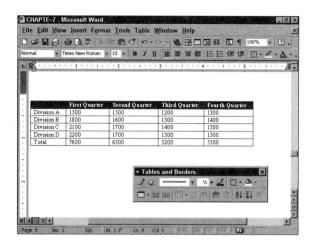

SET UP A TABLE

As you may have guessed, you can set up a table using one of several methods. The simplest way to create a table is to use the Insert Table button. This method works when you want a table with equal column widths.

When you create a table, select the number of columns and rows by dragging across the palette. For example, to create a table with three columns and two rows, drag across three columns and down two rows. Word displays the dimensions at the bottom of the palette. Using the Insert Table button, you can create a table no bigger than 4 by 5 (four columns by five rows).

You can easily add rows and columns, or change the column width once you create the table.

By default, each cell includes a border. You can change the look of this border or delete it, as covered later in this chapter.

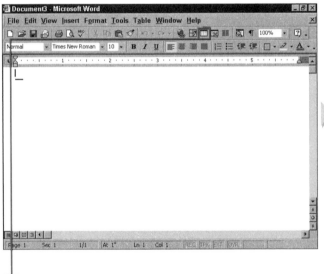

1 Click the Insert Table button.

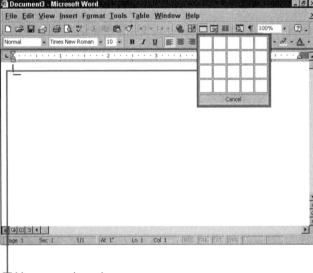

■ You see a drop-down palette of cells.

TIPS

What other method can I use to add a table to a document?

You can draw a table using the buttons on the Tables and Borders toolbar, as covered in the next task.

Which method is best?

Use the Insert Table button when you want a table with the same size rows and columns. Use the Tables and Borders toolbar when you want to format a table as you create it.

What if I already typed a tabbed list for the table?

If you have a typed list, you can convert it to a table. See the task "Convert a Table" later in this chapter.

How do I delete a table?

To delete a table, put the pointer within the table and then use the Table ⇨ Delete ⇨ Table command.

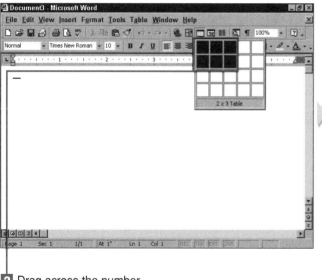

2 Drag across the number of columns and rows you want to include.

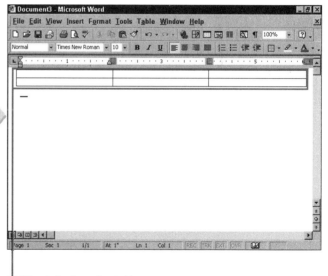

■ Word displays the table, a grid of columns and rows

DRAW A TABLE

If you are more visually inclined, you can draw a table using the Tables and Borders toolbar. Start by drawing the outside border. Then draw columns down the table and rows across. Make them any size you want.

Choose the line style using the Line Style drop-down list, the width using the Line Weight drop-down list, and the color using the Border Color palette, all from the toolbar. Note that the line width or weight is measured in points. You also can choose a shading. The default shading color is None, but you can display the Shading Color palette and choose a fill (color or shade of gray).

Use a different line style for each side by selecting the options you want before drawing the line.

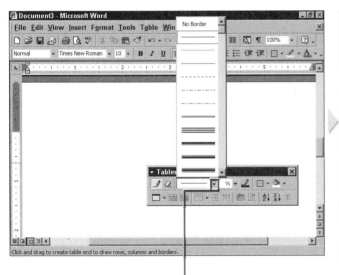

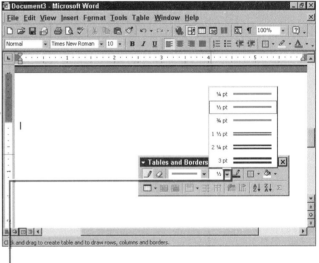

1 Click the Tables and Borders button.

■ You see the Tables and Borders toolbar. Word also automatically switches you to Print Layout view.

2 Display the Line Style drop-down list and choose a border style for the table.

3 Display the Line Weight drop-down list and choose the line thickness.

4 Display the Border Color drop-down palette and choose the color you want.

TIPS

How do I erase a line?

Click the Eraser button and then click the line you want to erase. To go back to drawing lines, click the Draw Table button.

I've erased the lines, but the table still appears.

The Eraser erases borders, not tables. To get rid of a table, you have to delete it. Use Table ➪ Delete ➪ Table.

Can I use the Tables and Borders button to modify an existing table?

Yes. Display the toolbar and then use the buttons to format or change the table.

How do I insert worksheet data?

If you have Excel and want to insert data from that program, do so by using Insert Microsoft Excel Worksheet. See Chapter 21.

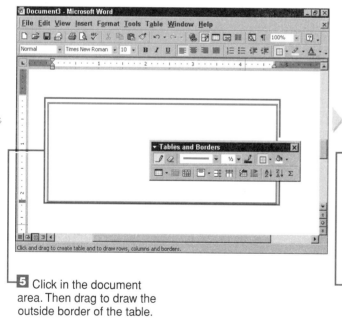

5 Click in the document area. Then drag to draw the outside border of the table.

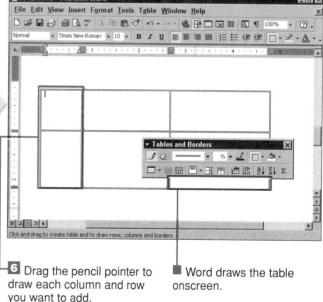

6 Drag the pencil pointer to draw each column and row you want to add.

■ Word draws the table onscreen.

ENTER DATA INTO A TABLE

No matter how you create a table, you follow the same method for entering text. Type the entries into the appropriate cells.

Basically, a table is a grid of columns and rows, and the intersection of a row and column is a *cell*. Word places the insertion point in a table's first cell.

To type something in a table, move to the cell you want. Click in the cell or use the arrow keys to move around. You also can press Tab to move forward through the cells or Shift+Tab to move backward through the cells.

When you type, you can enter a single word, a line, a paragraph, or several paragraphs. When you type a long entry, you don't have

to worry about pressing Enter to keep the text within the cell. When you reach the cell border, Word wraps the text to the next line and expands the cell. Press Enter if you want to create a new paragraph within the cell.

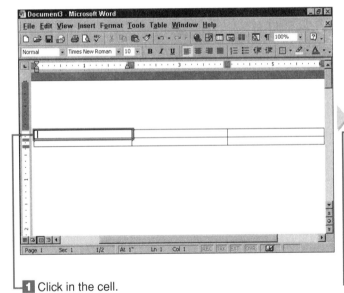

1 Click in the cell.

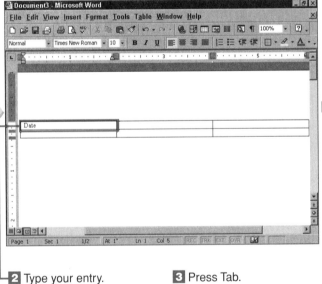

2 Type your entry.　　**3** Press Tab.

TIPS

How do I edit text?

 Use any editing features learned in preceding chapters. For instance, drag across text to select it, use Cut or Copy to rearrange table entries, and so on.

How do I format text?

 Make any formatting changes, as learned in preceding chapters. Remember that each cell is a paragraph, so you can use paragraph formatting options, such as setting tabs, indenting text, or changing the alignment of each cell.

I want to combine two cells into one for a table heading. Can I?

You can merge cells to add a table heading. See the task on table headings later in this chapter.

How do I delete an entry?

To delete a table entry, select it and press the Delete key. The cell remains, but the contents are erased.

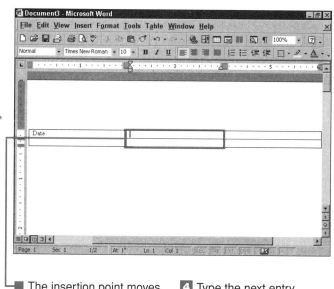

■ The insertion point moves to the next cell.

4 Type the next entry. Continue to do this until the table is complete.

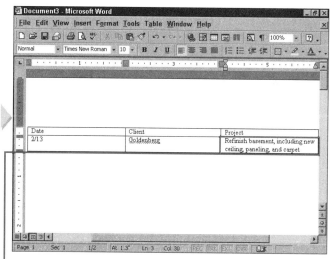

■ Notice that Word wraps the entry within the cell.

SELECT PART OF THE TABLE

Like formatting or editing text, you often need to select part of a table: a cell, a column, a row, or even an entire table. You may need to select a cell to make a formatting change,

or add a border or shading.

If you want to format a row or column, select that row or column. If you want to make a change to the entire table, select it.

New in this version of Word is the Select command in the Table menu. Use this menu to easily select the table element with which you want to work.

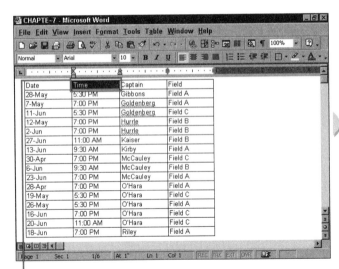

1 To select a cell, put the pointer in the cell and then use the Table ⇨ Select ⇨ Cell command.

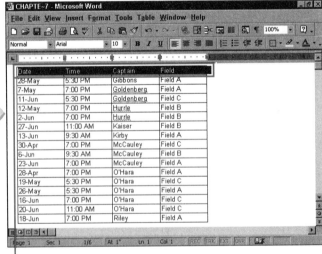

2 To select a row, put the insertion point within the row and then use the Table ⇨ Select ⇨ Row command.

How do I select text?

To select text within a table, drag across the text as you would in a normal document.

What are the shortcut keys?

You can press Alt+Num Lock 5 (the 5 key on the numeric keypad) to select an entire table.

The commands in the Table menu are grayed out. Why?

If most of the commands in the Table menu are dimmed, it probably means your insertion point is not within the table. The commands are available only when the insertion point is within the table. Put the insertion point somewhere in the table and try again.

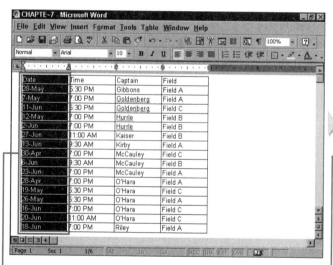

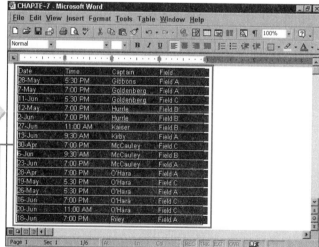

3 To select a column, put the insertion point within the column and then use the Table ⇨ Select ⇨ Column command.

4 To select the entire table, put the insertion point within the table and then use the Table ⇨ Select ⇨ Table command.

ADD A ROW OR A COLUMN TO A TABLE

You don't need to worry about guessing the number of rows correctly because it is easy to add a row. The simplest way to add a row is to press Tab in the last column of the last row in the table. Word adds a new row. You also can add a row in between two existing rows. Choose to place the new row above or below the current row.

Just as you can add rows, you can add columns. Add columns to the left or right of an existing column.

New with this version of Word is the Insert command within the Table menu. It not only enables you to insert columns or rows, but it also enables you to choose where a new row or column is placed.

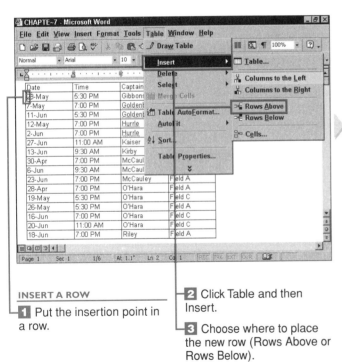

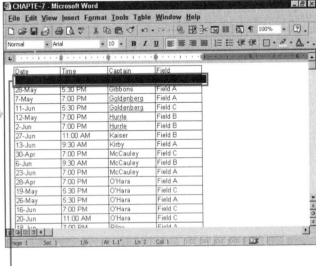

INSERT A ROW

1 Put the insertion point in a row.

2 Click Table and then Insert.

3 Choose where to place the new row (Rows Above or Rows Below).

■ Word inserts the new row.

TIPS

Can I sort rows?

Don't worry about getting the rows in a particular order. You can always sort by row or column, as covered later in this chapter.

How do I draw a new row or column?

Display the Tables and Borders toolbar button. Then choose the line style you want and draw the new row or column within the table.

How do I delete a row or column?

To delete a row or column (or even the entire table), use the Delete command. See the next task.

Can I insert more than one row or column?

Yes. To do so, determine how many rows or columns you want to insert in the table. Then use the Insert command.

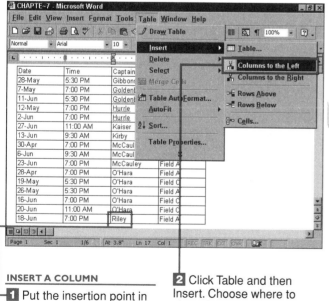

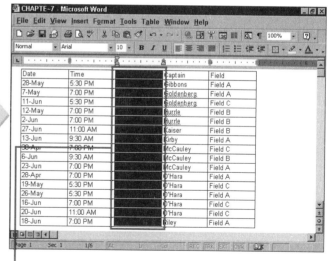

INSERT A COLUMN

1 Put the insertion point in a column.

2 Click Table and then Insert. Choose where to place the new column.

■ Word inserts a new column.

DELETE A ROW OR COLUMN FROM A TABLE

Just as you can add rows and columns, you also can delete them. The difference is that if you delete a row or column that contains data, you also delete the entries.

If you have rows that you no longer want to include, you can

delete them. If there's a column that's empty, or includes text that you don't need anymore, you can delete it.

In addition to covering how to delete rows and columns, this section describes how to delete an entire table. You can't just

select it and press Delete. Doing so deletes the data, but leaves the table framework.

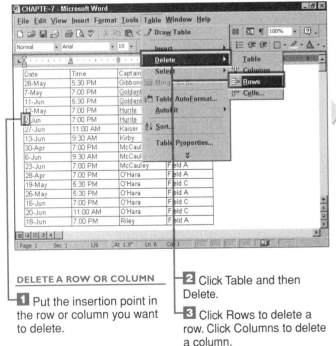

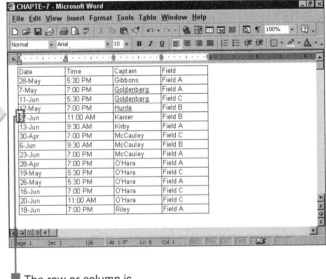

DELETE A ROW OR COLUMN

■1 Put the insertion point in the row or column you want to delete.

■2 Click Table and then Delete.

■3 Click Rows to delete a row. Click Columns to delete a column.

■ The row or column is deleted (here, the row).

TIPS

What's different in this version?

The Delete menu (within the Table menu) is new in this version of Word. Before, you had to select the row or column and then give the command. Now you can simply place the insertion point and then give the command.

How do I undo a deletion?

Use the Undo button or the Edit ➪ Undo command to undo a row, column, or table deletion.

How do I rearrange columns?

To rearrange columns, select the entire column and then cut it with the Edit ➪ Cut command or the Cut button. Click where you want to paste the column and go to Edit ➪ Paste Columns.

How do I delete several rows or columns?

If you have more than one row or column to delete, select the rows or columns to delete. Then use the Delete command.

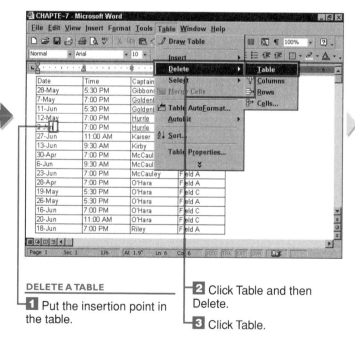

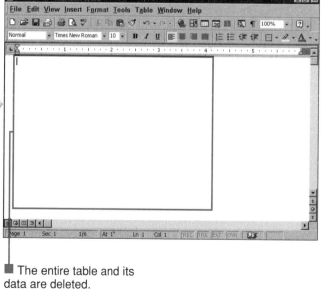

DELETE A TABLE

1 Put the insertion point in the table.

2 Click Table and then Delete.

3 Click Table.

■ The entire table and its data are deleted.

CHANGE THE COLUMN WIDTH

When you create a table using the Insert Table button, Word bases the column width on the size of the page margins and the number of columns you have. Each column is the same size. You can adjust the column width if necessary.

Adjust the column width by dragging the border to the size you want. You can see how wide or narrow to make a column. If you want a column wide enough for the longest entry (or the size of the window), use AutoFit. As another alternative, have Word

make selected rows or columns the same size.

Use the commands in the Table menu. If the Tables and Borders toolbar is displayed, use the buttons there.

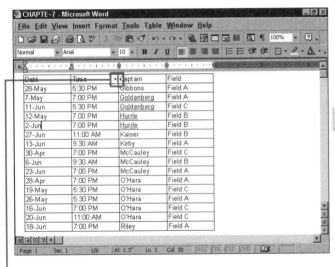

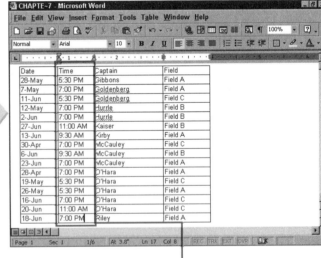

DRAG A COLUMN TO RESIZE

1 Place the mouse pointer on the right border of the column you want to change.

■ The pointer should have two vertical lines with an arrow on either side.

2 Drag the border to resize the column width.

■ The column is resized.

TIPS

What's the command for setting column size?

You can use the Table ➪ AutoFit ➪ Fixed Column Width command to set the column width. This method is not all that useful because you have to enter precise measurements for each column. It's much easier to drag the border.

How do I make a table bigger?

You can make a table bigger by expanding the last column.

I wanted to resize a column, but only one cell changed. What happened?

If you didn't have the pointer in the right spot, you probably dragged a cell border rather than the entire column. Make sure the pointer appears as two vertical lines with an arrow on each side. Undo the change and try again.

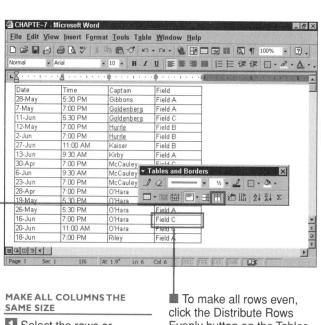

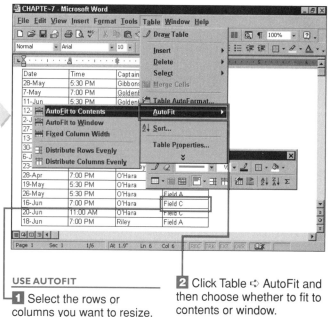

MAKE ALL COLUMNS THE SAME SIZE

1 Select the rows or columns you want to resize.

2 To even out all columns, click Distribute Columns Evenly on the Tables and Borders toolbar.

■ To make all rows even, click the Distribute Rows Evenly button on the Tables and Borders toolbar.

■ All the rows or columns are made the same size (here, the columns).

USE AUTOFIT

1 Select the rows or columns you want to resize.

2 Click Table ➪ AutoFit and then choose whether to fit to contents or window.

USE A TABLE FORMAT

You can take the time to format a table — aligning the headings, adding borders, possibly shading certain rows or columns. Manual formatting is covered in the following sections. Before you take the long route, though, try the short one.

Word provides several predefined table formats called AutoFormats, which include borders, shading, column settings, special formatting for table headings, and more.

You can view — and choose — these AutoFormats. Choose from simple, classic, colorful, and other styles. You can even affect which autoformatting elements are applied.

If the AutoFormats aren't what you want, there are other methods for formatting a table. For example, you can manually format different elements of a table.

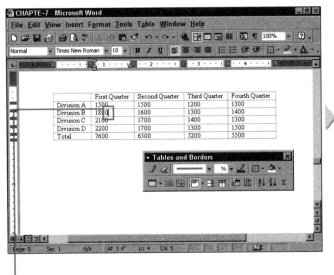

1 Click within the table.

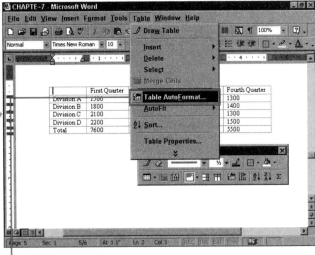

2 Click Table and then Table AutoFormat.

What if I don't want to apply all the formats?

 If you want to use some but not all of the format options, uncheck those in Formats to Apply that you don't want.

What are the special formats?

Often a table includes column headings in the rows, and list items in the first column. You may want to format these items differently. To do so, make sure special formats for the Headings rows and First column are checked. Turn off these items if your table does not include these elements.

I have total rows. How can I specially format them?

 If the last row or column in your table includes a total or other summary information, you can check the Last row or Last column checkboxes to apply special formatting to these elements.

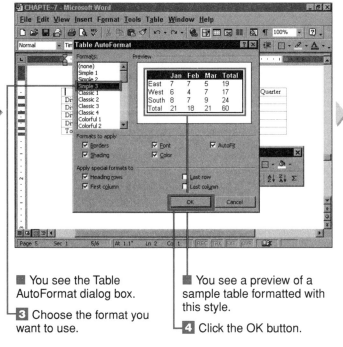

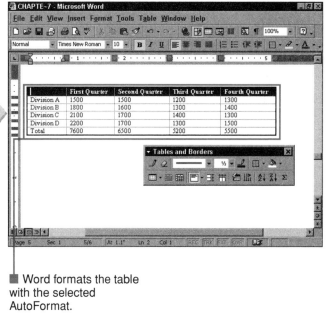

■ You see the Table AutoFormat dialog box.

3 Choose the format you want to use.

■ You see a preview of a sample table formatted with this style.

4 Click the OK button.

■ Word formats the table with the selected AutoFormat.

CHANGE THE TEXT ALIGNMENT

I f one of the AutoFormats doesn't give you exactly what you want, you can format the table yourself. One change you may want to make is how text aligns in a cell.

You can change how text aligns vertically (top to bottom)

and horizontally (left to right). You also can change how text reads in a cell (across, down, and up).

To make these changes, use the buttons on the Tables and Borders toolbar. Change the alignment using the Align

button, which includes combinations for top and bottom, and left-, center-, and right-aligned entries. To change how text flows in a cell, use the Change Text Direction button.

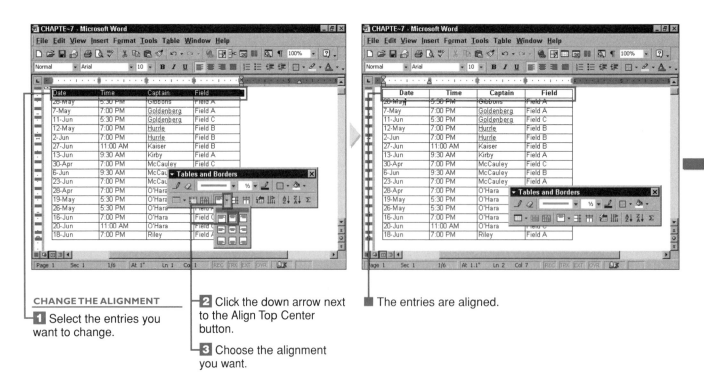

CHANGE THE ALIGNMENT

■1 Select the entries you want to change.

■2 Click the down arrow next to the Align Top Center button.

■3 Choose the alignment you want.

■ The entries are aligned.

What if the Tables and Borders toolbar is not displayed?

Display it by clicking the Tables and Borders button on the Standard toolbar.

What other formatting changes can I make to entries?

As mentioned, use any of the other formatting features. Make text bold, italic, or underlined. Change the font. Use an indent, and so on. To do so, select the text and then use the appropriate button or command to make the change.

How do I undo a change?

If you make a change and don't like it, undo it with the Undo button.

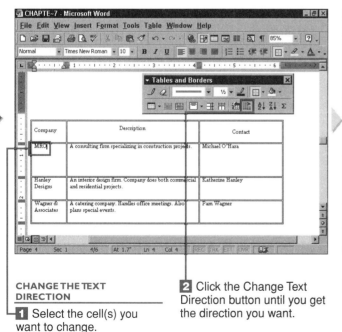

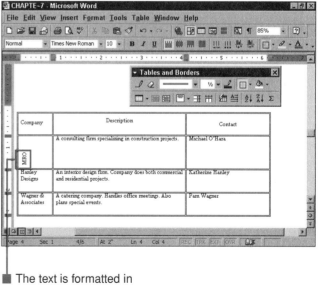

CHANGE THE TEXT DIRECTION

1 Select the cell(s) you want to change.

2 Click the Change Text Direction button until you get the direction you want.

■ The text is formatted in that direction.

CHANGE THE TABLE ALIGNMENT

As another formatting option, you can choose a table alignment. You can center a table, align it with the left margin, or align it with the right margin. You also can determine how text wraps around a table. To make either of these changes, use the Table Properties dialog box.

This dialog box offers margin options for each cell. You can set the top, left, bottom, and right margins, as well as add spacing between cells.

The Table Properties dialog box also includes Row, Column, and Cell tabs. Use these tabs to set a specific row height or column weight. Also choose whether rows or columns break across pages.

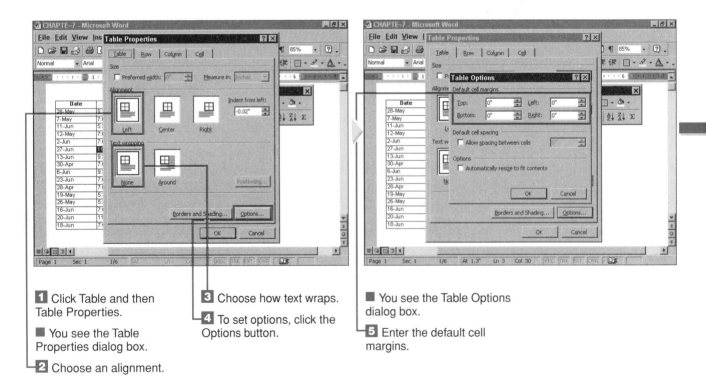

1 Click Table and then Table Properties.

■ You see the Table Properties dialog box.

2 Choose an alignment.

3 Choose how text wraps.

4 To set options, click the Options button.

■ You see the Table Options dialog box.

5 Enter the default cell margins.

TIPS

What is the Borders and Shading button used for?

Click this button to display the Borders and Shading dialog box, which you can use to change the borders of each line in the table.

How do I undo a change?

If you make a change and don't like it, undo it with the Undo button.

What other formatting changes can I make to entries?

As mentioned, use any of the other formatting features. Make text bold, italic, or underlined. Change the font. Use an indent, and so on. To do so, select the text and then use the appropriate button or command to make the change.

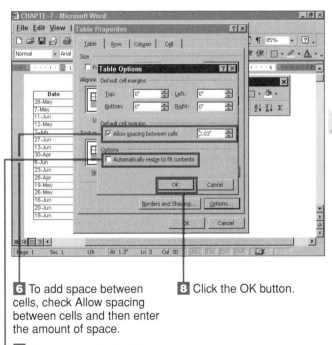

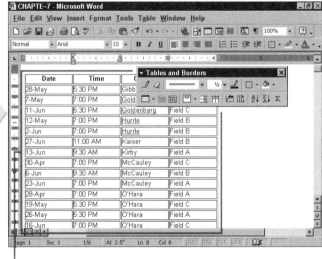

6 To add space between cells, check Allow spacing between cells and then enter the amount of space.

7 Check or uncheck other options.

8 Click the OK button.

■ The table is formatted with the selected options.

CHANGE THE TABLE BORDERS

In addition to changing text directions, you can change table borders. The easiest way is to use the buttons on the Tables and Borders toolbar. From this toolbar, choose a different style, thickness (measured in points), or color for each of the

lines in a table. Choose from several line styles, including double lines and dashed lines.

You also can apply shading to a cell, row, or column. The default shading is None, but you can choose a different color, shade (or gray), or pattern.

Make these changes using the Format ➪ Borders and Shading command. Using this method, make your selections for borders on the Borders tab and selections for shading on the Shadings tab.

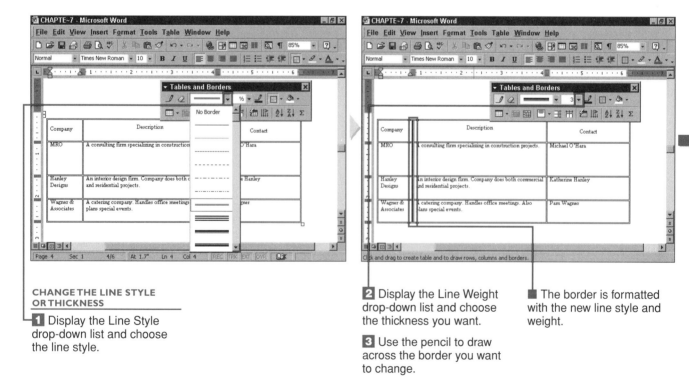

CHANGE THE LINE STYLE OR THICKNESS

1 Display the Line Style drop-down list and choose the line style.

2 Display the Line Weight drop-down list and choose the thickness you want.

3 Use the pencil to draw across the border you want to change.

■ The border is formatted with the new line style and weight.

TIPS

What if the Tables and Borders toolbar is not displayed?

Display it by clicking the Tables and Borders button on the Standard toolbar.

How do I undo a change?

If you make a change and don't like it, undo it with the Undo button.

How do I turn off gridlines?

Even if you don't have any table borders, Word displays gridlines indicating each cell. Turn these off by using the Table ⇨ Hide Gridlines command. Go to Table ⇨ Show Gridlines to turn them back on. Note that gridlines do not appear in a printed document. Table gridlines print only if you add borders to a table.

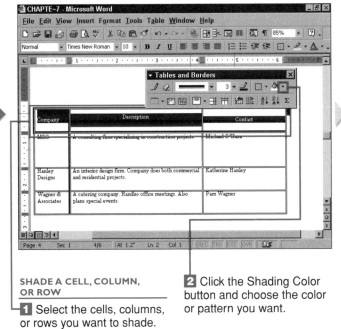

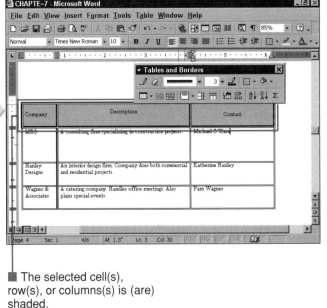

SHADE A CELL, COLUMN, OR ROW

■1 Select the cells, columns, or rows you want to shade.

■2 Click the Shading Color button and choose the color or pattern you want.

■ The selected cell(s), row(s), or columns(s) is (are) shaded.

247

SORT A TABLE

I f you need to keep table entries in a certain order, don't worry about typing them in order. Enter information any way you want and then sort the list.

You can sort by any of the columns in the table, and even sort using more than one column.

You also can choose a sort order (descending or ascending).

If your table has headings, you don't want to sort them. (Word usually recognizes a header row.) Choose whether your list has a header row if you need to make a change.

When you use the Sort command, Word also reviews the selected text and chooses an appropriate type: Text, Date, or Numbers for each of the columns.

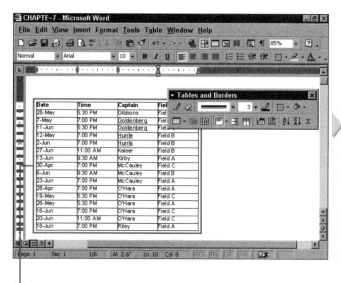

1 Put the insertion point somewhere within the table.

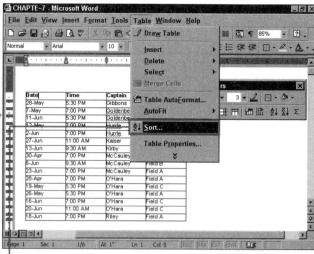

2 Click Table and then Sort.

TIPS

Can I sort only tables?

No. You also can sort regular text. See Chapter 4 for information on sorting text.

What's a shortcut?

If you want to sort one column, use the Sort button on the Tables and Borders toolbar.

How do I sort more than one column?

Display the Then By drop-down list and choose the next column you want to sort. You also can use the next Then By list to choose another sort column.

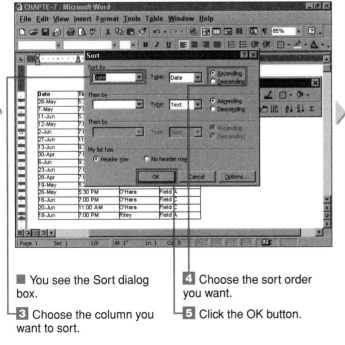

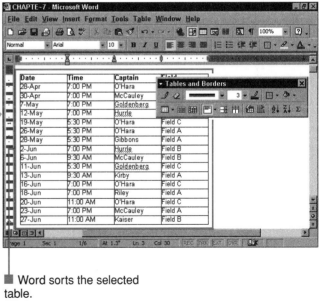

■ You see the Sort dialog box.

3 Choose the column you want to sort.

4 Choose the sort order you want.

5 Click the OK button.

■ Word sorts the selected table.

CALCULATE A TOTAL IN A TABLE

Often a table includes numeric entries, and you may want to calculate a simple total. Do so quickly using the AutoSum button from the Tables and Borders toolbar. This button inserts a sum formula that totals all entries in a particular column.

If you need a more complex formula, build one using the Formula dialog box. You can type an equation and use special features such as a function or number format. To use this feature, you should know how to build formulas. (If you use a spreadsheet program such as Excel, you probably know how to create an equation. If not, consult Word's online help.)

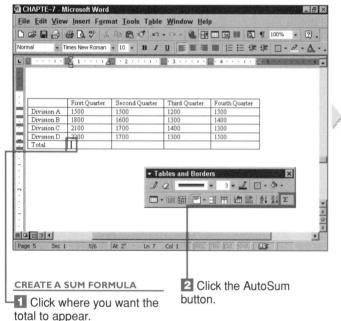

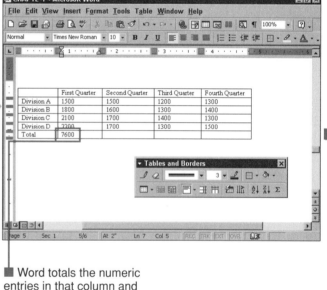

CREATE A SUM FORMULA

1 Click where you want the total to appear.

2 Click the AutoSum button.

■ Word totals the numeric entries in that column and displays the total.

TIPS

How do I recalculate?

If you change an entry included in the formula, you can recalculate. Select the formula (which is really a field). Then press F9. The formula is recalculated.

What if I have many formulas?

If you have many numeric entries to include and you have Excel, consider inserting a worksheet instead of a table. Find information on inserting worksheets in Chapter 15.

What is a number format?

A number format controls how data appears in the table. You can choose currency, percentage, and other formats from the drop-down list.

What is a function?

A function is a prebuilt formula. If you have used Excel, you may be familiar with functions. For instance, use the AVERAGE function to calculate an average.

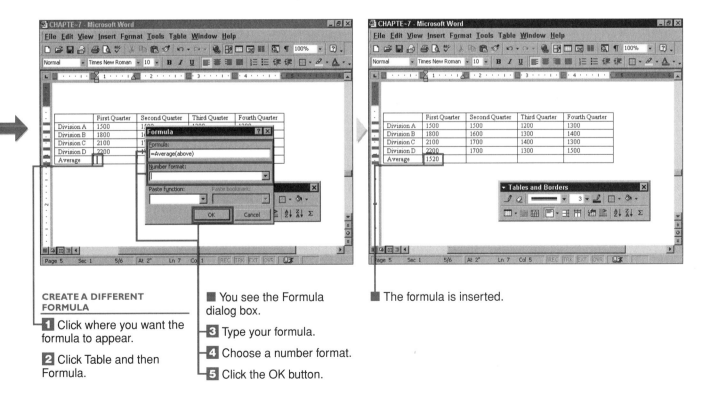

CREATE A DIFFERENT FORMULA

1 Click where you want the formula to appear.

2 Click Table and then Formula.

■ You see the Formula dialog box.

3 Type your formula.

4 Choose a number format.

5 Click the OK button.

■ The formula is inserted.

251

ADD A TABLE HEADING

I n some cases, you may want to merge cells to make one larger cell. For instance, you may include a heading as part of a table and want this heading centered over the entire table. (To

insert a heading in an existing table, insert a blank row.)

You can merge an entire row of cells or just a few cells and then make an entry in the combined cell.

You also can do the reverse, that is, split two cells. For example, to divide an existing cell in two, use the Table ⇨ Split Cells command. You also use this command to undo a merge.

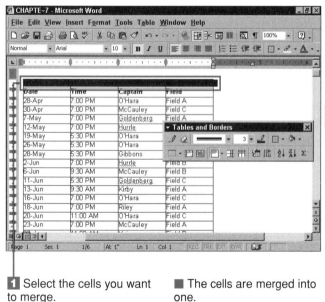

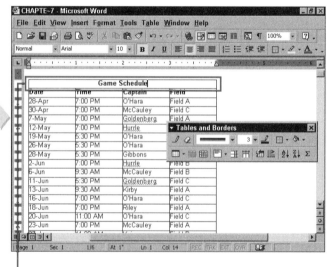

1 Select the cells you want to merge.

2 Click Table and then Merge Cells.

■ The cells are merged into one.

3 Type your heading. Make any formatting changes (such as centering the title).

■ The heading is added to the table.

ADD A TABLE CAPTION

In a long document, you may want to add a caption to your table to identify it. You can do so choosing text, placement, and numbering options for the table.

If you start with the insertion point within a table, Word

should use Table as the caption type. If not, display the Caption drop-down list and choose Table.

As for the position, you can place the caption above or below the selected table.

Word automatically numbers each table and makes changes to

the numbering if you add or delete a table. To make changes to the formatting of the numbering, use the Numbering button in the dialog box.

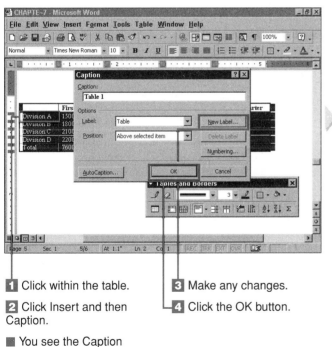

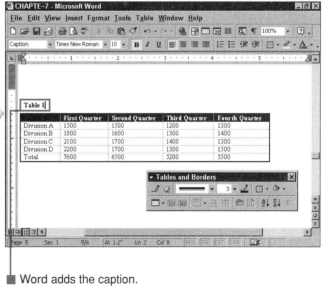

1 Click within the table.

2 Click Insert and then Caption.

■ You see the Caption dialog box.

3 Make any changes.

4 Click the OK button.

■ Word adds the caption.

CONVERT A TABLE

Perhaps you didn't discover tables until after setting up a tabbed list. You typed all the entries, but now want to include them in a table. How do you convert this list to a table? Do you have to retype it? No. As

long as the list is separated by a tab, paragraph, or other delimiter, such as a comma, you can convert it.

For the most part, Word guesses the numbers of columns and rows, as well as the way text

is separated. If the program doesn't choose the right options, you can control how the text is converted.

You also can do the reverse — convert a table to regular text.

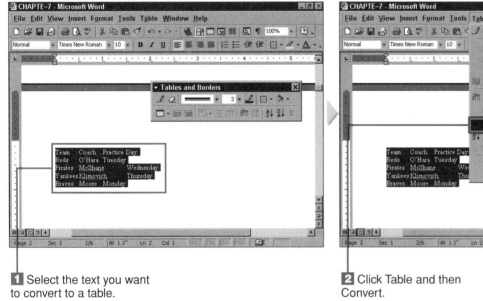

1 Select the text you want to convert to a table.

2 Click Table and then Convert.

3 Choose the Text to Table command.

TIPS

My table entries didn't divide up correctly. How do I fix this problem?

 Make sure that you correctly chose how the text was separated (by paragraphs, tabs, commas, or other characters). Also, make sure you chose the correct number of columns. You also may need to do a little cleanup on the table to get everything just right.

How do I convert a table to text?

 To convert a table to text, select the table. Then choose Convert Table to Text.

What are the AutoFit options?

 You can choose which AutoFit option Word uses for the cells: fit to a set column width, fit to window, or fit to contents.

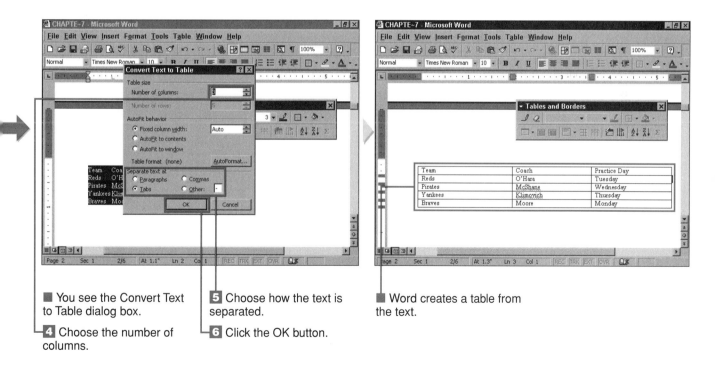

■ You see the Convert Text to Table dialog box.

4 Choose the number of columns.

5 Choose how the text is separated.

6 Click the OK button.

■ Word creates a table from the text.

CREATING COLUMNS AND SECTIONS

Once you master the basics of Word, you can try your hand at creating documents such as newsletters, brochures, manuscripts, and so on. In these types of documents, you may want to experiment with some of the page layout features of Word so you can set up the page just how you want.

Creating Columns

For instance, you may want to divide your document into columns. Create a newsletter and break it into two or more columns. You can use columns for other types of documents as well; they work for documents other than just newsletters.

If your work requires you to send out information, you may want to create a brochure. A brochure is basically a three-column document in landscape layout. You can change the layout, divide the document into columns, print, and then fold the document to create a brochure.

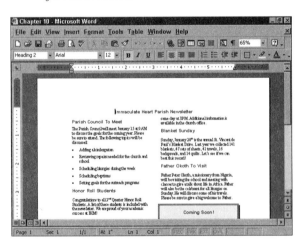

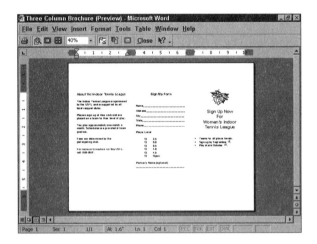

Creating Sections

If you want to vary the page settings from page to page, divide the document into sections. For instance, you might have a title page with bigger margins. In a report, you might want a large table to print in landscape orientation, but have all the other pages to print in portrait orientation. Any time you want to vary the settings, you create a new section.

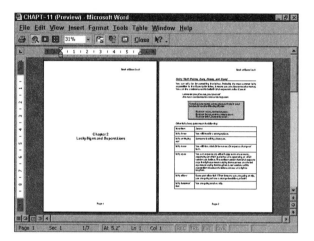

In addition to formatting, you can change how pages are numbered and also create different headers and footers for each section in your document.

Combining Columns and Sections

You can combine sections and columns. For instance, you may want a two-column format for the first page of a newsletter and a three-column format for the second page. To create this layout, you set up columns and sections, as described in this chapter.

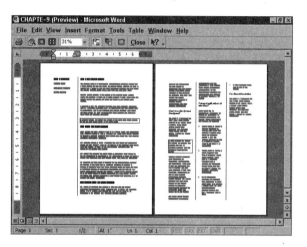

SET UP EVEN COLUMNS

For certain documents, you may want to vary the look of the page by using columns. You can create two, three, four, or more columns of the same size or different sizes. You can set up the columns first and then type the document. Or you can format an existing document into columns.

If you want four or fewer columns of the same size, the fastest method is to use the toolbar. If you want to set up more than four columns, or if you want to set up different sizes from the start, use the menu command. (You can always modify the columns you have set up with the toolbar, such as changing the size, for instance.) To create columns, you must be in Print Layout view. If you forget to switch to this view, Word switches to this view automatically.

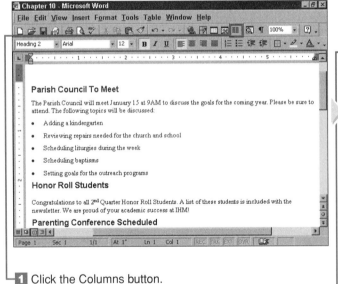

■1 Click the Columns button.

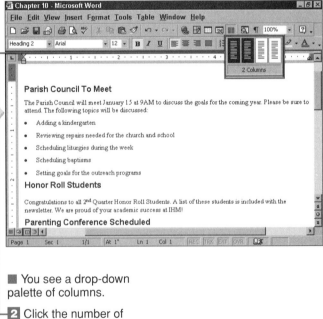

■ You see a drop-down palette of columns.

■2 Click the number of columns you want.

TIPS

Can I format just part of the document into columns?

If you want, you can format just part of a document into columns. For instance, you can have text that spans the entire page, have a section with two columns, and then have another section with three columns. To do so, you divide the documents into sections (covered later in this chapter). Select the text you want to format into columns. Click the Columns button and select the number of columns you want. Just the selected text is formatted into columns. Word also sets up sections and inserts appropriate section breaks.

How do I move around?

The next section, "Setting Up Different-Sized Columns," explains how to add text and move around in the document.

What does the Col indicator mean?

This indicator shows you which column the insertion point is currently within.

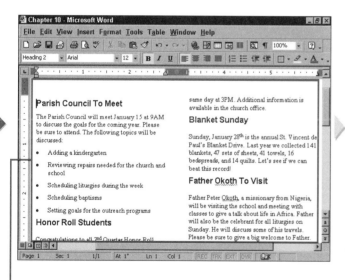

■ If you are formatting a document you have already created, you see the text broken into columns.

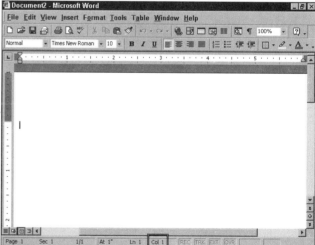

■ If you have not typed text, you may have a hard time telling the document is now formatted into columns. Notice that the Col indicator appears in the status bar, and that, if present, the ruler at the top shows the margins of the two columns.

SET UP DIFFERENT-SIZED COLUMNS

If you want to use more than four columns, or if you want to use columns of unequal widths, use the Columns command to format a document into columns. You can do any of the following:

▸ Select from some preset column formats

▸ Set the size for each column and make them all equal

▸ Set the size for each column, making each one a different size

▸ Select the amount of space between columns

Use this command to set up new columns, or when you want to change the columns you have created with the toolbar.

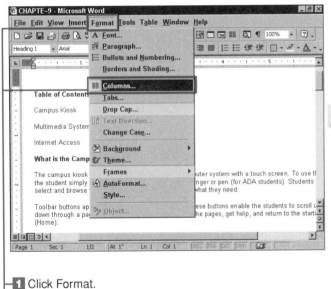

1 Click Format.

2 Click Columns.

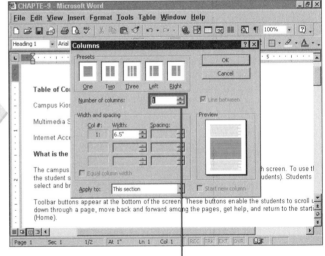

■ You see the Columns dialog box.

3 Enter the number of columns you want in the Number of columns spin box.

I'm not sure what size columns I want.

If you aren't sure how the columns will affect the document, check the preview in the dialog box. It gives you an idea of how the selected options will look when used in your document.

How do I add space between the columns?

To change the spacing between columns, click in the Spacing text box for the column you want to change. Enter a new width or use the spin arrows to select the value you want. Do this for each column you want to change.

Do I have to make all the columns different sizes if I use this method?

No. To use the same width for all columns, check the Equal column width checkbox and then enter the width you want in the Width spin box.

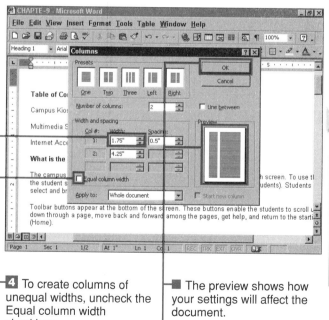

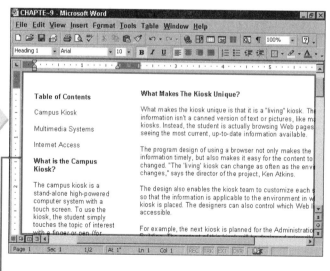

4 To create columns of unequal widths, uncheck the Equal column width checkbox.

5 Click in the Width spin box for each column you want to change and enter a new width.

■ The preview shows how your settings will affect the document.

6 Click the OK button.

■ Word reformats the document.

TYPE IN COLUMNS

If you set up columns in a blank document, you can simply start typing to create the document. Word keeps the text aligned within the columns. If you fill up one column, Word automatically moves you to the next column. Continue typing until you complete the document.

Use any of the editing and formatting features covered in this book. You can copy, move, delete, or add text. You can change the font, apply styles, make text bold, add borders, insert graphics, and so on.

To make an editing change, use the mouse to position the insertion point and then edit as you normally do. You can also use the keyboard to move through the document, but keep in mind that pressing the right arrow key will *not* move you to the next column. You have to go to the end of that column and then up to the top to move through the document. It's faster to use the mouse.

If you want to move to the next column, you may be tempted to press Enter until you jump to the column. But you shouldn't do this because the blank lines will make a mess of the breaks if you add or delete text. Instead, insert a column break when you want to force a column break.

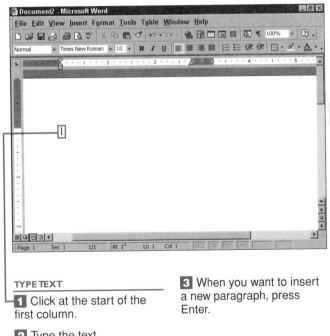

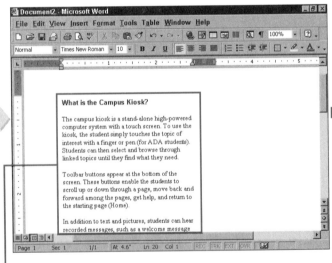

TYPE TEXT

1 Click at the start of the first column.

2 Type the text.

3 When you want to insert a new paragraph, press Enter.

■ The text wraps within the column borders in Print Layout view.

TIPS

What other kinds of breaks are possible?

You can also use the Break dialog box to insert line, page, and section breaks. The later tasks in this chapter cover these section breaks.

Can I format the text?

You can use any of the formatting and editing features on the text. The only difference is how the text wraps within the column. You can still center a line, add bullets, and so on to the paragraphs of text.

I don't see my columns!

In Normal view, the columns are shown in one single column down the page. Normal view works well when you are typing because Word doesn't have to constantly adjust the columns and redisplay the screen (which can be visually disorienting). When you are formatting the document and want to see the columns side-by-side, change to Print Layout view using the View ➪ Print Layout command.

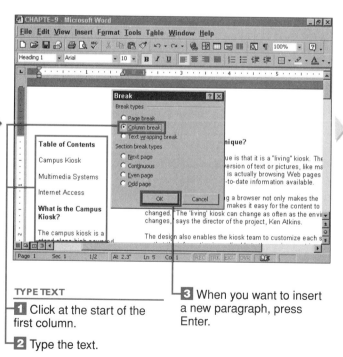

TYPE TEXT

1 Click at the start of the first column.

2 Type the text.

3 When you want to insert a new paragraph, press Enter.

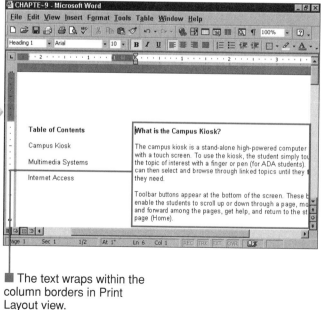

■ The text wraps within the column borders in Print Layout view.

CHANGE THE COLUMN SIZE

When you created the columns, you decided the column size. If you used the Columns button to set them up, all columns are the same size. (The size is determined by the number of columns and the margins.) If you used the Columns command, you entered the size and space you wanted between the columns. You can always make a change.

Make changes using the Columns dialog box. Select the Format ⇨ Columns command and then make any changes. Or use the ruler and visually make a change, as covered here.

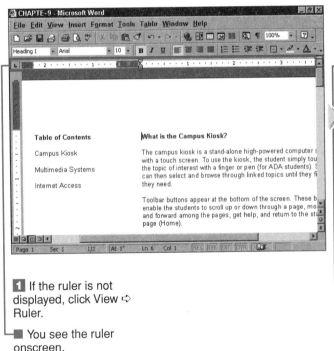

1 If the ruler is not displayed, click View ⇨ Ruler.

■ You see the ruler onscreen.

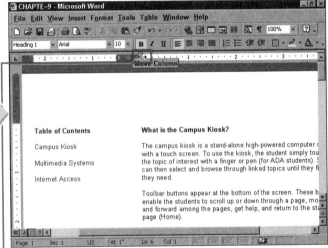

2 To change the width by increasing the space between the columns, put the pointer on the border and drag.

I have a lot of columns. How can I fit more on the page?

If you have a lot of columns, change to Landscape orientation using the File ⇨ Page Setup command. This orientation gives you more room across the width of the page.

How else can I change the column size?

You can also change the column size by using the Format ⇨ Columns command. Make any adjustments to the size and space between each column and then click OK.

What's another way to fit more on the page?

Keep in mind that there's only so much room on the page. When you increase the size of one column, you leave less room for other columns. To get more room, you can make the left and right page margins smaller. You can also decrease the amount of space between the columns.

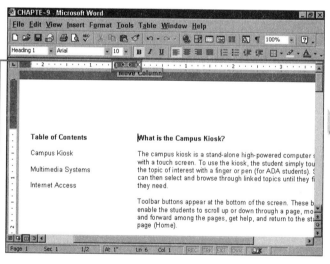

3 To change the width but keep the space between the columns the same, put the pointer on the gray area indicating the space between columns and drag.

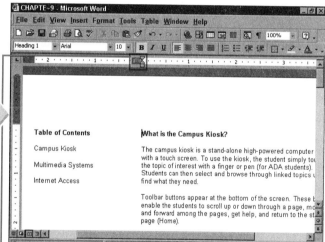

■ The columns are resized.

FORMAT COLUMNS

You can use any text and formatting paragraph options within the columns. For instance, you can create numbered lists, bulleted lists, indents, and so on. You can make the text bigger, use styles, and so on. Simply select the text and make the change.

One special change you may want to make is to add a border between each column. You can do so using the Format Columns dialog box.

As another special formatting idea, you may want to include a one-column banner or heading that spans all the columns. You can do this by formatting that heading as one-column text.

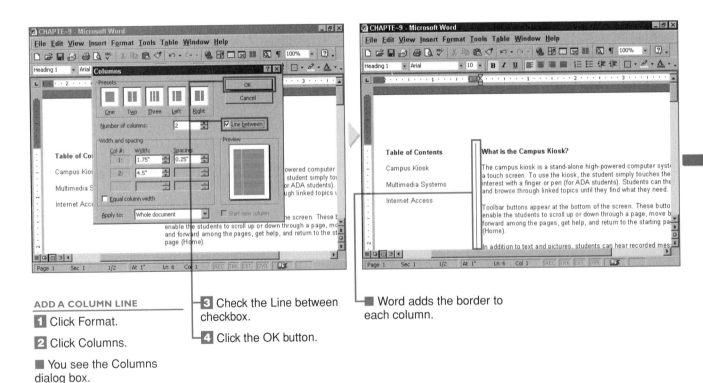

ADD A COLUMN LINE

1 Click Format.

2 Click Columns.

■ You see the Columns dialog box.

3 Check the Line between checkbox.

4 Click the OK button.

■ Word adds the border to each column.

TIPS

What happens to the document when I format the heading across all columns?

Technically, you set up two sections — one for the heading in a one-column format, and one for the rest of the document, which is two columns. You learn more about sections in the next part of this chapter.

How else can I add a line?

You can also add a line by drawing one, as covered in Chapter 14. You can also add lines to the paragraphs (Chapter 8) or to the page (Chapter 9).

The column heading isn't centered over the columns. Why?

Remember that all text is left-aligned. If you type a new title and then use it for a one-column banner, that text will still be left-aligned. You can select that line and center it using the Center button in the toolbar. (The example banner is centered.)

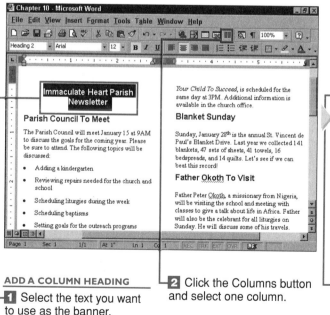

ADD A COLUMN HEADING

■1 Select the text you want to use as the banner.

■2 Click the Columns button and select one column.

■ The text is formatted as one column and goes across all the columns.

DIVIDE YOUR DOCUMENT INTO SECTIONS

As you get more and more skilled, you may create more complex documents. In doing so, you may need to vary the page formats for the document.

For instance, you may want to have a title page that is one column (that is, spans the entire page). You may want to format the rest of the document using two columns.

As another example, you may create a newsletter with a banner that spans the entire page and have the rest of the page in two columns. The second page is broken into three columns.

If you have a really long document (such as a book manuscript), you may have broken that document into sections. You may want to use different headers and footers for each section, or separate page numbering for each section.

For reports, you may want to include the title page and most report pages in portrait orientation. For some pages—those including wide tables—you may want to use landscape orientation.

For the first page of a document, you might want to center the page. For the remaining pages, you may want to use smaller margins.

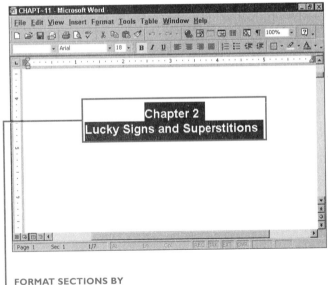

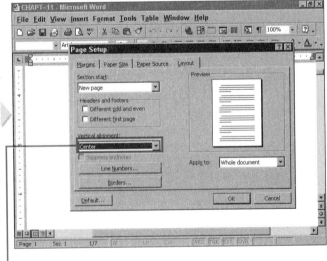

FORMAT SECTIONS BY SELECTING THE TEXT

1 Select the text you want to format with the special settings.

2 Make the change in the Page Setup dialog box.

TIPS

What if I don't set up sections?

If you don't insert sections in a document, then you basically have a one-section document.

How do I delete a section break?

To delete a section break, place the insertion point immediately after the break and press Backspace, or place the insertion point immediately before the break and press Delete.

Something wacky happened to my sections. How can I fix it?

Just as paragraph formatting is stored in the paragraph marker, section formatting (margins, columns, and so on) is stored with the section break. If you delete the section break, the section takes on the formatting of the following section. Undo the deletion if this happens.

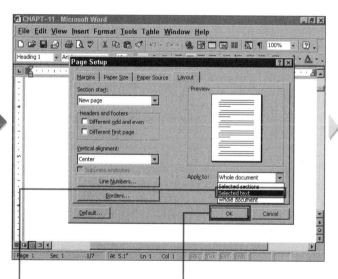

3 Display the Apply to drop-down list and select Selected text.

4 Click the OK button.

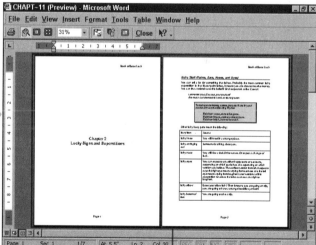

■ The document is divided into sections, and the selected text is formatted with the appropriate page settings.

■ You can preview the pages side by side to see the difference (here the first page is centered and the following pages have normal margins).

CONTINUED ▶

DIVIDE YOUR DOCUMENT INTO SECTIONS CONTINUED

These examples give you some idea of when you might want to vary formatting from page to page. When you want to do so, set up a section for each part of the document with different formatting. A section may be just part of the page, a whole page, or several pages.

You can set up sections using one of two methods. Create sections automatically by selecting the text you want to format. For instance, select the text to which you want to apply different margins. Then use the command to make the formatting change. Word applies the formatting to just that section

and creates the appropriate sections. You don't have to fuss with setting the breaks manually.

As the other method, you can manually insert section breaks to break up the document. You can then move to each section and format them as you want.

FORMAT SECTIONS BY INSERTING SECTION BREAKS

1 Place the insertion point where you want to start the new section.

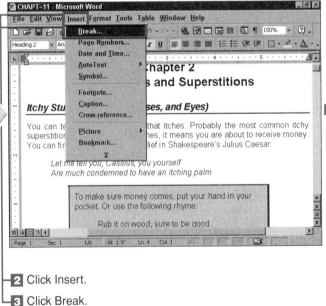

2 Click Insert.

3 Click Break.

TIPS

How do I start a new page?

To have the new section start on a new page, select Next page.

What if I don't want to start a new page?

To keep the section on the same page, select Continuous.

Can I select an odd or even page break?

Yes. To have the section start on the next odd-numbered page, select Odd page. To have the section start on the next even-numbered page, select Even page.

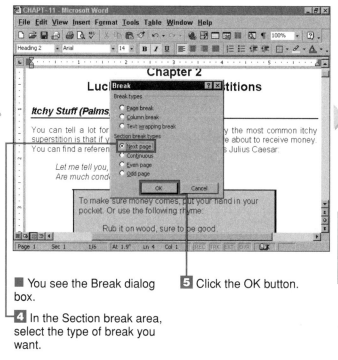

■ You see the Break dialog box.

■4 In the Section break area, select the type of break you want.

■5 Click the OK button.

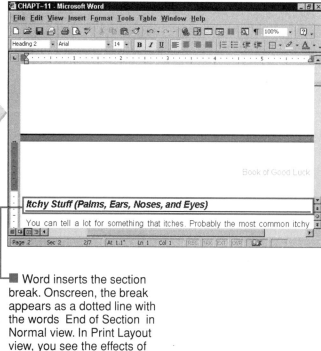

■ Word inserts the section break. Onscreen, the break appears as a dotted line with the words End of Section in Normal view. In Print Layout view, you see the effects of the break.

FORMAT SECTIONS

Once you have created the section breaks, you can format each section the way you want. Most of the Page Setup options (margins, orientation, vertical alignment) can apply to the entire document or just a section. You can vary these options for each section.

As another example, you can set up a different number of columns for sections. (Columns are covered in the first half of this chapter.)

If necessary, create different headers and footers for each section. You can also use different page numbering for

sections. For instance, you may want to start numbering each section with the number 1.

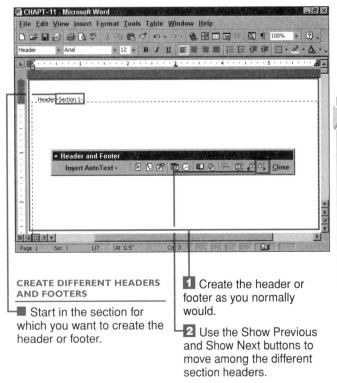

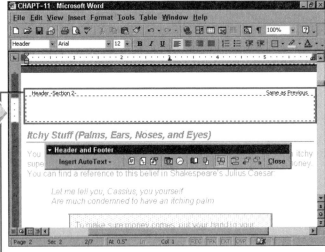

CREATE DIFFERENT HEADERS AND FOOTERS

■ Start in the section for which you want to create the header or footer.

1 Create the header or footer as you normally would.

2 Use the Show Previous and Show Next buttons to move among the different section headers.

3 Create the header or footer for that section.

TIPS

Where can I find more information on headers and footers?

 For more information on creating headers and footers, see Chapter 9 on formatting pages.

Where can I find more information on formatting page numbers?

 Chapter 9 also covers inserting page numbers into a document. Turn to this chapter if you need help with inserting and formatting page numbers.

What if I inserted the page number when I created a header or footer?

 If you inserted the page number while creating a header or footer and you want to change the formatting, you can display the Page Number Format dialog box. To do so, click the Page Number Format button on the Header and Footer toolbar.

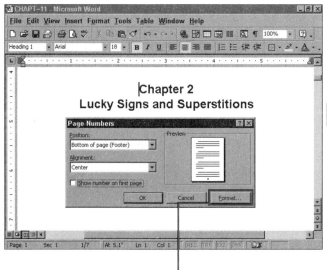

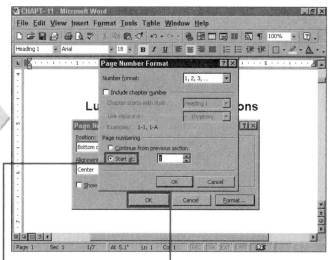

CHANGE PAGE NUMBERS FOR SECTIONS

1 Insert the page number.

2 In the Page Numbers dialog box, click the Format button.

3 In the Page Number Format dialog box, click the Start at option button and then enter the number with which you want to start.

4 Click OK twice.

CREATING SPECIAL TEXT EFFECTS

So far you have learned all different kinds of ways to make your text, paragraphs, and pages look nice. For common changes and simple documents, you may find these tools are all you need. But if you need to create flashier documents with some special effects, you may want to start with some of the available text effects.

Start a Chapter with a Drop Cap

For a simple change to a manuscript, consider adding a drop cap to the first character in the chapter. You can select the font style, size, and placement of the drop cap. Not only does this feature add flair to a page, but it also helps the reader note when each new chapter starts.

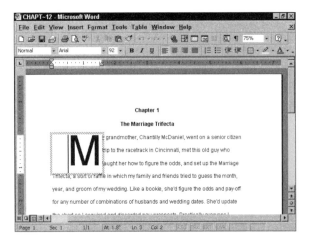

Place Text Anywhere on the Page

If you want a good deal of control over the placement of a text element, use a text box. You can draw this element anywhere on a page and add as much or as little text as you want. You can also format the text and the box itself; for example, you can change the border or add shading.

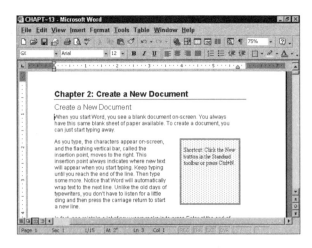

Add WordArt Text

When you want some really jazzy text, consider using WordArt, a special type of text in various sizes, colors, shapes, shades, shadows, slants, and so on. You can choose from an entire gallery of styles. And you can make changes to the font, size, color, border, and more.

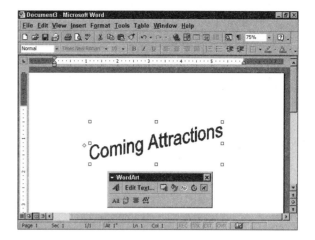

CREATE A DROP CAP

When you want to add some visual pizzazz to your document, you have several choices. For instance, you might consider using a drop cap. A drop cap is commonly used for the first character in a chapter opener.

Think of all those old medieval manuscripts with the fancy illustrations. You can include a little of this flair in your document with a drop cap.

When you create a drop cap, you can select the position, font, lines to drop, and distance from the text. The Drop Cap dialog box gives you a good idea of what each option looks like.

Basically, a drop cap is a frame with one character inside. If you want to edit the character, click in the frame and make a change.

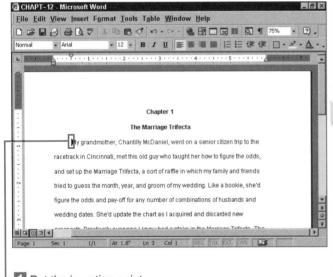

1 Put the insertion point before the character you want to use as the drop cap.

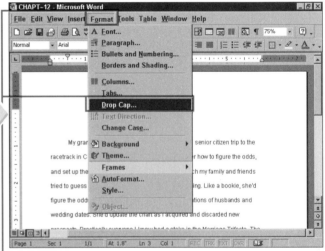

2 Click Format.

3 Click Drop Cap.

TIPS

How do I change the font of a drop cap?

If you want to use a different font for a drop cap, display the Font drop-down list in the Drop Cap dialog box and select the font you want to use.

What does "Lines to drop" mean?

The Lines to drop box indicates the size of the drop cap. You can drop fewer lines to make the drop cap smaller. Increase the number of lines to make the drop cap larger.

I want more space between a drop cap and text.

If you want more space between a drop cap and text, increase the value in the Distance from text box.

How do I remove a drop cap?

Click the letter to display the frame. Next, click the frame around the letter and press Delete. You then need to manually retype the letter in the document.

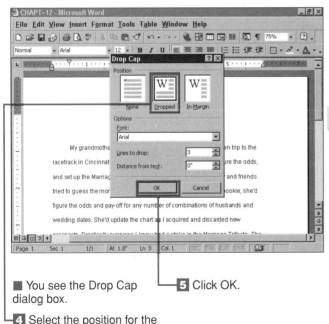

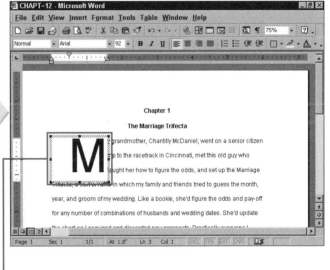

■ You see the Drop Cap dialog box.

5 Click OK.

4 Select the position for the drop cap.

■ The drop cap is added.

INSERT A TEXT BOX

Sometimes it is difficult to position text just where you want. You try indents, margins, borders, font changes, and so on, but the text just won't go where you want it. If this is the case, consider adding a text box.

You can draw a text box anywhere on a page, and then move and resize it as necessary.

This capability gives you a great deal of control over the placement of text in a document. You can use a text box to create special sections of text such as margin notes or other elements that would otherwise be hard to place.

You can include as much or as little text as you want in a text box. This task covers how to

create a text box. You'll learn other ways to edit and change the appearance of the text box in later tasks.

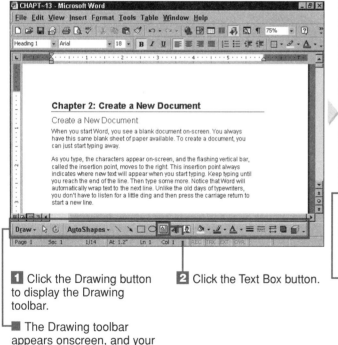

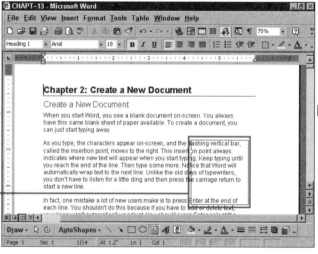

1 Click the Drawing button to display the Drawing toolbar.

■ The Drawing toolbar appears onscreen, and your document is switched to Print Layout view (if it isn t already in this view).

2 Click the Text Box button.

3 Click within the document area and drag to draw the text box.

TIPS

How do I edit text?

To edit the text in a text box, click within the text box and then use the movement keys to place the insertion point. Make your change and click back in the document text.

Can I format text in a text box?

Yes. You can make any changes to the appearance of the text in a text box. You can make text bold, change the font, and so on.

I can't see my document text!

The text box may be placed on top of the text. Don't worry. You can change how document text wraps around a text box. See the task titled "Format a Text Box" later in this section.

How do I get rid of a text box?

To delete a text box, click the box itself. You should see selection handles around the edges. Press Delete.

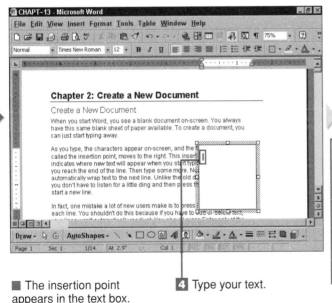

■ The insertion point appears in the text box.

4 Type your text.

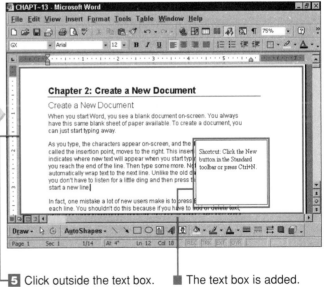

5 Click outside the text box.

■ The text box is added.

FORMAT A TEXT BOX

When you draw a text box, it is placed as a layer over your document. To make the document text flow around the text box, use the Layout tab of the Format Text Box dialog box.

You may also want to change the border used for the text box. You may want to use a different border style or color, or no border at all. As another option, you may want to shade the text box. Make these changes on the

Colors and Lines tab in the Format Text Box dialog box.

You may also want to set margins for the interior of the text box, which you can do using the Text Box tab.

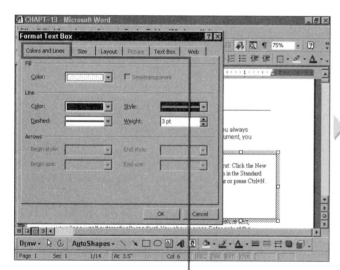

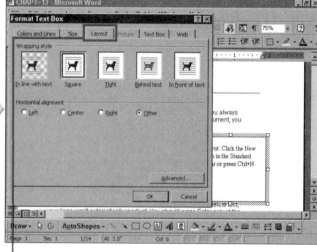

1 Double-click the text box itself.

■ You see the Format Text Box dialog box.

2 On the Colors and Lines tab, make any changes to the appearance of the borders.

3 Click the Layout tab and select how text wraps around the text box.

TIPS

When I double-clicked the text box, the dialog box did not appear. Why not?

Be sure to double-click the text box itself, not inside the text box. Try again.

Why would I use the Size tab?

You can select a specific size for the text box on the Size tab. However, it's easier to drag the selection handles of the text box to change the size. See the task titled "Move and Resize a Text Box" later in this chapter.

What types of lines can I select?

You can select not only the color, but also the style and weight of the line used for the border. Use the Dashed drop-down box to select a dash style.

What options are available on the Web tab?

If the document you are creating is a Web page, you may want to insert alternative text in the text box. For more information on Web publishing, see Chapter 23.

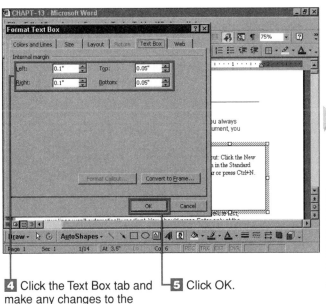

4 Click the Text Box tab and make any changes to the margins of the text inside the text box.

5 Click OK.

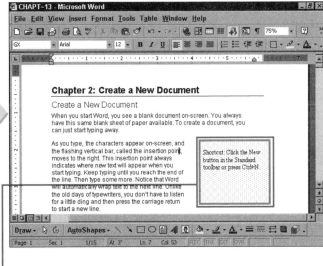

■ The text box is formatted with the selected options.

MOVE OR RESIZE A TEXT BOX

As mentioned previously, one of the greatest benefits of using a text box is how easy it is to move the text box around in a document. You can simply drag and drop it where you want.

You can also change the size of a text box. If you have too little

text in the box, you may want to make the text box smaller. If not all the text fits, you can make the text box larger. You can also change the dimensions of the text box.

The easiest way to make a change is to drag in order to move and resize. You can also

change the size using the Format Text Box dialog box.

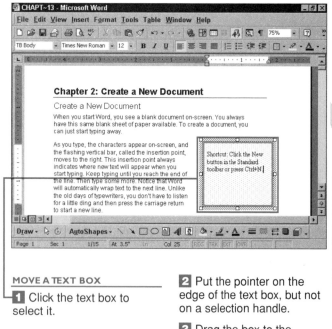

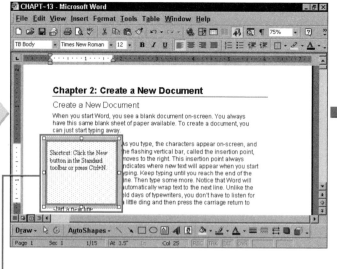

MOVE A TEXT BOX

1 Click the text box to select it.

2 Put the pointer on the edge of the text box, but not on a selection handle.

3 Drag the box to the location you want.

■ The box is moved.

I can't get the box to move!

Be sure that you have selected the text box and then put the mouse pointer on the border. The pointer should look like a four-headed arrow.

How else can I resize a text box?

If you want to select a particular height and width for a text box, you can use the Format Text Box dialog box. Double-click the text box and then click the Size tab. Enter the dimensions for the text box and then click the OK button.

What are the selection handles?

The selection handles are small white squares that appear around the edges of a text box when it is selected. You can drag any of these handles to resize the text box. Drag the bottom and top selection handles to change the height of the box. Drag the left and right selection handles to change the width of the box. You can also drag any of the corner handles to change both the height and width at the same time.

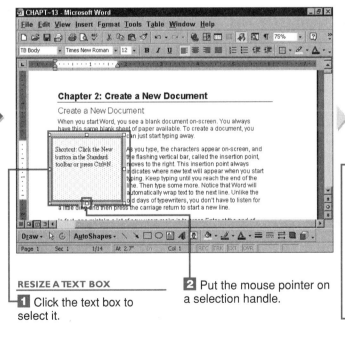

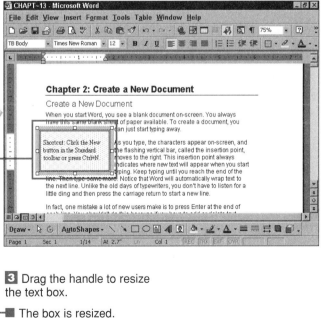

RESIZE A TEXT BOX

1 Click the text box to select it.

2 Put the mouse pointer on a selection handle.

3 Drag the handle to resize the text box.

■ The box is resized.

283

CHANGE TEXT DIRECTION IN A TEXT BOX

By default, all text reads left to right in a text box. That is probably the most common alignment and works for boxes with text that contains more than a few words.

For a special effect — for short words or phrases, for instance —

you may want to rotate the text. This type of text is more of a design element than part of the document to be read. For example, you can position the banner of a newsletter or other document down the side of the page.

In any case, the best way to add this special effect is to draw a text box and then change the rotation of its text.

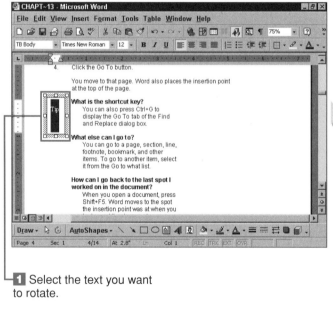

1 Select the text you want to rotate.

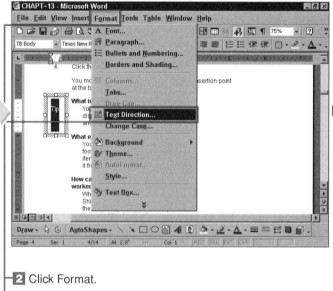

2 Click Format.

3 Click Text Direction.

What other changes can I make?

When you rotate the text, you may need to resize and move the text box. You may also want to change the text wrapping option. As a final idea, change the border, or add a fill to make the text stand out.

Can I change the direction of text in a document?

No. You can change the direction of text in text boxes and in table cells, but not in a regular document.

How do I undo the change?

You can use the Edit ⇨ Undo command or the Undo button. Or, select the text box and follow the same steps you used to change the direction to return the text to its original state.

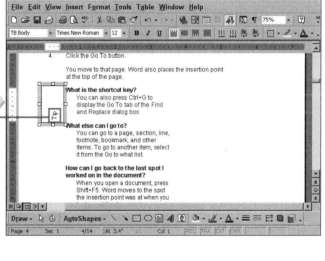

■ You see the Text Direction dialog box.

4 Select the orientation you want.

5 Click OK.

■ The text is rotated.

INSERT WORDART

When you want to get really fancy with text, insert a WordArt object. This object is really graphical text. You can select from several formats, colors, alignments, and more.

The benefit of the WordArt object, besides being an attractive addition without a lot of effort, is that you can move and resize the object and place it anywhere on the page, just like a text box.

The downside of WordArt is that it can take a long time to print. Don't clog up a document with a lot of WordArt text unless you have a fast printer. Instead, use it only for special emphasis.

This task explains how to add WordArt text to a document. See the later tasks in this chapter for help on editing and formatting a WordArt object.

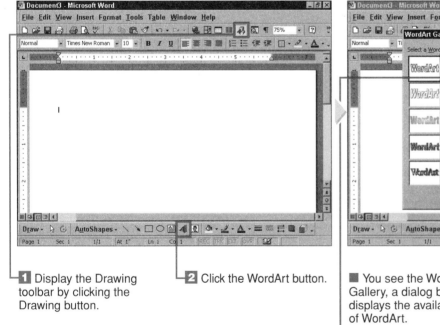

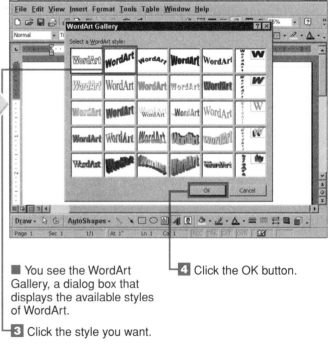

1 Display the Drawing toolbar by clicking the Drawing button.

2 Click the WordArt button.

■ You see the WordArt Gallery, a dialog box that displays the available styles of WordArt.

3 Click the style you want.

4 Click the OK button.

TIPS

What else can I draw with the Drawing toolbar?

You can draw other shapes using the Drawing toolbar. For more information on drawing in a document, see the next chapter.

What other method can I use to insert a WordArt object?

You can also insert a WordArt object using the Insert ⇨ Picture ⇨ WordArt command.

How do I delete a WordArt object?

A WordArt object is like any other object you draw in a document. To remove it from the document, click the object once to select it and then press the Delete key.

How do I move a WordArt object?

To move a WordArt object, click it once to select it. Then, put the pointer on a border (not a selection handle). Drag the object to the location you want.

 ■ You see the Edit WordArt Text dialog box.

 6 Click the OK button.

5 Type your text.

■ The text is added to your document.

EDIT WORDART TEXT

Because the WordArt text is special text, you cannot edit it by clicking and then typing. Instead, you have to use the dialog box for editing the text. You can easily access this dialog box from the WordArt toolbar or by double-clicking the WordArt text.

In either case, you see the Edit WordArt Text dialog box. Using the dialog box, you can change existing text, delete text, add more text, replace text, and so on. In addition to changing the text, you can select the font and size of the text, and style the text bold or italic.

You can also make changes to the text's appearance (rotation, color, and so on). For help on making these changes, see the other tasks in this chapter.

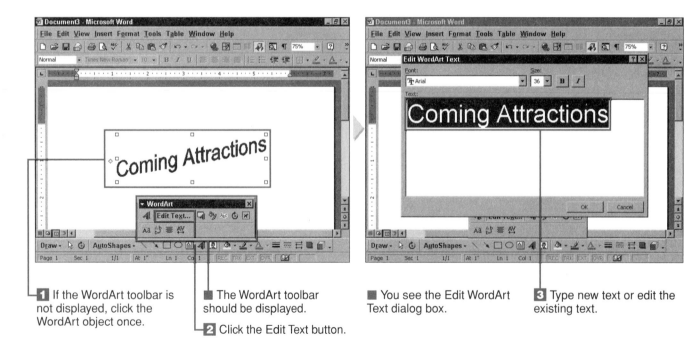

■ ■ If the WordArt toolbar is not displayed, click the WordArt object once.

■ The WordArt toolbar should be displayed.

■ Click the Edit Text button.

■ You see the Edit WordArt Text dialog box.

■ Type new text or edit the existing text.

Can I use the Formatting toolbar to change the font?

No. When you select a WordArt object, the Font, Font Size, and Style buttons are dimmed on the toolbar. You cannot use these buttons to change the font. You must use the Edit WordArt Text dialog box.

Is there a shortcut?

You can double-click the WordArt object to display the Edit WordArt Text dialog box.

What are the other buttons in the WordArt toolbar used for?

You can use the other buttons to change the style of the object, format the object, change the shape of the object, rotate the text in the object, set text wrapping options, and more. To see the name of a button, put the pointer on the button's edge. The rest of this chapter covers making changes with some of the other buttons.

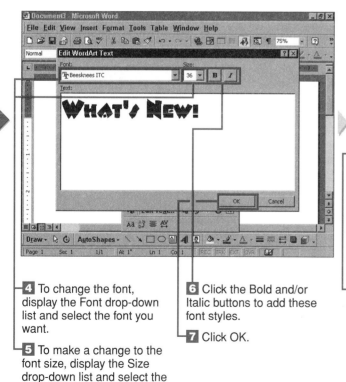

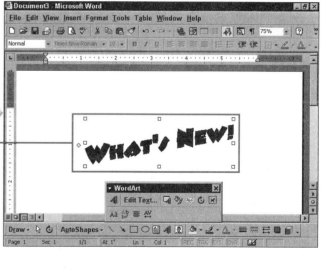

 4 To change the font, display the Font drop-down list and select the font you want.

5 To make a change to the font size, display the Size drop-down list and select the size you want.

 6 Click the Bold and/or Italic buttons to add these font styles.

7 Click OK.

■ The edited text is inserted in the document.

CHANGE THE STYLE OR SHAPE OF WORDART TEXT

When you first create a WordArt object, you see the WordArt Gallery, where you select the style you want. If you change your mind, display the Gallery to select another style. Select from several shapes, colors, sizes, directions, fills, shadows, 3-D effects, and more.

The WordArt Gallery shows a preview of each of the different styles so that you can get an idea of what the text looks like.

You can also change the shape of the text. There's no easy way to describe the many different shapes, but you make an educated guess from the toolbar palette. For instance, if the

button shows an arch, the text appears arched. If the button shows a circle, the text is in a circle.

If you can't figure out the shape, simply experiment until you find a shape that you like.

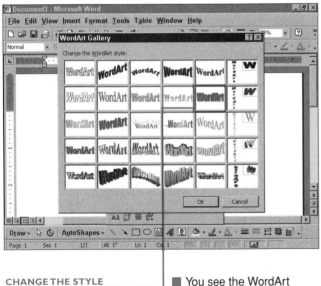

CHANGE THE STYLE

1 Click the WordArt object you want to change.

2 Click the WordArt Gallery button in the WordArt toolbar.

■ You see the WordArt Gallery dialog box.

3 Select the style you want.

4 Click OK.

■ The WordArt object is updated to the new style.

How do I undo a change?

You can use the Edit ⇨ Undo command or the Undo button. Or, you can follow the same steps you used to select a different style or shape to return the object to its original state.

What other special character changes can I make?

You can use the other buttons on the toolbar to fine-tune the character spacing (WordArt Character Spacing) and letter height (WordArt Same Letter Heights).

I want text to go down the page. How do I make this change?

You can select a shape that goes the direction you want. Or, use the WordArt Vertical Text button in the WordArt toolbar to change the text from horizontal to vertical.

Can I rotate text?

If you want to rotate text, click the Free Rotate button and then drag the rotation handles to rotate the text to the degree you want.

CHANGE THE SHAPE

1 Click the WordArt object you want to change.

2 Click the WordArt Shape button in the WordArt toolbar.

3 Click the shape you want.

■ The WordArt object is updated to the new shape.

291

CHANGE THE COLORS OF WORDART TEXT

S ome styles include a color as part of the WordArt object. Does that mean you are limited to just that selection? No. You can change the color, add a pattern, and even apply a texture or gradient to the color. You can do this for WordArt that is black or any color.

You can also select the color, weight, and style of the line used to draw the characters (the character border).

To make these changes, use the Format WordArt button in the WordArt toolbar. The Format WordArt dialog box includes tabs for making several changes.

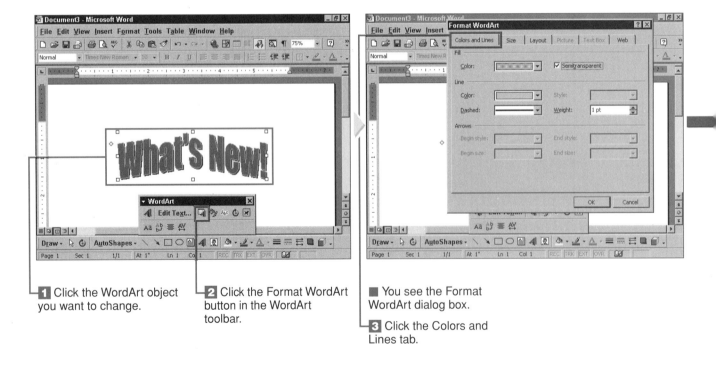

1 Click the WordArt object you want to change.

2 Click the Format WordArt button in the WordArt toolbar.

■ You see the Format WordArt dialog box.

3 Click the Colors and Lines tab.

I changed the color, but it didn't turn out as I intended. What happened?

Sometimes the color of an object is the combination of the line color and fill color. To get the effect you want, you may need to change the line color. To do so, display the Color drop-down list and select the color you want.

My colors don't print! Why not?

Colors print only if you have a color printer. If you have a black-and-white printer, the colors print in shades of gray.

How do I add a texture or pattern?

To add a texture, pattern, or gradient, select the Fill Effects command from the Color drop-down list. Then select the appropriate tab. Select the type of fill you want and click OK.

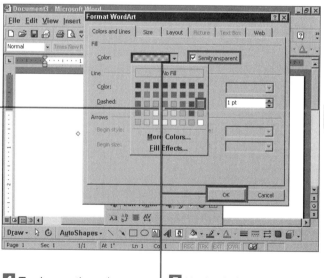

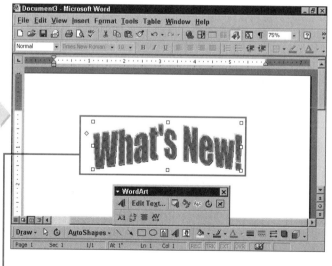

■4 To change the color, display the Color drop-down list and select the color you want.

■5 Uncheck the Semitransparent checkbox to use a solid color.

■6 Click OK.

■ The new color is used.

SIZE AND PLACE WORDART TEXT

When you create a new WordArt object, the object is a particular size depending on the font size you selected. You aren't stuck with this size, though. To resize the object, you can change the font size (covered earlier) or you can drag the selection handles.

As for placement, you can simply drag the object to the spot you want. You can also control how text wraps around a new WordArt object placed on top of the text. If you want text to wrap around the object, you need to make a change.

The easiest way to make a change is to use the WordArt toolbar, but keep in mind that you can also make changes using the Format WordArt dialog box.

(To display this dialog box, click the Format WordArt button.)

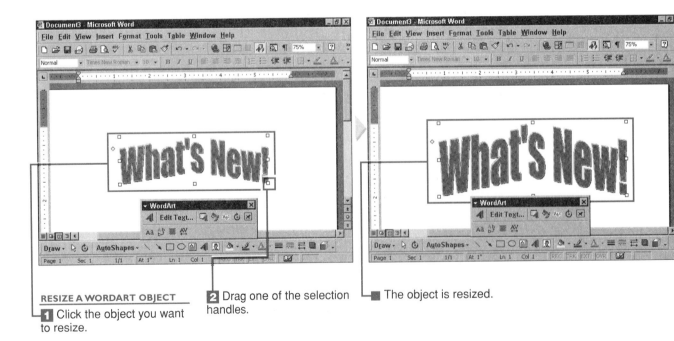

RESIZE A WORDART OBJECT
1 Click the object you want to resize.

2 Drag one of the selection handles.

■ The object is resized.

TIPS

How do I change the font size?

To change the font size, double-click the WordArt object. Then select the size you want from the Size drop-down list. Click OK.

How do I enter a precise measurement for a WordArt object?

If you want to use a precise measurement for an object, display the Format WordArt dialog box and click the Size tab. Enter the height, weight, and rotation (if any), and then click OK.

What are the different text wrapping options?

You can have the object appear behind, in front of, or through the text; the text runs right through the WordArt object for these wrap styles.

You can also wrap the text in a square around the object, tight to the object shape, or above and below the object.

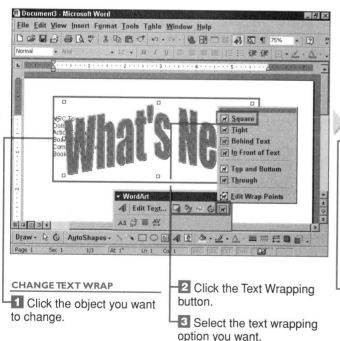

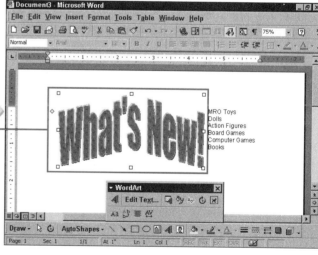

CHANGE TEXT WRAP

■1 Click the object you want to change.

■2 Click the Text Wrapping button.

■3 Select the text wrapping option you want.

■ The text wraps around the object as you selected.

DRAWING IN YOUR DOCUMENT

In the previous chapter you learned how to create special effects with text. Another way to enliven a document is to insert your own drawings. Use a simple illustration to explain something, or create a shape to use as a special design feature. This chapter covers using the Drawing tools in your document.

Note that you also can insert pictures in your document. That's the topic of the next chapter.

Let Word Draw the Shape

If you aren't much of an artist, don't worry. You can choose from several of Word's predrawn shapes, called AutoShapes. Choose different lines, basic shapes, arrows, flowchart symbols, stars, banners, call-outs, and more. Decide on the shape you want and simply click and drag to draw.

Draw the Shape Yourself

If you can't find an AutoShape that works, draw what you want using the Drawing tools. The Drawing toolbar includes buttons for drawing lines, rectangles and squares, ovals and circles, and arrows. Choose the color and special effects for these shapes. You can even combine them to create simple illustrations.

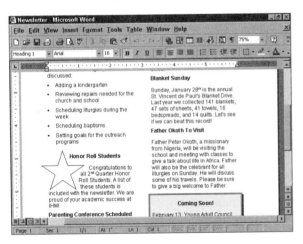

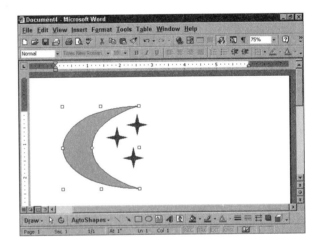

Change the Shape

Once a shape is added to a document, you can make changes. Here are some ways to edit a shape:

- ▸ Move the shape to a different location in the document.
- ▸ Resize the shape by dragging or entering a precise size.

- ▸ Change the line colors and styles.
- ▸ Add a fill color or pattern.
- ▸ Rotate or flip the shape.
- ▸ Add special effects such as 3-D or a shadow.
- ▸ Copy a shape.

This chapter covers these tasks and more. (For information on using the Text Box tool, see Chapter 13.)

UNDERSTAND THE DRAWING TOOLS

Word includes several drawing tools, which you can use to add drawings to your document. Add an AutoShape, a line, a rectangle, a square, an oval, a circle, or an arrow. Use this toolbar to insert a text box, a WordArt object (covered in Chapter 13), or a clip-art image (covered in Chapter 14).

The Drawing toolbar also includes buttons for manipulating added objects. For instance, use the Draw menu to choose how text wraps around a drawing. Use the Fill Color button to add color to an object. The following table lists the buttons on the Drawing toolbar and describes what each one does.

Drawing Toolbar Buttons

Button	Button Name	Description
	Draw	Click to display the Draw menu, which includes commands for manipulating an object.
	Select Objects	Use this tool to select objects you have drawn.
	Free Rotate	Use this tool to rotate an object.
	AutoShapes	Click this tool to insert an AutoShape.
	Line	Draw a line in your document with this tool.
	Arrow	If you want an arrow, use this tool.
	Rectangle	To draw a rectangle or square, use this tool.
	Oval	Draw an oval or circle using this tool.
	Text Box	Draw a text box with this tool.
	Insert WordArt	Click this button to display the WordArt Gallery and add a WordArt object to your document.
	Insert Clip Art	Display the Clip Art Gallery by clicking this button. Then choose to add a clip art image to your document.

Drawing Toolbar Buttons (continued)

Button	Button Name	Description
	Fill Color	Choose a color from the color palette drop-down list and then click an object to fill it with color.
	Line Color	Choose a different color for the lines of an object using this tool.
	Font Color	If your object contains text, choose a font color using this tool.
	Line Style	Use this to choose a style for the lines in an object.
	Dash Style	Use dashed lines for the lines.
	Arrow Style	If you drew an arrow, choose a style for it using this tool.
	Shadow	Click this button to add a shadow effect to an object.
	3-D	If you want a 3-D effect, click this button.

INSERT AN AUTOSHAPE

An easy way to add a simple drawing to your document is to use an AutoShape. Word includes several predrawn shapes including several styles of lines, basic shapes, arrows, flowchart symbols, stars, banners, and callouts. Choose the type of shape and then pick a style from the pop-up menu.

After you decide on a shape, simply click and drag to draw. Once you've drawn the shape, use any of the tools on the Drawing toolbar to change the shape's appearance. Change how text wraps around it, add a fill color, use a different color for the lines, add a 3-D effect, and more. Keep in mind that an AutoShape functions as a drawn object; you

can do anything to it, as covered in the rest of this chapter.

In addition to drawing single AutoShapes, you can combine the shapes to create a line drawing, such as an organizational chart.

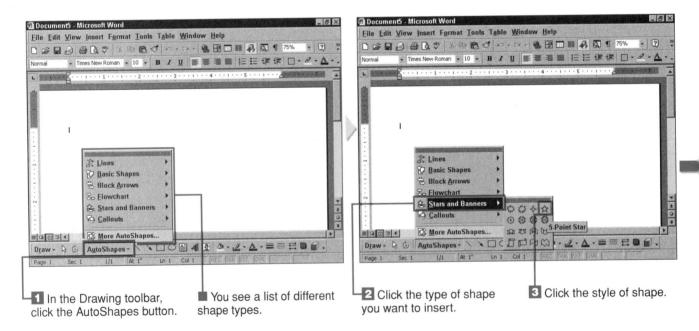

1 In the Drawing toolbar, click the AutoShapes button.

■ You see a list of different shape types.

2 Click the type of shape you want to insert.

3 Click the style of shape.

TIPS

What if I don't see the shape I want?

Display additional shapes using the More AutoShapes command in the menu. Then choose from several clips: simple illustrations of a computer, paper, a monitor, and more. (Note that if you did not install these, you may be prompted to do so.)

What are call-outs?

Call-outs are similar to cartoon captions. You draw them and then type in text.

Can I change the AutoShape size?

Yes. To do so, click the shape once to select it. Then drag one of the selection handles. For more information, see "Move or Resize a Shape" later in this chapter.

How do I get rid of a shape?

To delete a shape, click it. You should see selection handles around the edges. Then press Delete.

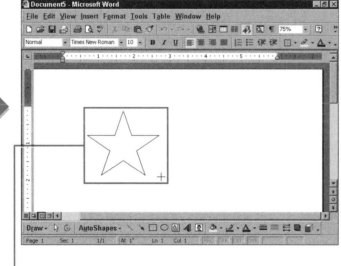

4 Put the pointer in the document and click and drag to draw the shape.

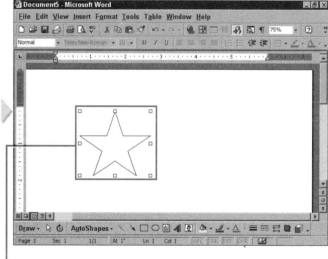

■ The shape is added to the document.

DRAW A SHAPE

The Drawing toolbar includes several tools for drawing shapes. You can draw a line, an arrow, a rectangle, a square, an oval, or a circle. The process of drawing any object is the same: choose the tool and then click and drag to draw.

You can make changes to a line after it is drawn (as covered later in this chapter), such as adding a color to a rectangle, a circle, an oval, or a square, or changing the color of the lines. You can also add a special effect such as 3-D or a shadow.

You don't have to worry about making a shape the right size or getting it in the right spot when you draw. You can easily resize or move a shape as needed.

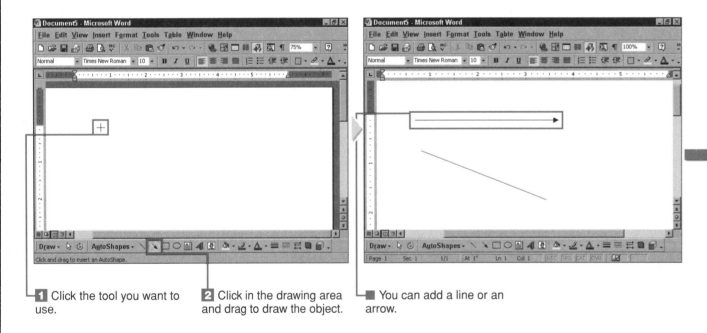

■1 Click the tool you want to use.

■2 Click in the drawing area and drag to draw the object.

■ You can add a line or an arrow.

I can't see my text! What happened?

A shape is like another layer on top of your document. If you want text to flow around a shape, you can change the text wrapping options, as covered in the section "Control Text Wrapping" later in this chapter.

How do I draw a straight line?

To draw a straight line, click the Line tool and then hold down the Shift key as you drag to draw the line.

How do I draw a circle or square?

To draw a circle, use the Oval tool but hold down the Shift key as you drag. To draw a square, use the Rectangle tool. Hold down the Shift key as you drag to draw a perfect square.

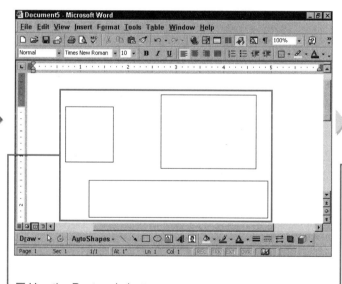

■ Use the Rectangle button to draw squares or rectangles.

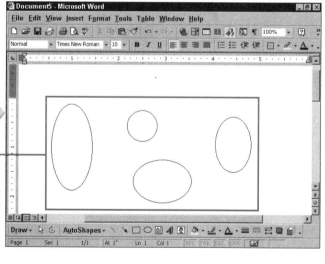

■ Add circles or ovals using the Oval tool.

MOVE OR RESIZE A SHAPE

As mentioned, you don't have to worry about getting the location of a shape just right. Drag and drop a shape to easily move it around a document.

You also can change the size. Drag the top or bottom selection handles to make an object taller. Drag the left or right selection handles to make an object wider. If you want to expand an object in both directions, drag one of the corner selection handles.

You can make some changes to the size using the Format AutoShape dialog box. (It's called the AutoShape dialog box for all kinds of shapes — whether they're AutoShapes or shapes you've drawn yourself.)

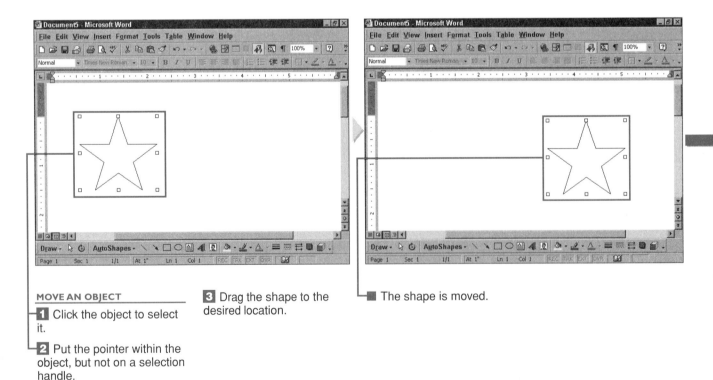

MOVE AN OBJECT

1 Click the object to select it.

2 Put the pointer within the object, but not on a selection handle.

3 Drag the shape to the desired location.

■ The shape is moved.

I can't get the shape to move!

Make sure you selected the object and put the mouse pointer on the border. The pointer should appear as a four-headed arrow.

What are selection handles?

Selection handles are the small white squares that appear around the edges of an object when it is selected. Drag any of these handles to resize an object.

How else can I move an object?

Click an object and then use the cursor movement keys to move it.

How else can I resize an object?

If you want to choose a particular height and width for a shape, use the Format AutoShape dialog box. Double-click the text box and then click the Size tab. Enter the object dimensions and then click the OK button.

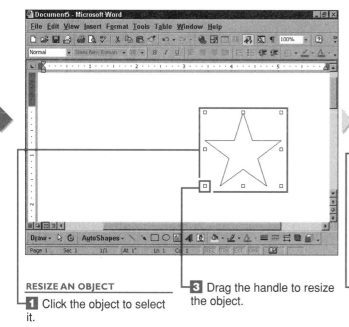

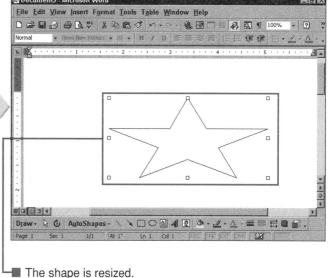

RESIZE AN OBJECT

◤ Click the object to select it.

◢ Put the mouse pointer on a selection handle.

◢ Drag the handle to resize the object.

◢ The shape is resized.

305

DELETE A SHAPE

When you first start using the Drawing tools, you may need to experiment. Use your document as a doodle pad to draw all kinds of fun shapes. Add a banner here, a star there, a circle in the center.

When you are done "playing," you may need to clean up the document. Get rid of any shapes you don't need. You may want to delete a shape and start over if you don't get the shape right the first time.

If you delete something and then change your mind, undo the deletion using the Undo button or the Edit ➪ Undo command.

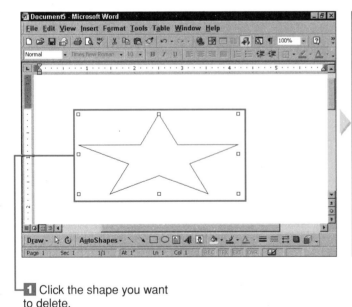

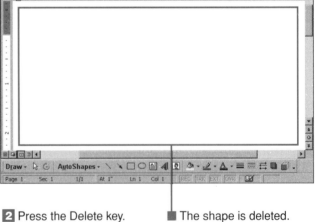

1 Click the shape you want to delete.

2 Press the Delete key.

■ The shape is deleted.

COPY A SHAPE

Often a simple illustration is composed of the same or similar shapes. If you draw and format an object and want to use it again, don't re-create it, copy it instead.

The easiest way to copy an object is to drag a copy from the original (as covered in the following steps). You also can use the Edit ➪ Copy and Edit ➪ Paste commands to copy and paste an object.

If you do spend the time putting together a line drawing, you may want to group all the individual objects into one. Do so by using the Group command on the Draw menu. See the section "Group Shapes" later in this chapter.

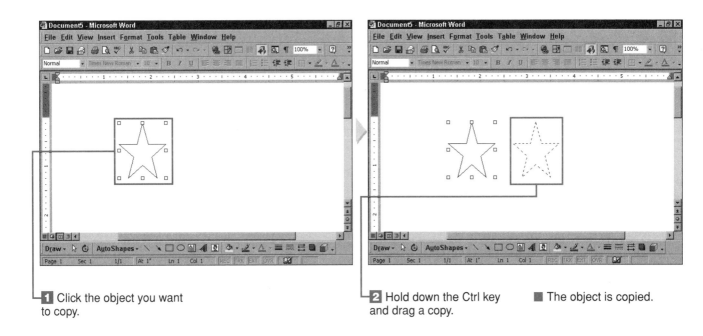

1 Click the object you want to copy.

2 Hold down the Ctrl key and drag a copy.

■ The object is copied.

CHANGE THE LINE STYLE

All objects are composed of lines. When you draw an object, Word uses a single thin line. After you've drawn the object, you can change the line style.

Line style choices include lines of different thickness (measured in points), as well as double lines.

As another option, you can choose from several styles of

dashed lines. If the object you are changing is an arrow, choose an arrow style. To do this, choose the type of arrow and where it points.

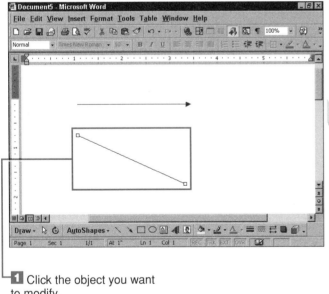

1 Click the object you want to modify.

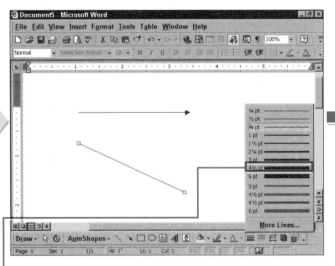

2 To change the line style, click the Line Style button and choose the style you want.

TIPS

Can I change the color of the lines?

 Yes. Information on changing line color (and adding a fill color) is in the next section of this chapter.

I can't get the object selected!

Sometimes it can be tricky to click an object to select it, especially lines. If you have trouble selecting an object, try using the Select Objects button. Click the button and then try clicking the object.

What if I don't want a line for the borders?

 If you don't want to use lines around an object, click the Line Color button and choose No Line. If your object contains nothing but lines, it will disappear. Therefore, this change works best for filled objects, text boxes, or call-outs.

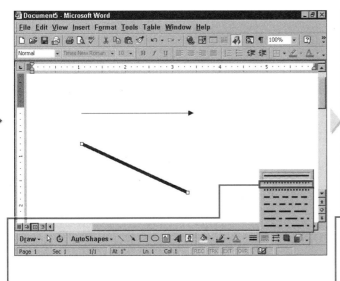

3 To use a dashed line for the object, click the Dash Style button and then choose the style you want.

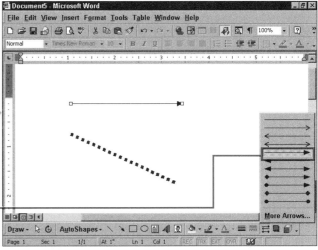

4 If you chose an arrow for step 1, you can click the Arrow Style button and choose an arrow style.

CHANGE THE SHAPE COLOR

When you draw a new object, Word uses black for the line color, and the inside of the object has no color. You can change both.

To start, change the line color. Choose from a palette of common colors, or try something really fancy such as a pattern.

For contained shapes (not lines or arrows), you can add a fill color. As with line color, you can choose from one of several colors, or try such fill effects as patterns, textures, or gradients.

The Drawing toolbar also includes a Font color button. Use this button to change the color of text in text boxes and call-outs.

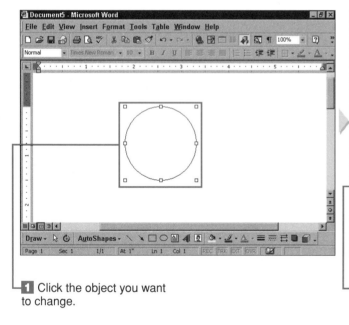

1 Click the object you want to change.

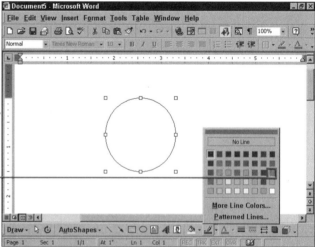

2 To change the line color, display the Line Color drop-down list and choose the color you want.

I changed the color, but it didn't turn out how I intended. What happened?

Sometimes the color of an object is a combination of the line color and fill color. To get the effect you want, you may need to change both the line color and fill color.

How do I add a texture or pattern?

To add a texture, pattern, or gradient, choose the Fill Effects command from the drop-down list. Then click the appropriate tab. Choose the type of fill you want and click the OK button.

My colors don't print! Why not?

Colors print only if you have a color printer. If you have a black-and-white printer, colors print in shades of gray.

I clicked the button, but nothing happened. What's going on?

To choose a color, you have to click the down arrow next to the button. If you click the button itself you change to the color displayed on the button.

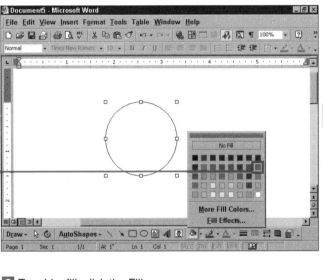

3 To add a fill, click the Fill Color button and choose the color you want.

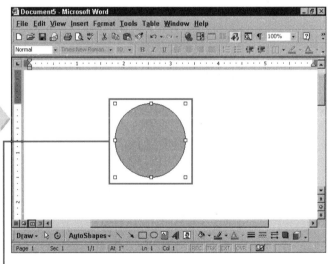

■ The new color is used.

USE SPECIAL EFFECTS

The Drawing toolbar includes two other buttons for changing object appearance: the Shadow button and the 3-D button.

Click the Shadow button to choose from several shadow shades. Basically, you decide where a shadow will fall around an object. For instance, you can add a shadow to the top left corner or the top right corner. You also can determine the degree of shadow. The palette gives you a good idea of each shadow option.

As another option, click the 3-D button and to choose from several 3-D versions of an object. Again, the viewing angle of the 3-D object and the size vary. The palette gives you a good idea of what each style will look like.

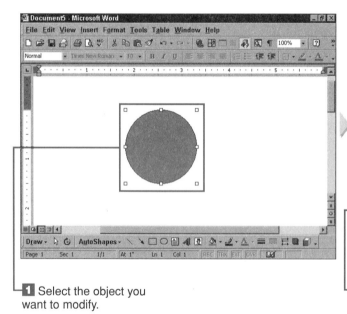

1 Select the object you want to modify.

2 Click the Shadow button and choose a shadow style.

TIPS

How do I undo a change?

To undo a change, use the Undo button or the Edit ➪ Undo command. You also can click the Shadow button and choose No Shadow, or click the 3-D button and choose No 3-D.

What are shadow settings?

If you want ultimate control over the placement of a shadow, click the Shadow Settings command. You see the Shadow Settings toolbar. Use the button to nudge the shadow on each side of an object. You also can choose a shadow color.

What are 3-D settings?

As with shadow settings, you can click the 3-D Settings button to display the 3-D Settings toolbar. Use the buttons in this toolbar to tilt a 3-D effect to the left or right, up or down. You also can set the depth, color, and direction of a 3-D effect.

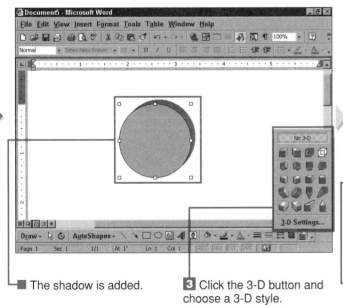

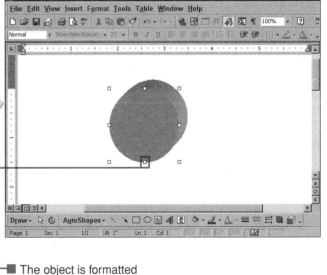

■ The shadow is added.

3 Click the 3-D button and choose a 3-D style.

■ The object is formatted with your selections.

CONTROL HOW TEXT AND OBJECTS OVERLAP

When you draw an object, it is placed as a layer on top of your document. You can change this to make document text flow around an object. To do so, use the Text Wrapping command on the Draw menu. (You also can use the Layout tab of the Format AutoShape dialog box.)

An object can appear behind, in front of, or through text — text runs right through an object with these wrap styles.

You can make text wrap in a square around an object, tight to an object's shape, or above and below an object.

If you have several objects, you can control how they stack on top of each other. To do so, use the Order command.

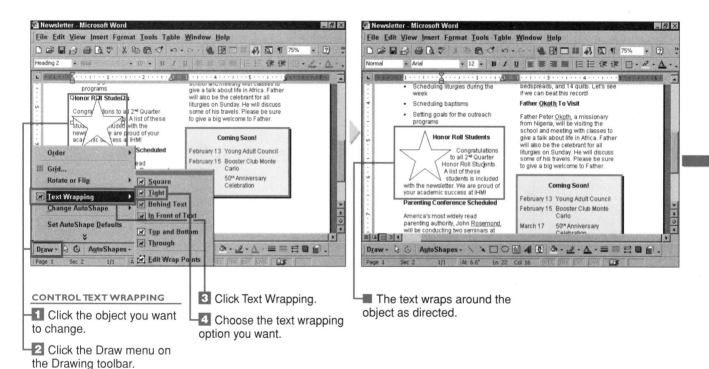

CONTROL TEXT WRAPPING

1 Click the object you want to change.

2 Click the Draw menu on the Drawing toolbar.

3 Click Text Wrapping.

4 Choose the text wrapping option you want.

■ The text wraps around the object as directed.

What other method can I use to format an object?

The Drawing toolbar buttons provide the easiest way to make a change to an object. But you can double-click the object to display the Format AutoShapes dialog box. Use the tabs in this dialog box to make a change. For instance, to set the text wrap, click the Layout tab and make a change.

What are the order options?

You can choose to place an object behind or in front of text. The pictures next to the menu commands give you some idea of how the options work.

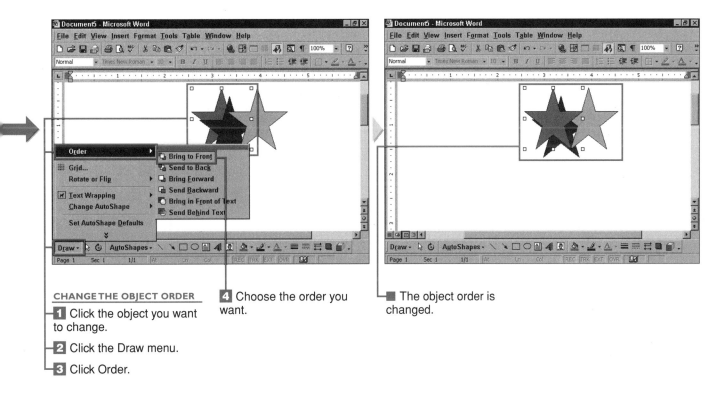

CHANGE THE OBJECT ORDER

1 Click the object you want to change.

2 Click the Draw menu.

3 Click Order.

4 Choose the order you want.

■ The object order is changed.

ROTATE OR FLIP AN OBJECT

Want another way to change an object? Rotate it. You can rotate an object 90 degrees to the left or right. If neither of these rotations suits you, drag to the amount of rotation you want. To use this method, choose Free Rotate and then drag the special selection handles to change the degree of rotation.

Similar to rotating is flipping, which is rotating 180 degrees. You can choose to flip an object horizontally or vertically. Access these commands with the Draw menu on the Drawing toolbar.

If you prefer to set a specific amount, use the Format AutoShape dialog box to make a rotation change. Use the Rotation spin box on the Size tab.

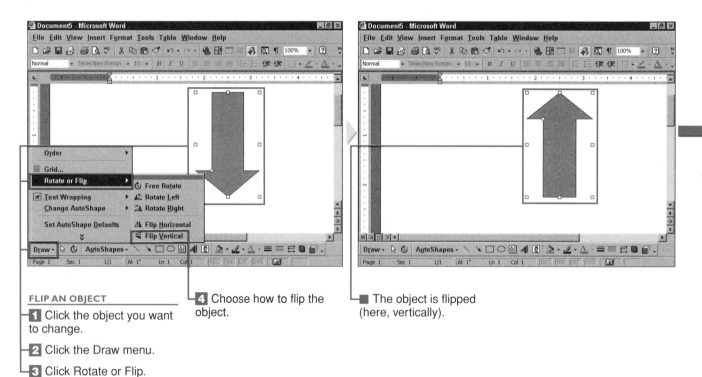

FLIP AN OBJECT

1 Click the object you want to change.

2 Click the Draw menu.

3 Click Rotate or Flip.

4 Choose how to flip the object.

■ The object is flipped (here, vertically).

TIPS

What's Free Rotate?

If you don't want to rotate to the left or right, you can rotate the number of degrees you want using Free Rotate. When you choose this command, selection handles appear as dots on the object. Drag one of these handles to rotate the object.

How do I undo a flip or rotation?

To undo a flip or rotation, click the Undo button or use Edit ⇨ Undo. You also can click the Draw menu and choose the command to go back to the original orientation.

How do I set a specific amount of rotation?

If you want to rotate an object a specific number of degrees, double-click the object to display the Format AutoShape dialog box. Then click the Size tab. In the Rotation spin box, enter how many degrees to rotate. Click the OK button.

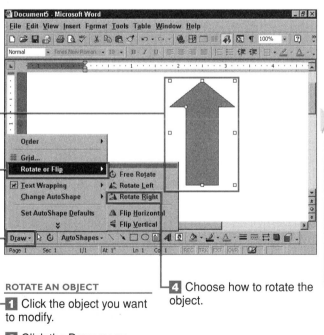

ROTATE AN OBJECT

1 Click the object you want to modify.

2 Click the Draw menu.

3 Click Rotate or Flip.

4 Choose how to rotate the object.

■ The object is rotated (here, to the right).

GROUP SHAPES

When you create an illustration composed of several shapes, you draw each shape individually. Then you can select that individual shape and format, move, resize, and so on as needed.

Once all of the objects are placed how you want them, you may want to group them as one object. Then you can make changes to the entire drawing. For instance, you can drag the grouped object instead of moving each object individually. You also can copy an object, delete it, resize it, and so on.

You can choose which items are grouped, and you can ungroup them if you need to change an individual object.

To select multiple objects, click the first object. Then hold down the Shift key and click each object you want.

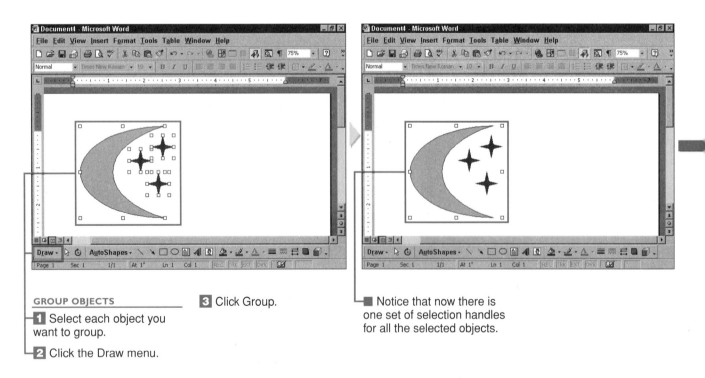

GROUP OBJECTS

1 Select each object you want to group.

2 Click the Draw menu.

3 Click Group.

■ Notice that now there is one set of selection handles for all the selected objects.

TIPS

What's a shortcut?

If you group objects and then need to ungroup them to make a change to an individual object, you don't have to go through the process of selecting and grouping again. Instead, select one of the objects that was grouped and then choose Draw ⇨ Regroup.

I don't see the Drawing toolbar.

If the Drawing toolbar is not displayed, click the Drawing button on the Standard toolbar. You can move the toolbar to another location onscreen. To do so, drag a blank area (not a button) of the toolbar.

What's an easy way to align objects?

By default, objects snap to an underlying grid. You can display the gridlines and also control the grid settings. To do so, click Draw and then the Grid command. Make any changes and then click OK.

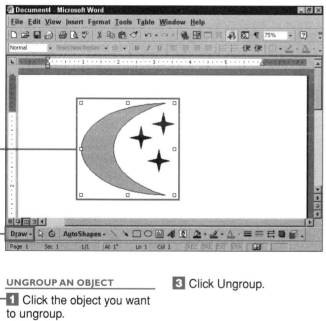

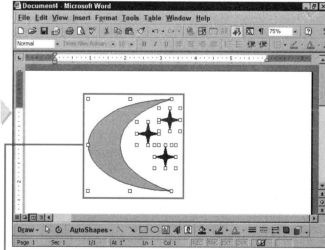

UNGROUP AN OBJECT

1 Click the object you want to ungroup.

2 Click the Draw menu.

3 Click Ungroup.

■ The object is now divided into its individual parts.

USING PICTURES AND CHARTS

D rawn shapes are okay for simple illustrations, but when you want something more complex, you may want to insert a picture or chart. You have a myriad of picture choices, including graphic files, clip art, scanned images, and more. You also can use other Word add-on applications to create a chart or an equation.

Use Clip Art

Word comes with a lot of canned art called clip art. If you want an illustration to liven up a document, try one of these images. Choose from animals, business images, buildings, flags, cartoons, and more. You can use any of the images provided with Word or the other programs you have. (For instance, if you have Microsoft Publisher, it also includes clip art). You can even purchase additional clip art to use in your documents.

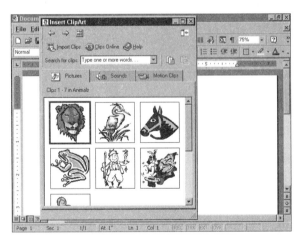

Insert a Graphic File

In addition to clip art, you can insert several other types of graphic files. You might be an artist and create illustrations with a drawing program such as Illustrator. Or perhaps you have taken photographs, scanned them, and saved them as graphic files. If you have a digital camera, the pictures are automatically saved as graphic files. You can insert these images.

As another example, look at the figures in this book. They are graphic files created with a special screen capture program and then inserted into the document.

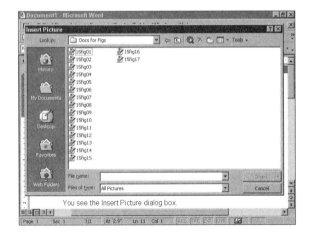

You see the Insert Picture dialog box.

Create a Chart

If you want to illustrate numbers, you may want to create a chart. Use the simple charting program included with Word. You can enter data into a datasheet and then choose from several chart types to represent the data.

Note that if you have Excel, you may want to use it to create charts and worksheets. You can easily insert Excel data. For information on inserting data from Excel and other programs, see Chapter 21.

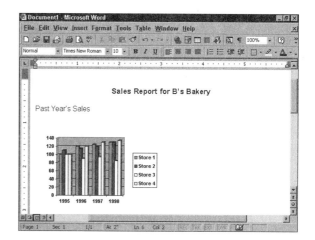

INSERT A CLIP ART IMAGE

You don't need artistic talent to use pictures in your documents. All you need are some clip art images, and Word has plenty.

Clip art are illustrations provided for your use in documents. There are clip art images for a wide variety of topics, including plants, sports, science, computers, business,

travel, food, home, government, and more. There are simple black-and-white drawings to full-color images. The pictures vary in style and complexity.

Some images may be installed on your hard disk; you also can insert your Word or Office CD-ROM and access even more images. If you need even more images, you can purchase

additional clip art packages. (Note that if you didn't install clip art, you can do so later as prompted.)

Once you've added a picture, you can change how text wraps around it, use a different line style for the picture border, and more. Just keep in mind that a picture functions the same as any object added to a document.

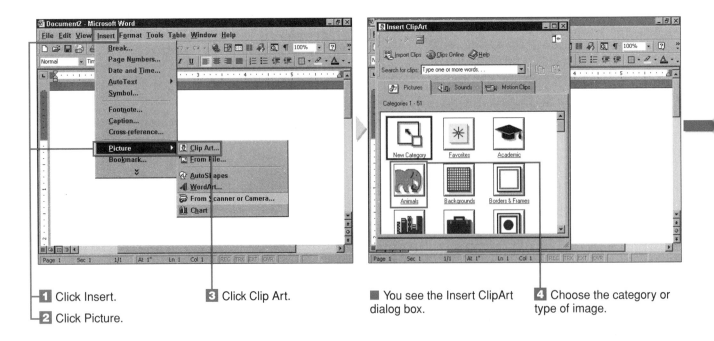

1 Click Insert.

2 Click Picture.

3 Click Clip Art.

■ You see the Insert ClipArt dialog box.

4 Choose the category or type of image.

The image isn't the size I want — or the location I want.

You can change the size and location of the image. You also can control how text flows around the picture. See the other sections in this chapter for more information on formatting the picture.

Where can I find other images?

If you insert your Word or Office CD-ROM and then choose the Insert ⇨ Picture command, you will see images from this disk as well as those on your hard drive. You also can look for clips online (if you have an online connection) using the Clips Online button.

Can I insert sounds and motion clips?

Yes. If you want to create a multimedia document, you can insert sounds or motion clips. These are most appropriate for documents sent via e-mail, or viewed on the Internet or an intranet. See Chapter 23 for more information on this type of document.

What's a quick way to find an image?

If you are looking for a particular image, type a word or phrase in the Search for clips text box that describes the image. Then choose from a list of images that match your search request.

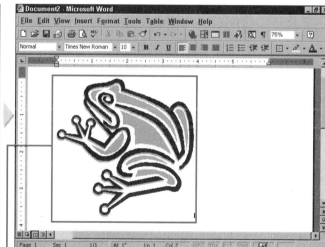

■ You see images in that category.

■ Click the dialog box s Close button.

■ The image is inserted into your document.

5 Click the image you want to insert and then click the Insert clip button.

INSERT A PICTURE FROM A FILE

In addition to clip art images, you can insert several other graphic file types, such as bitmap, JPEG, GIF, Kodak Photo CD, Paintbrush, TIFF, and others. By default, the Insert Picture dialog box lists all picture types, but you can display files of a certain type. (To do so, display the Files of type

drop-down list and then choose the file type you want.)

For instance, perhaps you created your own artwork with another program. You can insert this saved file into your Word document.

As another example, maybe you have photos that you scanned and saved as graphic

files, or saved with a digital camera. You can insert these images as well.

Once you insert a picture, you can move and resize it as needed. You can choose what type of border is used, whether the picture has a caption, and so on.

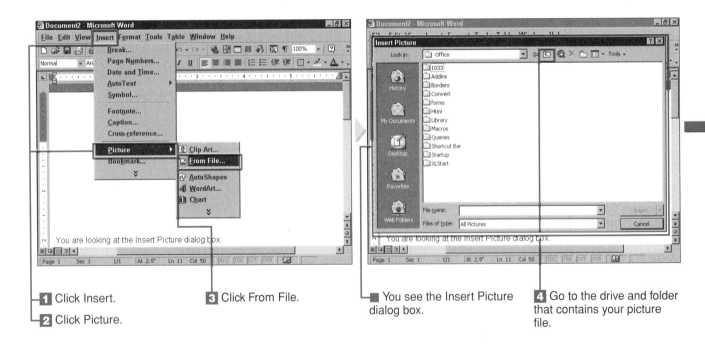

1 Click Insert.

2 Click Picture.

3 Click From File.

■ You see the Insert Picture dialog box.

4 Go to the drive and folder that contains your picture file.

TIPS

How do I change drives or folders?

 In the Insert Picture dialog box, display the Look in drop-down list to select another drive. To view picture files in another folder, double-click the folder on the list. You also can use the Up One Level button to back up a level in the folder structure.

I can't find the file!

If you can't find the file, try using a different view in the file list. You can display file details, which may help you find the file you want. Or display a preview. Click the Views button and then select the view you want.

What are the buttons along the left edge of the dialog box used for?

 Use the buttons along the left edge of the dialog box to display files in special folders, including Web Folders, your Favorites folder, and your My Documents folder. When you click the button you want, you see the contents of that file.

What other methods can I use for inserting files?

You also can insert objects from other programs. Use the features of a particular program to edit an image in Word. For information on inserting objects, see Chapter 21.

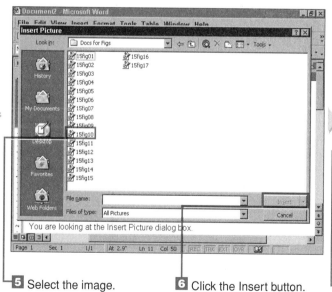

5 Select the image.

6 Click the Insert button.

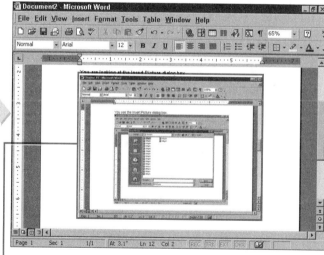

■ The picture is inserted. Here you see an image of a screen shot inserted into a Word document.

SET PLACEMENT AND TEXT WRAP

When you add a picture, it is placed inline with the text (as is a character). You can move an image within text, but not outside text.

This placement isn't very flexible. In most cases you want to be able to drag an image anywhere on a page. You can change the placement and choose how text wraps around a picture.

As for text wrap, you can have an object appear behind or in front of text. Text runs through an object with one of these wrap styles. You also can make text wrap in a square around an object or tight to the object shape.

If you select one of these text wrap styles, you can then drag the image around on the page.

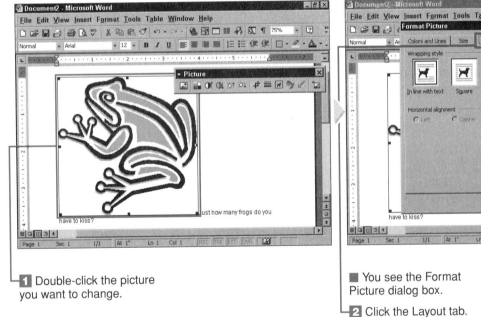

1 Double-click the picture you want to change.

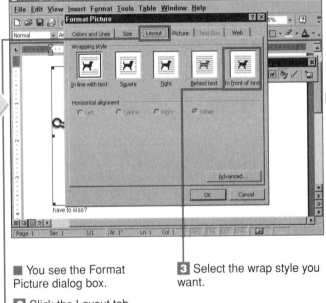

■ You see the Format Picture dialog box.

2 Click the Layout tab.

3 Select the wrap style you want.

TIPS

How do I select an alignment?

Choose a horizontal alignment using the Layout tab. Click Left, Center, Right, or Other.

How else can I make a change?

Use the Text Wrapping button in the Picture toolbar to choose a text wrapping style. From this menu you can choose square, tight, behind text, in front of text, top and bottom, and through. Click the button and then choose the style you want.

I can't drag the image or add a border! What's wrong?

Some options are not available for certain wrap styles, in particular when an image is in line with text. For this wrap style, you can move the image only within the text, and you cannot add a border. If you want more flexibility, choose one of the other wrap styles.

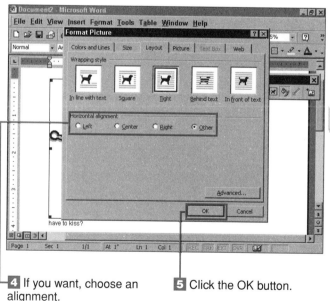

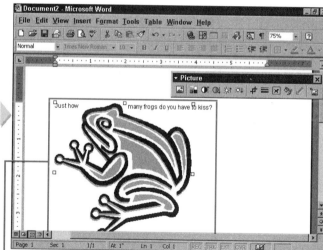

■4 If you want, choose an alignment.

■5 Click the OK button.

■ Text wraps around the picture as directed.

MOVE OR RESIZE A PICTURE

When you insert a picture, it is sized to the most appropriate shape and placed at the location of the insertion point. You may need to change this.

If an image is placed in line with text, you can move it around within the text. Drag it as you would drag a character. If

you change the wrap style (as covered in the preceding task), you can drag a picture to any spot on a page.

You can change the size of a picture. Drag the top or bottom selection handles to change the height. Drag the left or right selection handles to make a picture wider. If you want to

expand a picture in both directions, drag a corner selection handle.

You can make some size changes using the Format Picture dialog box. Using this dialog box, you can enter an exact size for a picture.

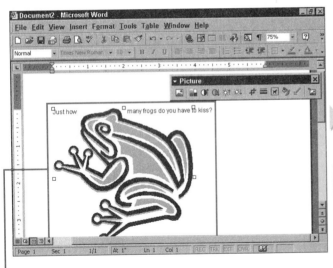

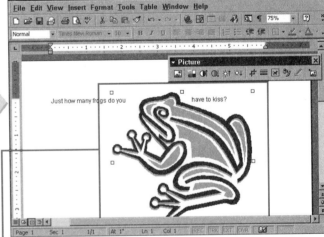

MOVE A PICTURE

1 Click the picture to select it.

2 Put the pointer on the edge of the picture, but not on a selection handle.

3 Drag the picture to the new location.

■ The picture is moved.

I can't get the image to move outside of the text. What's wrong?

If the wrap style is in line with text, you can move the image only within the text. To place the image anywhere on the page, change the wrap style, as covered in the section "Set Placement and Text Wrap."

How else can I resize an object?

If you want a particular shape height and width, use the Format Picture dialog box. Double-click the text box and then click the Size tab. Enter the dimensions for the object and then click the OK button.

 How do I undo a change?

Click the Undo button or choose Edit ➪ Undo to undo a move or resize. Or click the Reset Picture button on the Picture toolbar to reset a picture to its original settings (size, shape, brightness, and so on).

Can I cut out part of a picture?

 Yes. You can crop out part of an image. To do so, use either the Format Picture dialog box or the Crop tool. See the section "Crop a Picture" later in this chapter.

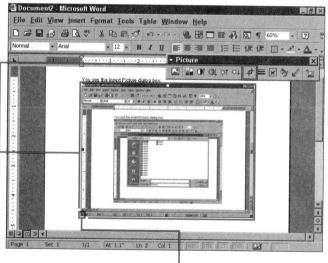

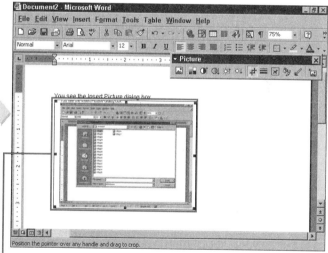

1 Click the picture you want to modify.

■ The Picture toolbar should be displayed. If it s not, right-click the picture and choose Display the Picture Toolbar.

2 Click the Crop button.

3 Click the selection handle on the side you want to crop and drag to remove that part of the picture.

4 Do this for each side you want to crop.

■ The picture is cropped.

CROP A PICTURE

In some instances, you may not want to use an entire image. This is especially true with photos or illustrations. You may want to use just part of an image and cut out the rest. This process is called cropping.

The easiest way to crop is to use the cropping tool (as covered here), but you also can choose a precise measurement. To use this method, double-click the image and then, using the Picture tab of the Format Picture dialog box, enter the amount to crop from the left, right, top, and bottom.

The image remains the same size in the file, but only the selected part of the image is included in the document. That is, the original illustration isn't modified, just the document view of it is.

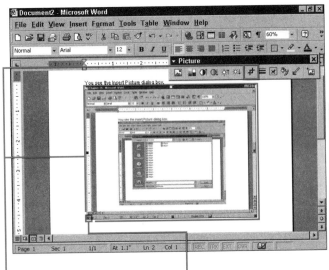

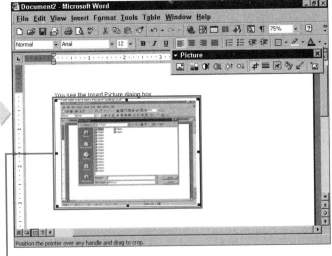

■1 Click the picture you want to modify.

■ The Picture toolbar should be displayed. If it s not, right-click the picture and choose Display the Picture Toolbar.

■2 Click the Crop button.

■3 Click the selection handle on the side you want to crop and drag to remove that part of the picture.

■4 Do this for each side you want to crop.

■ The picture is cropped.

DELETE A PICTURE

When you see the wealth of images that are available, you may go overboard adding illustrations to all of your documents. It's doubtful that your boss wants to see every memo decorated with cartoon workers. You can easily delete pictures that aren't needed.

When you delete an image, you remove it from the document. The file remains on your hard drive or CD-ROM so you can use it again.

If you delete something and then change your mind, undo the deletion using the Undo button or the Edit ➪ Undo command.

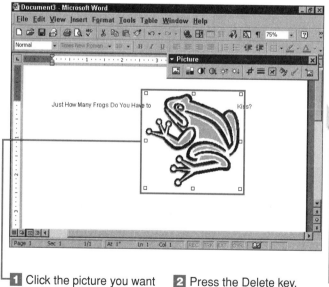

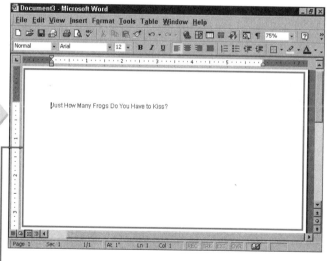

1 Click the picture you want to delete.

2 Press the Delete key.

■ The picture is deleted.

SET CONTRAST AND BRIGHTNESS

In addition to the size and placement of a picture, you can fine-tune other aspects. For instance, you may want to change the contrast or brightness. You can use more or less contrast. The same is true for brightness; you can adjust the brightness level up or down.

The easiest way to make a change is to use the buttons on the Picture toolbar. Or double-click the image to display the Format Picture dialog box. Click the Picture tab. Then adjust the settings in the Brightness or Contrast scroll bars, or enter percentages in the spin boxes.

Depending on the original settings and colors used in the image, you may see different effects. For instance, if you adjust the brightness of a color image, the colors may change to entirely different shades. Experiment until you get the setting you want. You may have to click more than once.

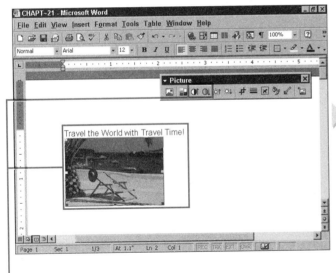

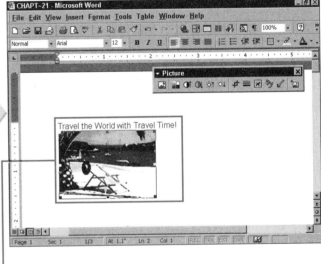

■ The contrast is adjusted.

ADJUST THE CONTRAST

1 Click the picture you want to change.

2 To change the contrast, click the More Contrast or Less Contrast buttons.

TIPS

Can I convert a color image to black and white?

 Yes. To do so, click the Image Control button and then choose Black & White. Use Grayscale to display an image in shades of gray.

Can I add a border to an image?

 If a picture is not an in-line image, you can choose a line style for the border. To do so, click the Line Style button and then choose the style you want.

How do I go back to the original settings?

 If you experiment with the brightness or contrast and don't like the results, you can undo the change using the Undo button. You also can reset an image to the original settings. To do so, click the Reset Picture button on the Picture toolbar.

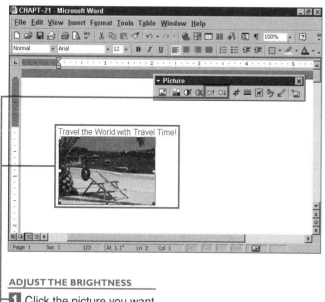

ADJUST THE BRIGHTNESS

1 Click the picture you want to change.

2 To change the brightness, click the More Brightness or Less Brightness buttons.

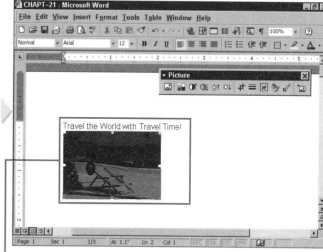

■ The brightness is adjusted.

ADD A FIGURE CAPTION

I n a long document or a document with several illustrations (such as a technical manuscript), you may want to add captions to figures. You can choose the caption text, placement, and numbering options. Or use the Caption dialog box to add a caption.

If you start with the picture selected, Word should use Figure as the caption type. If not, display the Caption drop-down list and choose Figure.

As for positioning, you can choose to place a caption above or below a selected item.

Word automatically numbers each figure and updates the numbering if you add or delete a captioned figure. You also can click the Numbering button to choose a formatting style.

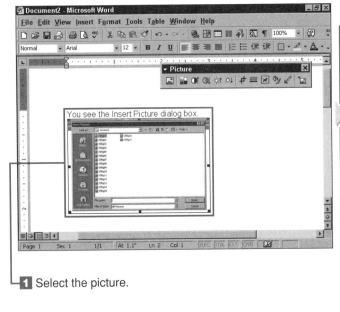

■1 Select the picture.

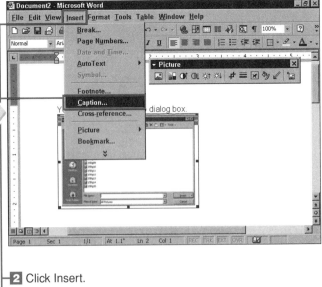

■2 Click Insert.

■3 Click Caption.

TIPS

How do I add a callout?

If you want to call attention to a particular part of an illustration, you can add a callout. Decide where you want the callout to point and then type text to identify that part of the picture.

To add a callout, display the Drawing toolbar and then click the AutoShapes button. Choose Callouts and then the callout style you want. Click in the document and then drag to draw the callout.

For more information on drawing, see Chapter 14.

How do I delete a caption?

A caption is just a text box added to a figure. Click the text box and press Delete to get rid of the caption.

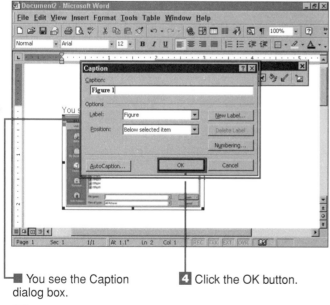

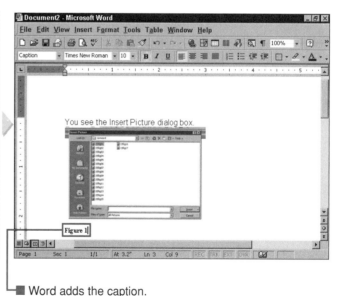

■ You see the Caption dialog box.

3 Make any changes to the type of caption, label, or placement.

4 Click the OK button.

■ Word adds the caption.

INSERT A CHART

If your document includes numerical information, you may want to represent this data in a chart. Sometimes you can spot things in a chart that you would not immediately notice from the numbers themselves. For instance, you might spot a trend, or notice a drop or increase in sales.

If your needs are simple, use the charting program included

with Word. (If this feature was not installed when you installed Word, you can install it now.) For more complex spreadsheet features, consider using a program such as Excel. Chapter 21 covers how to insert Excel worksheets and charts into a Word document.

When you use the charting program, you see the datasheet with sample data and a sample

chart. The datasheet is a grid of columns and rows, and the intersection of each column and row (called a cell) is where you enter data. Click the cell you want or use the cursor movement keys to move around the datasheet.

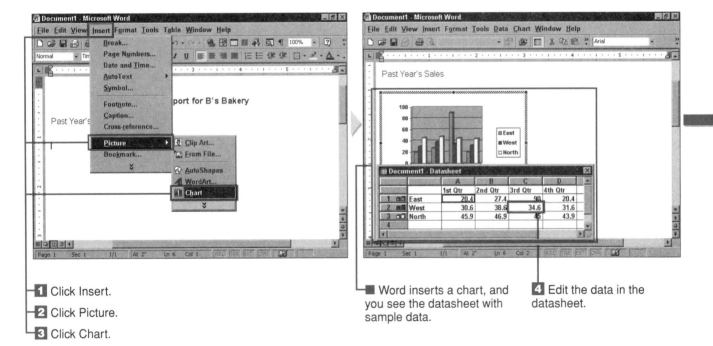

■1 Click Insert.

■2 Click Picture.

■3 Click Chart.

■ Word inserts a chart, and you see the datasheet with sample data.

■4 Edit the data in the datasheet.

My chart includes data that I didn't enter. What happened?

The chart starts out with sample data. You must edit this data or delete it so that the contents reflect your numerical data. Edit a cell by typing over the current entry. To delete an entry, select that cell and press Delete.

Can I include just three rows and four columns?

No. The datasheet includes entries for three rows and four columns, but you can make entries in the other rows and columns to include as much (or little) data as you need. Just click in the row or column and type the entry.

How do I use a different chart type?

The default chart type is a column chart. Choose from several other types, including bar, line, pie, area, stock, and more. See the section "Format a Chart" later in this chapter for information on changing the look of a chart.

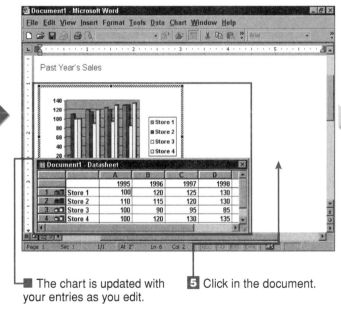

 The chart is updated with your entries as you edit.

5 Click in the document.

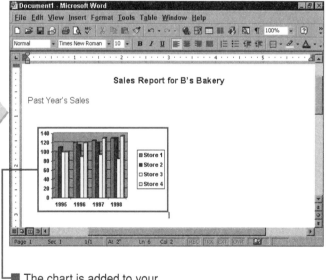

■ The chart is added to your document.

EDIT A CHART

After you add a chart, you may need to make changes to its content. (See the next section for help on changing the look of a chart.) For instance, you may need to update the numerical data. Or maybe you want other data in the chart.

To make a change to the content, display the datasheet. As you edit the datasheet, the chart in your document is updated.

To edit a cell, first select the cell you want to modify. You can click the cell or use the cursor

movement keys to move to the cell you want.

Close the datasheet by clicking its Close button or by clicking in the document.

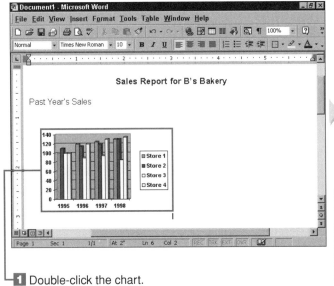

1 Double-click the chart.

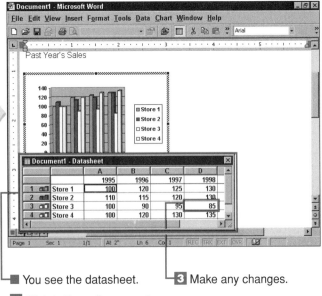

■ You see the datasheet.

2 Click in the cell you want to change.

3 Make any changes.

TIPS

Can I insert rows or columns within the datasheet?

 You can go to the next row or column to insert more data. Or insert a new row or column within existing data. To insert a new row, click the row number. To insert a new column, click the column letter. Then choose Insert ➪ Cells.

How do I select entries?

To select entries to edit (or format), drag across the cells you want to change.

How can I see more of the datasheet?

Drag the borders of the datasheet window to make it bigger (or smaller). You also can use the scroll bars to scroll through the data you've entered.

What keyboard shortcuts can I use to move around in the datasheet?

Press Home to go to the first cell in the current row. Press End to go to the last cell that contains data in the current row.

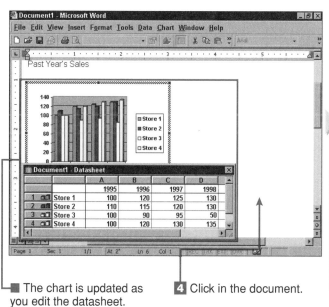

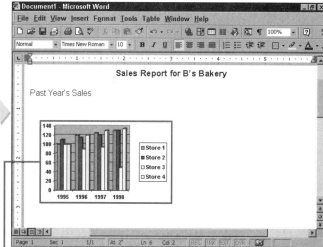

■ The chart is updated as you edit the datasheet.

4 Click in the document.

■ The chart is updated, and the datasheet is closed.

FORMAT A CHART

I n addition to the content, you have a great deal of control over the look of a chart. When a chart object is selected, you see a different set of menus. Use these menus to modify the chart and datasheet.

You can make any of the following changes: choose a font and column width for the datasheet entries, choose a style for the numbers in the datasheet and chart, choose how the data series are plotted, choose a

different chart type, or set chart options such as the placement of the legend and the format of the chart axes.

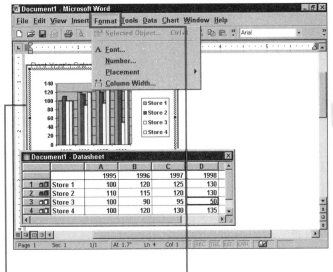

1 Double-click the chart.

2 Use the Format menu to choose the Font, Number style, or Column Width for the datasheet.

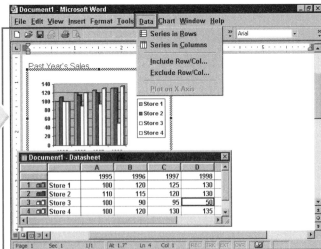

3 Use the Data menu to determine how data is charted.

TIPS

What chart type should I choose?

Depending on the message you want to convey, different chart types are appropriate. For instance, line charts shows trends over time. Column and bar charts are good for comparisons. Use the options in the dialog box to get help. Or experiment until you find a chart type you like.

How can I make a chart bigger?

To make a chart bigger, click the chart once to select it. Then drag one of the selection handles.

What chart options can I change?

You can add a chart title using the Titles tab. To select the primary axis, click the Axes tab. To control how gridlines appear, use the Gridlines tab. If you want to change the placement of the legend, click the Legend tab.

To include data labels, click the Data Labels tab. Finally, you can choose to display the datasheet itself by checking the Show data table checkbox on the Data Table tab.

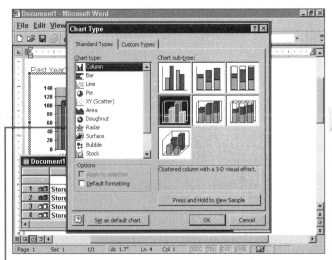

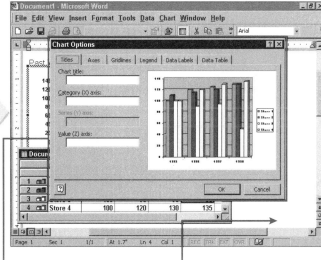

4 Click Chart and then Chart Type to choose the chart type.

5 Click Chart and then Chart Options to make changes to the chart titles, axes, legend, and other options.

6 When you are done making changes, click in the document.

SECTION IV

CREATING SPECIAL DOCUMENTS

CREATING FORM LETTERS

Form letters or mail merges are a way to send the same letter to many people. Even though you may think this is "junk" mail, these types of letters can come in handy to you or your business.

For example, if you have a small business, you may want to send a letter to your clients announcing a new product or service. Or you may want to thank a customer for an order. If you are a real estate agent, you might want to send out a letter introducing yourself to your neighbors. If you mainly use Word for family functions, you may want to send a holiday letter to all your friends and family. Or you may be in charge of one of your child's sports teams and need to send the same information to other parents. The types of letters you might want to create are endless.

Word provides a convenient way to send the same letter — but personalized — to several people. Two files make up a basic merge procedure: the data source and the main document. This introduction gives you an overview of the process and explains what each document contains. The remaining sections tell you specifically how to create each document and then do the merge.

Set Up the Main Document

The main document contains the text of the letter — the information you want each letter to contain — and the field code for fields you want to include. For example, a last name field code tells Word to take the specific last name and insert it in that spot in the main document. You start this document first, create the data source, and then go back to complete the main document.

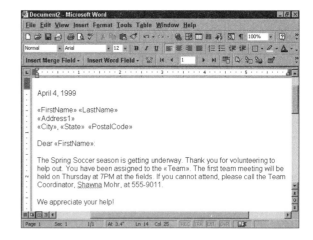

Create the Data Source

The data source is the list of variable information (usually names and addresses) that you want to use to personalize the main document. You can use an existing data source (such as an electronic address book or a database file), or you can set up a data source.

If you create the data source (within Word), you basically create a table. The first row of the table contains the name of the *fields* or variable information you want to insert in the main document. For example, you may have fields for the first name, last name, address, city, state, zip code, and so on. Each field has a name and appears in its own column. Word provides several predefined fields that you can use in the data source. Or you can create your own fields.

After you set up the data source, you then enter the specific information for each field. One set of fields (or a row) is called a record. For instance, in one row you would have the name and address of a specific person. You next enter the records using a data form. Enter a record for each person to whom you want to send the letter.

Merge the Two

After you create both documents, you then merge the two. Word creates one big document, with a personalized letter for each record in the data source. You can print or save the resulting document.

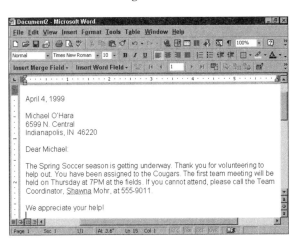

You may think that setting up a mail merge is complex because you do have to follow a lot of steps, but your hard work will be rewarded once you see the results.

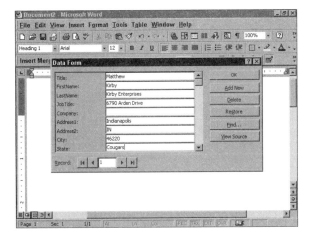

START THE MAIL MERGE

To lead you through the process of performing a mail merge, Word provides the Mail Merge Helper, which outlines the three steps you follow: create the main document, create the data source, and merge the data.

To start, you create a new blank document. This document will be the main document. You need this document open because Word makes a connection between the two documents (the main document and the data source).

Select the type of main document you want to create. You can create form letters, mailing labels (covered later), envelopes, or a catalog. After you make your selection, this information is listed under the Main document so you can keep track of what you've done so far.

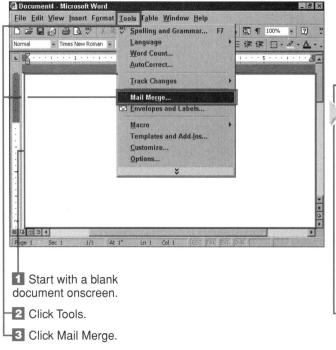

1 Start with a blank document onscreen.

2 Click Tools.

3 Click Mail Merge.

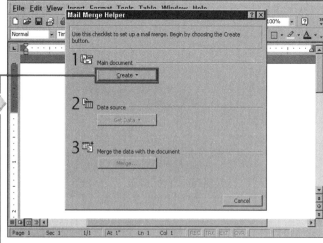

■ You see the Mail Merge Helper dialog box.

4 Click the Create button.

TIPS

How do I use a main document I've already created?

Open the main document. When you click Tools ⇨ Mail Merge, you see all the details of the main document and data source. Edit the main document or select another data source using the buttons in this dialog box.

What if I forget where I am in the process?

If you forget where you are in the process, display the Mail Merge Helper dialog box by clicking Tools ⇨ Mail Merge. You can see which of the steps you have completed.

Is that all for the main document?

No. You basically select which document is the main document, create the data source, and then go back and finish up the main document. The steps are a little misleading. See the later section, "Create the Main Document," for help on finishing this document.

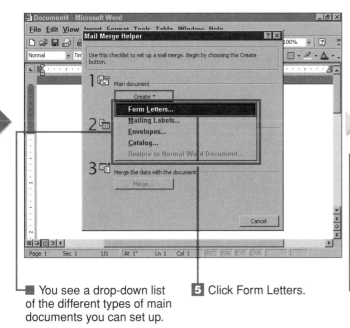

■ You see a drop-down list of the different types of main documents you can set up.

5 Click Form Letters.

◢**6** Click the Active Window button.

■ Word records the document type (form letters) and document window you are using for the main document.

■ The next step is to create the data source, as described in the next section.

CREATING SPECIAL DOCUMENTS

CREATE A DATA SOURCE

This section continues where the previous one left off. For your next step, you can choose to create the data source, open a data source, use the address book, or set header options. Here you create a data source.

The data source contains the header row (the top row) with names for each of the fields (each

piece of information you want to include). The data source also includes individual records for each person (or item or event). When you create the data source, you start by defining the fields to include. Then you enter the data.

Word includes some commonly used fields such as FirstName, LastName, Company, Title, City, State, HomePhone,

and so on. These fields are pretty self-explanatory. For instance, the FirstName field is used to enter first names. You can use any of these fields. You can also add your own fields.

After you add the fields, you can enter the data (covered in the next section).

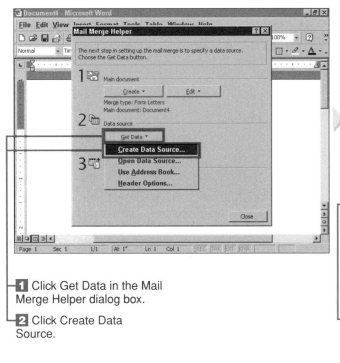

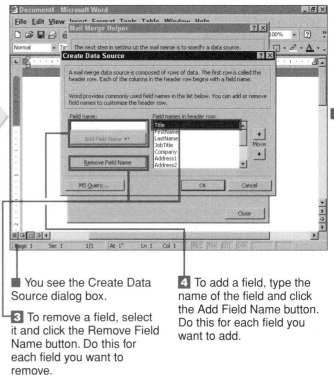

1 Click Get Data in the Mail Merge Helper dialog box.

2 Click Create Data Source.

■ You see the Create Data Source dialog box.

3 To remove a field, select it and click the Remove Field Name button. Do this for each field you want to remove.

4 To add a field, type the name of the field and click the Add Field Name button. Do this for each field you want to add.

TIPS

How do I use a data source I've already created?

In the Mail Merge Helper dialog box, click the Get Data button and select Open Data Source. You see the Open Data Source dialog box. Select the file you want to use. Word lists this file name in the Mail Merge Helper dialog box. You can then create the new main document you want to use.

Can I use data from other programs?

Yes. For information on using other data sources — such as an Access database — see Chapter 21.

Which fields do I need?

To come up with your list of fields, think about each individual piece of data you want to include. Which of the predefined fields are appropriate? Which additional fields do you need to include? You may want to make a list of all the fields. For instance, in this example, a field for team is added.

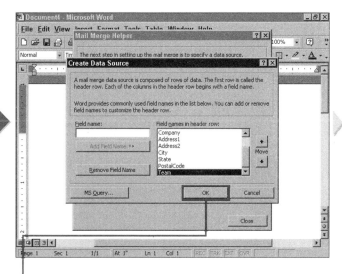

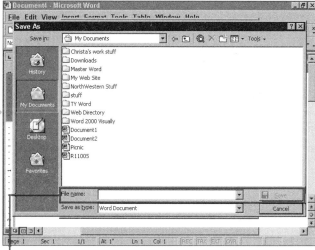

5 When you finish adding or removing fields, click the OK button.

6 Select a drive and folder, type a file name, and click the Save button.

■ Word then prompts you to edit the main document or data source. You want to edit the data source, adding the records to your data table. This is the topic of the next section.

ENTER THE DATA FOR THE DATA SOURCE

After you set up the fields, you next enter the specific information for each person to whom you'll send a letter. For instance, if you wanted to send out ten letters, you would enter the specific name and address information for those ten people.

To help you, Word creates a data form, with text boxes for each of the fields you set up in the data source. To create a record, you type an entry for each field. Press Tab to move from field to field. (You can also press Shift+Tab to move backward through the fields.)

Once the record is complete, you click the Add New button to add this record and go to a new blank record. Type the data for this record and click Add New again. Do this until you've added all the records in your data source.

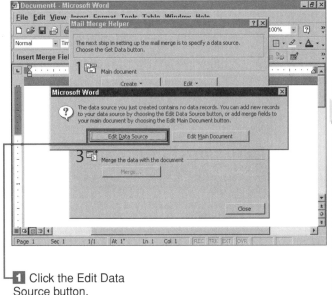

1 Click the Edit Data Source button.

■ You see the Data Form, with a text box for each of the fields.

2 Type the information for the first field and press Tab.

3 Continue entering information for all the fields until you complete the record.

TIPS

How do I edit a record?

In the data form, use the scroll buttons at the bottom-left to display the record you want to change. Make your changes and then click OK.

How do I delete a record?

In the data form, display the record you want to delete. Then click the Delete button.

I accidentally closed the Data Form. How do I reopen it?

Click Tools ➪ Mail Merge to display the Mail Merge Helper dialog box. Under Data source, click the Edit button and then click the file name. The data form is redisplayed. You follow this same procedure if you want to edit the records — make a change or add records.

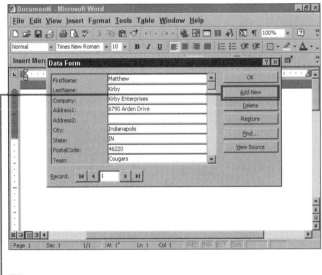

4 Click the Add New button.

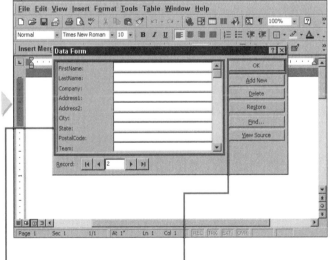

■ The record is added, and a new blank record is displayed.

5 Follow Steps 2 through 4 for each record you want to add.

6 When you have completed all the records, click the OK button.

■ You see the main document onscreen. The next section describes how to complete this document.

CREATE THE MAIN DOCUMENT

Congratulations! You've completed the first step of the mail merge. Now you are on to the second step — creating the main document. When you finish adding records, Word displays the main document. You can then type the text of the document as well as insert the merge fields.

You type your document — in this case, a mail merge letter —

just like a normal document, including the text and formatting you want. The difference is that when you want to insert variable data from the data source, you insert a merge code.

For instance, for a letter, you would include the merge codes for the name, address, city, state, and zip codes. To insert these items, use the Insert Merge Field button and select the field.

The field appears in brackets in the document and is actually a code that tells Word where to merge data from your data source. You insert these merge codes at any spot in the document, and you can use them more than once. On the other hand, you don't have to use all the fields — only the ones you need in this document.

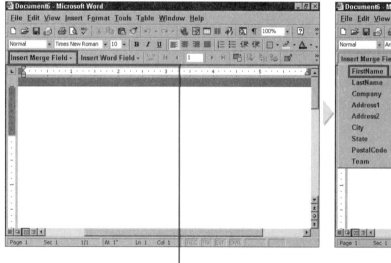

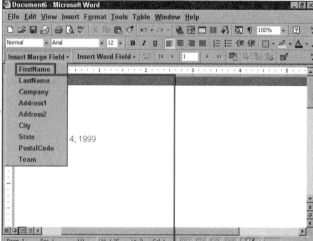

1 Type the text of the letter.

2 When you get to a spot where you want to insert variable information, click the Insert Merge Field button.

■ You see a list of fields you have set up in the data source.

3 Click the field you want to insert.

How do I delete a merge code?

If you add a merge code and want to delete it, drag across it to select it and then press the Delete key.

What are the other toolbar buttons?

When you are working in the main document, the Merge toolbar is displayed. You can use this toolbar to not only insert merge fields, but also to display the Mail Merge Helper, check the main document for errors, perform the merge, and edit the data source. If you aren't sure what a button does, put the mouse pointer on the button. The button name should pop up.

Can I just type the brackets to insert the merge code?

No. You can't just type the merge codes within brackets. You have to insert them using the toolbar button.

What's a common mistake?

A common mistake is to forget to include punctuation, such as commas or spaces, between the merge fields. For example, be sure to press the spacebar in between the FirstName and LastName fields so that there's a space when you do a merge.

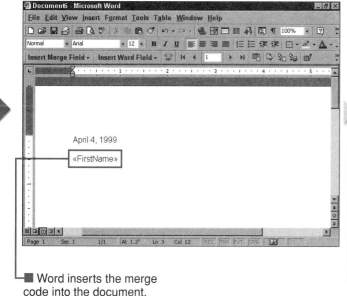

■ Word inserts the merge code into the document.

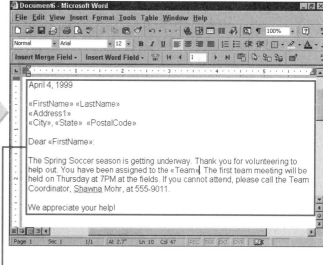

■4 Continue typing and inserting fields until you complete the document.

■5 Save the main document.

■ Now that both the main document and data source are completed, you can merge the two.

MERGE THE DOCUMENTS

The final step is the easiest. You select a few commands and Word performs the merge. Word takes your main document and pulls the specific information from each record in the data source, creating a custom letter for each record in the data source.

When you start the merge, you see the Mail Merge Helper

dialog box. All the selections you made and the file names for each file are listed. You can select how to perform the merge, whether to merge to a new document or to send it to the printer, and whether to merge all or just selected records.

I usually recommend merging to a new document so you can see the letters first before

printing. If the letters are acceptable, print them using the File ➪ Print command. If you see a mistake, you can correct it and then perform the merge again.

You don't have to save the merged letters because you have the data source and main document; you can always merge again to create the letters if necessary.

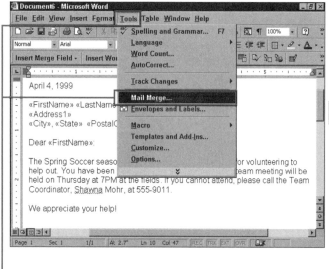

1 Click Tools.
2 Click Mail Merge.

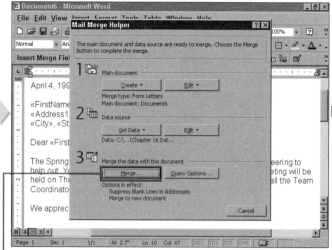

3 Click the Merge button.

Can I print the letters directly?

To merge directly to the printer, click the Merge to Printer button on the Merge toolbar. Or in the Merge dialog box, display the Merge to drop-down list and select Printer. You can also select Electronic mail.

Do I have to merge all the records?

No. To merge only selected records, select the From option button and then enter the record numbers you want to use in the merge. You can use Query Options to select which records are merged.

How are blank lines handled?

If Word encounters a blank field or line, it does not print the line. If you want to print this line, select the Print blank lines when data fields are empty option button in the Merge dialog box.

How can I check for errors?

You can use the Check Errors button to have Word check for common merge errors. Make any corrections and then perform the merge again.

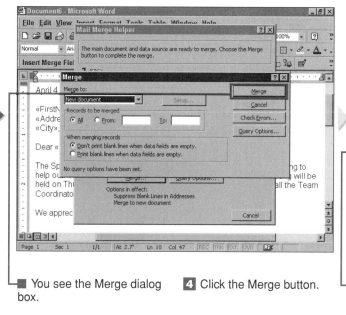

■ You see the Merge dialog box.

4 Click the Merge button.

■ Word merges the letters and displays each one on a separate page.

CREATE MAILING LABELS

You save all that time creating the letters, but what about addressing them? Word can save you time with this task, too. You can easily set up mailing labels, using the names and addresses in the data source.

You don't have to worry about setting up the columns and layout for the page because you can select from common label layouts. The most common type of labels are made by Avery. Many other labels are compatible with Avery labels, too.

You don't have to type each label. Instead, you can use a data source to create a merge. Set up a new data source or use an existing one (as covered here).

When you use a data source, you set up the merge fields for the address label. That is, you use merge codes to specify where each piece of address information goes on the label. Most labels are all codes. Be sure to insert spaces in between each part of the address!

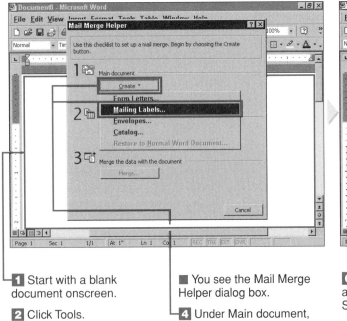

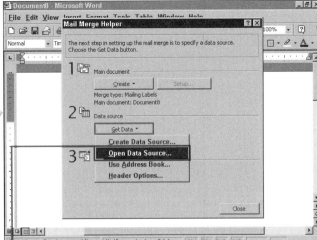

1 Start with a blank document onscreen.

2 Click Tools.

3 Click Mail Merge.

■ You see the Mail Merge Helper dialog box.

4 Under Main document, click the Create button and select Mailing Labels.

5 Click the Active Window button.

6 Click the Get Data button and select Open Data Source.

TIPS

What are the dimensions of the label?

When you select a particular label, the dialog box lists the dimensions. You can view more detailed information by clicking the Details button. You see a dialog box that shows the margins, number of labels across and down the page, and the width and height of the labels.

How do I know what type of label I have?

Check the label box for the product number. Also, if you don't have Avery labels, many other brands list the Avery product with which they are compatible.

My addresses weren't spaced correctly. What happened?

Be sure to include appropriate spaces and punctuation in between each of the merge fields. Otherwise, the fields will run together. Instead of John Smith, you'll get JohnSmith.

How do I change the printer information?

If necessary, you can change the printer information. Select the type of printer (dot matrix or laser and ink jet) as well as the tray that contains the labels.

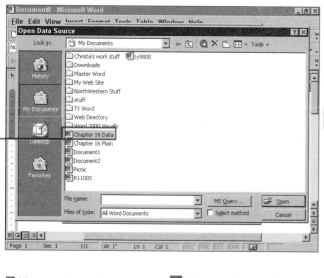

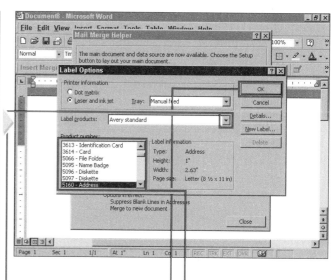

■ You see Open Data Source dialog box.

7 Change to the drive and folder that contains the data source. When you see the file listed, double-click it.

8 Click the Set Up Main Document button.

■ You see the Label Options dialog box.

9 Display the Label products drop-down list and select the brand of label you are using.

10 In the Product number list, select the name of the labels you are using.

11 Click the OK button.

CONTINUED ▶

357

CREATE MAILING LABELS CONTINUED

Once you've set up the labels, you can merge the label document with the data source to create the labels. Like a regular mail merge, you can merge to a new document or directly to the printer.

If you merge to a new document, you see the label document onscreen. (Keep in mind that your final document will look different depending on the label type you are using.) You can check them to be sure they look as you intended. Then you can insert the labels into the printer and select the File ⇨ Print command to print the labels.

If you aren't sure which way to insert the labels, check your printer manual. You can also print a test sheet. (I put an X on one side of a blank piece of paper and then print that. From this printout, I can tell which side the printer prints on so I insert the labels the right way.)

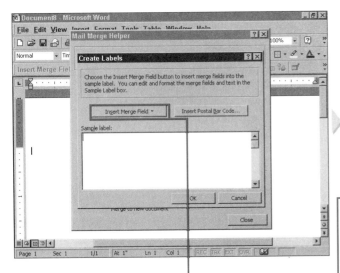

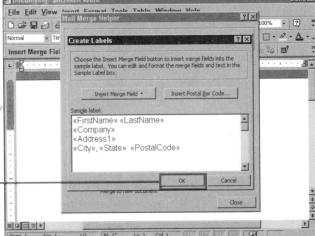

■ You see the Create Labels dialog box.

12 Click the Insert Merge Field button and select the merge field to include in the address label. Do this for each part of the address.

└ When you finish setting up the sample label, click the OK button.

■ You are returned to the Mail Merge Helper.

CREATING SPECIAL DOCUMENTS

IV

Can I print the labels instead of creating a new document and then printing?

Yes. In the Merge dialog box, display the Merge to drop-down list and select Printer. When you click Merge, the documents are sent directly to the printer.

My labels didn't print correctly. What happened?

If they printed on the wrong side, print them again, but switch the paper around. If they printed outside the labels, be sure you have selected the right label type. If there's a mistake with the merge codes, edit the main document and remerge.

How do I create envelopes?

The process for creating envelopes is the just about the same, only you select Envelopes under Main document. You also select the envelope size and printing options for the delivery and return addresses.

Do I have to save the merged document?

No. I usually don't save the merged document, only the main document and data source. If needed, you can easily perform the merge again, so you don't need the merged labels.

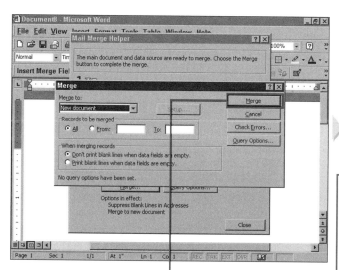

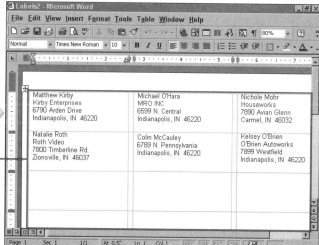

" Click the Merge button.

15 Click the Merge button again.

■ Word creates a document based on the label size and includes an address for each label.

PUTTING TEMPLATES AND WIZARDS TO WORK

So far you have learned how to save time entering text into your document. You also learned shortcuts for using the same set of formatting options. What if you want to do both — save time typing text and formatting? Then consider a template.

Think of one type of document you create over and over, say something simple such as a memo. When you create this document, you most likely include the same text in every memo: the memo heading and the to, from, date, and subject lines. You probably also format the text the same way. Perhaps you center and make the memo header bold. Maybe you also make bold and set up tabs for the to, from, date, and subject lines. If you create a lot of memos, you do these same monotonous tasks over and over.

When you find yourself creating the same document over and over, you should think *template*. A template is a document that includes text and formatting already set up. You simply open the template and then add the text you want to include to complete the memo. Think of a template as a fill-in-the-blank document.

To start, you may want to check out some of the templates provided with Word. You may find one that meets your needs. If not, you can always set up your own template.

Use Word's Templates and Wizards

Word provides two tools for quickly adding text and formatting to documents: a wizard and a template. The difference is in how they work. A wizard is an automated document. When using a wizard, Word leads you through the process step-by-step, prompting you to make selections and enter text. Follow each step and when you finish, you have a completed document. Word provides wizards for many document types — faxes, letters, mailing labels, envelopes, legal pleadings, newsletters, résumés, and more.

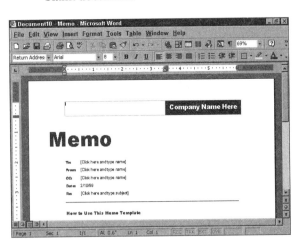

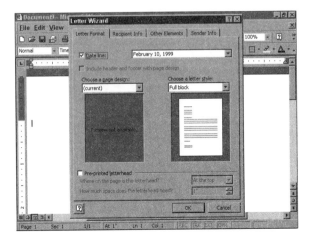

When you use a template, you select the template you want. You then see a new document based on the template, basically a document skeleton, that includes the text and formatting appropriate for that document type. In addition to having several wizards, Word provides many templates that you can use to create a professional-looking document.

Create Your Own Templates

You can use a template for any type of document. A memo, for instance, is a good type of document for a template. You might also use a template for letters, reports, invoices, fax cover sheets, press releases, newsletters, and so on. For example, I have templates for invoices, faxes, and my letterhead. Each one includes some text that I always want included in the template. The document is also formatted just the way I want. When I use one of these templates, I don't have to enter the same text over and over again. I just have to fill in the "blanks" for each document.

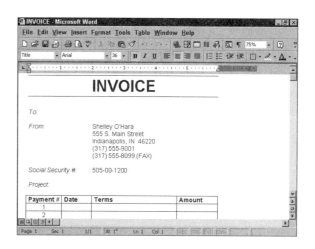

This chapter covers how to use Word's templates and wizards as well as create your own.

USE A WIZARD

If you like the step-by-step approach to creating a document, try one of the many wizards provided with Word. Here are just a few of the wizards provided with Word: envelope, fax, mailing label, résumé, memo, newsletter, legal pleading, and Web page. (For information on Web pages, see Chapter 23.)

When you use a wizard, you are prompted in a series of dialog box tabs to make selections. For some steps, you are prompted to enter or select text to include or are prompted to select a style for the document. Word then takes your selections and creates a document.

In the resulting document, some text is already entered, and the document is pretty much formatted for you. The document may also include some filler text (in brackets). You can replace the text in brackets with the appropriate text for your document. You can also make any changes to the text and formatting already included in the document.

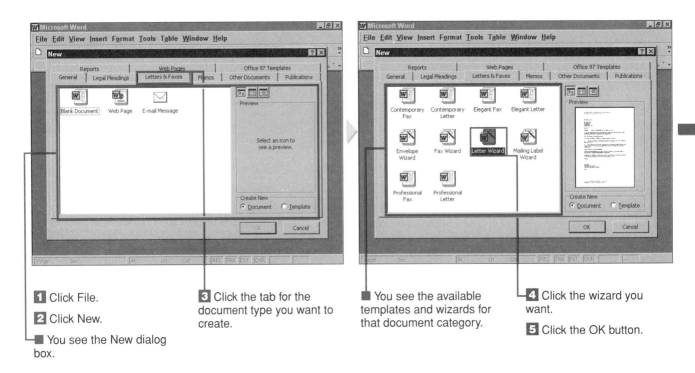

1 Click File.

2 Click New.

■ You see the New dialog box.

3 Click the tab for the document type you want to create.

■ You see the available templates and wizards for that document category.

4 Click the wizard you want.

5 Click the OK button.

How can I tell the difference between wizards and templates?

 You can tell which ones are wizards because they say wizard.

What if I make a mistake?

If you make a mistake or change your mind, click the Back button to go back through your selections and make changes. To get help, click the Help button.

What else does each wizard include?

Most templates include several styles set up for each of the document elements. Use these styles for other text in the document. You can also modify the styles. For more information on styles, see Chapter 10. The template may also include macros. For more information on macros, see Chapter 27.

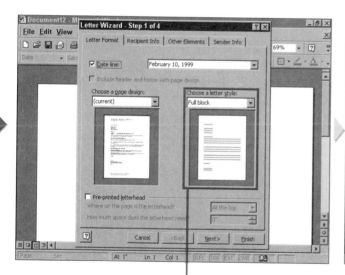

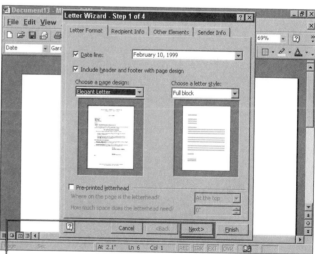

■ Depending on which wizard you select, you see a different series of dialog box tabs.

6 Follow the instructions in the dialog box. For the letter wizard, you select a letter style.

7 After you complete the step, click the Next button to display the next step.

CONTINUED ▶

USE A WIZARD CONTINUED

When you are using a template or wizard, the Office Assistant may appear to prompt you for selections such as whether you want to create an envelope for the label or redo the wizard.

Click any of these options to have the Assistant display pertinent help on the process.

After you complete the document, you can save and print the document. When you use File ➪ Save to save the

document, the document is saved as a separate file, with the name you assign. You can open and edit this document as needed. The original template remains untouched on disk so you can use it again.

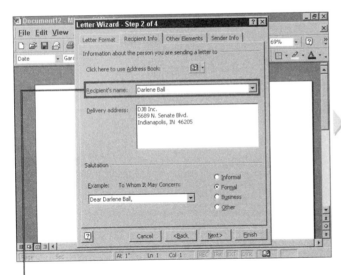

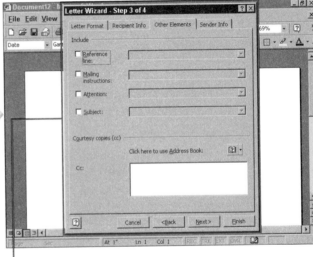

8 Continue moving through the tabs, making selections. For the letter, you complete the recipient information and then click Next.

9 For the letter wizard, select any other elements to include and click Next.

Why does the Office Assistant keep popping up?

 The Office Assistant appears and asks whether you want help with particular tasks. For example, after you complete the letter wizard, the Assistant asks whether you want to make an envelope or mailing label. Close the Assistant by clicking the Cancel button.

What other elements can I include in a letter or memo?

You can include a reference line, mailing instructions, attention line, subject, and CC lines. To add these to the letter, check the appropriate box on the Other Elements tab.

What if I use letterhead?

 If you use letterhead, check the Pre-printed letterhead checkbox on the Letter Format tab. Then select where the letterhead appears and how much space it takes. Word will format the letter from the wizard accordingly.

Can I select addresses from my Address Book?

 Yes. If you have your electronic Address Book set up, you can click the Address Book button on the Recipient Info tab and then select the name and address you want to use.

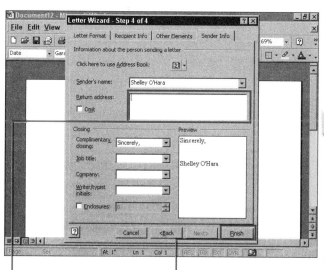

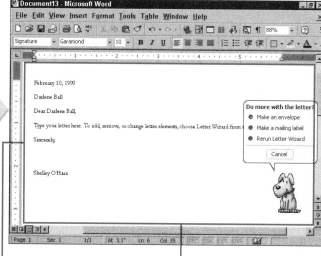

10 For the letter wizard, complete the sender information and click Next.

11 Click the Finish button to complete the document, adding your own text and making any needed changes.

■ You see your finished document onscreen.

12 Complete the document.

USE A TEMPLATE

As mentioned, a template is like a fill-in-the-blank document. The document skeleton includes the text and formatting, and you fill out this skeleton to complete the document. Word includes many different templates. You can select from several document types as well as different styles of each type.

Here's a few of the templates included with Word: blank document or Normal template (the default), faxes in several styles (contemporary, elegant, and professional), letters and memos in the same styles, reports, Web pages, résumés, and more.

Like a wizard, some templates include text, such as the document title, subject fields, and date for the fax. Other text appears in brackets, indicating that you need to replace this "filler" text with your "real" text.

You can make any editing and formatting changes to the document, as necessary. Then save and print the document. This new document is saved as a separate file; the template remains unchanged so you can use the template again.

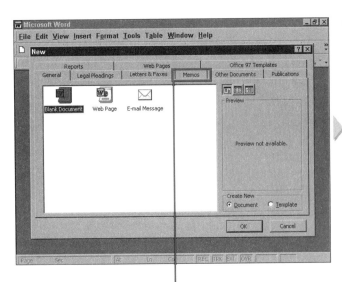

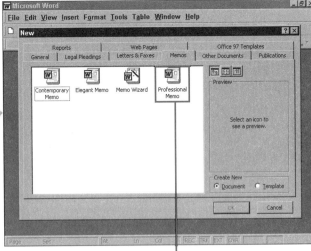

1 Click File.

2 Click New.

■ You see the New dialog box.

3 Click the tab for the document type you want to create.

■ You see the available templates and wizards for the document category you selected.

4 Click the template you want to use.

TIPS

What if I don't like the formatting?

 If you don't like how the document is formatted, you can make changes. You can select different styles, use different fonts, and basically make any changes you would in a "regular" document.

What template style is best?

Word offers three basic styles for most templates: professional, elegant, and contemporary. You can select one that suits you. If you don't find any style that you like, create your own template, as explained later in this chapter.

Can I update one of the templates?

 Yes. You can edit one of Word's templates to create your own personalized version of that template. Then you don't have to make the same changes again and again (such as typing the company name). See the section "Modify a Template" later this chapter.

How do I edit filler text?

Click the text you need to replace and type the actual text. Do this for each section of text that needs to be completed.

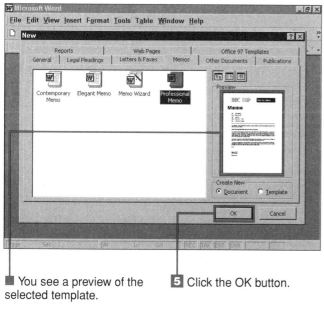

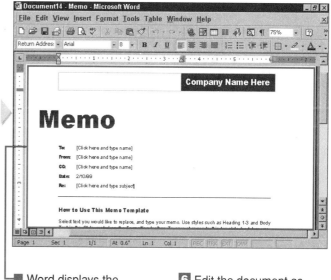

■ You see a preview of the selected template.

5 Click the OK button.

■ Word displays the template document onscreen.

6 Edit the document as needed.

CREATE YOUR OWN TEMPLATE

It's easy to create a template. You just create the document as you would normally and then use a special procedure to save the document as a template.

You can include any of the following in a template: any text that all documents should include (company name, document title, address, date code, and so on); any graphic image that all documents should include (company logo, for example); formatting for the existing text and other elements such as the page margins, layout, border, and so on; styles, macros, and other customized options.

When you save the template, you save it to a special folder. You can also select the folder (tab) where you want the template to appear. This folder matches the tab used in the New dialog box.

After you create a template, you can create new documents based on this template. All new documents you start with this template will include all the formatting and text you include.

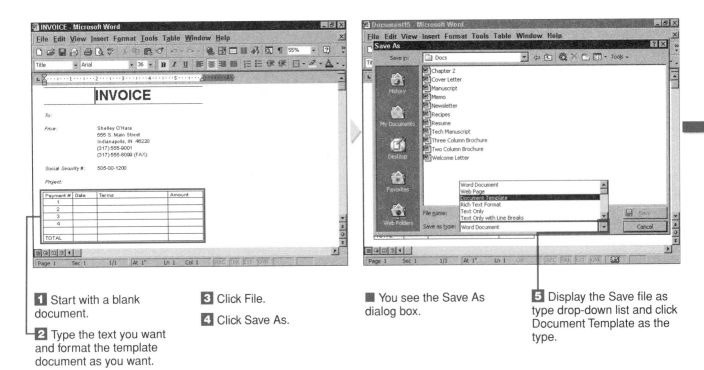

1 Start with a blank document.

2 Type the text you want and format the template document as you want.

3 Click File.

4 Click Save As.

■ You see the Save As dialog box.

5 Display the Save file as type drop-down list and click Document Template as the type.

TIPS

CREATING SPECIAL DOCUMENTS

IV

Can I use an existing document?

You can start with a document you have already created and formatted. If you do so, be sure to delete any text that you don't want to include in the template.

What should I name the template?

Use something descriptive that reminds you of the template's contents and purpose.

How do I use this new template?

Open the File menu and select the New command. Click the tab for the template. This is the folder where you placed the template when you saved it. You should see your template listed. Click the template name. Click the OK button.

Can I create a template from an existing template?

Yes. If one of the predefined templates is close to what you want, you can save time by creating a new template based on an existing one. Select File ➪ New and select the template you want to use. In the Create New area, instead of Document select Template. This step tells Word to create a template (rather than a document) based on the selected template. Click the OK button. Modify the existing template to create your new template. You can make any editing and formatting changes to the existing template. When you finish, save the template using the File ➪ Save command.

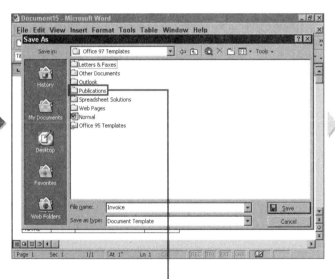

■ Word automatically selects the Templates folder where you must place your templates to make them available.

-6 Select the folder where you want to place this template.

7 Type a name for the template.

8 Click the Save button.

■ Word saves the document as a template.

MODIFY A TEMPLATE

Getting your template set up exactly right may take some trial and error. As you use the template, you may notice some elements you want to change. You might want to get rid of text that isn't appropriate for every document based on that template. Or you might want to add text or formatting that you do want to include.

When you use the template, remember that you are creating a new document. The original template remains unchanged. When you want to actually work on the template, you need to open the actual template file and then modify it. You need to follow a special procedure to open the actual template.

Remember that the templates folder has several subfolders for different document types (memos, reports, and so on). When you saved your template, you selected one of these folders. Select that same folder when you are looking for the template.

After you save the template, it is updated. The next time you use this template to create a document, it will include all the editing and formatting changes you made. Any previous documents based on the template remain unchanged.

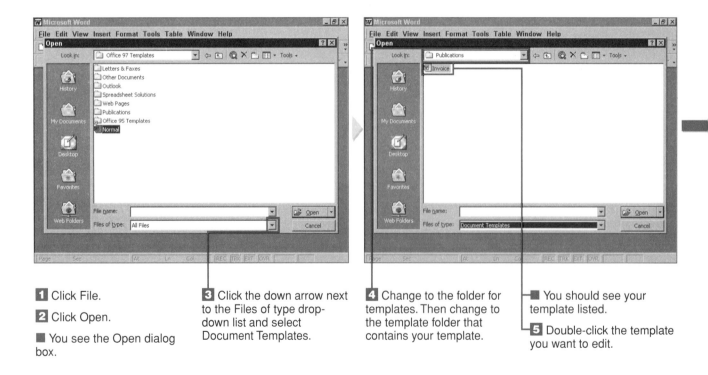

1 Click File.

2 Click Open.

■ You see the Open dialog box.

3 Click the down arrow next to the Files of type drop-down list and select Document Templates.

4 Change to the folder for templates. Then change to the template folder that contains your template.

■ You should see your template listed.

5 Double-click the template you want to edit.

TIPS

Where are templates stored?

The templates are stored in a special folder on your system. Use the Up Level button to move through the folders on your system to get to the templates folder.

How do I delete a template?

To delete a template, display it in the Open dialog box. Then right-click the file and select Delete.

Are existing documents updated?

No. Only new documents based on this template are updated. You can reapply the new template to update the document. See the next section in this chapter.

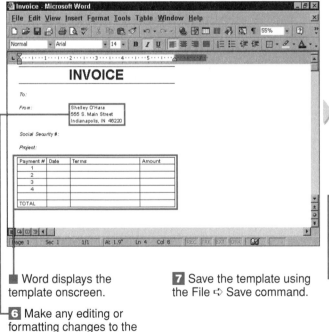

■ Word displays the template onscreen.

6 Make any editing or formatting changes to the template.

7 Save the template using the File ⇨ Save command.

■ Word saves the template in the same folder with the same name.

APPLY A NEW TEMPLATE

Y ou can easily modify a template, as covered in the preceding section. But what if you want to use a different template on an existing document? Do you have to start over? No. You can apply a new template and have Word update the document.

You can't open a new template using File ⇨ New because that creates a new document. Instead,

you use a special command to apply the new template.

You can select any of the templates on your system, including Word's templates or any templates you have created. To select the template you want, you move to the folder where it is stored.

When you apply the template, Word leaves the existing text of the document unchanged, but

updates the styles (if styles have been applied). Word also updates other formatting options such as the page margins, the document font, and so on. You also will have available for your use all the styles and macros in that template.

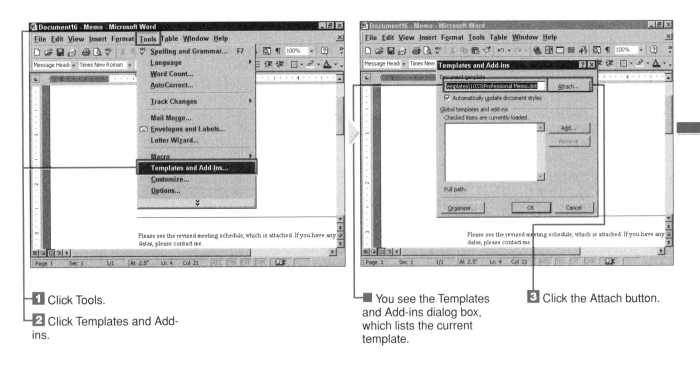

1 Click Tools.

2 Click Templates and Add-ins.

■ You see the Templates and Add-ins dialog box, which lists the current template.

3 Click the Attach button.

What if I don't want to replace the styles?

If you don't want to update the document styles, but leave them as they are currently formatted, uncheck the Automatically update document styles checkbox.

What is the Organizer?

The Organizer is a feature for managing the macros, styles, and templates on your hard drive. See the next section for information on copying styles from one document to another.

What is the default template?

The default template is named Normal. This is the template that Word uses if you select File ➪ New and select Blank Document or click the New button. This template is displayed on the General tab.

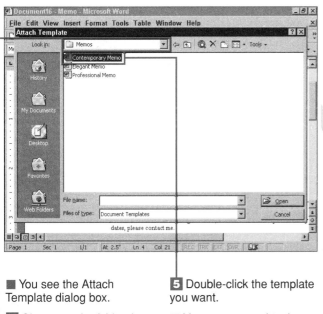

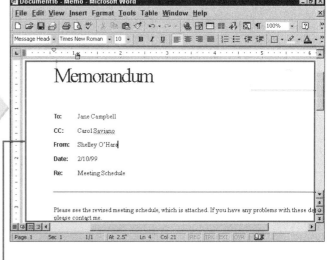

■ You see the Attach Template dialog box.

4 Change to the folder that contains the template you want to apply.

5 Double-click the template you want.

■ You are returned to the Templates and Add-ins dialog box.

6 Click the OK button.

■ Word applies the new template and styles.

COPY STYLES FROM A TEMPLATE

As mentioned, templates can contain text, macros, and styles. You can apply a new template and have access to all of these features. As an alternative, you can copy styles from one document to another.

You might want to copy styles if you have set up and saved styles in one document and want to use them in another. Or you might want to copy new styles from one template to the Normal template (the default template) or any other template. Select both the document or template that contains the styles and the document or template that you want to receive the styles.

The dialog box lists the styles in each document so you can keep track of what you've copied. You also see a description of the selected style when you click it in the dialog box.

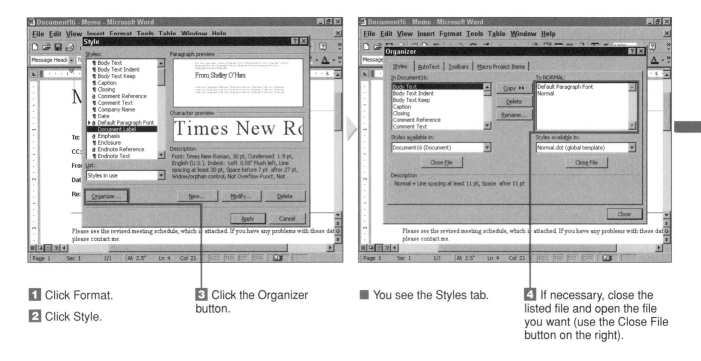

1 Click Format.

2 Click Style.

3 Click the Organizer button.

■ You see the Styles tab.

4 If necessary, close the listed file and open the file you want (use the Close File button on the right).

TIPS

What if the wrong documents are listed?

If the wrong documents are listed, you can close that file and open the correct one. Click the Close File button. That file is closed, and the button changes to say Open File. Click this button and then open the document you want to use. You can do this for both the document with the styles and the document to which you want to copy the styles. They both have Close File buttons listed under the file details.

What else can I copy?

You can also copy AutoText entries, custom toolbars, and macros from one document or template to another document or template.

How do I delete a style?

You can delete listed styles. Click the style you want to delete and then click the Delete button.

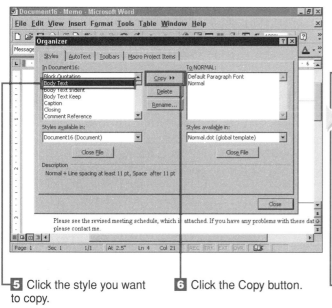

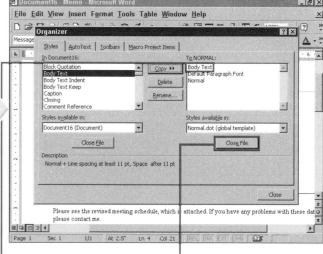

5 Click the style you want to copy.

6 Click the Copy button.

■ The file is added to the list of styles in the To document.

7 Copy each style you want to add.

8 Click the Close button.

ORGANIZE WITH AN OUTLINE

An outline is a good way to organize a document, especially a longer document. You can plan what topics and sections are included. You can think about the logical order of those topics. You can check the content to ensure it covers the subject comprehensively. Did you leave anything out? Does the document have any unnecessary sections? You can also check the consistency of your headings. Are all level-2 headings of equal weight? Is the wording parallel? Do the headings make sense?

You aren't limited to just outlines for documents. You can also outline a presentation or create an agenda. Again, you can check the content and flow of the presentation.

Word includes an Outline view, which you can use to create, view, edit, rearrange, and format outlines.

Create an Outline

Typing an outline is easy. Just change to Outline view and then type the document headings. Press Tab to indent a heading (make it a lower level heading). You can unindent a heading to make it a higher level heading (press Shift+Tab). You can include up to nine levels of heading. Not only does Word organize the sections for you in an easy-to-view document, but the program also applies appropriate heading styles to each heading.

You don't have to start with a blank document. You can change an existing document into an outline. You can do so by changing to the appropriate view and then assigning the appropriate headings.

View an Outline

In Outline view, you can tell the major headings and how each subheading relates to that heading by the indents (and also the formatting). The Outline toolbar includes buttons for selecting how many levels are displayed. You can, for instance, choose to display just the top-level headings. Or you might want to collapse the view of a particular branch of an outline. Change the view so you can work and concentrate on just the area you want.

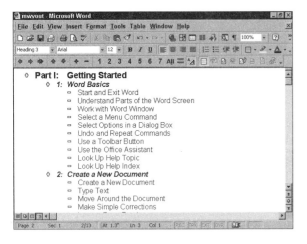

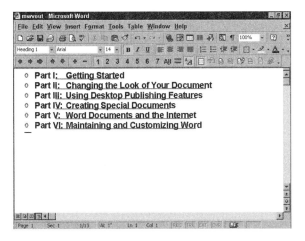

Rearrange an Outline

Not only is the Outline view a good tool for checking your document's organization, but you can also use this view to easily make changes. Move a section and its contents with one simple drag-and-drop action. You can work on the order until the presentation is just perfect.

Format an Outline

As mentioned, Word applies appropriate heading styles for each heading. If you don't like how the styles are formatted, you can modify the style. You can also add outline numbers to the outline, selecting from several numbering styles.

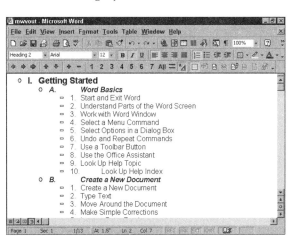

CREATE AN OUTLINE

You can use either of two methods for creating an outline. You can change to Outline view and type your outline, assigning headings as you go. You can press Tab to indent a heading, which automatically assigns the appropriate heading level. Press Shift+Tab to demote a heading and assign the appropriate heading level.

As an alternative, you can assign Heading styles to existing text to create an outline for an existing document.

In either case, an outline consists of text formatted with specific heading styles. The top-level heading is heading 1, and Word applies the Heading 1 style. The next is level 2, for which Word uses the Heading 2 style, and so on. As already

mentioned, you can include up to nine levels of headings in an outline. Word also indents each heading in Outline view so you can see how the current topic relates to other levels in the overall structure.

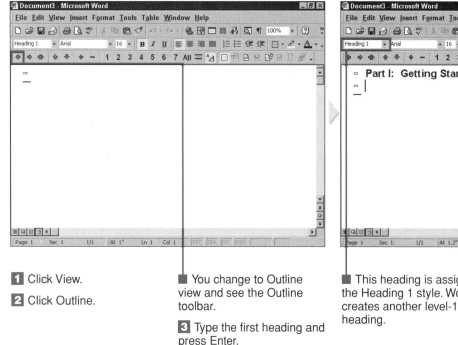

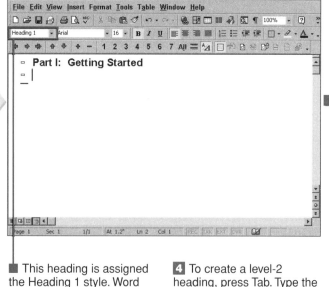

■1 Click View.

■2 Click Outline.

■ You change to Outline view and see the Outline toolbar.

■3 Type the first heading and press Enter.

■ This heading is assigned the Heading 1 style. Word creates another level-1 heading.

■4 To create a level-2 heading, press Tab. Type the heading and press Enter.

How do I create an outline from existing text?

Select each heading and assign the appropriate style (Heading 1 for level-1 headings, Heading 2 for level-2 headings, and so on). The easiest way to assign a style is to use the Style drop-down list in the toolbar. To view your outline, select View, Outline.

Can I include regular text in an outline?

Yes. Not all of the outline text has to have a heading style assigned. For text that is part of the document (not the outline), assign the level Body Text.

I pressed Tab too many times and now the level is wrong. How can I fix this?

As you type an outline, you can press Tab to indent a heading. If you tab over too far, press Shift+Tab to go back a level. You can also change the level headings as covered in the "Reorganize an Outline" section later in this chapter.

What's a shortcut for switching views?

You can also click the Outline view button in the lower-left corner of the status bar to switch to this view.

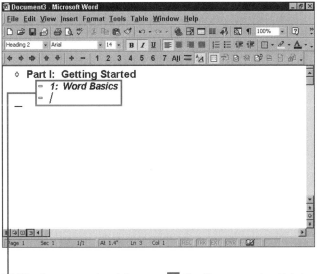

■ Word creates a level-2 heading, assigns the Heading 2 style, and creates another paragraph with the same style.

5 Continue pressing Tab to assign the appropriate heading levels. Press Shift+Tab to back up a level.

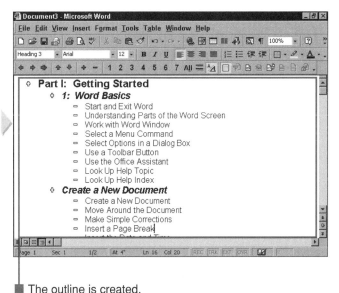

■ The outline is created.

VIEW AN OUTLINE

The benefit of creating an outline is that you have so much control over viewing and organizing a document. You can view, for instance, all the top-level headings and check them for consistency. You can expand a particular branch of an outline to work on the content of that section.

Any section that contains subheadings is indicated with a plus sign. You can view more of an outline or less. The easiest way to make a change is to use the toolbar buttons, and you have two basic ways to make a change.

One method is to click the Show Heading button for the level you want. For instance, click the Show Heading 2 button to show all Heading 2 and higher levels in the outline. Click the All button to show all text in the outline.

Another method is to select a particular branch of an outline and then click the Expand or Collapse button to expand (show subheadings) or collapse (hide lower level headings) the outline.

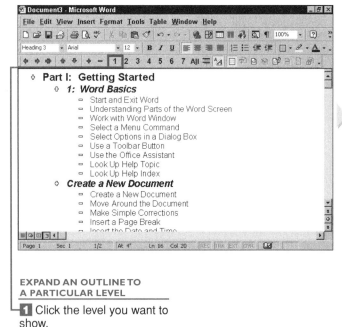

EXPAND AN OUTLINE TO A PARTICULAR LEVEL

1 Click the level you want to show.

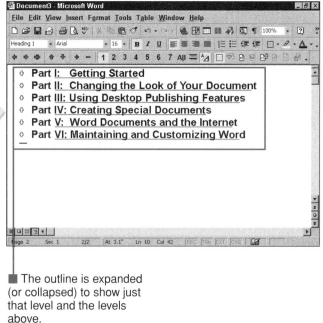

■ The outline is expanded (or collapsed) to show just that level and the levels above.

What's another method for viewing the overall organization of a document?

 You can also use the Document Map feature, as covered in Chapter 2. With the Document Map, you see the headings in the document in a separate document pane (as well as other text). You can navigate from one section to another using this mini-outline.

I clicked a button, but nothing happened. Why?

 If you try to expand a branch that is already expanded, nothing will happen. The same is true if you try to display more levels than you have. If you have just three levels, nothing changes if you click Show Heading 4, 5, 6, or 7.

Can I make changes to the outline?

 Yes. You can edit an outline. For instance, you can demote or promote the headings. You can also rearrange them. Word moves the entire section of the document when you make a change. See the next section, "Reorganize an Outline."

What happens to my outline if I change to Normal view?

 Nothing. The outline remains, only you don't see the indented levels or the Outline toolbar. You do see the headings as well as the formatting for that heading. (Each heading style has a different set of formatting options.)

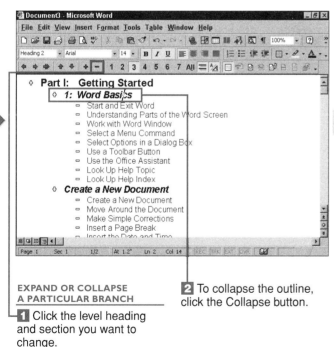

EXPAND OR COLLAPSE A PARTICULAR BRANCH

1 Click the level heading and section you want to change.

2 To collapse the outline, click the Collapse button.

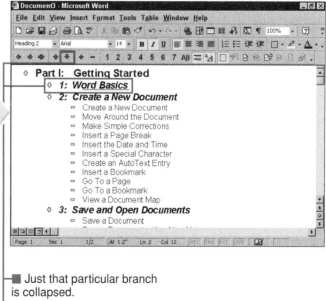

■ Just that particular branch is collapsed.

3 To expand the branch, click the Expand button.

REORGANIZE AN OUTLINE

The reason you create an outline is to help your writing. You may want to check the organization to make sure the document flows logically. One change you may want to make is to rearrange the order of some sections. It's simple to move a section to another location. Word moves not only the heading, but any subordinate text as well (any headings or body text beneath that heading).

You may also check the consistency of the headings and sections. For instance, are all level-2 headings the same in importance? Do you need to make adjustments? If necessary, you can promote or demote headings so they have the proper place in the overall structure. When you make this type of change, Word adjusts just that heading.

To make either of these changes, use the buttons on the Outline toolbar.

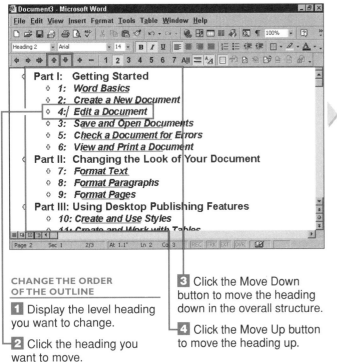

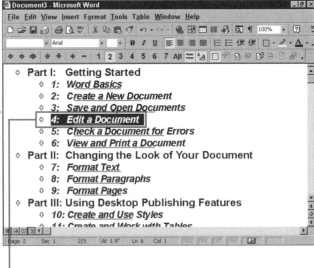

CHANGE THE ORDER OF THE OUTLINE

1 Display the level heading you want to change.

2 Click the heading you want to move.

3 Click the Move Down button to move the heading down in the overall structure.

4 Click the Move Up button to move the heading up.

■ The heading (and all its associated subheadings and text) are moved.

Can I change several headings at once?

Yes. To do so, simply select the headings you want to change. Then click the Demote or Promote button to assign a lower (Demote) or higher (Promote) level.

What level should I use for regular text?

For text that is part of the document itself (not a heading), change that level to Body Text. Word includes a button for this level next to the Promote and Demote buttons so you can quickly assign the Body Text level.

I thought I rearranged the outline, but the entire section was not moved. What happened?

If you are viewing just the headings, Word will move the heading and all associated text. If you are viewing the heading and lower headings, Word moves just the selected item. To move them all, change the view or select the headings you want to move.

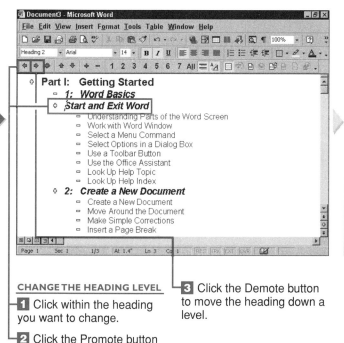

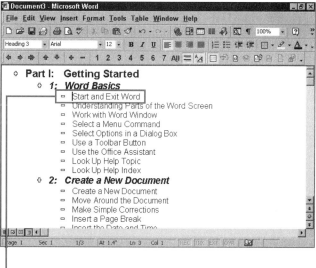

CHANGE THE HEADING LEVEL

1 Click within the heading you want to change.

2 Click the Promote button to move the heading up a level.

3 Click the Demote button to move the heading down a level.

■ That heading is adjusted.

FORMAT AN OUTLINE

You can make changes to any of the text in an outline. If you want to use a different look for the headings, the easiest way to do so is to modify the style. Modify the style once, and Word updates all text formatted with that style. You can select a different font, alignment, font size, style, border, and so on.

As another formatting change, you can add numbers to your headings. Word does not automatically number an outline (although you can type numbers when you create an outline). If you don't want to bother with typing the numbers, you can assign numbers to each level using the Bullets and Numbering command. You can select from several numbering styles, specifically suited for outlines.

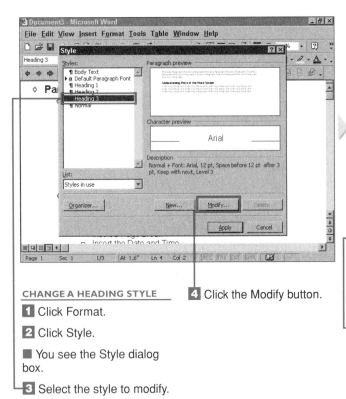

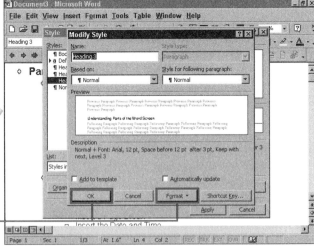

CHANGE A HEADING STYLE

1 Click Format.

2 Click Style.

■ You see the Style dialog box.

3 Select the style to modify.

4 Click the Modify button.

■ You see the Modify Style dialog box.

5 Make any changes (click the Format button to change various formats) and click OK.

6 Click Close to close the Style dialog box.

TIPS

How do I modify styles?

When you click the Modify button, you can then click the Format button and select any of the formatting commands, such as Paragraph, Font, and so on. Make your selections in the dialog box that appears and then click OK. For more information on styles, see Chapter 10.

What if I want to use a custom numbering style?

To use a custom numbering style, click the Customize button. Then select the number format for each level in the document. You can also select the number position and text position. The preview gives you an idea of how your selections will affect the headings.

What are other ways to number lines?

You can use the Numbering tab to add lines to the paragraphs. Chapter 8 covers adding paragraph numbers. As another alternative, you can insert a field code that is automatically numbered. And you can add line numbers. Chapter 19 covers both of these features.

How do I undo the numbering?

Click the Undo button or select Edit ⇨ Undo. If you cannot undo the change, select the entire outline (or just the lines where you want to remove numbers). Then click Format ⇨ Bullets and Numbering. Click the Outline Numbered tab and select None as the style. Click OK.

CREATING SPECIAL DOCUMENTS

IV

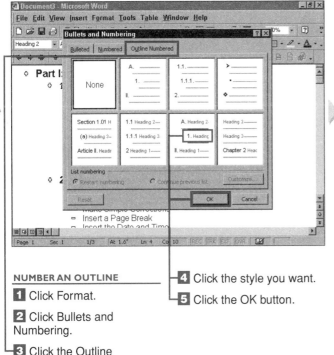

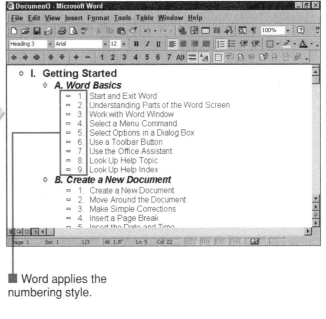

NUMBER AN OUTLINE

1 Click Format.

2 Click Bullets and Numbering.

3 Click the Outline Numbered tab.

4 Click the style you want.

5 Click the OK button.

■ Word applies the numbering style.

ADDING DOCUMENT REFERENCES

Word is great for simple documents such as memos and letters, as well as complex documents such as manuscripts, reports, papers, contracts, and scripts. For these longer documents, you may want to use some document reference features, as covered in this chapter.

Add Footnotes or Endnotes

In any type of research, you often need to refer to your source, whether you are creating a simple term paper or a paper on biochemical research. You can include two types of references in your document: footnotes or endnotes.

Footnotes are printed at the bottom of the page that has the reference. Endnotes are printed on a separate page (or pages) at the end of the document. When you use Word to create either, it takes care of numbering and setting up pages for proper printing.

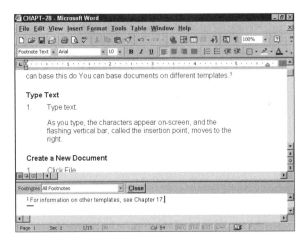

Create a Table of Contents

A table of contents helps your audience not only find a particular topic but also get an idea of a document's overall content and structure. You don't have to manually type a table of contents. Instead, have Word generate one for you, including headings and page numbers. If you make a change, you can even update the table.

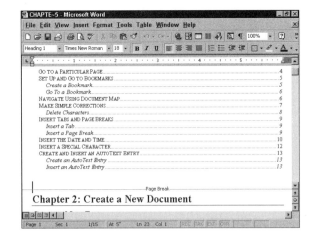

Create an Index

When creating a long document, in addition to a table of contents, you may want to include an index to help your reader find a particular topic. You can mark the terms you want to include and then have Word compile the index, including the appropriate references and page numbers.

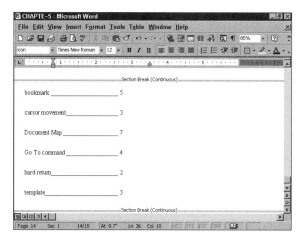

Use Other References

As another reference, you may want to number the lines in your document (scripts are sometimes numbered). Or maybe you want to number a legal contract. Line numbers help your reader refer to a particular place in a document.

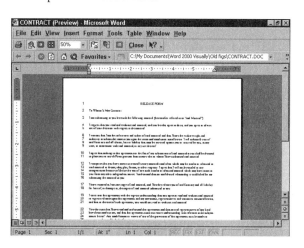

You can also include other references, including field codes for numbers and document information.

INSERT A FOOTNOTE

If you need to cite a reference or clarify a particular point, you may want to use footnotes. You can insert a footnote reference (called the *note reference mark*) and then type the reference or note text.

Footnotes are printed at the bottom of the page. Word inserts the footnote number in the text and in the note itself. Word also takes care of setting up the page so that there's room to print the footnote.

Not only does Word make it easy to set up a page for footnotes, but it also takes care of numbering. If you make a change — such as deleting a footnote — Word updates the numbering.

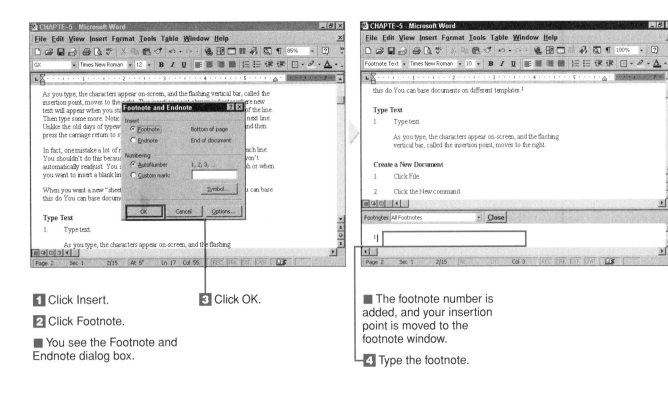

1 Click Insert.

2 Click Footnote.

■ You see the Footnote and Endnote dialog box.

3 Click OK.

■ The footnote number is added, and your insertion point is moved to the footnote window.

4 Type the footnote.

How are footnotes numbered?

Word automatically numbers footnotes. If you want to use a custom mark, choose this option and then click the Symbol button. Choose the symbol you want to use and then click OK.

How can I see what the footnote will look like on the page?

If you want to see how the footnote will appear, preview the page using File ➪ Print Preview. You can see how Word adjusts the page to make room for the footnote.

How long can I make the footnote?

You can type as much text as you want. You can even press Enter to include more than one paragraph in the footnote. If the text doesn't fit, Word moves some of it to the next page.

Can I format the text?

Yes. You can select the text to make it bold, change the font, and so on. If you want to change some of the text, make the change individually. If you want to change all the footnotes, update the style.

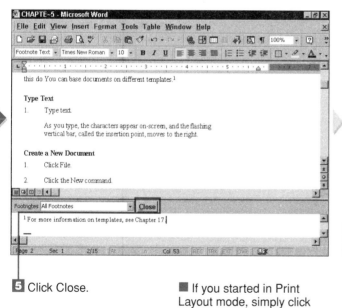

5 Click Close.

■ If you started in Print Layout mode, simply click the main part of the document.

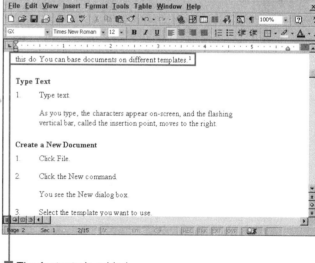

■ The footnote is added.

INSERT AN ENDNOTE

For most formal papers, you have certain guidelines for document structure. You also may receive instruction on how to handle sources. Some instructors or publishers, for instance, may want footnotes. Others may prefer endnotes.

Both serve the same purpose: they enable you to provide additional notes or source information. The difference is how they appear in a document.

Endnotes print at the end of a document. As with footnotes, endnotes are numbered with both a text reference and then the matching note number and note. The endnotes print on the last page of a document, with a separator line above each one.

Note that you can insert a page break if you want endnotes to print on a separate page.

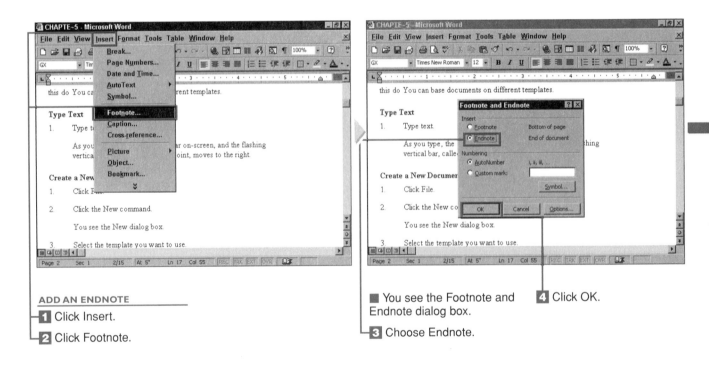

ADD AN ENDNOTE

1 Click Insert.

2 Click Footnote.

■ You see the Footnote and Endnote dialog box.

3 Choose Endnote.

4 Click OK.

TIPS

I changed my mind and want endnotes instead of footnotes. Can I make a change?

 Yes. You can convert footnotes to endnotes and vice versa. To do so, click the Options button in the Footnote and Endnote dialog box. Then click the Convert button.

How do I view endnotes?

View endnotes by previewing the document. Choose File ⇨ Print Preview or click the Preview button on the toolbar.

Can I use both footnotes and endnotes?

 Yes. You may want to use, as online help mentions, footnotes for descriptive or explanatory notes and endnotes to cite sources. Just create both sets. That is, insert the footnotes and then insert the endnotes. They are numbered separately.

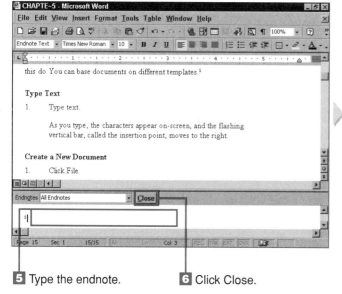

5 Type the endnote.   **6** Click Close.

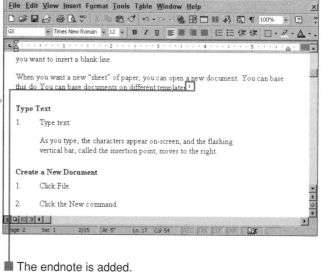

■ The endnote is added.

EDIT A FOOTNOTE OR ENDNOTE

As you edit your document, you may need to make a change to a footnote or endnote. Perhaps you need to add clarification. Or maybe you need to change a source.

In any case, you can easily view and edit footnotes or endnotes. As a shortcut for viewing note text, put the pointer over the reference number. The note appears at the bottom of the page.

To make a change, display the footnote pane and then edit the text accordingly.

If you have several footnotes, you can quickly move to a particular footnote or endnote using the Go To command.

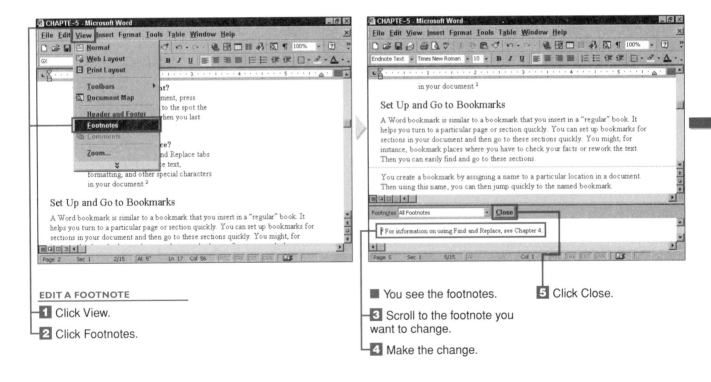

EDIT A FOOTNOTE

1 Click View.

2 Click Footnotes.

■ You see the footnotes.

3 Scroll to the footnote you want to change.

4 Make the change.

5 Click Close.

What's a shortcut for going to the footnote text?

Double-click the footnote reference mark to jump to the footnote text. Double-click the footnote reference in the footnote text to go to the text reference.

Can I change how footnotes appear?

Yes. You can make changes to the separator lines that appear, as well as the footnote placement. See the section "Format Footnotes" later in this chapter.

How do I delete a footnote?

Select the reference number in the text and press Delete. The reference and the footnote itself are deleted. If you simply delete the text, the footnote reference remains. You must delete the reference in the text.

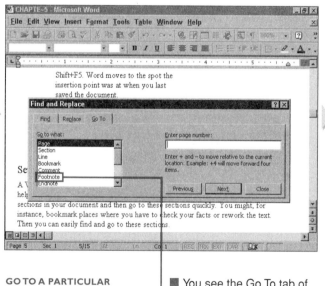

GO TO A PARTICULAR FOOTNOTE

1 Click Edit.

2 Click Go To.

■ You see the Go To tab of the Find and Replace dialog box.

3 Choose Footnote.

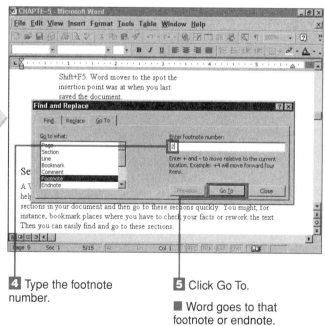

4 Type the footnote number.

5 Click Go To.

■ Word goes to that footnote or endnote.

FORMAT FOOTNOTES

If you like how the footnotes print, then you don't need to make a change. If you want, though, you can make a change to footnote placement and numbering. Choose to place footnotes at the bottom of the pages or directly below text.

You can choose a number format from several different numbering styles. Word starts numbering with 1, but you can set a different starting number and choose whether numbering is continuous, restarts each section, or restarts each page.

By default, Word uses a separator line. You can edit this line and use something different (or nothing at all).

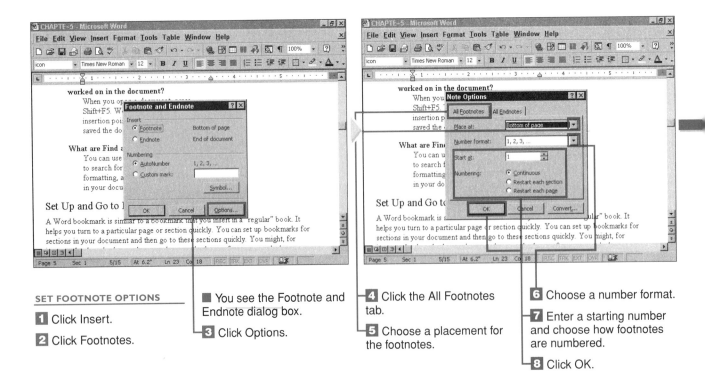

SET FOOTNOTE OPTIONS

1 Click Insert.

2 Click Footnotes.

■ You see the Footnote and Endnote dialog box.

3 Click Options.

4 Click the All Footnotes tab.

5 Choose a placement for the footnotes.

6 Choose a number format.

7 Enter a starting number and choose how footnotes are numbered.

8 Click OK.

How do I use a different symbol for the footnote reference?

In the Footnote and Endnote dialog box, choose Custom mark. Then click the Symbol button. Choose the symbol you want and click OK.

How is the text formatted?

Word applies the style Footnote Text to the note text and Footnote Reference to the reference number. You can individually format text or modify the style.

What if I don't want to use a separator line?

If you don't want to use a separator line, select it and press Delete.

What are continuation lines?

If a footnote doesn't fit on a page, Word uses a different line length for the separator. You can edit this line as well as the text that appears for the continued footnote.

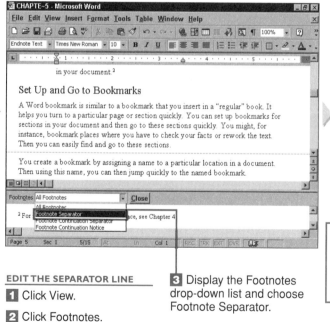

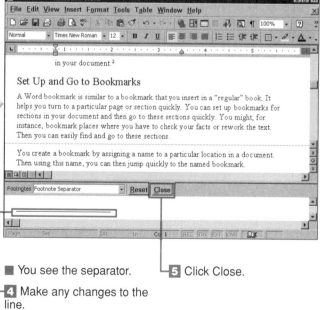

EDIT THE SEPARATOR LINE

1 Click View.

2 Click Footnotes.

■ You see the footnote pane.

3 Display the Footnotes drop-down list and choose Footnote Separator.

■ You see the separator.

4 Make any changes to the line.

5 Click Close.

FORMAT ENDNOTES

As with footnotes, you can set other options for how endnotes print. First, you can choose where they print: at the end of the document or at the end of each section.

Second, you can choose a number format. Word uses lowercase Roman numerals (i, ii, iii). This numbering style, for one thing, helps you distinguish between footnotes and endnotes. However, you can choose another style. You may want to use letters or some other character.

Finally, you can enter the starting number and choose whether numbering is continuous or restarts at each section.

Word uses the same separator line to mark the start of an endnote. You can edit this line and use something different (or nothing at all).

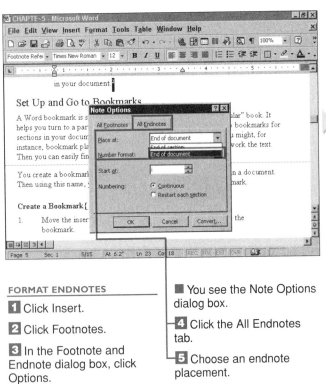

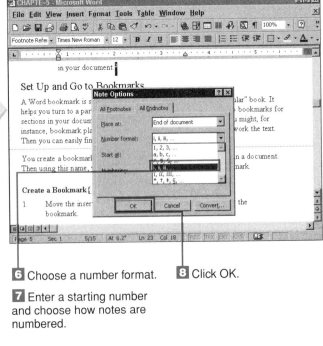

FORMAT ENDNOTES

1 Click Insert.

2 Click Footnotes.

3 In the Footnote and Endnote dialog box, click Options.

■ You see the Note Options dialog box.

4 Click the All Endnotes tab.

5 Choose an endnote placement.

6 Choose a number format.

7 Enter a starting number and choose how notes are numbered.

8 Click OK.

CREATING SPECIAL DOCUMENTS

What does the separator line contain?

 The separator line is just a row of dashes. You can type another character, such as an asterisk.

How do I go back to the original separator line?

 Click the Reset button in the endnote pane to go back to the original separator line.

How is endnote text formatted?

 Endnotes are formatted with the selections associated with the Endnote Text style. You can modify this style to change the formatting. You can also make individual changes to endnotes — that is, format specific text according to your preferences.

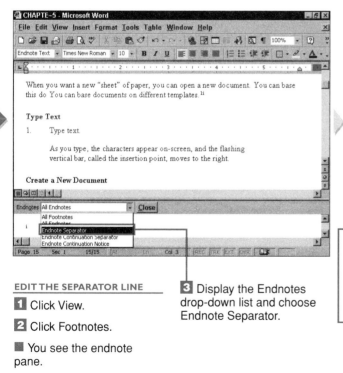

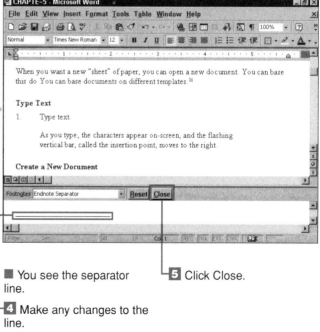

EDIT THE SEPARATOR LINE

1 Click View.

2 Click Footnotes.

■ You see the endnote pane.

3 Display the Endnotes drop-down list and choose Endnote Separator.

■ You see the separator line.

4 Make any changes to the line.

5 Click Close.

CREATE A TABLE OF CONTENTS

In a long document, you may want to include a table of contents for your reader. A table of contents can serve two purposes. First, it can help your reader find a particular section in a document. A table of contents can list main headings, subheadings, and page numbers. Second, a table of contents can give your reader an overall view of document content and structure.

The easiest way to create a table of contents is to use Word's heading styles (Heading 1, Heading 2, and so on) to organize a document and format headings. Then Word can automatically use these headings for table of contents entries. If you use other styles, you can generate a table of contents, but you have to go through the process of specifying which style matches which head level.

Word includes the top three heading levels, but you can include more or fewer headings in a table of contents. You can also choose whether page numbers are included.

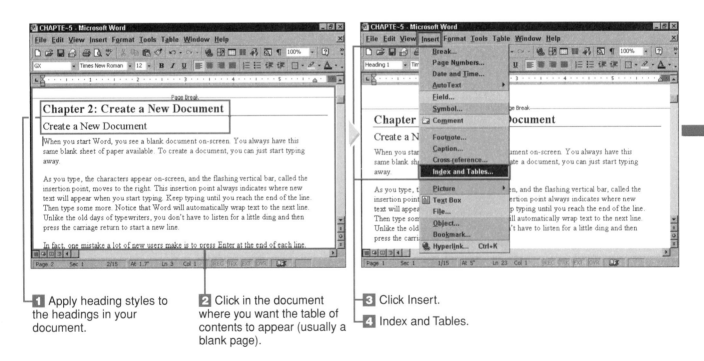

1 Apply heading styles to the headings in your document.

2 Click in the document where you want the table of contents to appear (usually a blank page).

3 Click Insert.

4 Index and Tables.

Can I edit the table of contents?

The text is composed of field codes, which you cannot directly edit. To make a change, edit the heading itself and then update the table of contents. Or convert the table of contents to regular text (select it and press Ctrl+Shift+F9) and then edit it. Keep in mind that once the table is converted to regular text, you cannot update the headings by changing a heading and updating the table.

How do I update a table of contents?

Select the table of contents and press F9. Choose to update the entire table or just the page numbers. Then click OK.

What if I don't use such styles as Heading 1, 2, and so on?

You can build a table of contents from the styles you used. Click the Options button on the Table of Contents tab in the Index and Tables dialog box. You see a list of available styles. Next to each style, enter the TOC level for that style. Click OK.

What other kinds of tables can I insert?

You can insert a table of figures or a table of authorities. Consult online help for more information on these table references.

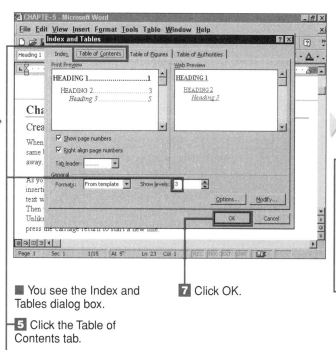

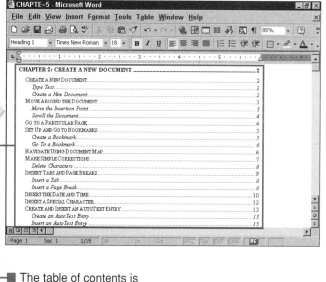

■ You see the Index and Tables dialog box.

5 Click the Table of Contents tab.

6 Choose the number of levels to include.

7 Click OK.

■ The table of contents is added.

FORMAT A TABLE OF CONTENTS

Word uses the default style from the template for table of contents entries. Usually page numbers are included, are right-aligned, and have a dot leader. You can change any of these options. For instance, you don't have to include page numbers. Or you may want a different tab leader.

If you want an entirely different look for your table of

contents, use another set of formats. If you just want a different look for some of the heading levels, consider modifying the styles. (Each table of contents heading level has its own style. Modify the style to change the formatting of the heading in the table.)

If you want to use the heading styles, but don't like how they look, remember that you can

apply them and modify these styles as well, selecting any formatting you want. Use the Style dialog box instead of making changes manually (as covered here).

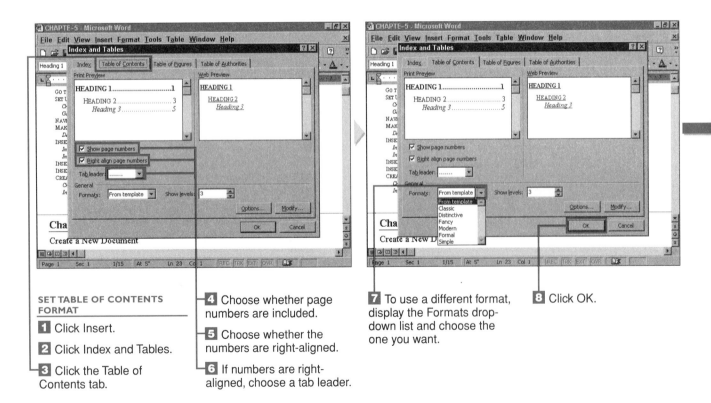

SET TABLE OF CONTENTS FORMAT

1 Click Insert.

2 Click Index and Tables.

3 Click the Table of Contents tab.

4 Choose whether page numbers are included.

5 Choose whether the numbers are right-aligned.

6 If numbers are right-aligned, choose a tab leader.

7 To use a different format, display the Formats drop-down list and choose the one you want.

8 Click OK.

TIPS

What determines the styles used for the table of contents?

The template determines the styles used for the table of contents. You can choose another template to use its table of contents styles. See Chapter 17 for more information on applying a different template.

Which format is best?

It depends on your personal preference and the type of document. Try to pick a style that matches the content.

How do I delete a table of contents?

Select the table of contents and press Delete.

I chose a different format, but now I can't modify the style. Why not?

If you choose a format, the heading styles no longer apply; therefore, the Modify button is not available. To update the look using this method, you must use the formats from the template.

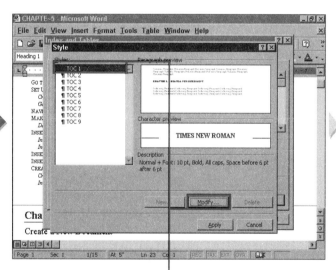

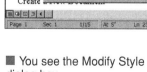

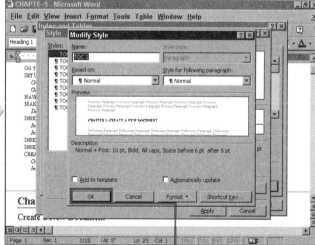

MODIFY THE STYLES USED FOR THE TABLE OF CONTENTS

1 Click Insert.

2 Click Index and Tables.

3 Click the Table of Contents tab.

4 Click Modify.

■ You see the Style dialog box.

5 Pick the style you want to change.

6 Click Modify.

■ You see the Modify Style dialog box.

7 Make any changes to the formatting of the styles. Use the Format button to choose the appropriate Format command.

8 Click OK.

MARK AN INDEX ENTRY

Another type of reference to include in a document (especially a longer document) is an index. Creating an index is really a two-step process. For the first step, you mark the terms (or sections) to include in the index. When you mark a term, you enter the main entry and any subentry. Word notes the location of the insertion point and uses this place for the page reference.

When you mark an entry, you basically insert a hidden code. This code includes XE to indicate "index" and also includes the main entry you typed as the index reference. When field codes are displayed, you see these codes in the document. (They do not print.)

After you mark the first entry, the dialog box remains open so you can continue to mark other entries. Move the insertion point

to each term or section you want to mark and type the index entry for that section. You have to mark each entry you want to include. (Creating an index is a more involved process than creating a table of contents.)

After all entries are marked, you can generate the index. (Generating an index is covered in the section "Compile an Index.")

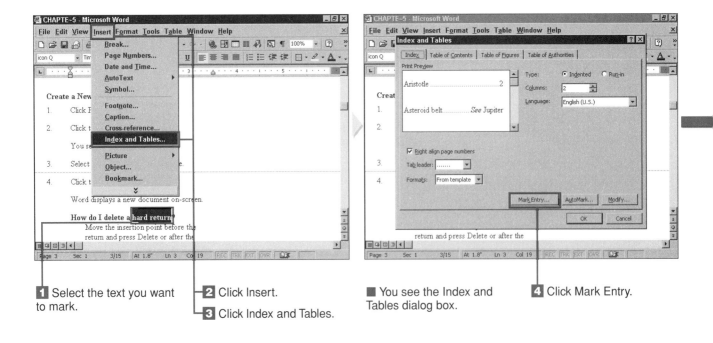

1 Select the text you want to mark.

2 Click Insert.

3 Click Index and Tables.

■ You see the Index and Tables dialog box.

4 Click Mark Entry.

TIPS

Why did the screen change?

When you work with index entries, Word displays special characters such as paragraph marks, spaces, tabs, and field codes. Turn these off by clicking Show/Hide ¶ on the toolbar.

How do I edit an index entry?

You can click within the index code to make a change. You can update the main entry. To delete an index entry, select the entire code and press Delete.

What options can I use when I mark an entry?

You can choose to insert a cross reference (*See also*). You can also choose to reference a page range.

Can I change how page numbers appear?

Yes. For instance, maybe you want to boldface a key entry. To change the page number format, check Bold or Italic when you mark the index entry.

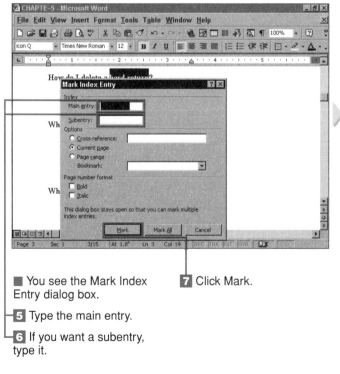

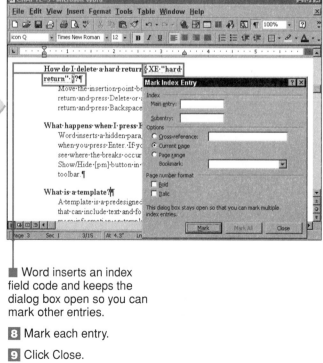

■ You see the Mark Index Entry dialog box.

5 Type the main entry.

6 If you want a subentry, type it.

7 Click Mark.

■ Word inserts an index field code and keeps the dialog box open so you can mark other entries.

8 Mark each entry.

9 Click Close.

COMPILE AN INDEX

After you mark all the references for the index, you can compile it. Word finds the references and pulls the text you entered for the main entries and subentries, as well as the relevant page numbers, creating an index.

You can choose how an index prints. Choose the number of columns, the placement of the page numbers, and the tab leader (if page numbers are right-aligned).

When you create an index, Word creates a new section and places the index in that section. You can make any changes to this section. (See Chapter 12 for more information on columns and sections.)

If you make a change (such as adding other terms, deleting terms, or changing the page numbers), you need to update the index. Word recompiles it and makes any adjustments.

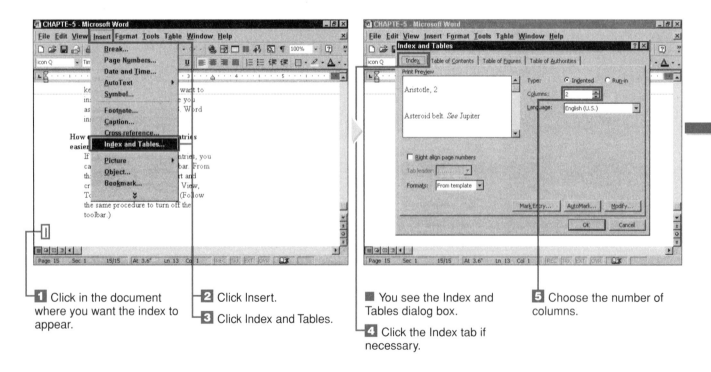

1 Click in the document where you want the index to appear.

2 Click Insert.

3 Click Index and Tables.

■ You see the Index and Tables dialog box.

4 Click the Index tab if necessary.

5 Choose the number of columns.

TIPS

How do I update an index if I add terms?

Select the entire index and then press F9.

What options can I change for the index look?

You can select to right align page numbers by checking the Right align page numbers checkbox. You can choose whether subentries are indented (the default) or run-in with the main entry.

How do I delete an index?

To delete an index, select it and press Delete.

Can I edit an index?

Yes. You can edit index entries, but if you manually edit the index, index codes are not updated. It's a better idea to edit the codes themselves by displaying the hidden text and editing the index entries.

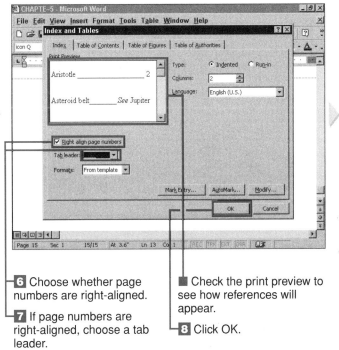

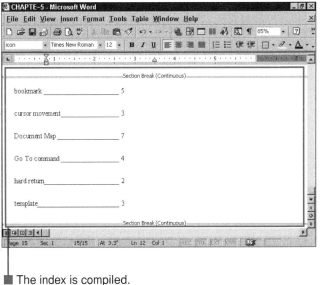

■6 Choose whether page numbers are right-aligned.

■7 If page numbers are right-aligned, choose a tab leader.

■ Check the print preview to see how references will appear.

■8 Click OK.

■ The index is compiled.

FORMAT AN INDEX

As with a table of contents, you can choose how an index appears. You can make changes in several ways.

First, if you don't like the overall look, choose a different format for the index. You can choose from several predefined formats.

Second, if you like the overall style but want to make minor adjustments, you can update the style. Word applies index styles to each index entry. Modify a style to change the appearance of the index itself.

Another option is to format the index section. Word creates the index in a separate section, which you can format. For more information on sections, see Chapter 12.

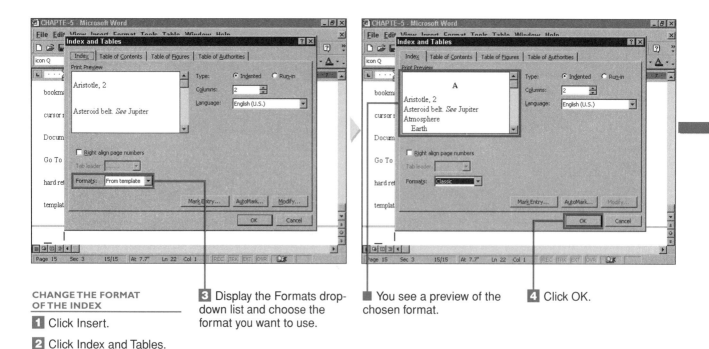

CHANGE THE FORMAT OF THE INDEX

1 Click Insert.

2 Click Index and Tables.

3 Display the Formats drop-down list and choose the format you want to use.

■ You see a preview of the chosen format.

4 Click OK.

TIPS

What determines the styles used for an index?

The template determines the styles used for an index. You can apply a different template or copy other index styles, as covered in Chapter 17.

What formats are available?

You can choose classic, distinctive, centered, or format. Check Print Preview to see how each one looks.

What type of changes can I make to a style?

You can change the font, the font size, the color, and the style. You can use a different paragraph format (indent, border, and so on). You can basically make any change to the look of the index that you want. For more information on styles, see Chapter 10.

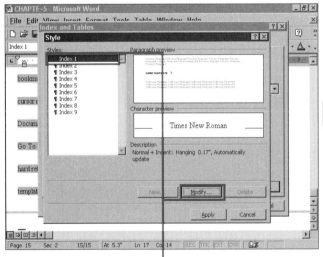

MODIFY THE STYLES USED FOR THE INDEX

1 Click Insert.

2 Click Index and Tables.

3 Click Modify.

■ You see the Style dialog box.

4 Choose the index style you want to change.

5 Click Modify.

■ You see the Modify Style dialog box.

6 Make any changes.

7 Click OK.

CREATE AN AUTOSUMMARY

Some documents include an executive summary . This summary may highlight key points or outline the overall structure of the document. You can manually create a summary. Or have Word create one for you using AutoSummary.

With AutoSummary, Word reviews the text in your document and then creates a summary. The summary is created by analyzing the words used most frequently and then honing in on the sentences with these words.

You can choose from several summary styles, including highlighting key points or creating an abstract. You can choose to create a new document and place a summary there. As a final option, you can choose to hide everything but the summary. (The original document is still there, it's just hidden.)

When you create a summary, you choose its type as well as its length.

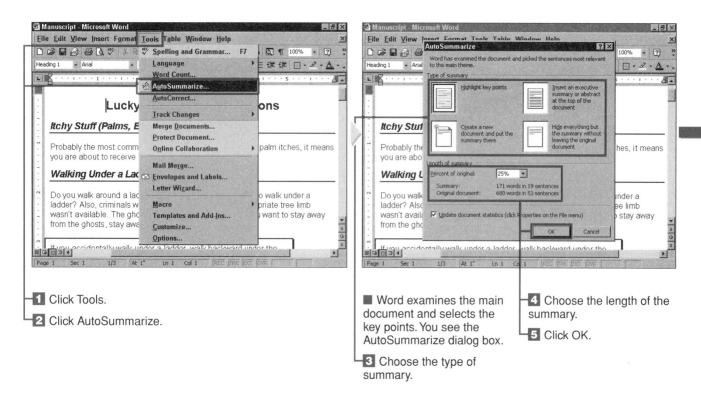

1 Click Tools.

2 Click AutoSummarize.

■ Word examines the main document and selects the key points. You see the AutoSummarize dialog box.

3 Choose the type of summary.

4 Choose the length of the summary.

5 Click OK.

What if the summary doesn't make sense?

You may need to edit the summary to include the points you want to make. Consider the summary as a starting place, not as something that's ready to go.

I think text disappeared in my document. What happened?

You can hide all the text and show just the summary. Click the Highlight/Show Only Summary button on the AutoSummarize toolbar.

How do I make a change to what is summarized?

Use the AutoSummarize toolbar to change the size of the summary — it is measured as a percentage of the full document size. Choose a higher percentage to show a larger summary. Choose a lower percentage to include less in a summary.

How do I undo a summary?

Click Undo or delete the summary and start over.

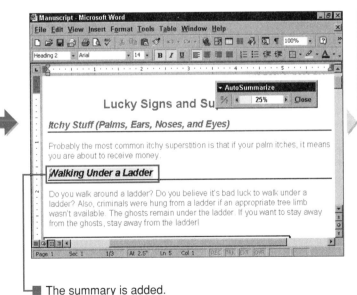

■ The summary is added.

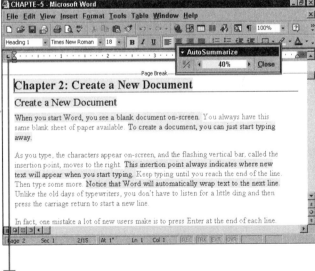

6 Use the AutoSummarize toolbar to change the summary (for the highlighted version).

INSERT DOCUMENT INFORMATION

Word keeps track of information about a document, including its file name, size, number of characters, author, and so on. In some documents, you may want to include this type of information. Rather than type it manually, insert a field.

You can choose from several fields, including author, comments, file name, file size, keywords, and others. When Word inserts a field code, what you see is the actual information. For instance, if you choose file name, Word uses the name of the file. For instance, I often include

the document file name in the header or footer so my editor knows what file to use.

If you change the name of a file, update the field so Word uses the new file name. This is one reason why using field codes is better than manually typing text!

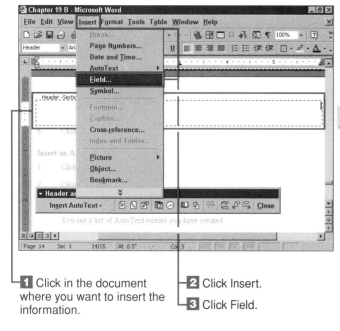

1 Click in the document where you want to insert the information.

2 Click Insert.

3 Click Field.

■ You see the Field dialog box.

4 In the Categories list, choose Document Information.

What options can I set?

Click the Options button to control the formatting of a field. You can determine the case (uppercase, lowercase, First capital, or Title case).

How do I insert the date and time?

Use the Insert ➪ Date and Time command to quickly insert the date and time. You can insert the date and time as regular text or a field. You can also choose Date and Time in the Categories list to pick dates and times for the creation, print, and save dates, as well as the current date and time.

What is user information?

Choose User Information to insert the User Address, User Initials, or User Name. This information is pulled from the Tools ➪ Options ➪ User Info tab.

Where can I find more information on mail merge?

Use mail merge codes to create a more sophisticated type of mail merge (where you are prompted for information, for instance). Mail merge is the topic of Chapter 16. Use online help for more information on mail-merge field codes.

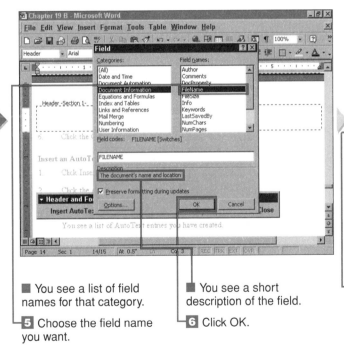

■ You see a list of field names for that category.

5 Choose the field name you want.

■ You see a short description of the field.

6 Click OK.

■ The field is inserted in the document (here, the file name is inserted in the document header).

INSERT NUMBER FIELDS

Another type of field to investigate is numbering fields. These fields automatically number items. You can create a task list or a product list, numbering the items. You can also include chapter numbers in a rough outline. If you delete one of the entries, the others are updated. If you add another number field, the others are updated.

Choose to insert automatic numbering, page numbering, section pages, legal numbering, and other types of number fields.

Some number fields are automatically numbered (and formatted). Others, such as SEQ (short for sequence), require a bookmark name. You can tell which field code format to use — it is listed in the Field dialog box.

1 Click where you want to insert the number field.

2 Click Insert.

3 Click Field.

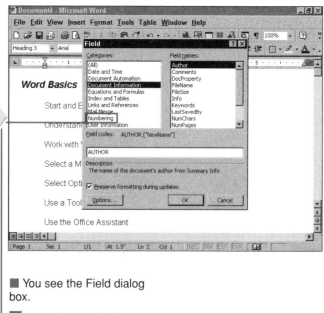

■ You see the Field dialog box.

4 In the Categories list, choose Numbering.

TIPS

How do I convert the code to regular text?

Select the field(s) and then press Ctrl+Shift+F9.

What other types of fields can I insert?

You can insert document automation fields, index and table fields, mail merge fields, links and references fields, and date and time fields. If you aren't sure what a particular field does, click the Help button in the dialog box and then click the entry with which you want help.

How do I update fields?

Select the field(s) you want to update. Then press F9. To delete a field, select the entire field and press Delete.

What about paragraph numbering?

You can use the Numbering button to number the paragraphs in a document. For information on this procedure, see Chapter 8.

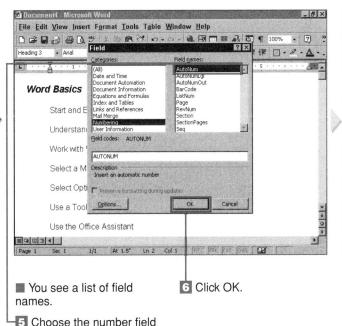

■ You see a list of field names.

5 Choose the number field you want.

6 Click OK.

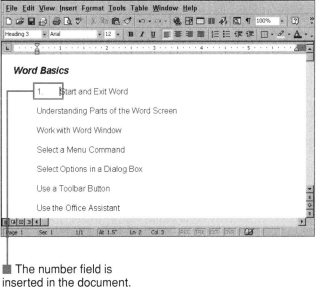

■ The number field is inserted in the document.

NUMBER LINES ON A PAGE

If you need a precise method of referring to part of a document, you may want to use line numbers. Contracts, for instance, sometimes include line numbers. Scripts and other documents where keeping track of location is important may include line numbers. You can say, "Refer to line 9," and your audience will know the exact place.

Word makes it easy to add line numbers. When you add the numbers, you can choose the starting number, the interval used to number the lines, and whether numbering is restarted at each page, restarted at each section, or is continuous.

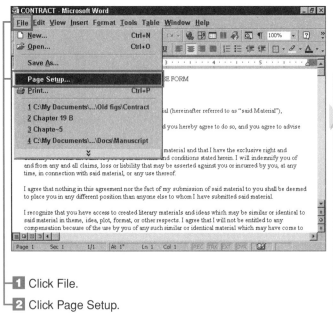

1 Click File.

2 Click Page Setup.

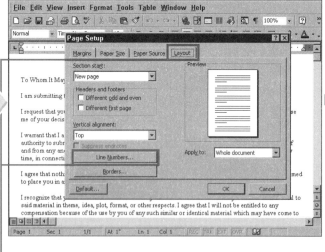

3 Click the Layout tab.

4 Click Line Numbers.

How do I undo line numbering?

Follow the same procedure, but uncheck Add line numbering in the Line Numbers dialog box.

Do I have to start with the number 1?

No. You can choose another starting number. Enter that number in the Start at spin box. You can also choose to restart numbering at each page or section. Or choose continuous numbering.

How do I number paragraphs?

When you add line numberings, each line is numbered. If you want just paragraphs numbered, use the Format ➪ Bullets and Numbering command. See Chapter 8 for more information.

What's another use for numbering?

You can create an outline and add numbers to it. See Chapter 18 for help with outlines.

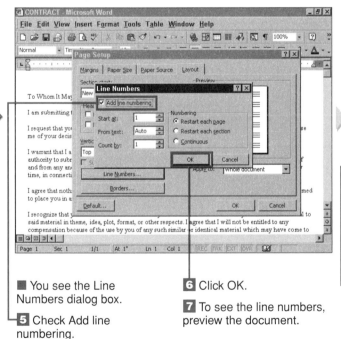

■ You see the Line Numbers dialog box.

5 Check Add line numbering.

6 Click OK.

7 To see the line numbers, preview the document.

■ The line numbers are added.

COLLABORATIVE EDITING

Document creation is often a collaboration. Take this book for instance. Even though the author's name is on the cover, many other people contributed and made changes to the book. The development editor read and made comments on content and structure. The technical reviewer read and made comments on technical inaccuracies. The copy editor worked with the words, phrases, and sentences to make the manuscript as readable as possible. And then the production staff took the text and figures and laid them out into a book.

I'll take the blame for any mistakes, but I have to credit everyone else for the many the good things about the book. If you also collaborate on projects, you may want to look into some of the powerful group editing features included with Word, as covered in this chapter.

Add Comments

Do you wish you could stick a little sticky note right on a particular page? Maybe to remind you to check something? Maybe to make a note to someone else to add his or her thoughts? You want a note, but you don't want that note as part of the text. If so, try adding comments. You can insert a hidden comment in the document text. These comments are displayed in a separate pane.

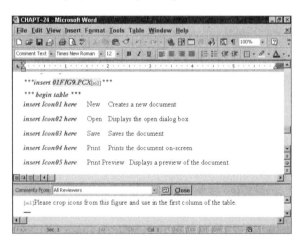

Save File Versions

If your work goes through multiple versions, you may want a way to keep track of these versions. If so, you can save each version of the file as you create it. All the versions are saved in the same file. If necessary, you can go back and view another version.

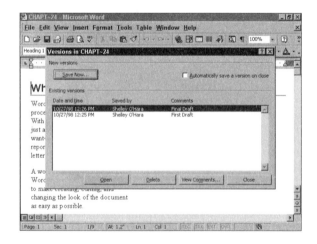

Mark Document Changes

If you want to know exactly what editing changes were made to your document, turn on Word's track changes feature. Any text that is deleted or added will be marked. You can then go through and review all the changes, selecting to accept or reject each change. Using this feature is a good way to see the results of an edit or review.

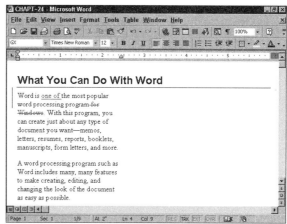

INSERT COMMENTS

If you want a way to insert a note without having that note become part of the document, you can insert a comment. You may insert a comment to yourself if you need to go back to review or check certain facts in the document. If you are working on a group project, you may want to insert a note to a coworker asking for an opinion or explaining additions or revisions.

Word keeps track of each added comment by inserting the user's initials and a number. Each comment is numbered sequentially.

By default the comments don't appear in the document, but you can choose to display and print them when needed.

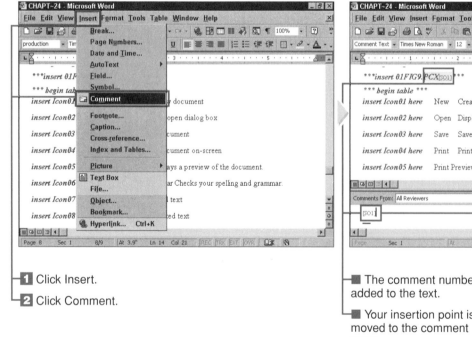

1 Click Insert.

2 Click Comment.

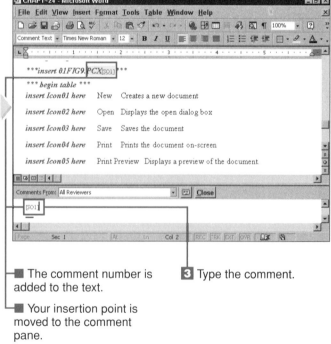

■ The comment number is added to the text.

■ Your insertion point is moved to the comment pane.

3 Type the comment.

TIPS

How can I call attention to text with a comment?

You may want to use highlighting to call attention to the text in question. Use the Highlight button to select the text and then insert the comment right after that text.

How do I delete a comment?

If you want to delete a comment, you can't delete the comment itself. You must delete the comment indicator in the text. View the comment and then select the comment indicator. Press Delete.

How are comments numbered?

Word automatically numbers the comments and adds the user initials so you can keep track of comments from multiple reviewers.

Can I record a sound comment?

Yes. If you have a microphone hooked up to your PC, you can record a message. Click the Record button in the Notes toolbar. Then use the Sound Recorder to create your message. Click Stop when you are done recording.

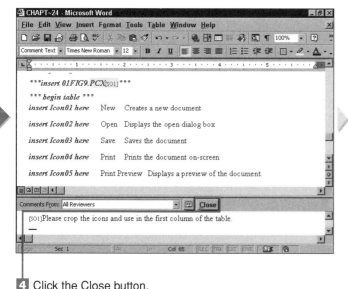

■4 Click the Close button.

■ The comment is added, and the word next to the insertion point is highlighted. You won t notice anything different about your document, but Word has added a hidden comment indicator in the text.

VIEW AND PRINT COMMENTS

C omments do not normally appear in the document, but you can display them in their own pane. You can then easily review each comment in the document. To move to other comments, you can scroll

through the comment pane, or you can use the buttons in the Comment toolbar to move to the next or previous comment.

The comments are not normally printed when you print the document. But if you want to

review hard copy with the comments, you can have Word print them. The comments are printed on a separate page. This page includes the page the comment appears on, the comment number, and the comment itself.

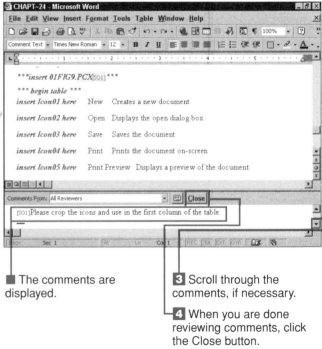

VIEW COMMENTS

1 Click View.

2 Click Comments.

■ The comments are displayed.

3 Scroll through the comments, if necessary.

4 When you are done reviewing comments, click the Close button.

How else can I print comments?

 You can also print the comments by opening the Print dialog box. Display the Print what drop-down list and then select Comments.

Select Tools ➪ Options and click the View tab. Check the Hidden text checkbox and then click OK.

How can I view comments from just one reviewer?

If multiple reviewers have added comments, you can choose to display comments from just one reviewer. (By default, comments from all reviewers are displayed.) In the Comment pane, display the Comments From drop-down list and select the particular reviewer.

 How else can I view comment indicators?

You can also view the comment by choosing to display hidden text. You can then double-click the comment indicator to display that comment.

Select Tools ➪ Options and click the View tab. Check the Hidden text checkbox and then click OK.

How can I move from comment to comment?

 You can use the toolbar buttons in the Reviewing toolbar to move to the next or previous comment. Click the appropriate button.

CREATING SPECIAL DOCUMENTS

IV

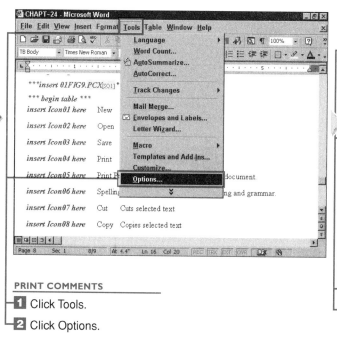

PRINT COMMENTS

1 Click Tools.

2 Click Options.

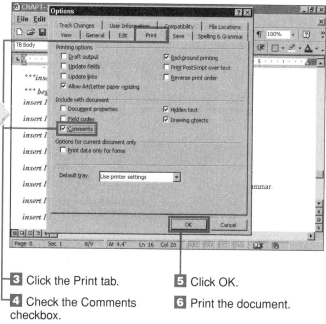

3 Click the Print tab.

4 Check the Comments checkbox.

5 Click OK.

6 Print the document.

421

SAVE FILE VERSIONS

Another feature handy for group editing or editing where the document may evolve through several stages is to save each version of a file. For example, an author might create a rough draft and save this version. The author may then make some changes and save the next version as Draft 2.

As another example, the author might save the first version. The editor then reviews and makes changes to this file, saving it as a different version. The final reviewer makes changes and saves yet another version.

All the versions are saved together in the same file, and you can easily open, delete, or view any of the versions.

Not only do versions help you keep track of when a change was made, but you can also go back to a previous version if necessary. You can track the progress or updates in a document by using this feature.

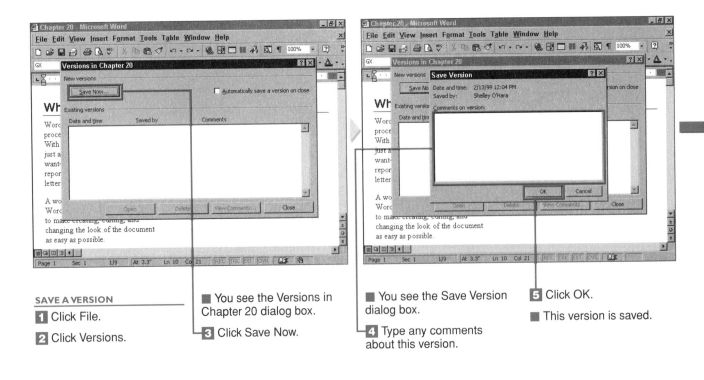

SAVE A VERSION

1 Click File.

2 Click Versions.

■ You see the Versions in Chapter 20 dialog box.

3 Click Save Now.

■ You see the Save Version dialog box.

4 Type any comments about this version.

5 Click OK.

■ This version is saved.

TIPS

Can I automatically save versions each time I close?

Yes. To do so, check the Automatically save a version on the Close button in the Versions dialog box.

How do I view additional information about a version?

Word displays the date and time for each version as well as the start of each comment. If you want, you can display the entire comment by clicking the document version and then clicking the View Comment button.

How can I save one of the versions?

After a version is saved, you cannot save it again using File, Save. If you want to save a version, use File ⇨ Save As and type a new name. This saves the document as a separate file.

Can I delete a version?

Yes. Display the document versions and click the one you want to delete. Click the Delete button. Confirm the deletion by clicking Yes.

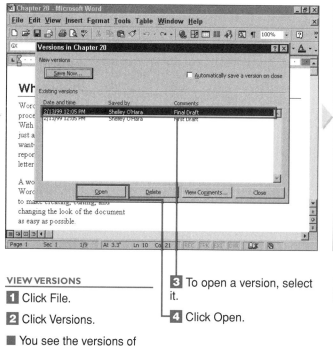

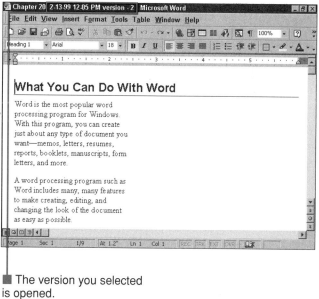

VIEW VERSIONS

1 Click File.

2 Click Versions.

■ You see the versions of the available document.

3 To open a version, select it.

4 Click Open.

■ The version you selected is opened.

TRACK DOCUMENT CHANGES

M ost of the editing features so far involve marking or noting the change or version. What if you want something more automatic? You can have Word track the changes.

You can turn on this feature (often called revision marking or something similar). Then Word will note every change made to the document — editing changes, deletions, new text, and so on.

Deleted text is marked with strikethrough. New text appears underlined. Both appear in a different color. Each time another review with track changes is on, another color is used. Word also adds a line to the left margin to indicate where changes have been made.

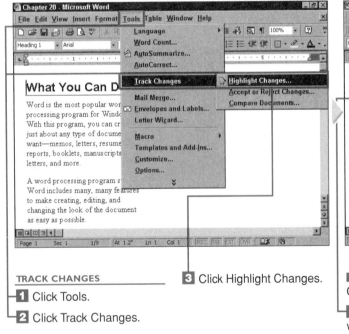

TRACK CHANGES

1 Click Tools.

2 Click Track Changes.

3 Click Highlight Changes.

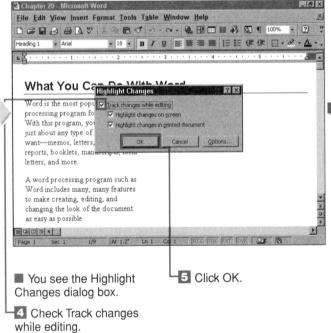

■ You see the Highlight Changes dialog box.

4 Check Track changes while editing.

5 Click OK.

Does Word note formatting changes?

No. You will not see any indication of formatting changes to a document by default. You can choose to have Word track these changes, though, by clicking the Options button in the Highlight Changes dialog box and setting the option to track changes to formatting.

How do I get rid of these tracking marks?

To get rid of the tracking marks once they have been made, you need to go through and accept or reject each change.

What options can I select for tracking changes?

If you don't like how changes are formatted, you can select a different way to mark the text. You can select how inserted text, deleted text, changed formatting, and changed lines are marked. Click the Options button in the Highlight Changes dialog box. Then make your selections for each change and click OK.

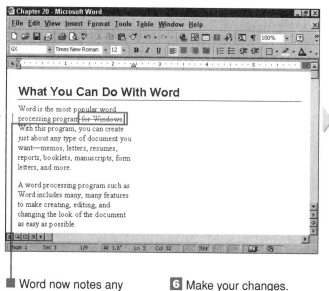

■ Word now notes any editing changes you make to your document.

6 Make your changes.

■ Notice that the margin is marked with a vertical bar when a change is made. Also, deleted text is marked with strikethrough, and new text is underlined.

CONTINUED ▶

TRACK DOCUMENT CHANGES CONTINUED

If someone goes to the trouble of marking changes, you will probably take the time to review the changes. You can have Word move from one change to another. You can then select to accept that change, reject the

change, or leave it marked. You can move through each change in the document, verifying the edits one by one.

You can also choose to accept all or reject all the revisions. If you do this, proofread your

document to make sure the edits are accurate. That is, do the text deletions make sense? Are the additions formatted properly?

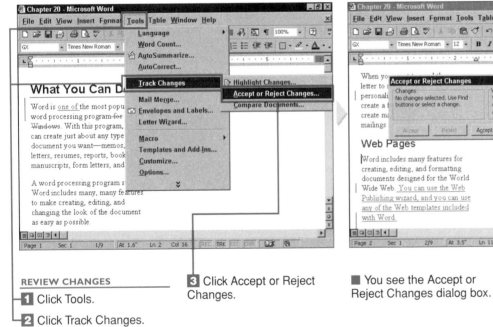

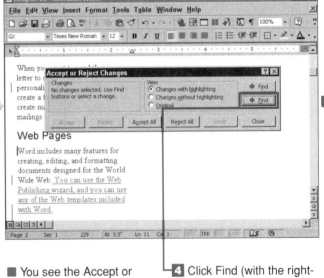

REVIEW CHANGES

1 Click Tools.

2 Click Track Changes.

3 Click Accept or Reject Changes.

■ You see the Accept or Reject Changes dialog box.

4 Click Find (with the right-pointing arrow) to move to the first change.

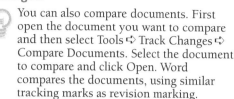

How do I undo an accepted change?

Click the Undo button if you change your mind and want to undo an accepted change.

Can I accept all the changes? Or reject them all?

Yes. To accept all the changes without going through them one by one, click the Accept All button. To reject all the changes, click Reject All.

Will these revision marks be printed?

Yes. When you print the document, the marked changes will be printed.

What's another method for tracking changes?

You can also compare documents. First open the document you want to compare and then select Tools ⇨ Track Changes ⇨ Compare Documents. Select the document to compare and click Open. Word compares the documents, using similar tracking marks as revision marking.

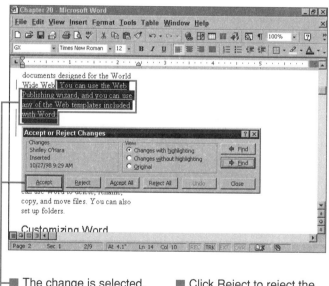

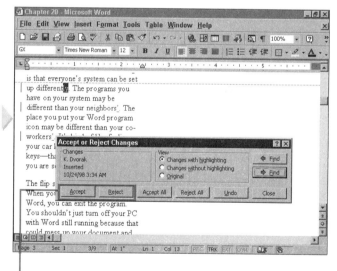

■ The change is selected.

5 Click Accept to accept this change.

■ Click Reject to reject the change.

■ Word updates the document accordingly and moves to the next change.

6 Continue accepting or rejecting changes until you check the entire document.

PROTECT A DOCUMENT

I f you've spent a lot of time getting a document just right, you may not want someone to come in and make changes to your work of art. You can protect a document from further changes in a couple of different ways.

You can assign a password so the person must type the password to even open the document.

You can assign a password so the person must type the password to modify the document.

And as another option, you can let a reviewer make changes, but only to tracked changes or comments. You can assign a password here also.

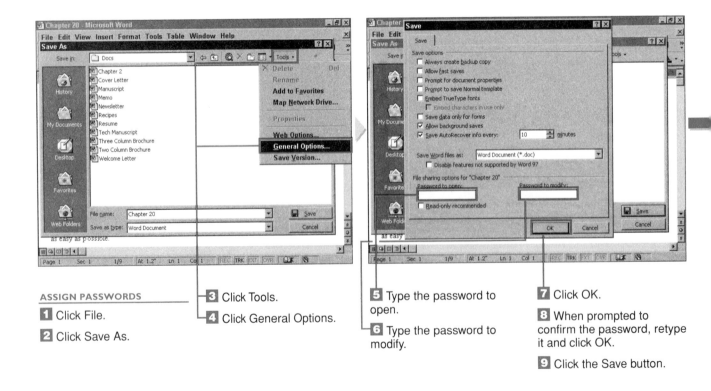

ASSIGN PASSWORDS

1 Click File.

2 Click Save As.

3 Click Tools.

4 Click General Options.

5 Type the password to open.

6 Type the password to modify.

7 Click OK.

8 When prompted to confirm the password, retype it and click OK.

9 Click the Save button.

What happens when I assign a password?

If you assign a password, Word displays the Password dialog box when you open or modify the file. Type the password and click OK.

How do I get rid of a password?

Follow the same procedure for assigning a password, but delete it from the Password text box.

What if I forget the password?

You may be out of luck because the password cannot be recovered. Try calling Microsoft Word Support and asking for help from one of the support staff.

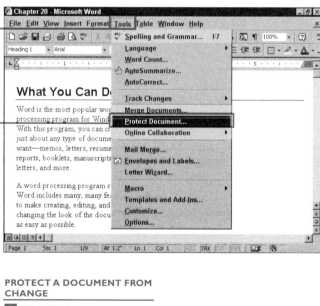

PROTECT A DOCUMENT FROM CHANGE

1 Click Tools.

2 Click Protect Document.

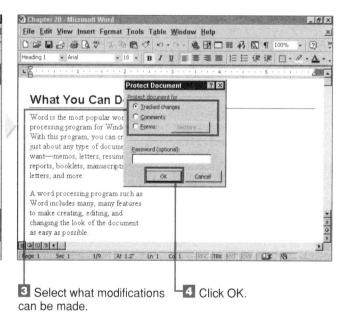

3 Select what modifications can be made.

4 Click OK.

INTEGRATING DIVERSE DATA

You probably use programs other than Word to create many types of documents. For instance, you or your office may have purchased Word as part of the Microsoft Office package. If so, you probably have access to several other programs. Or you may just have Excel, a spreadsheet program. Perhaps you have a separate database program.

As you get more skilled with Word, you may want to create a document that incorporates data from these other applications. For example, you may have created a budget worksheet or a chart showing sales growth. You may keep track of your clients using Access, a database program. You may also create presentations using PowerPoint, or want to use data from these other programs in your Word documents. That's the topic of this chapter.

You can use any of several methods to incorporate data from another program. Which one works best for you depends on the type of document you are creating and the results you want.

Copy Data

You can simply copy data from one application to another. For instance, you can copy an Excel worksheet and paste it as a table into Word. With this type of data sharing, the two files remain separate. If you change the worksheet in Excel, the data in Word is not updated. You also cannot use any of Excel's commands and features to modify the worksheet once it is placed in the Word document. Copy and pasting is the simplest type of data sharing.

Link Data

You can also insert a linked object. With this type of data sharing, the two files remain separate, but if you change the source file, the destination file is also updated. For instance, if you insert a linked Excel worksheet into Word and then change the worksheet, the worksheet is updated as well. Basically, the Word document includes only the location of the source file and pulls the data from this file. Use this method when you want to keep the data in sync.

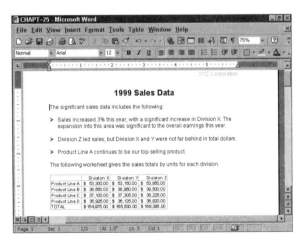

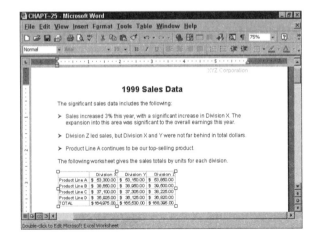

Embed Data

You can also insert an embedded object (from existing data or by creating a new embedded object). With this type of data sharing, the embedded object becomes part of the destination file. For instance, if you embed an Excel worksheet into Word, that worksheet becomes part of the Word file. You can use the Excel commands and features to modify the worksheet, but if you modify the original Excel worksheet, the embedded worksheet is not updated. Use this method when you don't need to keep the data in sync and when you want one file with both types of data.

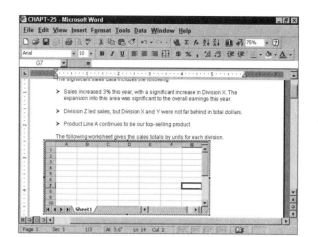

COPY DATA

Copying and pasting data is the simplest way to share data. Use this method when you don't need to update the information and when you want the data inserted as part of the Word document.

To start, go to the application that contains the data you want

to copy. Then select the data. If you aren't sure how to select data in that program, check the online help for that program. To switch among applications, click the application you want in the taskbar.

Depending on what you copy, you'll get different results. Data

from Excel worksheets and Access databases is pasted as a table. Pictures such as an Excel chart or a PowerPoint object are pasted as objects by default. The program pastes the data in an appropriate format.

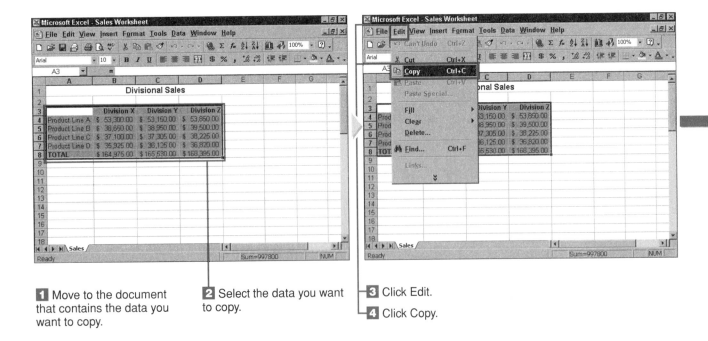

1 Move to the document that contains the data you want to copy.

2 Select the data you want to copy.

3 Click Edit.

4 Click Copy.

TIPS

What are some shortcuts?

You can also use the toolbar buttons for cut, copy, and paste. If you prefer the keyboard, use the keyboard shortcuts: Ctrl+X for cut, Ctrl+V for paste, and Ctrl+C for copy.

How do I switch from one application to another?

You can use the taskbar to switch applications. Click the button for the program you want.

What if I want to move the data to the program?

To move data from one program to another, select it and then choose Edit ⇨ Cut instead of Edit ⇨ Copy. Move to the program and then select Edit ⇨ Paste.

Can I edit the data?

Yes. The data you copy and paste becomes part of the document. You can edit it using any of the features of Word, but not the features of the original program.

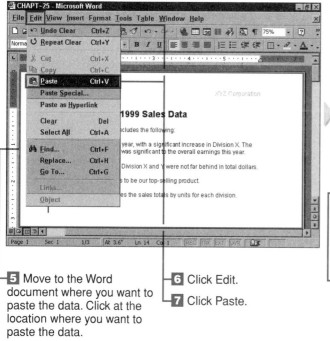

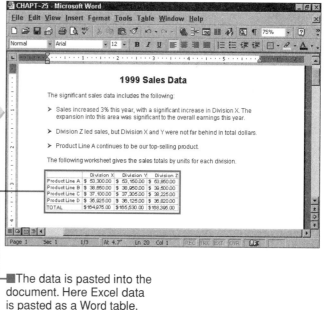

5 Move to the Word document where you want to paste the data. Click at the location where you want to paste the data.

6 Click Edit.

7 Click Paste.

■The data is pasted into the document. Here Excel data is pasted as a Word table. (You may need to adjust the size of the table or the column widths.)

LINK DATA

Sometimes the data you insert will change, and you will want to keep the Word document updated. For instance, you might include a worksheet in a sales report in Word. To ensure that the sales worksheet is the current, you can link the data.

You can then select how the object is pasted: as an object,

formatted text, unformatted text, picture, bitmap, or hyperlink.

If you paste the data as an object, it is like a picture. You can move it around within the document, but you cannot edit the data from within Word.

If you want to make a change to the data, edit the original file. You can do so by double-clicking the object. With a linked object,

double-clicking opens the source application and displays that file. You can then make a change and go back to the Word document. Contrast this with double-clicking an embedded object, covered next.

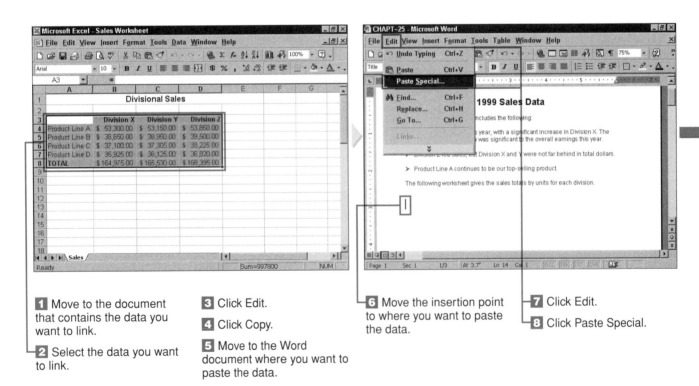

1 Move to the document that contains the data you want to link.

2 Select the data you want to link.

3 Click Edit.

4 Click Copy.

5 Move to the Word document where you want to paste the data.

6 Move the insertion point to where you want to paste the data.

7 Click Edit.

8 Click Paste Special.

SPECIAL DOCUMENTS

How do I change the file used as the link?

 You may decide to use another file as the linked data source. Or you might also need to update the file location of the linked file if you change where it is saved. To make a change to which source is used, right-click the linked object and then select Edit Worksheet Link. Click the Change Source button, make the change, and then click OK.

How do I update the link?

 The link is updated when you make a change to the original file. You can also manually update a link. Right-click the linked object and select Update Link.

How do I undo the link?

 If you no longer want to keep the two files linked, you can break the link. Select Edit ➪ Links. Select the link you want to break and then click Break Link. Click OK.

Can I edit the linked data?

Yes, but to do so, use the original application and update the original file (the file from which you copied the data). The Word document that contains a link to this data will be updated automatically.

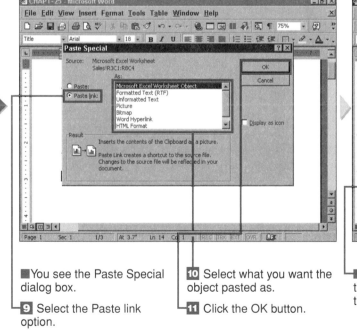

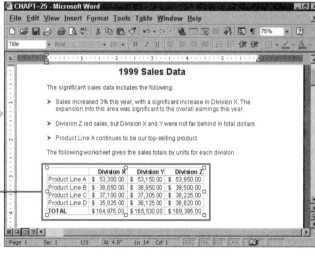

■ You see the Paste Special dialog box.

9 Select the Paste link option.

10 Select what you want the object pasted as.

11 Click the OK button.

■ The data is pasted into the document and linked to the source.

EMBED DATA

In some cases you will want to be able to manipulate the data using the source program (the program you used to create the data). But you won't need to keep two separate files. In this case, you can embed the data as an object into the document.

This process is similar to pasting a link, only you do not select the Paste link option.

Although the results look the same as pasting a link, they are not. Unlike linked data, if you make a change, the Word document is *not* updated. Also, you can double-click the object to edit it using the original program. For instance, if you embed an Excel object, you can double-click that object to edit the worksheet. You see the Excel commands and toolbars and a

mini-worksheet within the Word document.

You can insert several types of embedded objects, depending on the programs you have. Some of these have already been covered, such as inserting a chart. Both of these involve embedded objects. When you save the document, the embedded object is saved as part of the Word document.

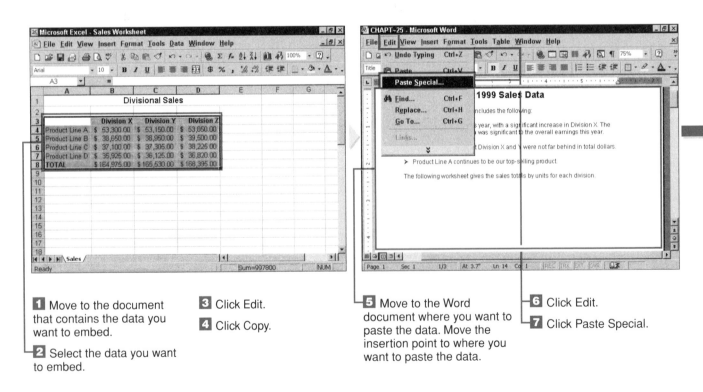

1 Move to the document that contains the data you want to embed.

2 Select the data you want to embed.

3 Click Edit.

4 Click Copy.

5 Move to the Word document where you want to paste the data. Move the insertion point to where you want to paste the data.

6 Click Edit.

7 Click Paste Special.

TIPS

What if the object isn't in the location I want?

You can move the object around and also change how text flows around the object. This object is just like a picture you've inserted. Refer to Chapter 14 for more information on formatting and working with objects.

How do I save the embedded object?

The object is saved with the Word document. There are not two separate files when you embed data. You can access the pasted data only from the Word document.

If I update the original document, is the Word document updated too?

No. If you embed an object, the original file and the copied data are not linked.

How do I get rid of the embedded data?

Click the object to select it and then press the Delete key.

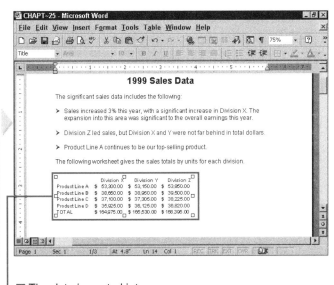

■ You see the Paste Special dialog box.

8 Select the type of embedded object.

9 Click the OK button.

■ The data is pasted into the document.

INSERT A NEW OBJECT

If you haven't already created the embedded object, you can create it within Word. You can create several different types of objects (as long as you have those applications). For instance, you can insert an Excel chart or worksheet, organization chart, graph, picture, and so on. Some of these objects will be specific

to your system (the programs you have installed), some are included with Word, and some are part of Windows.

When you select the file type, you can use any of that program's features to create the file. But remember that the object is not saved in a separate file. When you save the Word document, this object is saved with the document.

You can easily edit the object by double-clicking it. Doing so displays the menus and toolbars for that program, so although you may think you are still working in Word, you are really working in that program. Make your changes and then click back in the Word document.

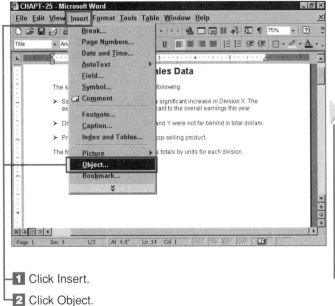

1 Click Insert.

2 Click Object.

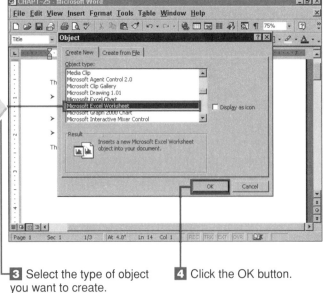

3 Select the type of object you want to create.

4 Click the OK button.

What types of objects can I insert?

It depends on the applications you have, but you can insert many types of objects including WordArt (covered in Chapter 13), equations, WordPad documents, drawings, sounds, video and animation clips, and others. The dialog box will list all of the installed programs you can use to insert objects.

Why would I insert the object as an icon?

One of the options when you create the object is to insert it as an icon. You may want to do this for documents that will be viewed online. Rather than show the content, the icon is displayed. Readers can double-click the icon to view the content of the object.

Can I link this new object?

No. If you want to link the object, start with the existing file (use the From File tab) or copy the data.

What is OLE?

OLE stands for Object Linking and Embedding and pertains to any programs that supports linking and embedding, as covered here.

CREATING SPECIAL DOCUMENTS

IV

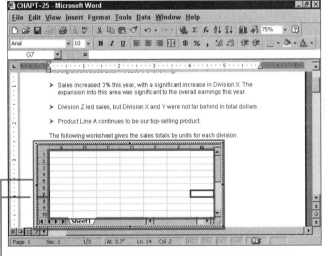

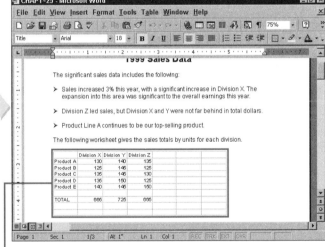

■ Word starts the selected application, and you see a blank document for that application, such as a blank Excel worksheet.

■ Create the object (within Word) using any of the tools from that application.

■ Notice that the Word menu and toolbars are replaced by the application s menu and toolbar.

■ After you create the object, choose File ➪ Close & Return to document.

■ The object you just created is inserted into the Word document.

21

INSERT A FILE INTO A DOCUMENT

The preceding sections focus mainly on adding data from other programs, but you may also want to combine Word documents. Perhaps you need to insert the content of one document into another, for instance, if you want to combine two documents.

As one method, you can open both documents. Select the data from one document and then copy it. Move to the other document and then Paste.

But as a shortcut, if you want to insert all the text from a document, simply insert the file. Word inserts the contents of the

selected file at the insertion point. (Note that if the file is not a Word document, you need to be able to translate or directly import that file. When you install Word, you select which formats you can directly import.)

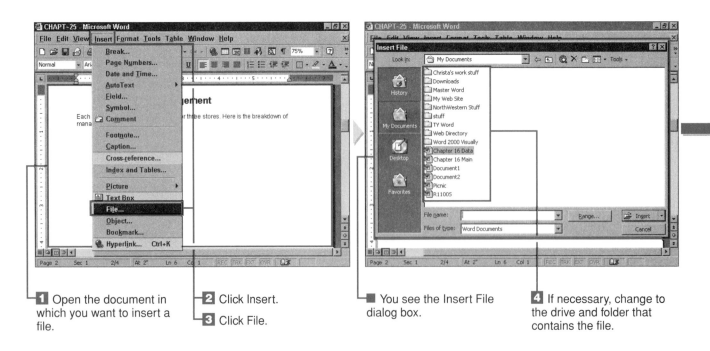

1 Open the document in which you want to insert a file.

2 Click Insert.

3 Click File.

■ You see the Insert File dialog box.

4 If necessary, change to the drive and folder that contains the file.

What if I want to be able to edit the file?

If you want to be able to edit the file, particularly if the file is from another application, insert it as an object. Select Insert ➪ Object. Click the Create from File tab. Type the file name or select it using the Browse button. Then click OK.

How do I get rid of the inserted file?

Select the text and press Delete.

Can I edit the file and update the Word document?

No. The file is inserted and saved as part of the Word document. If you edit the original file, the Word file is not updated.

5 Double-click the file.

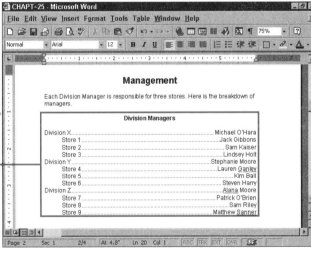

■ That document is inserted into the current document.

USE A DATABASE FILE FOR A MAIL MERGE

If you track of a lot of data, you may use a more sophisticated database program. For example, you might use Access, the database program included with Microsoft Office. Or you might use a simpler database program. Often one of the databases you use is a list of names and addresses. For instance, you may track customers or clients. You might

have a list of sales associates in your area. You might keep a membership roster.

If you want to use this same list to create a mail merge letter, you don't have to go to the trouble of setting up a new data source. Instead, you can use your database with Word to create a mail merge letter.

You can set up form letters, labels, or envelopes. When you

use a database, Word sets up links and reads the data records. You can then use any of the fields from the database in the main document. Word creates letters for each of the records in the database.

Note: For complete information on performing mail merges, refer to Chapter 16.

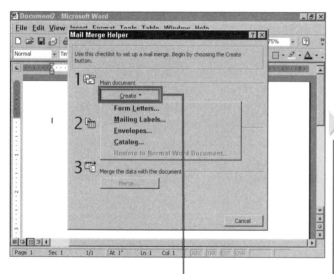

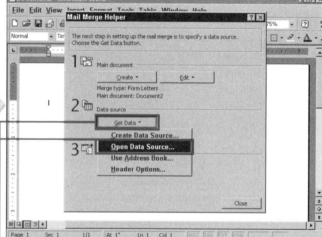

1 Start in Word with a blank document onscreen.

2 Click Tools.

3 Click Mail Merge.

■ You see the Mail Merge Helper dialog box.

4 Under Main document, click the Create button and select what you want to create.

5 Click the Active Window button.

6 Click the Get Data button.

7 Click Open Data Source.

Can I paste a database table into Word?

Yes. To do so, in Access, display the database in Datasheet view. Select the records you want to copy. Click Edit ➪ Copy. Move to the Word document where you want to paste the data. Click Edit ➪ Paste. The Access data is pasted as a table.

What fields can I use?

You can use any of the fields from your database. They should all be listed when you click the Insert Merge Field button.

How many letters will be created?

If you set up a form letter, Word will create letters for each record in the database. If you want only selected records, you can use the Merge dialog box to select a range of records.

What is a DDE link?

When you use some programs, in particular Access, Word also establishes a DDE (Dynamic Data Exchange) link so that the data is linked. This may take a while.

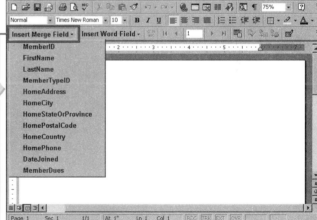

■ You see Open Data Source dialog box.

8 Change to the drive and/or folder that contains the file you want to use. Then display the Files of type drop-down list and select the type of file.

9 Double-click the database file.

■ When you set up the main document, you can click the Insert Merge Field button to insert fields from this database.

SECTION V

USING E-MAIL AND FAX CAPABILITIES

Now you can communicate with others in a myriad of ways — via the old-fashioned telephone, cell phones, pagers, car phones, e-mail, and faxes. There's no excuse for being out of touch! Word, of course, keeps up to date with all these messaging options. You can use Word to send both e-mail messages and faxes.

Send an E-mail

E-mail is short for electronic mail, and you can use this method of communication to send messages, memos, documents, and other files to anyone with an e-mail address. You might be hooked up internally at your office to all your coworkers. You can send messages to any of them, without leaving your office. Your company might have several offices, all connected via the Internet. Again, you can send messages to your coworkers.

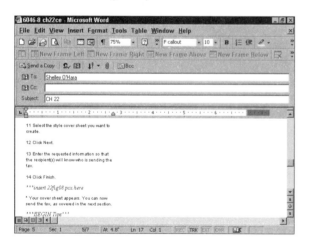

You might also have friends and family that you communicate with via the Internet or some other online service such as America Online. Create documents in Word and send them as e-mail messages. To do so, you need the following:

▸ An e-mail account with an Internet Service Provider (ISP) or some other network connection

▸ The e-mail address

▸ A mail/fax program that works with Word. Some popular programs include Microsoft Exchange, Microsoft Messaging, or Microsoft Outlook. Exchange is part of Windows 95, and Outlook is included as part of the Office package, so you may already have these programs.

Keep in mind that you cannot use Word to receive e-mail messages. You must have an e-mail program for retrieving and reading messages. (If you have Office, you can use the mail program Outlook Express.)

Send a Fax

Another way to send messages or documents to others is via fax. You can use your fax program to fax to any fax system, either another computer fax modem or a regular fax machine. You simply need a fax modem (or access to one via your network) and this fax modem must be set up on your system.

As with e-mail, you cannot use Word to receive faxes. You need to use a separate fax program or mail program such as Outlook Express. You may be able to view faxes with Word, though, by opening them within Word.

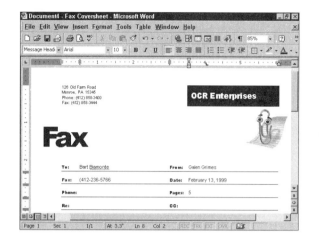

SEND A DOCUMENT VIA E-MAIL

I f you've ever sent a Word document to someone as an e-mail attachment, then you already understand the convenience of being able to send the document directly from Word. First save the document, and then open your e-mail client program, create and address your e-mail message, attach the

Word document to the e-mail message, and then send the message to its intended recipient.

Now, to send a Word document you simply select the Send To command right from the document window. Then address the document to its intended recipient and click Send.

Keep in mind that you need to have installed an e-mail program and set up this program for use with your specific e-mail server. You can use Outlook (included with Microsoft Office), or the mail program included with Windows (Microsoft Exchange or Microsoft Messaging).

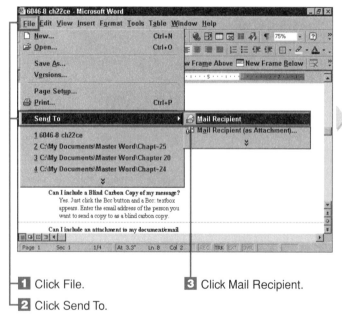

-■1 Click File.

-■2 Click Send To.

■3 Click Mail Recipient.

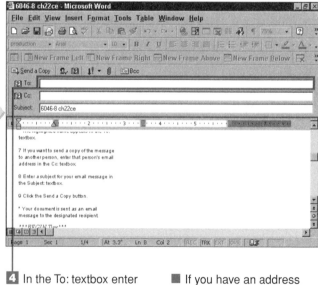

■4 In the To: textbox enter the e-mail address of the message recipient.

■ If you have an address book set up under Microsoft Exchange or Outlook, click the Address Book button to open the Address Book.

Can I include a Blind Carbon Copy of my message?

 Yes. Just click the Bcc button and a Bcc: textbox appears. Enter the e-mail address of the person you want to send a copy to as a blind carbon copy.

Can I include an attachment to my document/e-mail message?

 Yes. Click the Attach File button and enter the file name of the file you want to include as an attachment.

Can I designate different priorities for my e-mail documents?

 Yes. Click the Set Priority button and select High, Normal, or Low priority for your document.

Is it really necessary to include a subject?

Subjects are optional, but helpful. A subject is a polite way of letting the recipient know what the message is about.

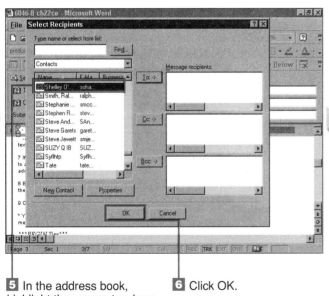

5 In the address book, highlight the person to whom you want to send the document.

6 Click OK.

■ The highlighted name appears in the To: textbox.

7 If you want to send a copy of the message to another person, enter that person's e-mail address in the Cc: textbox.

8 Enter a subject for your e-mail in the Subject: textbox.

9 Click the Send a Copy button.

■ Your document is sent as an e-mail message to the designated recipient.

COMPOSE A FAX USING THE FAX WIZARD

I f you have a fax modem and have set up a fax program (such as Microsoft Fax), you can use Word to create your faxes. Word has several fax templates and a Fax Wizard that will show you how to create the faxes you will send out.

The Fax Wizard helps you create a fax cover sheet. This cover sheet can contain a note to the fax recipient or have a document attached. Once you become familiar with the Fax Wizard, you can bypass it and create your fax cover sheet from one of the fax templates.

Word then "prints" the document to the fax modem, sending it to the fax number you enter. The wizard prompts you to enter the recipient information.

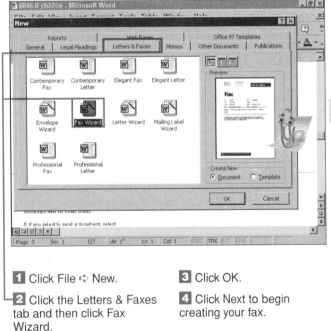

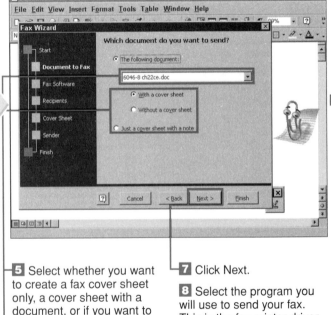

■1 Click File ➪ New.

■2 Click the Letters & Faxes tab and then click Fax Wizard.

■3 Click OK.

■4 Click Next to begin creating your fax.

■5 Select whether you want to create a fax cover sheet only, a cover sheet with a document, or if you want to just fax a document with no cover sheet.

■6 If you select to send a document, select the document you want to send.

■7 Click Next.

■8 Select the program you will use to send your fax. This is the fax printer driver you previously installed.

■9 Click Next.

TIPS

Do I need to use the Fax Wizard or one of the fax templates to create a cover sheet?

No. You can create any type of cover sheet you like. The wizard and templates are only there to assist you and make it easier and quicker to produce a professional-looking cover sheet.

Is a cover sheet really necessary?

Cover sheets are a courtesy to the recipient. They let the recipient know who sent the fax and (usually) what the fax is about.

Can I modify any of the existing fax templates?

Yes. The fax templates are fully modifiable. If you like the changes you make you can save them in a new template for future use. You can find more information on templates in Chapter 17.

Can I create my own fax cover sheet templates?

Certainly. Just create a fax template the same as you would any Word template. Chapter 17 explains how to create your own templates.

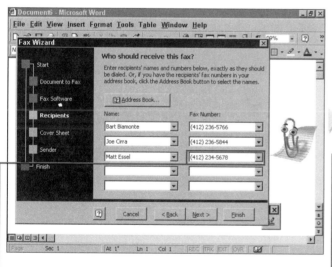

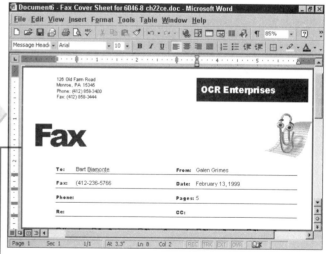

-10 Select the fax recipient(s) you are sending your fax to and then click Next.

11 Select the style cover sheet you want to create.

12 Click Next.

13 Enter the requested information so the recipient(s) will know who is sending the fax.

14 Click Finish.

■ Your cover sheet appears. You can now send the fax, as covered in the next section.

SEND A FAX

Now that you've set up your PC to send faxes, and you've learned how to create fax cover sheets for your faxes, you're ready to send your first fax from Word.

Sending a fax is literally no different from printing a document. In fact, you select the Print command to send the fax. The only difference is that you select the fax driver instead of your printer. Word then "prints" to this fax driver, which dials the appropriate fax number and transmits your document to the receiving fax machine. Remember that you can fax to another computer with a fax modem or to a "regular" fax machine.

Before you begin make sure that no other program or application is using your fax modem. Also, you need to be sure you get connected. If you get a busy signal, try again.

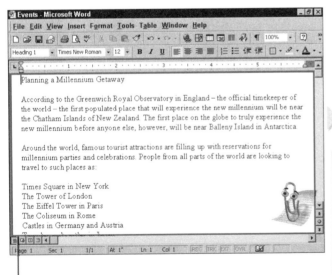

1 Open the document you want to send as your fax.

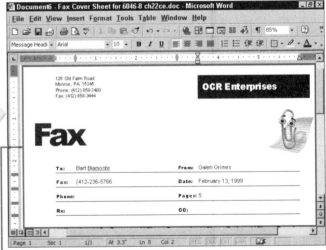

2 Use the Fax Wizard to create a cover sheet for your fax.

I have a rather slow fax modem. What can I do to transmit my faxes more quickly?

Keep it simple! Keep your faxes short and avoid a complex cover sheet. Avoid using graphics on your cover sheets and delete all unnecessary text.

Will Word work with any fax modem? Besides Word, can other Office 2000 applications send faxes?

Word will work with any fax modem that has software that installs as a print driver. And yes — because the fax software installs a print driver in Windows, any Windows application can send faxes.

Is it necessary to install third-party fax software to send my faxes?

Word has no provisions for actually sending your faxes using your fax modem. You need to install software specifically designed to work with the fax modem installed in your PC. You can use the program that came with your fax modem, purchase a fax program, or use Microsoft Fax, which comes with Windows.

Can I use Word to receive faxes?

Your fax modem is capable of receiving faxes, but to view and open them, you should use the software for your particular fax modem.

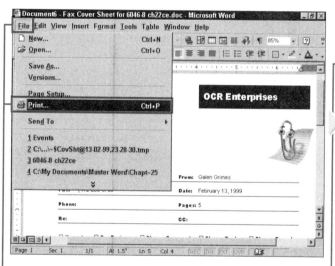

3 Click File ⇨ Print.

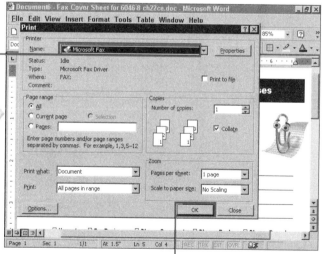

4 Select the driver for your fax modem in place of your printer as the destination for your document.

5 Click OK to send your fax.

WEB PUBLISHING

Documents are no longer simply printed. Instead, a whole new method of publishing has come into its own: Web publishing. To distribute information on the Internet or a company intranet, you can create your own Web pages.

What Is the Internet?

The Internet is a network of networks, all loosely connected. When you have access to one network, you can get access to the others. You can review information from countless sources, all without leaving your desk. You can check stock prices, read breaking news stories, research a topic of interest, find out what the weather is like on Grand Cayman, look up a movie review, order a book from an online bookstore, and more.

To take advantage of the Internet and all it has to offer, you need an Internet connection. Most connections are made using a modem, a phone line, and an Internet Service Provider (ISP). You may have a different setup, especially if you are connected through a business. You also need a browser. Two of the most popular browsers include Netscape's Navigator and Microsoft's Internet Explorer.

What Is a Web Page?

A Web page is probably the most popular method for publishing information on the Internet. A Web page is more than just text. A Web page can include graphics, sounds, animations, movies, and most importantly, links to other pages.

A link (or hyperlink) is a special feature of Web pages. When you click a link, the Web page associated with that link is displayed. You may see another page within the same Web document, another document at that Web site, or a page from another site entirely.

A Web page is formatted with a special formatting language called HTML (HyperText Markup Language). This language controls how the text and graphics appear as well as other features of the page such as links.

Why Should I Create a Web Page?

You may decide to get interested in Web publishing for your own personal page or for your business. You can publish the page through your company intranet (an internal network for a company or business) or through other Web hosting services. (Ask your ISP for more information about Web publishing.) Word includes many Web-friendly features. You can experiment with Word to get started on your Web publishing path.

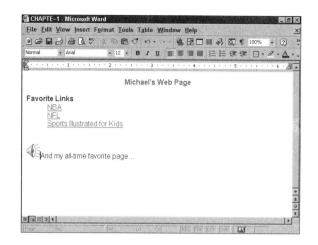

VIEW A WEB DOCUMENT

Microsoft has made a determined effort to make all of the applications in Office 2000 "Web-aware." In Word, this means that you can now work with Web documents just as if they were standard Word documents.

One of the simpler tasks you can perform on Web documents using Word is viewing them,

much as you would with your Web browser. Although Word is no replacement for your Web browser, you can use Word to quickly and easily preview Web documents, especially simple Web documents you are creating with Word.

Because Word is not an actual Web browser, it won't always display pages exactly the same as they are displayed in Web

browsers such as Internet Explorer. If you want to see how your page will look when displayed by a Web browser, use Word's Web Page Preview feature. The Web Page Preview feature automatically starts Internet Explorer, takes the page you have opened in Word, and displays that page in Internet Explorer.

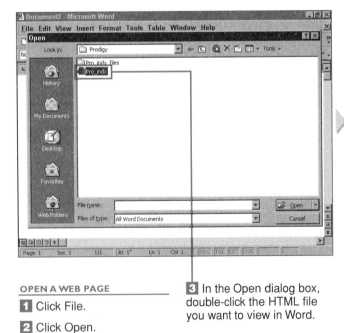

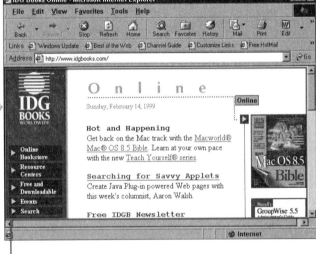

OPEN A WEB PAGE

1 Click File.

2 Click Open.

3 In the Open dialog box, double-click the HTML file you want to view in Word.

■ The file you selected is displayed in Word.

Can I edit documents I am viewing?

Yes, but only documents you are viewing in Word. You cannot edit files you are previewing in Internet Explorer.

Do Web page hyperlinks work while I am previewing a document?

Yes. When you preview an HTML file in Word, Word's built-in hyperlinks feature will work with any hyperlinks in the document you are viewing.

Can I select a Web browser for Web Page Preview other than Internet Explorer?

Yes. Open the Tools menu and select Options. From the Options dialog box, select the General tab. Select the Web Options button and then select the browser you want to use in the Browser drop-down list box.

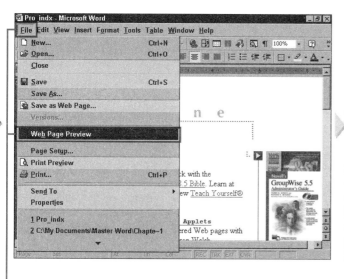

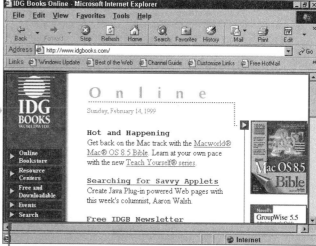

PREVIEW A WEB DOCUMENT

1 Click File.

2 Click Web Page Preview.

■ Word starts Internet Explorer and loads the file.

CREATE A WEB DOCUMENT

Although Word is not likely to provide much competition for heavy duty HTML editors, you can use it to create simple Web documents.

Most Web documents consist mainly of text, images, and hypertext links, all of which you can add to your documents using Word.

Adding text and images to Word documents has always been fairly simple, and Word makes it just as easy to add hypertext links. You are not limited to only adding links to other Web pages. You can also add links to files on FTP sites and even add mailto: links to e-mail addresses. (Click the link,

and you automatically create a mail message addressed to the appropriate e-mail address.) Word even lets you attach links to image files embedded in your files.

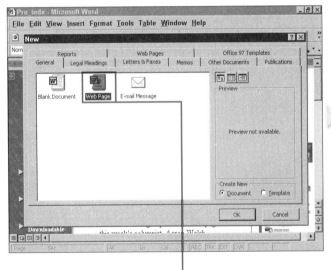

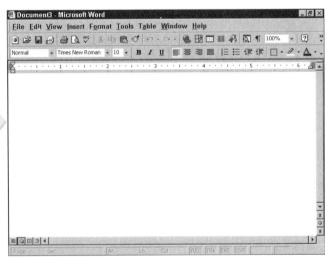

CREATE A WEB PAGE

1 Click File.

2 Click New.

3 In the New dialog box, select Web Page.

4 Click the OK button.

5 Type and format the text for the page.

TIPS

How do I create a hyperlink to an e-mail address?

When the Insert Hyperlink dialog box is open, click the E-mail Address icon to display the textbox for entering e-mail addresses and then enter the e-mail address you want inserted in your hyperlink.

Can I create Web pages containing forms?

No. Word is limited to creating static Web pages. You cannot create a form. A form contains entries for data that you can then submit to the Web site.

Does Word contain any preformatted Web page templates?

Yes. Word contains seven preformatted Web page templates and a Web page wizard that you can also use to create Web pages.

A Web page wizard is an Office 2000 wizard designed to help you through the preliminary steps needed to create a Web page. The wizard designs the foundation for your page based on how you respond to a series of questions and prompts.

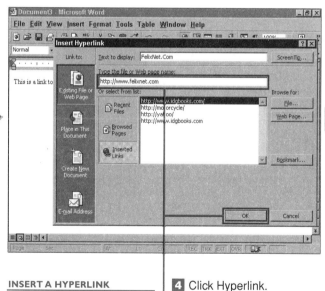

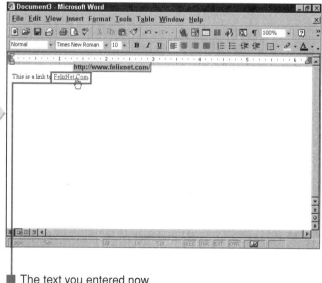

INSERT A HYPERLINK

■1 Enter the text you want to use for your hyperlink.

■2 Highlight the text for the hyperlink.

■3 Click Insert.

■4 Click Hyperlink.

■5 Enter the URL for your hyperlink in the textbox.

■6 Click OK.

■ The text you entered now contains a hyperlink to the designated URL.

CONTINUED ▶

CREATE A WEB DOCUMENT CONTINUED

Formatting your Web document in Word is pretty much the same as formatting any document in Word. You just have to remember which Word formatting features are available in HTML.

Generally, any text formatting feature you can use in Word is safe to use in Web page documents. The only caveat is that not all font styles will be available to all browsers, so you should stick to using only common fonts styles such as Times Roman and Arial.

Because the document will be displayed, you can use colors for the text, background, and borders. You may also want to jazz up the page with images, sounds, and motion clips. (Adding images to a document is covered in Chapter 15.) You can use the Insert ➪ Picture command to insert these types of added elements.

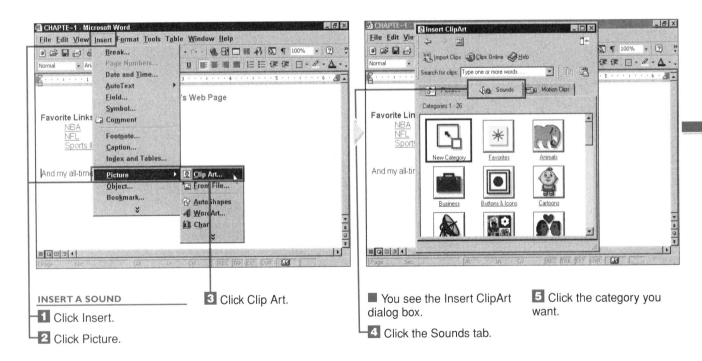

INSERT A SOUND

1 Click Insert.

2 Click Picture.

3 Click Clip Art.

■ You see the Insert ClipArt dialog box.

4 Click the Sounds tab.

5 Click the category you want.

TIPS

What if I don't have any sounds available?

You can import sounds from the other folders on your system or from the Word CD-ROM. Click the Import Clips button and then select the drive or folder that contains the clips.

How do I insert a motion clip?

Follow the same procedure as inserting a sound, only click the Motion Clips tab in the Insert ClipArt dialog box. Then select the file you want to add.

Can I use any images or sounds?

You can use any images, sounds, or motion clips that you've created yourself. If someone else created the item, you must have permission to use the images, sounds, and motion clips on your Web page. Check with the source of the image.

How do I play the sound?

To play the sound, double-click the sound icon.

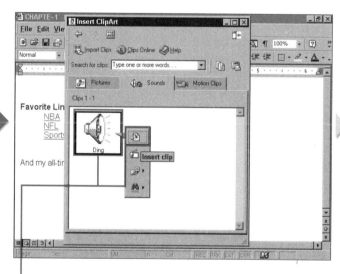

6 Click the sound you want to insert and then click the Insert clip button.

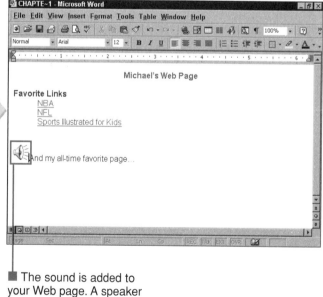

■ The sound is added to your Web page. A speaker icon indicates the sound.

SAVE A WEB DOCUMENT

After you've spent time creating your Web page in Word, don't forget to stop at some point and save your work. When you save your file you need to make sure you save it as a Web document, not simply as a Word document. Word provides a special menu selection for saving files as Web documents to make sure you save your file in the correct format. Basically, you save the document as an .HTM file. (HyperText Markup Language, remember, is the Web formatting language.)

You can also set the page title while you are saving your Web page document. This title helps identify the pages for other users that browse or search the page. The title also appears in the title bar of the browser window when you display this page.

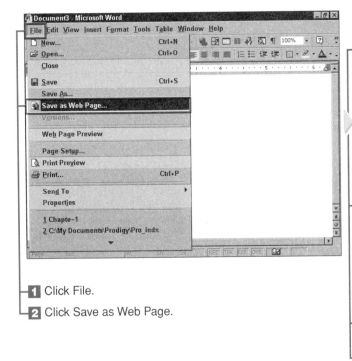

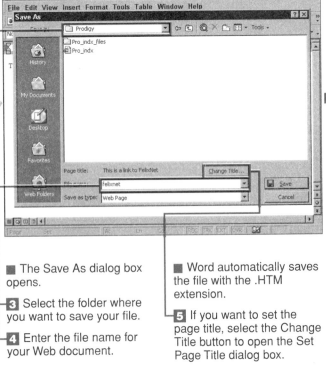

■1 Click File.

■2 Click Save as Web Page.

■ The Save As dialog box opens.

■3 Select the folder where you want to save your file.

■4 Enter the file name for your Web document.

■ Word automatically saves the file with the .HTM extension.

■5 If you want to set the page title, select the Change Title button to open the Set Page Title dialog box.

TIPS

Can I save my file with an .HTML file extension?

By default Word saves Web page documents with an .HTM file extension. If you prefer to use the .HTML file extension you will need to rename the file.

What's the purpose of a page title?

Primarily, the page title is used to help identify your page when it is indexed by a search engine. Search engines use other means to identify and index your pages, but the title is one of their criteria so it helps to use a descriptive title.

Are there any restrictions to where I can save my Web page documents?

No. Wherever you can save a file you can save your Web page documents.

Why can't I save a Web page document in the Word document format?

Web page documents are simple text files with no formatting codes. Word formatted files contain formatting codes, among other things. These codes would not be read by Web page browsers and also would likely produce errors in Web page browsers.

■6 Enter the title you want to set for your Web page.

■7 Click OK.

■8 Click the Save button to close the dialog box and save your document as a Web document.

DIVIDE A WEB DOCUMENT INTO FRAMES

As mentioned previously, Word is by no means serious competition for high-end HTML editors and Web page creation tools, but it does have a few advanced features. One of these advanced features in the capability to create frames on the pages you create with Word.

Word enables you to create both horizontal and vertical frames on your pages and lets you freely adjust the frame sizes. You can then display different parts of the document in each frame.

Word also enables you to create frames within frames, but you should exercise restraint in creating frames on your Web pages.

The easiest way to create frames is to use the buttons on the Frames toolbar.

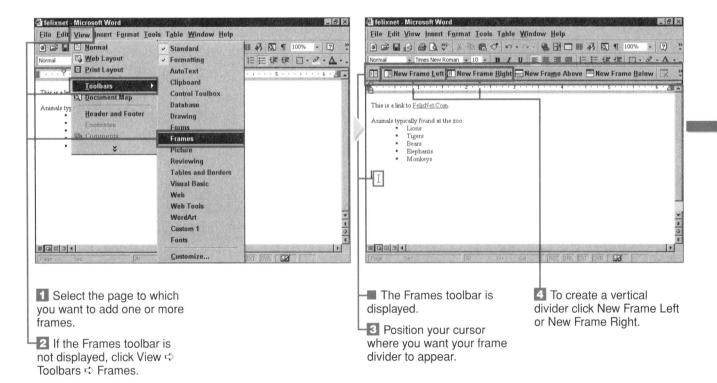

1 Select the page to which you want to add one or more frames.

2 If the Frames toolbar is not displayed, click View ⇨ Toolbars ⇨ Frames.

■ The Frames toolbar is displayed.

3 Position your cursor where you want your frame divider to appear.

4 To create a vertical divider click New Frame Left or New Frame Right.

V

Is the number of frames I can create limited?

 You can create a seemingly infinite number of frames but you should exercise some restraint in creating frames. Too many frames are confusing for viewers and hard to manage when you want to modify your pages.

How do I decide when to use frames?

 Frames should be used only when they add value or functionality to your page. If you don't know for sure that you need frames on a page, then you probably don't.

My frames are not the size I want. How can I adjust them?

Position your mouse cursor on the frame divider. A resize bar appears. Hold down your left mouse button and drag the frame divider to the position where you want it to be. Release the mouse button.

If I create more frames than I want, is it possible to remove or delete them?

Yes. Just place your cursor in the frame you want to delete and then click the Delete Frame icon.

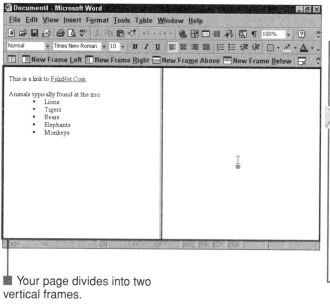

■ Your page divides into two vertical frames.

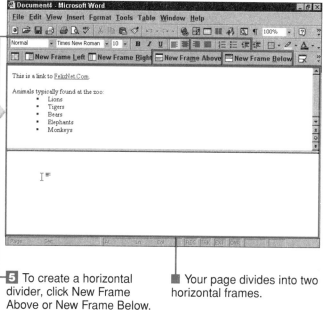

5 To create a horizontal divider, click New Frame Above or New Frame Below.

■ Your page divides into two horizontal frames.

SECTION VI

24 MANAGING DOCUMENTS

25 SETTING UP SHORTCUTS

AND CUSTOMIZING WORD

KEEP TRACK OF YOUR DOCUMENTS

W hen you first start using Word, you'll probably have just a few documents. You'll easily recognize each one, and know exactly where each one resides. Think of this as moving into a nice new office and having to keep track of just four or five sheets of paper.

Fast-forward a few months. Now you have 50 or so documents to keep track of — maybe more —

and your nice new office doesn't look so nice and new anymore. Where is everything? What the heck is this file named MWVISW2K? Why can't you find anything?

As you create more documents, you will want to learn some skills for organizing and keeping track of these documents. That's the topic of this chapter.

Saving Files

To start, you learn a few additional features of Save. For one thing, you can save a document as another file type. Why? Perhaps you share the file with someone that does not use Word. You can also set Save options such as summaries (additional file information).

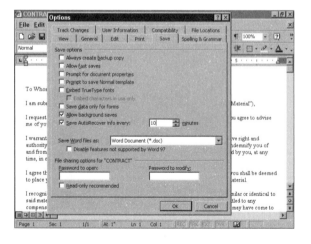

Organizing Folders

So that your files are easy to find, you should spend some time organizing your document folders. You can set up folders for each type of document you create. Or perhaps you want to use a different organization scheme, such as organizing documents by project. You can create new folders, select a default folder, and use shortcuts to view often-used folders.

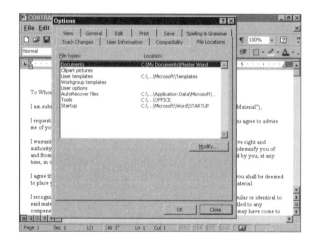

Managing Files

Setting up files is only part of file management housekeeping. You also can use Word to manage the files. You no longer have to use a separate file management program to work with files. All Microsoft programs enable you to work with files within the Open and Save dialog boxes.

You can do any of the following right from Word:

- ► Copy files to another folder
- ► Copy files to another disk
- ► Move files to another drive or folder
- ► Change the names of files
- ► Delete files you no longer need
- ► Restore files you delete by accident

Finding Files

There's nothing more frustrating than knowing that you created a file but being unable to remember where you saved it, or even what you named it. If this happens to you, use Word's Find command to locate a particular file. You have lots of available search options, such as searching for a file based on name or content.

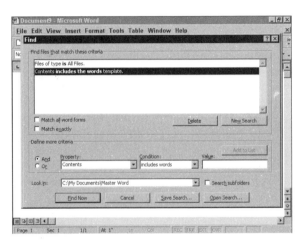

24

SAVE FILE SUMMARIES

When you have a gazillion files on your computer, sometimes telling what a file contains by the name — even if it is descriptive — is difficult. You may want to keep and review other information about the document, such as a title or keyword.

You can enter and save additional information about a file including a title, subject, author, manager, company name, category, keyword, or comment. Word automatically completes some fields such as the Author. Word may also suggest entries for other text boxes. You can

change any of the entries when you review this information.

The benefit of using summaries is that in addition to being able to review them, you can also search them to find a particular file. See the section titled "Find a Document by Content" later in this chapter.

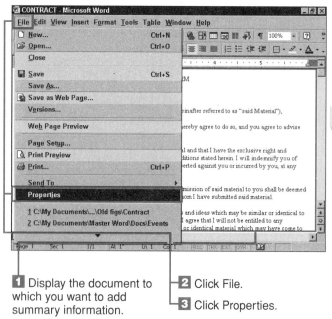

1 Display the document to which you want to add summary information.

2 Click File.

3 Click Properties.

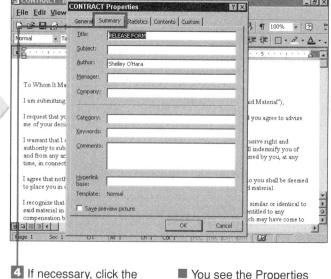

4 If necessary, click the Summary tab.

■ You see the Properties dialog box for the document.

What if I want to be reminded to save this information?

 If you want, you can be prompted to enter document information each time you save. See the section titled "Set Save Options" later in this chapter.

What entries should I make?

 On the Summary tab, complete the entries that are most pertinent to that document. For instance, if the document is a proposal, you may want to note the company name.

Another change you may want to make is to check the Save preview picture checkbox. When you check this option, you can preview the first page of the file in the Open dialog box.

In what other ways can I use the Properties dialog box?

 You can also use the Properties dialog box to display other information about the document, such as document statistics, general file information, and so on. To do so, click the appropriate tab.

How do I display properties?

You can display the properties of an open file by selecting File ⇨ Properties. If you want to find a file by checking its properties, select File ⇨ Open. Click the Views button and then select Properties.

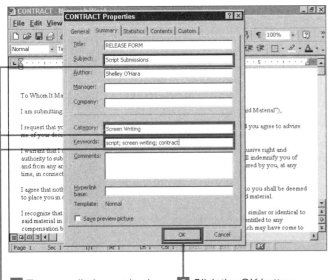

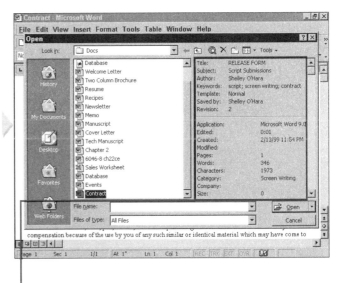

■5 Type or edit the entries in any of the text boxes.

■6 Click the OK button.

■ You can also view properties of the file in the Open dialog box.

SAVE A DOCUMENT AS ANOTHER FILE TYPE

I f you work in an office, you may not use the same word-processing program at home that you use in your office. Perhaps you have an older version of the program at home. Or, you may need to share a document with a friend or coworker that uses a different program. If so, you can use Word to save the document as another file type.

You can select from lots of different formats including plain text, Word 2, WordPerfect, Windows Write, Word for DOS, Works, and several others. (You must install the proper translation filters during installation to access these file types.) Just find out the file format needed and then perform the following steps to save the document as that type of file.

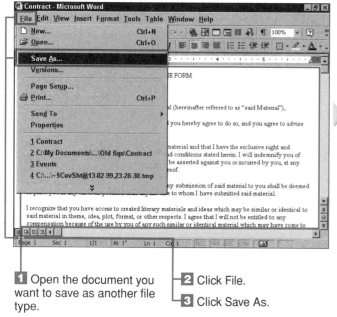

1 Open the document you want to save as another file type.

2 Click File.

3 Click Save As.

■ You see the Save As dialog box.

4 Display the Save as type drop-down list.

Will all the formatting be saved?

It depends on the format you selected as the new file type and the features used in the document. If there's a conflict, you will see an error message. You can choose to click Yes to save anyway and possibly lose some formatting. You can click No to try another format. Click Help to see what formatting might be lost.

Can I save a document as a Web page?

Yes. To do so, use the Save as Web Page command. For more information on this topic, see Chapter 23.

How do I open files in other formats?

Select File ➪ Open and then change to the drive and folder that contains the file. Display the Files of type drop-down list and select the appropriate file type. Double-click the file you want to open.

What formats should I use if I don't know what will work?

Plain text translates to almost any program. Another common popular file format is Rich Text Format, which can be used with Macintosh word-processing programs.

■ You see a list of the different file formats.

5 Click the type of file format you want.

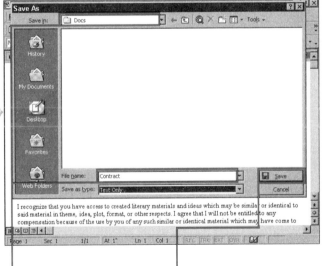

6 If necessary, select the drive and folder where you want to save the new file. Also, you can type a new name in the File name text box.

7 Click the Save button.

■ Word saves the document in the new format.

SET OTHER SAVE OPTIONS

Like most other Word options, you can control how saves are carried out. You can change, for instance, how often the AutoRecover information is saved. This is a special file that is saved periodically, and that opens if you lose power or your computer crashes. You can set the interval for how often the file is saved.

You can set a password to open a document; to simply open the document, you have to type the correct password when prompted. Or you can assign a password so that you have to type the password to modify a file.

If you want to be prompted to save file summary information, you can check the Prompt for document properties checkbox. You can also select other prompts or reminders.

As another option, you can select the default file format. You make all of these changes from the Save tab of the Options dialog box.

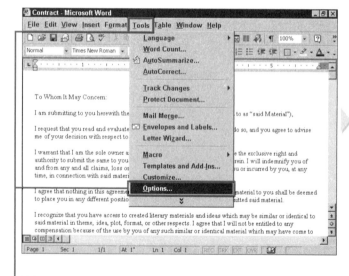

1 Click Tools.

2 Click Options.

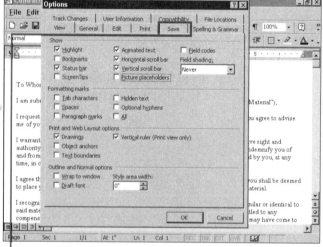

3 Click the Save tab.

TIPS

How can I find out more information about an option?

If you are not sure what an option does, right-click it and then select What's This? to view a pop-up explanation of the option.

How do I add a password?

To set a password for opening a file, type a password in the Password to open text box. To set a password for modifying a file, type a password in the Password to modify text box. When you click OK, you are prompted to confirm the password. Retype the password and click OK.

If the AutoRecover file is created for me, do I still have to save?

Yes. This is an emergency file and may not contain all of the data from a document. This file appears only when you restart Word after it has gotten stuck. You should still save your work frequently.

What's a backup copy?

With this feature on, you save two versions of the file. The original file becomes the backup file, and the new saved file becomes the new file. The backup file has the same name, but uses the extension .wbk.

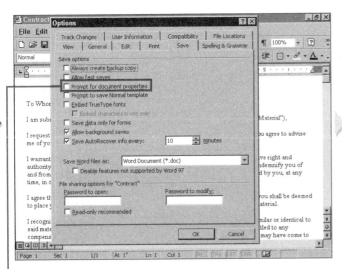

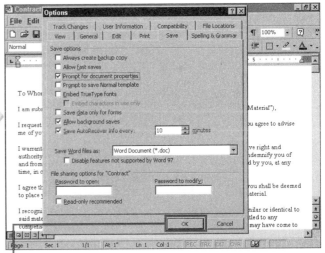

■ You see the various options you can use for saving documents.

4 To turn on an option, check its checkbox.

■ To turn off an option, uncheck its checkbox.

5 Click the OK button.

■ Word uses the save options you have set.

CHANGE THE DEFAULT FOLDER

E ach time you select the Save command, you may be surprised to see a different folder listed. In fact, it's easy to put a document into the wrong folder because you may not realize which folder is the current one.

When you first start Word and then save a document, the My Documents folder is selected as the default folder. You can then change to any other folder to save the document. The next time you save, Word goes back to the folder you most recently selected. For instance, the first time you use the Save command, you see the My Documents folder. Suppose that you change to a folder on your computer called Memos and save the document in this folder. The next time you use the Save command, Word displays the Memos folder.

You can do two things to avoid misplacing documents. First, always check that the appropriate folder is selected when you save. Second, select the default folder you want to use for saving documents, as covered here.

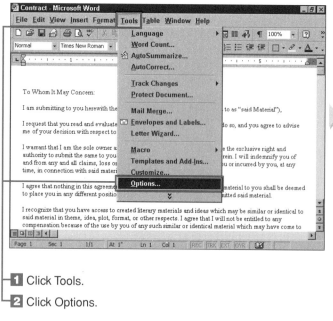

1 Click Tools.

2 Click Options.

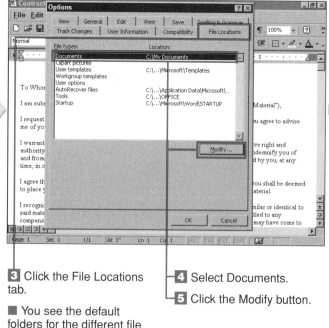

3 Click the File Locations tab.

■ You see the default folders for the different file types.

4 Select Documents.

5 Click the Modify button.

TIPS

Do I have to save all files to the default folder?

No. Just because you changed the default folder doesn't mean you have to save all documents to that folder. You can always select a different folder when you save. Also, Word does not go back to this folder each time you save a document — just the first time you select Save.

What other file locations can I set?

You can also select different folders for clip art, templates, tools, and your startup folder. Select the file type from the list and then modify the location.

How do I move to the folder I want?

You can double-click any folders listed on the side of the Open dialog box to open and select them. Use the Up One Level button to move up through the folder structure. You can also use the Look in drop-down list to change to a different drive.

MANAGING AND CUSTOMIZING WORD

VI

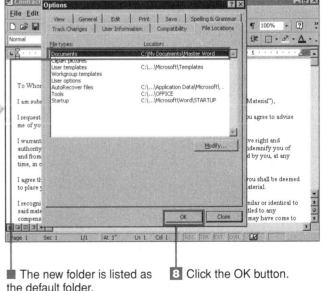

■ You see the Modify Location dialog box.

6 Select the folder you want to use.

7 Click the OK button.

■ The new folder is listed as the default folder.

8 Click the OK button.

477

USE FAVORITE FOLDERS

I f you are a good saver, you probably have several folders that you use. These may be scattered all over your system — on different drives and within different folders. Rather than navigate through your drives and folders to move to these folders, you can set up a list of your favorite folders and then quickly

move to these folders to save or open a document.

To start, add the folder to the Favorites list using the Open dialog box. To navigate to the folder, you can use the Up One Level button to move to a higher folder. You can double-click any folders listed to open and select that folder. Use the Look in drop-

down list to select a different drive.

When you want to save a document to one of your favorite folders, or open a document in one of these folders, you can use the Favorites button to quickly display the folders and files in the Favorites list.

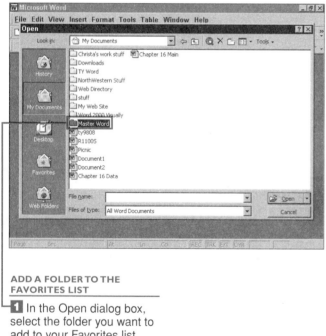

ADD A FOLDER TO THE FAVORITES LIST

1 In the Open dialog box, select the folder you want to add to your Favorites list.

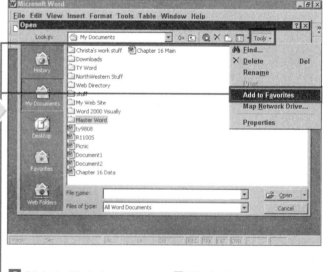

2 Click the Tools button.

3 Select Add to Favorites.

■ Word adds this folder to your list of Favorites.

TIPS

Can I add a Favorites folder when saving a document?

No. The Add to Favorites button is not available in the Save dialog box.

I see folders and Web sites. Why?

Keep in mind that these Favorites folders work for other Office applications and Windows. For instance, if you set up a Favorites folder for your Excel folders, it appears in this list. Also, any sites you have added to your Favorites list in Internet Explorer are displayed.

How do I remove an item from my Favorites folder?

Display the Favorites folder. Then right-click the item or folder and select Delete. Confirm the deletion by clicking Yes.

Can I add documents to the list?

Yes. You can add both files and folders to your Favorites list. Select the document and then click Tools ➪ Add to Favorites.

MANAGING AND CUSTOMIZING WORD

VI

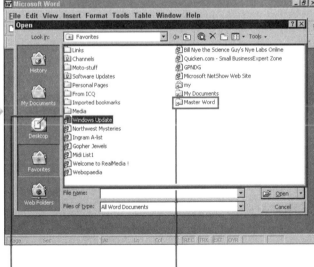

OPEN A FOLDER IN THE FAVORITES LIST

1 Click the Favorites button.

■ Word displays the folders in your Favorites list.

2 Double-click the folder you want to open.

SELECT FILES

For most commands, you can work with several files at once. For instance, you can select several files and copy them. Or, you may want to delete a group of files. As another example, you can select several files and open them together.

To start, select some files. Once the files are selected, you can then do any of the following:

▸ Open all of the selected files by clicking the Open button.
▸ Right-click any of the selected files and select the command you want. For instance, you

can select the Print command to print this group of files.
▸ Use any of the buttons in the dialog box to work with the files. For instance, click the Delete button to delete all the selected files.

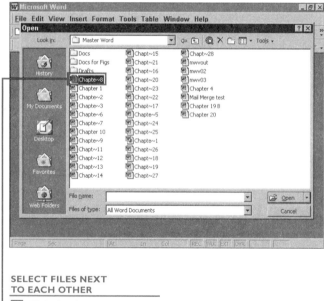

SELECT FILES NEXT TO EACH OTHER

1 Click the first file you want to select.

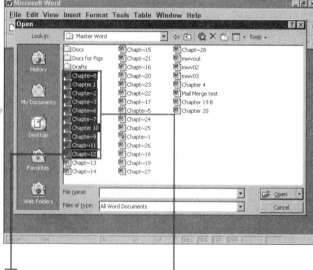

2 Hold down the Shift key and click the last file.

■ The first and last files and all files in between are selected.

TIPS

How do I deselect a file?

You can deselect a file by clicking outside the selected file.

Are there any commands that won't work on a group of files?

Yes. You cannot rename a group of files. If you select this command, only the current file is renamed.

What's another way to work with a group of files?

You can also change the type of files that are displayed. For instance, if you want to work with all text files, you can change the Files of type to text. Then only that type of file is displayed. You can easily select and work with just this file type.

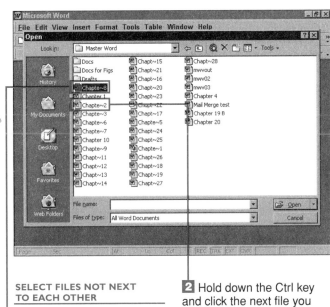

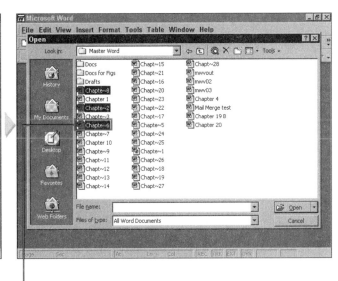

SELECT FILES NOT NEXT TO EACH OTHER

1 Click the first file.

2 Hold down the Ctrl key and click the next file you want to select. Do this for each file you want to select.

■ Each file you Ctrl+click is selected.

DELETE A DOCUMENT

Do you save every scrap of paper no matter what its significance or importance? Do you have every magazine you've ever received? If so, you are probably a pack rat on your PC too. You probably have every document you've ever created. Sooner or later, though,

you are going to run out of room. And you are going to need to do a little housekeeping.

You should periodically go through your documents and delete ones that you don't need.

Made a mistake? Deleted a file by accident? Don't panic. Windows doesn't really delete

documents; it simply moves them to a temporary holding spot called the Recycle Bin. As long as the Recycle Bin has not been emptied, you can retrieve your document from the "trash."

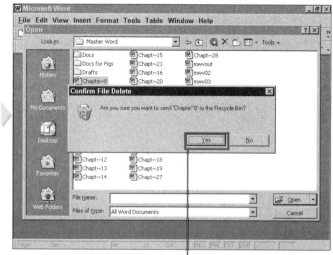

DELETE A DOCUMENT

1 Display the Open or Save As dialog box.

2 Right-click the document you want to delete.

■ You see a pop-up menu with commands for working with files.

3 Select Delete.

■ You are prompted to confirm the deletion.

4 Click the Yes button to delete the document.

How can I safeguard my files in case I need them again?

It's a good idea to make periodic backups of your work. Then if something goes wrong, you can use the backup files. You also don't have to worry so much when you delete something because you can always use your backup copy.

How do I permanently get rid of a file?

You can empty the trash. All documents are deleted and cannot be restored. The contents of the Recycle Bin take up disk space, so you should periodically clean it out to recover that space.

To empty the trash, double-click the Recycle Bin icon. Check the contents of the bin to be sure there's nothing you want to retrieve. Once you empty the trash, you cannot get the documents back (at least not without special software and some outside expertise). Select File ➪ Empty Recycle Bin. You are prompted to confirm the deletion. Click the Yes button.

Windows permanently removes the contents of the bin. Click the Close button to close the Recycle Bin window.

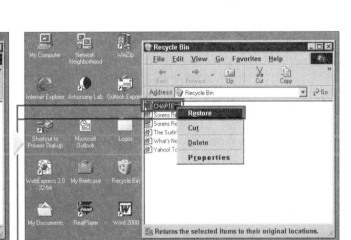

RESTORE A DOCUMENT

1 Go to the Windows desktop.

2 Double-click the Recycle Bin icon.

■ You see the contents of the Recycle Bin.

3 Right-click the file you want to restore.

4 Select the Restore command.

■ Word removes the document from the Recycle Bin and puts it back in its original spot.

5 Click the Close button to close the Recycle Bin window.

COPY A DOCUMENT

There are lots of reasons why you may want to copy a document and lots of ways to create that copy. You might want to copy a document so that you can keep the original and work from the copy. You might want to copy a document if you are creating something

similar and want to reuse text from the original document.

You can use the Copy and Paste commands to copy a document. Use this method when you are reorganizing files and moving them from folder to folder.

As another option, you can use the Send To command. Use

this command when you are copying the document to a floppy disk to take with you or to keep as a backup copy. See the section titled "Copy a Document to a Floppy Disk" for more information.

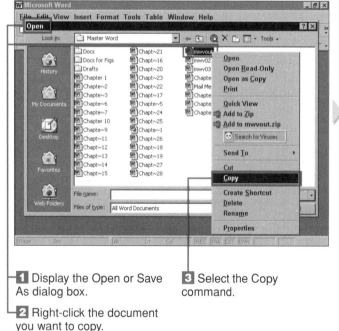

1 Display the Open or Save As dialog box.

2 Right-click the document you want to copy.

3 Select the Copy command.

4 Navigate to the folder where you want to place the copy of the document.

5 Right-click a blank area of the dialog box and select the Paste command.

■ Word copies the document to that folder.

COPY A DOCUMENT TO A FLOPPY DISK

Y ou may want to keep an extra copy of an important document on a floppy disk for safekeeping. Or, you may need to put a document on disk to take with you to your home or another business site. The fastest way to copy a document to a floppy disk is to use the Send To command.

Be sure to insert a floppy disk into the floppy disk drive of your computer before you select this command. If you don't, you will see an error message. If you see an error message, insert the disk and try again.

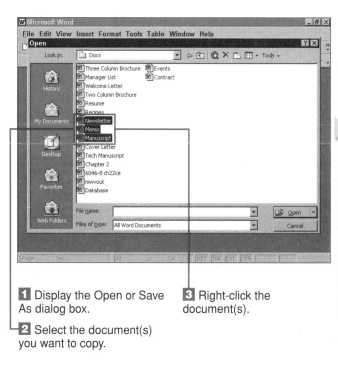

1 Display the Open or Save As dialog box.

2 Select the document(s) you want to copy.

3 Right-click the document(s).

4 Click Send To.

5 From the submenu, select your floppy disk drive.

■ Word copies the document(s) to this disk.

MOVE A DOCUMENT

When you save a document, you may accidentally save it in the wrong folder. If the document is not in the right location, you may want to move it to the right folder. Or, you may decide to

change how you are organizing your documents and need to move them to another folder.

Whatever the reason, you can use the Cut and Paste commands to move a document from one location to another. First, cut the

document from the original folder. Move to the new drive or folder and then paste the file. (It's like moving text.) You can move a single file or several files.

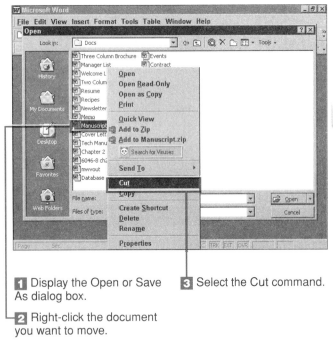

1 Display the Open or Save As dialog box.

2 Right-click the document you want to move.

3 Select the Cut command.

4 Navigate to the folder where you want to place the document.

5 Right-click a blank area of the dialog box and select the Paste command.

■ Word moves the document to that folder.

RENAME A DOCUMENT

With Windows 95 and 98 you are no longer restricted to the eight-character file name. You can type up to 255 characters, including spaces. No more decoding names like DECEXREP. You can use something descriptive like

December Expense Report instead.

Because I have been using a computer for so long, I have a hard time *not* limiting my file names to those eight characters. I either use a name that isn't descriptive enough such as

"RPTMTTOM," or I go overboard and use a name such as "Report on Tuesday's Meeting with Tom about the IUPUI Project." Luckily for me (and you too), you can easily rename a document.

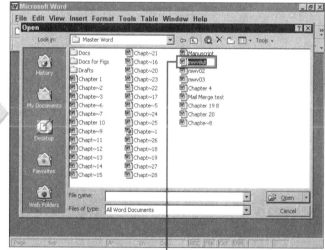

■1 Display the Open or Save As dialog box.

■2 Right-click the document you want to rename.

■3 Select Rename.

■ Word highlights the current name and displays a box around it.

■4 Type a new name and press Enter.

■ The file is renamed.

FIND A DOCUMENT BY FILE NAME

There's nothing more frustrating than knowing that you saved a document, but not being able to find it. Where is that document hiding? You can try looking through folders on a scavenger hunt, or you can search for the document using Word, a much better prospect.

Word offers several ways to search for a file. If you know part or all of the file name, but just can't remember which folder you saved the file in, you can search by file name. You can enter any part of the file name.

You can also select to search just the current folder, or that folder and any subfolders

(folders within the current folder). You can set other options, such as how matches are made.

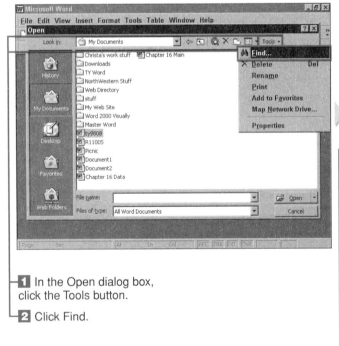

1 In the Open dialog box, click the Tools button.

2 Click Find.

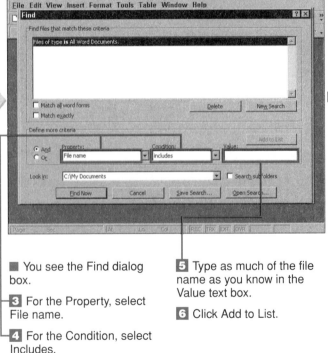

■ You see the Find dialog box.

3 For the Property, select File name.

4 For the Condition, select Includes.

5 Type as much of the file name as you know in the Value text box.

6 Click Add to List.

TIPS

How do I open a found file?

To open a found file, double-click it. To close the dialog box without opening a file, click the Cancel button.

Can I type part of a file name?

Yes. You can type all or part of a file name. For example, if you know you named the file something that started with "ch," you can type **ch**.

You can change how the values are matched by selecting a different condition. For file name, you can select Includes, Begins with, or Ends with. (The conditions vary from property to property.)

Why search all folders?

If you have a lot of files in the current folder, you may want to simply search it. But you probably could find the file if it was in the current folder, so most of the time, you will want Word to search through the subfolders too. To search the current folder and any other folders within that folder, check the Search subfolders checkbox.

Keep in mind that Word searches down — not up — through the folders. If you think the folder might be somewhere outside the current folder branch, select a higher folder from the Look in list.

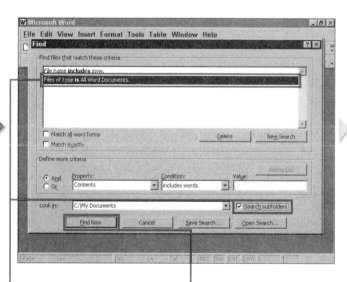

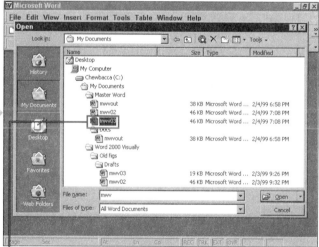

■ This criteria is added to the search list.

7 To search this folder and all subfolders, check Search subfolders.

8 Click the Find Now button.

■ You see the results of the file search.

FIND A DOCUMENT BY CONTENT

Say you can't even remember the file name, but you do remember some text within a document. In that case, you can search for the file based on its contents.

When you are searching for content, type a unique word or phrase. If you type something too common, you'll get too many matches and will never be able to find the file. If you type something unique, you limit the search.

You can search just the current folder, or that folder and any subfolders. You can also set other search options, such as how matches are made.

Note: To search by content, you must have installed the Find Fast feature during the initial installation of Word. If Find Fast is not installed, you are prompted to install it.

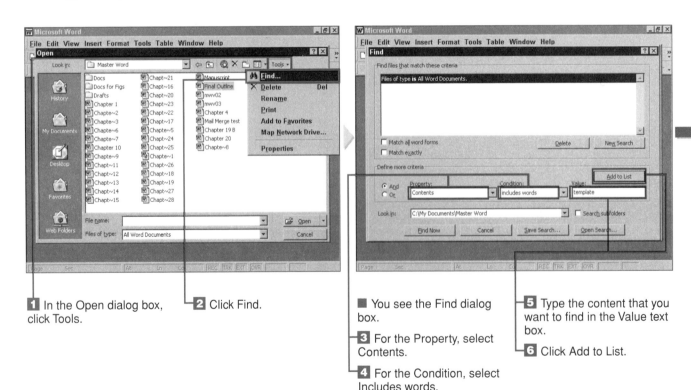

1 In the Open dialog box, click Tools.

2 Click Find.

■ You see the Find dialog box.

3 For the Property, select Contents.

4 For the Condition, select Includes words.

5 Type the content that you want to find in the Value text box.

6 Click Add to List.

How can I find a file on which I recently worked ?

If you still can't find a file, but you know that you worked on it sometime last week, try searching based on when the file was last modified. Select Date as the property and then select any of the date conditions. Enter the matching value.

I still can't find the file!

Make sure you started with the top-level file and try searching all subfolders. If you want to search a certain folder and any other folders within that folder, check the Search subfolders checkbox.

There are other search entries. How do I clear them?

Word remembers the last search you performed and keeps those conditions. If you want to clear them, click the New Search button.

What else can I search?

You can search any of the file properties displayed in the Property drop-down list, including date, company, author, keywords, last modified date, manager, and so on. Select the property and the condition and then enter the value you want to match.

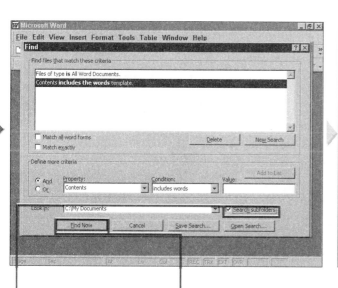

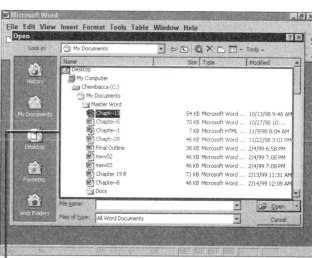

7 To search this folder and all subfolders, check Search subfolders.

8 Click the Find Now button.

■ You see the results of the file search.

MAKING THE MOST OF SHORTCUTS

Word may be a program you use all the time, or at least most of the time. You may, in fact, start your work day by starting Word. Rather than use the Start menu, you can use some shortcuts for starting the program. You can also use other timesaving features that are worth looking into.

Starting Word

You have several options for starting Word:

▸ If you want to be able to start Word from the desktop, you can create a shortcut icon. (That's how I start Word.)

▸ If you want to work on a particular document, you can open that document and start Word at the same time. I also use this method a lot when I want to edit a document on which I recently worked.

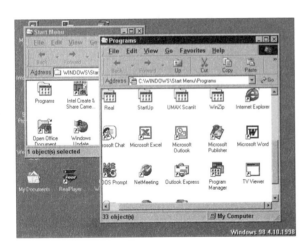

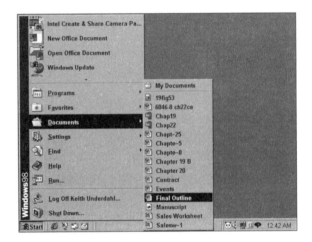

▸ If you use Word all the time, or most of the time, you may want to start the program each time you start Windows. This method is good if you exit Windows each time you quit. I don't use it because I keep Windows and my PC running all the time.

Setting Up the Toolbars

In addition to shortcuts for starting Word, you can use the toolbar. It is a convenient palette of shortcuts to commonly used commands. You may like the toolbars so much that you want to use others, or even create your own.

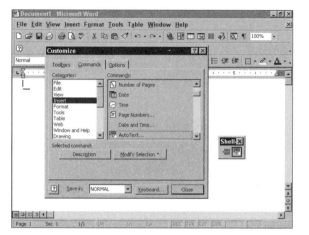

Using Shortcut Keys

Word has several shortcut keys. Rather than open a menu and select a command, you can press a key combination. As an example, you can press Ctrl+B to make text bold. The menus list many of the shortcut keys, and this book also highlights some of the best ones. If necessary, you can assign your own shortcut keys.

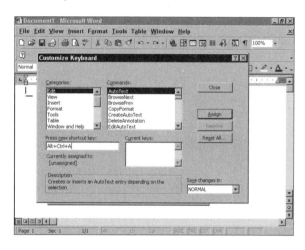

CREATE A SHORTCUT ICON

f you look around your "real"
desktop, you may see that
you have everything you need
close at hand. You can just reach
across the desktop, for instance,
and pick up your pen. Maybe you

have to shuffle some papers
around. Or maybe you have to
crawl under the desk to find the
pen. Or maybe it would take a
search-and-rescue team to find a
pen on your desk. You get the

idea, though. Stuff you use often
is right there on top of your desk.

If Word is a program you use
often, you can place access to it
on your Windows desktop,
making it easy to find and run.

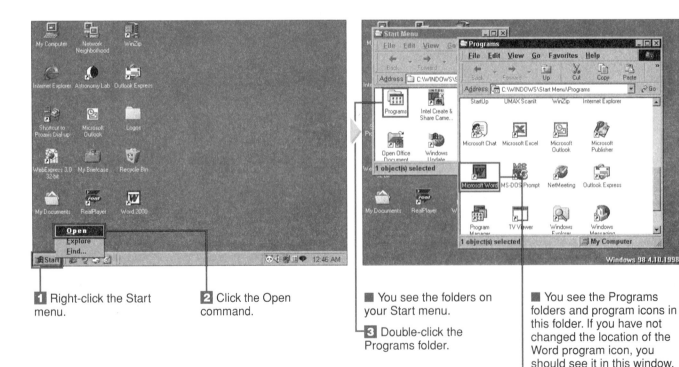

■1 Right-click the Start
menu.

■2 Click the Open
command.

■ You see the folders on
your Start menu.

■3 Double-click the
Programs folder.

■ You see the Programs
folders and program icons in
this folder. If you have not
changed the location of the
Word program icon, you
should see it in this window.

■4 Point to the Word icon
and click and hold down the
right mouse button.

TIPS

How do I start Word using this icon?

You can use the shortcut icon to start Word. To do so, double-click it.

How do I delete a shortcut icon?

You can delete a shortcut icon by dragging it to the Recycle Bin or by right-clicking the icon and selecting Delete. The program is not deleted, only the shortcut icon pointing to the program.

To what else can I create a shortcut?

You can also add shortcuts to folders and files that you frequently use. Display the folder or file in a file window and follow the same procedure: drag it to the desktop using the right mouse button and select Create Shortcut(s) here. If you double-click a file shortcut, the file is opened and the program started. Double-click a folder icon to view its contents.

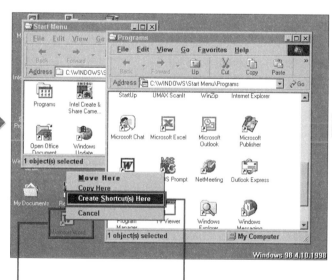

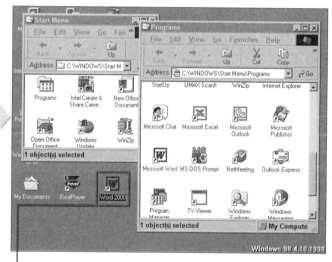

5 Drag the program icon to the desktop and release the mouse button.

6 Select the Create Shortcut(s) Here command.

■ Windows creates the shortcut and places it on your desktop.

START WORD AUTOMATICALLY

Maybe double-clicking a shortcut icon is too much work for you. Why not just start Word when you start Windows? If you use Word a lot, you can add a copy of the Word program icon to your StartUp folder. The StartUp folder is a special program folder created automatically by Windows. Each time you start Windows, it starts all the programs placed in the StartUp folder.

Don't go overboard adding a lot of programs. Doing so wastes your system resources. Also, remember that the programs are started only when you start Windows. If you don't exit and restart Windows after you've added Word and other programs to the StartUp folder, the programs will not be started.

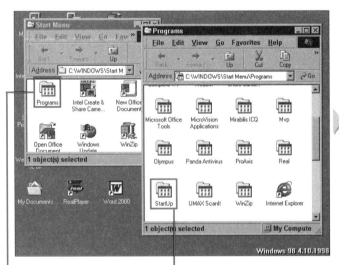

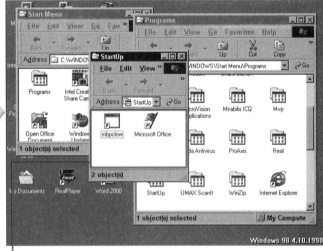

1 Right-click the Start menu and then select the Open command.

■ You see the folders on your Start menu.

2 Double-click the Programs folder.

■ You see the program folders and icons. If you have not moved the Word program icon, you should see it in this window. If you have moved it, select the folder that contains the program icon.

3 Double-click the StartUp folder.

■ You see a window with all program icons already in the StartUp folder.

What if I can't see both windows?

If necessary, arrange the windows so you can see both the Programs window and the StartUp window. You can move a window by dragging the title bar.

How do I remove a program from the StartUp folder?

If you change your mind and decide you no longer want to start Word each time you start Windows, delete the program icon from the StartUp folder. Open this folder, right-click once on the icon, and then select the Delete command.

What other programs are in my StartUp folder?

It depends on your system setup. You or other programs may have added programs to this folder. You will see the programs when you display the StartUp folder.

I added the icon to this folder, but Word didn't start. Why not?

Keep in mind that Word will start only when you restart Windows. If you have not turned your PC off and on, the programs in the StartUp folder will not be started.

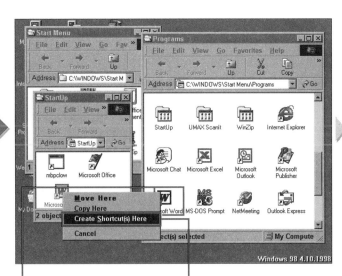

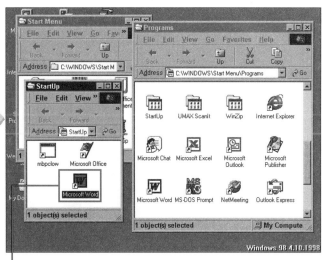

4 Use the right mouse button to drag the program icon from the Programs folder to the StartUp folder.

5 Select the Create Shortcut(s) Here command.

■ Windows creates the shortcut and places it in your StartUp folder. Each time you start Windows, Word will start as well.

START WORD AND OPEN A DOCUMENT

A lot of times you will start work by going back to a document on which you just worked. You could start Word and then find and open that document. Or you can use a shortcut.

Windows keeps track of the last 15 documents on which you

worked. You can select any of these documents from the Documents menu, start the program, *and* open that document at the same time.

When you display the Documents menu, keep in mind that you will see other document types besides Word. You see the

last 15 documents, regardless of type. You can usually tell by the document icon what program was used to create the document, and will be started when you select the document.

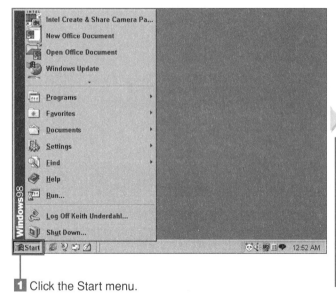

1 Click the Start menu.

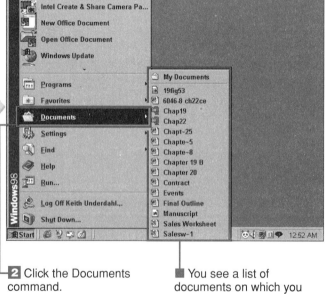

2 Click the Documents command.

■ You see a list of documents on which you have recently worked.

What if the document isn't listed?

If the document is not listed, it was not one of the most recent files on which you have worked. You'll have to open the document using the File ➪ Open command from within Word.

How else can I open a document from the Windows desktop?

You can also double-click the My Computer icon and then open the drive and folder that contains your document. When you see the document icon, double-click it. Windows starts Word and opens the document.

Can I clear the Documents menu?

Yes. To do so, click Start ➪ Settings ➪ Taskbar & Start Menu. Click the Start Menu Programs tab and then click the Clear button in the Documents menu area. Click OK.

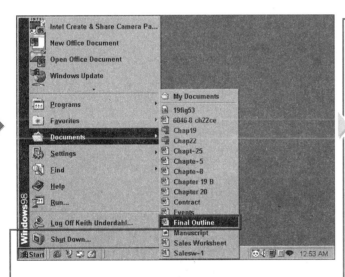

3 Click the document you want.

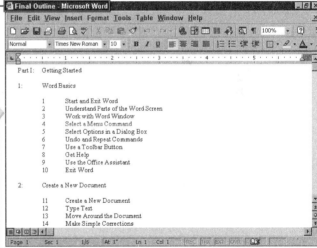

■ Windows starts that program (Word in this case) and then opens the document.

VIEW OTHER TOOLBARS

By default, you see the Standard and Formatting toolbars, which contain buttons for frequently used commands. If you use these items, you will find them quite handy. If you don't, you can turn off the toolbars and gain additional screen space.

You can also select to display other toolbars. You can select

from several different toolbars including ones for databases, drawing, WordArt, Web page creation, reviewing changes, and others.

Some toolbars are displayed when you click a button on the Standard toolbar. For instance, if you click the Drawing button, you see the Drawing toolbar. If you click the Insert Table button, you

see the Tables and Borders button. Some toolbars appear when you perform a certain action. For instance, when you create a merge letter, you see the Merge toolbar. You can also choose to display these and other toolbars at any time.

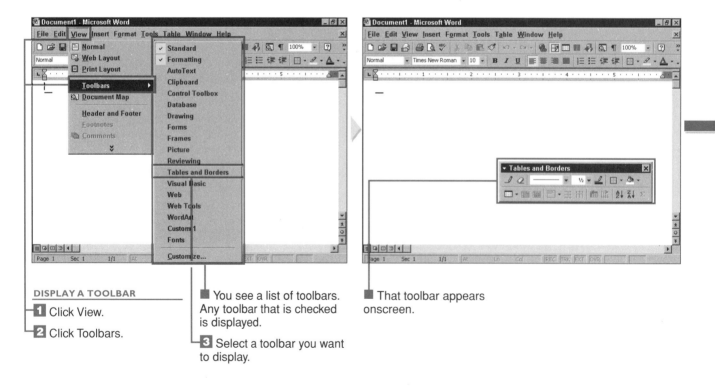

DISPLAY A TOOLBAR

1 Click View.

2 Click Toolbars.

■ You see a list of toolbars. Any toolbar that is checked is displayed.

3 Select a toolbar you want to display.

■ That toolbar appears onscreen.

TIPS

My Standard and Formatting toolbars appear as one row. How can I change this?

If the two default toolbars are on the same row, you should see a More Buttons arrow. Click this button to display additional buttons. If you don't like the cramped style of all the buttons on one row, select to view them as two rows. To do so, select Tools ➪ Customize. Click the Options tab. Uncheck the Standard and Formatting toolbars Share One Row checkbox and then click Close.

What's another method for viewing toolbars?

You can also right-click any toolbar to display the Toolbar menu. You can then check or uncheck any of the listed toolbars.

What other changes can I make?

You can also move and resize toolbars. You can add other buttons or delete buttons. See the other sections in this chapter.

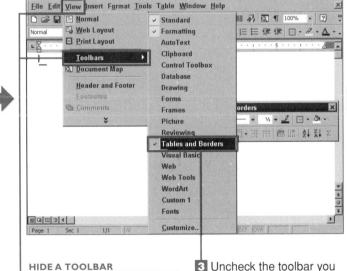

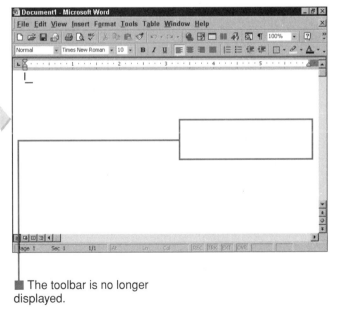

HIDE A TOOLBAR

1 Click View.

2 Click Toolbars.

3 Uncheck the toolbar you want to hide.

■ The toolbar is no longer displayed.

MOVE AND RESIZE A TOOLBAR

When you start Word, the Formatting and Standard toolbars are displayed right under the menu bar. If you don't like this placement, move them to another spot. You can have them float as a palette, or you can dock them against the edge of the screen.

When the toolbars aren't docked, you can also resize them, changing the size and shape. You may want to move the toolbars to a more convenient location. For example, you might want to have them as a boxed palette in the lower-right corner.

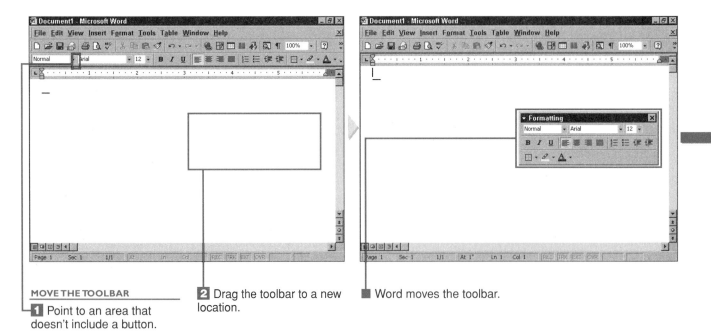

MOVE THE TOOLBAR

1 Point to an area that doesn't include a button.

2 Drag the toolbar to a new location.

■ Word moves the toolbar.

I can't get the toolbar to move. Why not?

To move the toolbar, you have to put the pointer on a blank area, and this step can be kind of tricky. You can't put the pointer on a button or you will select that button. Put it right between two buttons.

How do I close (or hide) a toolbar?

If the toolbar is not docked against a screen edge, it should have a Close button. To close the toolbar, click the Close button. Otherwise, right-click any toolbar then uncheck the toolbar's name to hide the toolbar.

How do I return the toolbar to its original location?

Drag the toolbar so it butts up against the edge of the screen.

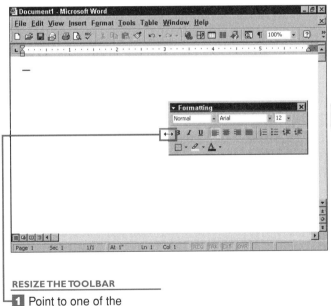

RESIZE THE TOOLBAR

1 Point to one of the borders.

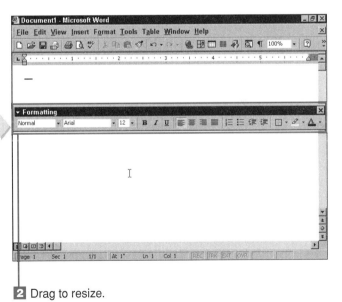

2 Drag to resize.

CUSTOMIZE AN EXISTING TOOLBAR

The Formatting and Standard toolbar each contain buttons for commonly used features. You may find that you use some buttons all the time. You may also find that you don't use some buttons at all. You can make changes to the toolbar if you want, to make it more suitable to how you use it. You can rearrange the buttons, putting them in a different order, delete buttons you don't use, or add buttons you do want.

You can customize any of the Word toolbars — not just the Standard and Formatting ones. To start, be sure that the target toolbar is displayed.

To make changes, you open the Customize dialog box. Once this dialog box is open, you can make a change.

If the command had an icon next to it and you add this command, that icon is used for the button. If the command doesn't have an icon, Word just uses a text button.

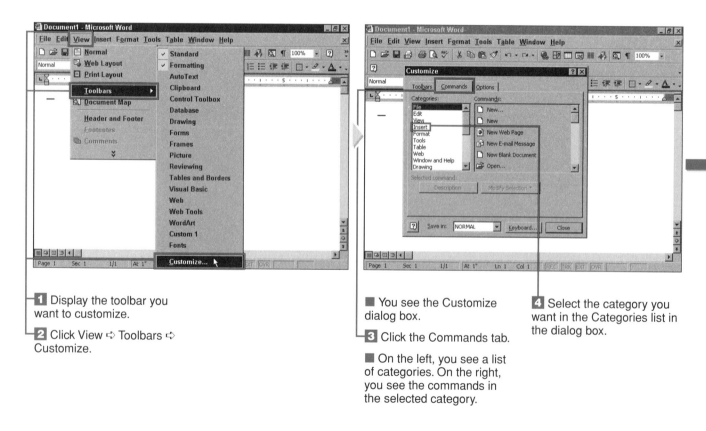

■1 Display the toolbar you want to customize.

■2 Click View ➪ Toolbars ➪ Customize.

■ You see the Customize dialog box.

■3 Click the Commands tab.

■ On the left, you see a list of categories. On the right, you see the commands in the selected category.

■4 Select the category you want in the Categories list in the dialog box.

TIPS

How do I move a button?

To move a button on a toolbar, display the Customize dialog box. Then drag the button to a new location on the toolbar.

How do I go back to the original set of buttons?

If you make a lot of changes and want to go back to the default, you can reset the toolbar. To do so, select View ➪ Toolbars ➪ Customize. On the Toolbars tab, select the toolbar you want to reset. Then click the Reset button. Word goes back to the default order and buttons. Close the dialog box by clicking the Close button.

How do I delete a button from a toolbar?

To delete a button on a toolbar, open the Customize dialog box. Then drag the button off the toolbar.

The button wasn't added. Why not?

If you try to add the button to the end of the toolbar, be sure it's right on the toolbar. You can tell when the pointer is in the right spot. If you see a plus sign, the button will be added. If you see an X, you are not on the toolbar.

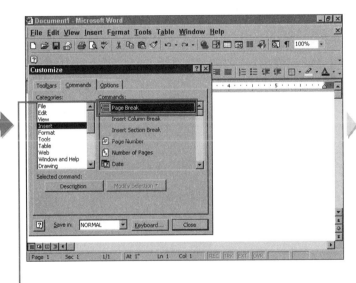

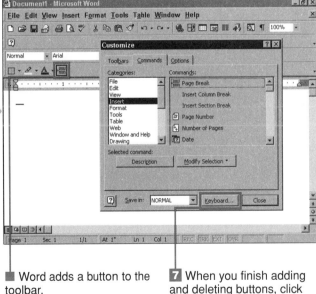

5 Select the command you want in the Commands list.

6 Drag the command from the Customize dialog box to the toolbar onscreen.

■ Word adds a button to the toolbar.

7 When you finish adding and deleting buttons, click the Close button.

CREATE A NEW TOOLBAR

Instead of changing the Standard and Formatting toolbars, you may want to leave them as is and create your own little box (in this case bar) of tools. You can create a new toolbar and then add the buttons you want.

To start, create the new toolbar. It will be blank. You can then add buttons from the different menus, from other toolbars, and for macros, fonts, AutoText entries, and styles. Simply select the item you want to add and then drag it to your toolbar.

If the command had an icon next to it, that icon is used for the button. If the command doesn't have an icon, Word uses a text button.

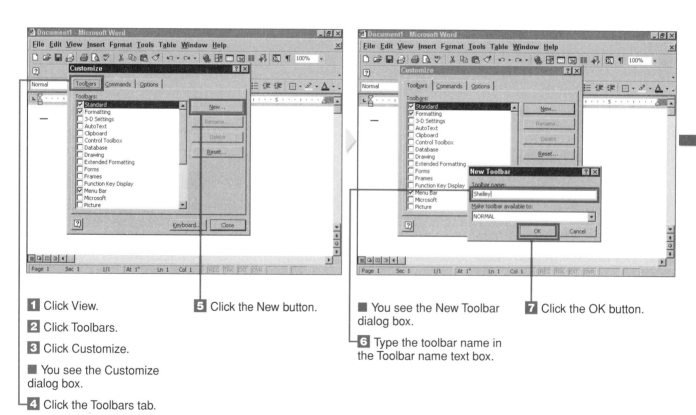

1 Click View.

2 Click Toolbars.

3 Click Customize.

■ You see the Customize dialog box.

4 Click the Toolbars tab.

5 Click the New button.

■ You see the New Toolbar dialog box.

6 Type the toolbar name in the Toolbar name text box.

7 Click the OK button.

TIPS

How do I delete a toolbar?

Select View ➪ Toolbars ➪ Customize. Click the Toolbars tab. Select the toolbar you want to delete, and then click the Delete button. When prompted to confirm the deletion, click the OK button.

When can I use the toolbar?

You can use the toolbar in any of the documents based on the Normal template (the default). If you want to make the toolbar available for a specific template, display the Make toolbar available to drop-down list and select the template you want.

What should I use for the toolbar name?

Type something that reminds you of the toolbar's purpose. If you don't like the name you used for a toolbar, you can rename it. To rename a toolbar, open the View menu and select the Toolbars command. Select Customize. Click the Toolbars tab. Select the toolbar you want to rename, and then click the Rename button. Type a new name and click OK.

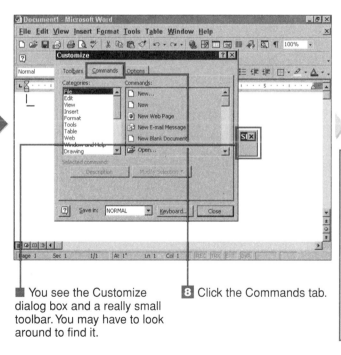

■ You see the Customize dialog box and a really small toolbar. You may have to look around to find it.

8 Click the Commands tab.

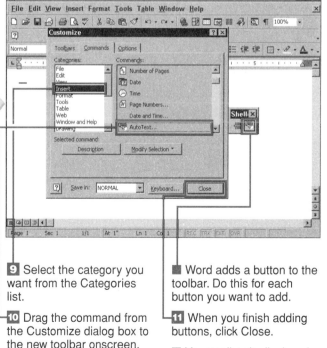

9 Select the category you want from the Categories list.

10 Drag the command from the Customize dialog box to the new toolbar onscreen.

■ Word adds a button to the toolbar. Do this for each button you want to add.

11 When you finish adding buttons, click Close.

■ Your toolbar is displayed onscreen.

ASSIGN SHORTCUT KEYS

I love shortcut keys. I'm a fast typist, and I don't like to have to move my hand away from the mouse to select a command or click a button. Plus, I learned to use a PC before a mouse was standard equipment, and before software was dolled up with all the buttons. To do something more quickly then, you *had* to learn keyboard shortcuts.

If you like keyboard shortcuts, too, you may want to review and/or change some of the keyboard assignments. For example, when I write a book, I have to assign styles to the different headings, bulleted lists, and numbered lists. To do so quickly, I assign shortcut keys to the styles I use most frequently.

You can assign shortcut keys to menu commands, toolbar

buttons, macros, fonts, AutoText entries, styles, and common symbols. The Commands list shows the available items. For example, if you select a menu, you see menu commands. If you select styles, you see a list of styles.

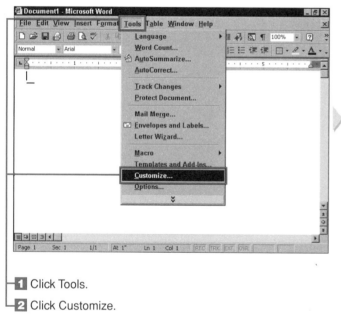

1 Click Tools.

2 Click Customize.

3 Click the Keyboard button.

TIPS

What key combinations can I use?

You can press any combination of Ctrl, Alt, Ctrl+Shift, Ctrl+Alt, Alt+Shift, or Ctrl+Alt+Shift with any of the number or character keys.

How do I reset the keyboard shortcuts?

You can reset all the shortcuts by clicking the Reset All button in the Customize Keyboard dialog box.

What if the key combination is already being used?

If you press a keyboard combination that is already used, you see the current assignment in the dialog box. You can either press Backspace to delete this key combination, and then press another key combination or reassign the current one.

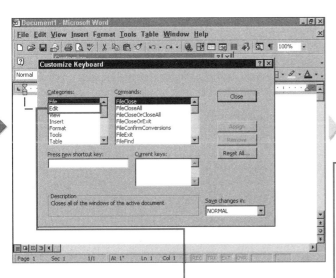

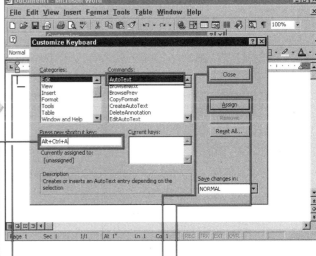

■ You see the Customize Keyboard dialog box.

4 In the Categories list, select the category.

5 In the Commands list, select the item to receive a keyboard shortcut.

■ You see current shortcut keys and short descriptions.

6 Click here and press the keys you want to use as the shortcut.

7 Click the Assign button.

8 Follow Steps 3 through 6 for each keyboard shortcut you want to assign.

9 When you finish making changes, click the Close button twice.

CUSTOMIZING WORD

Think about how you perform a task such as cooking a meal. Do you have everything going at once? Or do you make each meal item one at a time? Do you clean up as you go? Or do you leave it all for the end? Which utensils do you use? A food processor? Or chop by hand? Now think about how your mother, aunt, spouse, or neighbor cooks the same meal. It's likely that each person does the same task differently.

The same is true for creating documents. Each person has a certain job to do — certain documents or things to accomplish. Even if two people have the same job, they most likely do that job their own special way.

The makers of Word needed a way to accommodate how most people work. That's why certain options have defaults that work in the most common situations. Word also needed to be flexible so that if the defaults don't work, the user can make a change. This chapter discusses some of the changes you may want to make to how Word works.

Changing How the Program Looks

As one change, you can control what appears onscreen. You can hide everything so that you can concentrate on the writing. Or you can display other characters, such as nonprinting characters (returns, tabs, spaces, and so on). What's best? What *you* like.

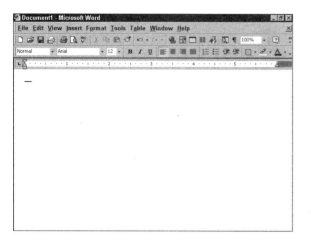

Changing How the Program Works

The look of the program is one change. How the program works is another. You have a great deal of control over several options: editing, printing, saving, user information, and so on. To make these changes, you use the tabs in the Options dialog box.

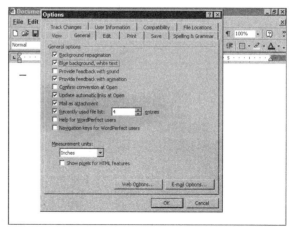

This chapter covers the View, Edit, General, and User Info tabs. You can find information on other tabs throughout the book:

- For information on save and file location options, see Chapter 24.
- For information on print options, see Chapter 6.
- For information on spelling and grammar options, see Chapter 5.
- For information on tracking changes, see Chapter 20.

You can also make changes to the menu options.

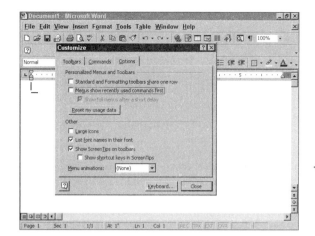

CHANGE WHAT APPEARS ONSCREEN

You can think of Word as your desktop, equipped with all the tools you need to write, edit, and change the look of your text. If you don't have the tools you need handy, you can change them.

You have a lot of control over what appears on your screen. You can hide or display items, such as the status bar, scroll bars, ruler, nonprinting characters, and other elements.

By default, Word shows drawings, animated text, ScreenTips, and highlighting. You can turn off each of these items by unchecking its checkbox. You can also choose to display hidden items such as bookmarks, field codes, picture placeholders, text boundaries, and object anchors. You can display characters for tabs, spaces, paragraph marks, optional hyphens, hidden text, or all of these characters. To display an item, check its checkbox.

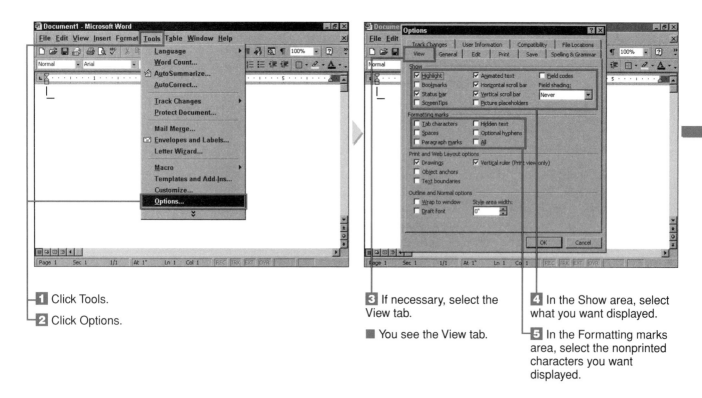

1 Click Tools.

2 Click Options.

3 If necessary, select the View tab.

■ You see the View tab.

4 In the Show area, select what you want displayed.

5 In the Formatting marks area, select the nonprinted characters you want displayed.

Everything is gone! What happened?

If you selected View ⇨ Full Screen, all the toolbars, rulers, and other elements are hidden. You should still see the Full Screen toolbar. Click the Close Full Screen button to go back to the regular view of the program window.

What changes can I make to the toolbars?

You can hide toolbars, or display other toolbars. You can also move them to another location onscreen. For help on making these changes, see Chapter 25.

How do I get a perfectly blank program window?

You may like just a plain old blank screen without any toolbars, menu bars, or other distractions, like a big clean piece of paper. If so, you can hide everything by selecting View ⇨ Full Screen.

What's a shortcut for displaying nonprinting characters?

You can click the Show/Hide ¶ to show returns, tabs, and spaces. Click this button again to hide these nonprinting characters.

6 Click OK.

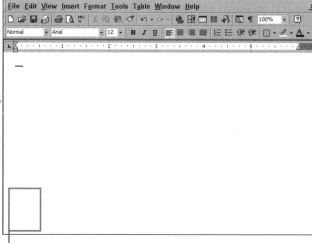

■ Word makes the change. Here the status bar and scroll bars are turned off.

SET GENERAL OPTIONS

Word includes many other program options that you can control. If you want to review some of the other available options, you can do so. For instance, you might want to make a change to some of the general program options, found on the General tab.

Here are a few changes worth considering:

- ▶ The default measurement unit is inches. If you

prefer a different measurement (picas, points, or centimeters), select it from the Measurement units drop-down list.

- ▶ The File menu lists the last four documents on which you worked. You can increase (or decrease) this number using the Recently used file list entries spin box.

- ▶ If you are a former WordPerfect user, you can make Word look and operate more like this program. Use the various WordPerfect options.

Remember that if you don't know what an option does, you can display a pop-up explanation. To do so, right-click it and then select the What's This? command.

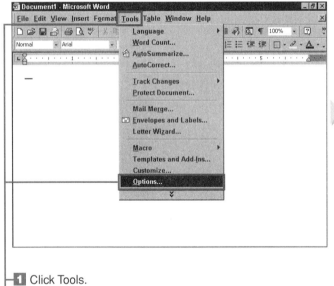

1 Click Tools.

2 Click Options.

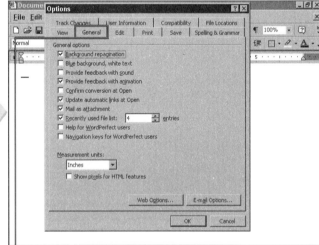

3 Click the General tab.

TIPS

What are the Web options?

You can click the Web options button to select the browser you use to browse the Web. For more information on Web publishing, see Chapter 23.

What are the e-mail options?

You can set up an e-mail signature (added to e-mail messages) and personal stationery using the E-mail Options button. For information on e-mailing documents, see Chapter 22.

How do I undo a change?

If you change your mind, select the Tools ➪ Options command again. Click the General tab and then check the option to turn it on, or uncheck it to turn it off.

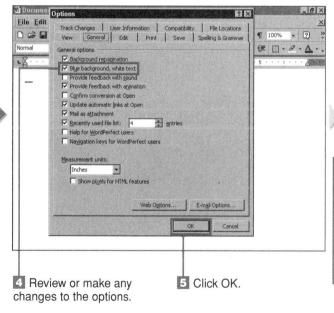

4 Review or make any changes to the options.

5 Click OK.

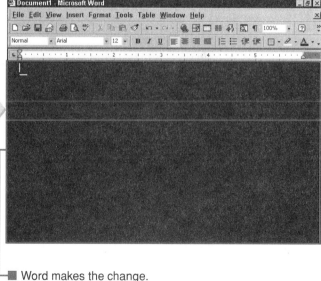

■ Word makes the change. Here you see a blue background.

SET EDIT OPTIONS

In addition to General options, you may want to review and make changes to some of the editing features. For instance, you can select to turn off drag-and-drop editing. If you press Tab, Word sets a left indent. If you don't want an indent, you can turn off this feature (tabs and backspace set left indents). You can also change to Overtype mode, rather than Insert mode.

As with other tabs, check an option to turn it on. Uncheck an option to turn it off. You can also get help on a particular option by right-clicking the option and selecting the What's This? command.

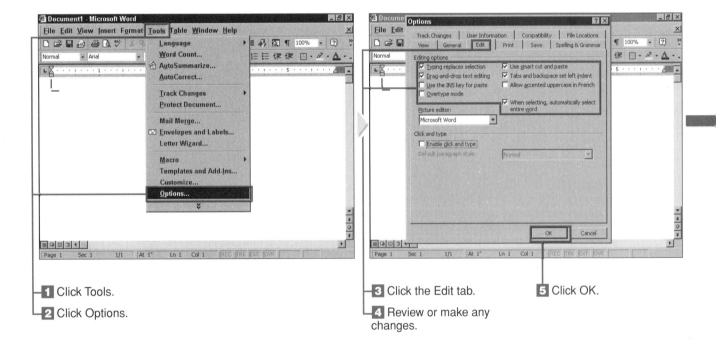

1 Click Tools.

2 Click Options.

3 Click the Edit tab.

4 Review or make any changes.

5 Click OK.

MODIFY USER INFORMATION

When you start typing your name, you may be surprised to see Word display a ScreenTip with the entire name. That's because Word creates an AutoText entry for your name, and it gets the name from the Name text box on the User Information. (You enter this information when you install the program.)

Word also uses your initials for comments added to a document and uses your address for envelopes. You can review and make any changes to this user information.

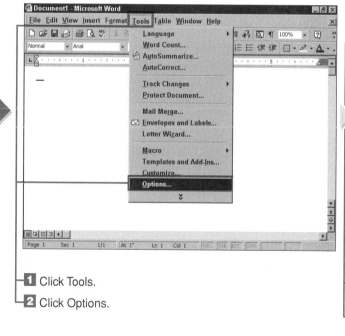

1 Click Tools.

2 Click Options.

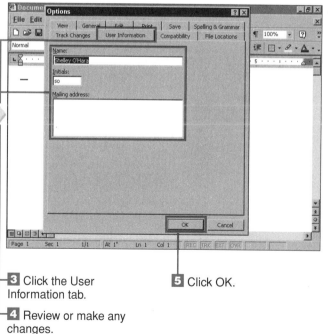

3 Click the User Information tab.

4 Review or make any changes.

5 Click OK.

CUSTOMIZE HELP

D o you use the Office Assistant? If so, you may want to modify the appearance of the Office assistance and set options for how it works.

You can set several options. For example, you can display the assistant when you press F1. You can play sounds. You can have the assistant move automatically if it is in the way. You can have the assistant guess help topics. Turn on or off any of these options on the Options tab.

You can also use a different character for the Assistant. Click the Gallery tab, and then use the

Back and Next buttons to scroll through the characters until you find the one you want.

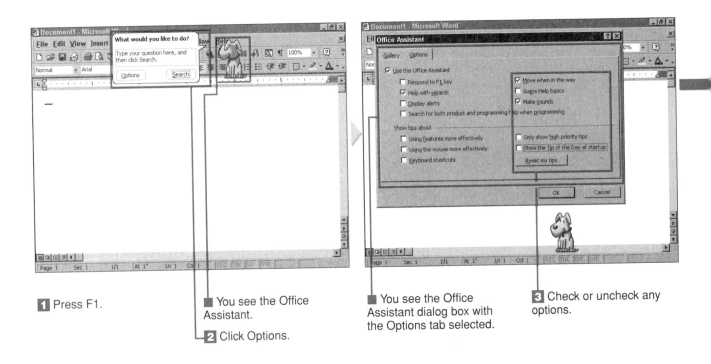

1 Press F1.

■ You see the Office Assistant.

2 Click Options.

■ You see the Office Assistant dialog box with the Options tab selected.

3 Check or uncheck any options.

TIPS

From what characters can I select?

You can select from a range of characters including Rover the dog, Mother Nature, The Genius, The Dot, and others. Select the one you like best.

How do I display the Office Assistant?

You can display the Office Assistant by clicking the Microsoft Word Help button in the toolbar.

How do I turn off the Office Assistant?

To turn off the assistant, click Help ➪ Hide the Office Assistant.

How do I use the Office Assistant to get help?

To use the assistant to get help, type your question and click Search. For more information on Word's help features, see Chapter 1 of this book.

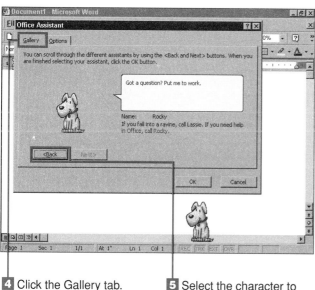

4 Click the Gallery tab.

5 Select the character to use by clicking the Back or Next button.

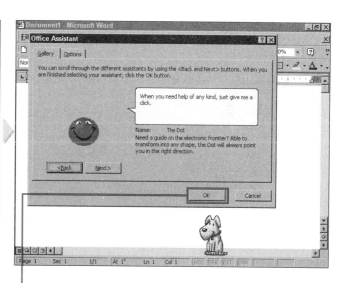

6 Click OK.

MANAGING AND CUSTOMIZING WORD

519

CUSTOMIZE THE MENUS

The menus work differently in this version of Word. When you open a menu, only some of the commands are displayed. If you keep your pointer on the menu, all the commands will appear. Or you can click the arrow at the bottom of the menu to display all commands.

If you don't like this feature, you can turn it off. You can also add menu animations.

You can also set other options including using large icons for the toolbar buttons, listing font names in their font, and showing ScreenTips. Make all these changes from the Options tab of the Customize dialog box.

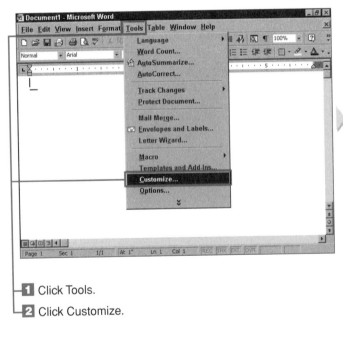

1 Click Tools.

2 Click Customize.

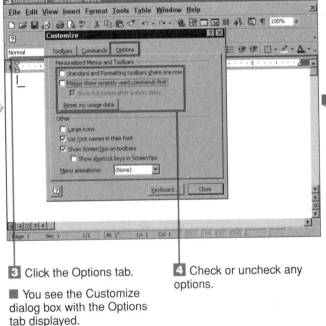

3 Click the Options tab.

■ You see the Customize dialog box with the Options tab displayed.

4 Check or uncheck any options.

TIPS

What menu animations are available?

You can select Random, Unfold, or Slide. The best way to understand them is to try out each one. The animations are fun at first, but can get tedious after a while.

Can I customize the toolbar?

Yes. You can rearrange the buttons on a toolbar, add new buttons, and delete buttons. You can even create a new toolbar with your own personal set of buttons. For information on changing the toolbar, see Chapter 25.

Can I also customize the menu commands?

Yes. Customize the menus by rearranging, adding, and deleting commands. For the most part, changing the menus can create a mess. This book, the online help, and other users assume that certain commands are available. If you make a change, you can end up lost. If you do want to make this type of change, use the Commands tab in the Customize dialog box. Consult online help for complete information.

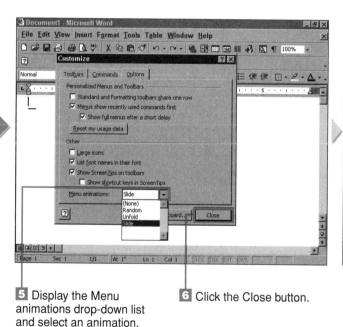

5 Display the Menu animations drop-down list and select an animation.

6 Click the Close button.

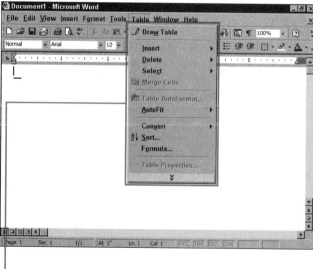

■ The menus appear with your selected options.

THE MAGIC OF WIZARDS

You used to have just one way to automate routine tasks in a word-processing program: macros. And you had to be somewhat of an expert to create and use macros. All of that is changed. First, macros are easy to record. Second, you can use other features for automating tasks.

What Is a Macro?

A macro is a series of keystrokes, commands, and mouse actions recorded so you can play the same set of commands again. Suppose, for instance, that for most documents you create a header with the file name and page number. This process involves several command selections. First you select View ⇨ Header and Footer. Then you type any text you want to include, tab to where you want the file name, and then use Insert ⇨ Field to insert the file name. Then you tab again and click the Insert Page Number button to insert a page number. In a book with 27 chapters, you would have to select these same commands 27 times. Instead, you can create a macro.

With a macro, you record the commands once and save them as a macro. All you do is turn on Macro Recording, select your commands, and then turn off the recorder.

Once you've recorded your macro, you can play it back at any time. You can select to play back the macro from the Macro list, from a keyboard shortcut, or from a toolbar button.

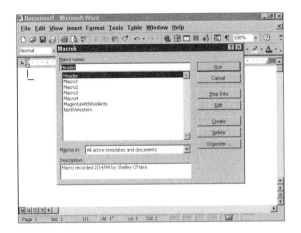

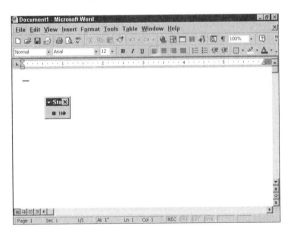

Macros versus Other Features

Macros are one way to automate tasks, but keep in mind that Word offers several automation features. Pick the one that is best suited for the task. Here are some other possibilities:

- If you simply want a way to enter the same word, phrase, or other text, you can set up an AutoText entry. See Chapter 2.

- If you want to use the same set of formatting on certain document elements (for instance, document headings), consider a style. You can create a style once, and then apply it to other text. If you need to make a change, update the style, and all paragraphs formatted with that style are automatically updated.

- If you create the same type of document — with particular margins, text entries, and formatting features — consider building a template. A template is a predesigned document. You open the template and have a head start on creating a new document.

Big-time Macros

Word includes a programming language, the same language used to create macros. This language, called Visual Basic, can also be used to create more sophisticated applications. If you are a programmer, or build custom applications for Word, you can use this language to expand the power of Word's features.

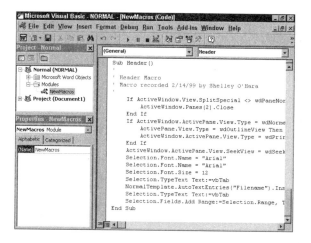

RECORD A MACRO

If you find yourself performing the same task over and over again, create a macro. Macros are a convenient means of automating a repetitive task. You might, for instance, create a macro that inserts the file name and page number in the header. You might have a formatting macro that makes several formatting changes at once. To create a macro, you simply start the macro recorder,

enter the keystrokes or select the commands, and then turn off the recorder. All the actions you perform are recorded.

When you create a macro, you assign a name. You also have the option of saving it as a keyboard macro or a toolbar macro. When you save your macro as a keyboard macro, you assign the macro to a certain key combination such as Ctrl+B or Alt+K so that when you later

press the assigned key combination, the macro containing your recorded actions is replayed.

When you save your macro as a toolbar macro, you assign the macro to a toolbar button on either an existing toolbar or a new toolbar you create. You can also run the macro using the Macro command.

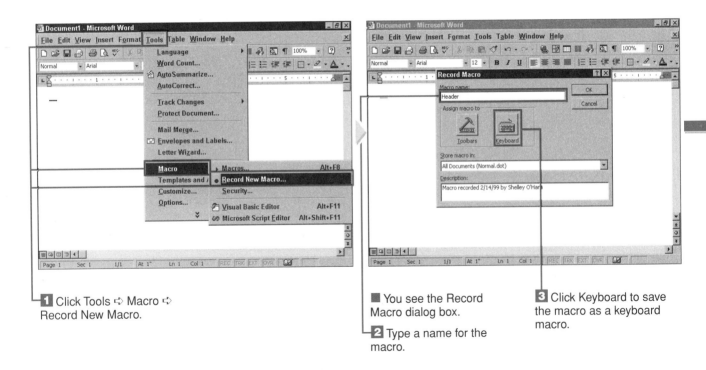

■1 Click Tools ➪ Macro ➪ Record New Macro.

■ You see the Record Macro dialog box.

■2 Type a name for the macro.

■3 Click Keyboard to save the macro as a keyboard macro.

What's the difference between a keyboard macro and a toolbar macro?

The macro is the same; the only difference is the action you perform to invoke the macro. Toolbar macros are assigned to toolbar icons; you need to click the icon to invoke the macro.

What should I name my macros?

If you don't supply a name, Word uses the default naming combination Macro1, Macro2, Macro3, and so on. Use a name that reminds you of the macro's contents or purpose.

Can macros include both keyboard and mouse actions?

Yes. Virtually any step you can perform in Word can be recorded as a macro. Some steps, such as changing to a specific folder, will not be recorded.

What happens if I select a key combination that is already in use?

Word notifies you that a key combination is already assigned to a particular operation, in which case you need to select another key combination.

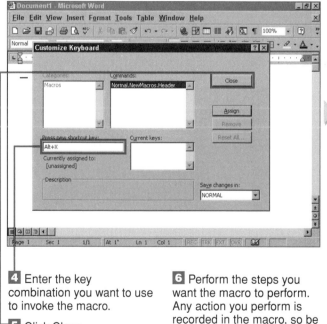

4 Enter the key combination you want to use to invoke the macro.

5 Click Close.

6 Perform the steps you want the macro to perform. Any action you perform is recorded in the macro, so be careful.

7 Click the Stop Recording button in the Macro toolbar.

■ The macro is created.

RUN A MACRO

After you create your macro, it is a good idea to test it. You can also play back the macro any time you want to issue the same set of commands. You have several ways to run a macro.

First, you can use the Macro command to select and run a macro.

Second, if you created a keyboard macro, you simply press the key combination you assigned to replay the macro.

Or, if you assigned the macro to a toolbar, make sure that toolbar is visible. Then click the icon to which the macro is assigned; doing so will run or replay the macro.

When your macro runs, it should perform the same keystrokes and mouse actions you performed when you created the macro.

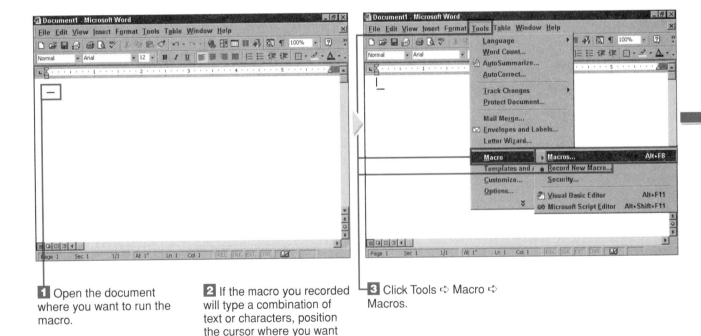

1 Open the document where you want to run the macro.

2 If the macro you recorded will type a combination of text or characters, position the cursor where you want the text to appear.

3 Click Tools ➪ Macro ➪ Macros.

If I create a macro in one document, can I run the same macro in another document?

 Yes. See the later section, "Organize Macros," about using the Organizer to transfer macros from one document to another.

Will I have trouble running macros created in Word 97?

No. Macros created using Word 97 will run in Word 2000 without modification or conversion. (You may have problems upgrading from Word 95 to Word 2000, though.)

Can I undo a macro after I have run it?

Yes. If you click Edit immediately after running the macro, you will see the Undo VBA Selection option. Click this option to undo the macro you just ran. (The name of the command will vary depending on the action recorded in the macro.)

Is there a limit on the number of times I can run a macro?

No. You can literally repeat a macro *ad infinitum*.

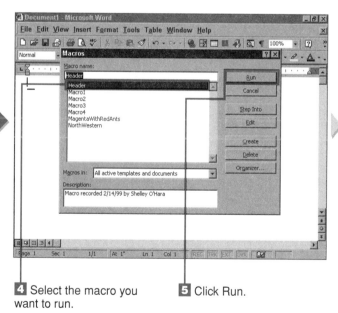

4 Select the macro you want to run.

5 Click Run.

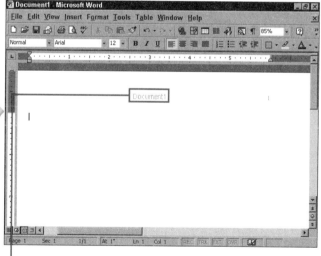

6 Examine the results to make sure the macro performed as you intended. Here you see the macro added a header with the document file name and page number.

527

EDIT A MACRO

If you create a macro and then change your mind about the steps you want the macro to perform, you can edit the macro. Occasionally problems do pop up with macros, and you may need to edit the macro to correct a problem.

When you edit your macros, Word displays the steps

programmed into the macro so you can see each individual step. You can review and make changes to the commands in the macro.

Word macros are written in Visual Basic. Although it isn't essential to know Visual Basic to make simple edits in your macros, if you intend to make complex

changes, you might want to consider learning Visual Basic. You can use this programming language in many Microsoft products, so your skills will come in handy for more than just Word.

Word also has a section in its online Help to help you troubleshoot problems with macros.

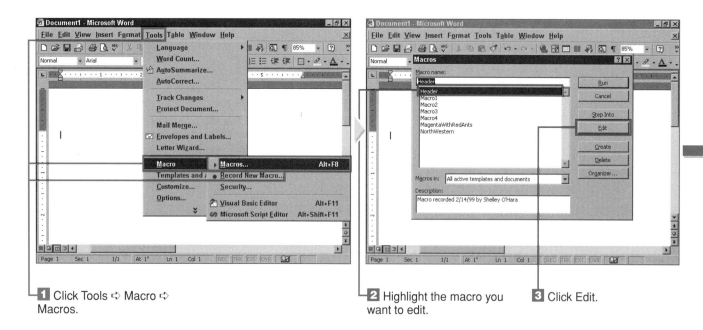

1 Click Tools ⇨ Macro ⇨ Macros.

2 Highlight the macro you want to edit.

3 Click Edit.

Where can I find out more about Visual Basic?

 You can get lots of useful information from Microsoft's Visual Basic Web site at *http://msdn.microsoft.com/vbasic/.* You can also click Help and search on macros. This takes you to a Help section Microsoft has included on troubleshooting the recording and running of macros.

When editing macros is it possible to add new steps or operations, or am I limited to simply correcting problems?

 No. You can add anything you want to your macros. You simply need to know enough about Visual Basic to add the functions to your macros. Type the appropriate commands to add the steps or tasks you want to perform.

When editing macros, is it possible to get the macro to perform step-by-step to see exactly how it is performing?

 Yes. In the edit screen click Debug ➪ Step Into or press F8 to step through your macro.

Can running macros ever present a problem?

 Yes. Because macros are written in Visual Basic they can be fairly powerful tools. Some less than scrupulous programmers have used Visual Basic to create what are called "macro viruses." Macro viruses are Visual Basic counterparts to computer viruses, and can potentially cause problems. Always make sure you are running an antivirus program that checks for macro viruses.

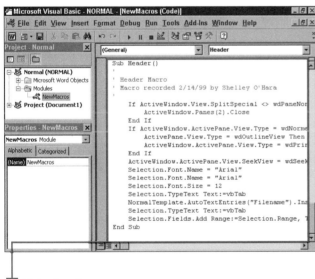

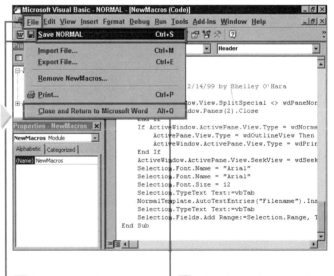

4 Make the changes you want to make in your macro.

5 Click File ➪ Save Normal to save your changes.

6 Click File ➪ Close and Return to Microsoft Word.

ORGANIZE MACROS

Word includes a tool, called Organizer, that you can use to help you organize and make better use of your macros. Organizer enables you to copy and/or transfer macros, toolbars, and template elements from one file or template to another.

You'll find the Organizer a great timesaver for transferring complex macros from one file or template to another. Transferring then lets you use the macros in other documents. With the Organizer, you can copy or transfer a macro without having to re-record or re-enter the macro by hand.

Start by opening the document with the macro and the document to which you want to copy the macro.

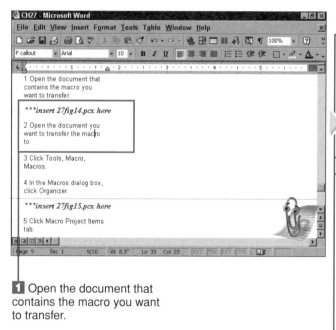

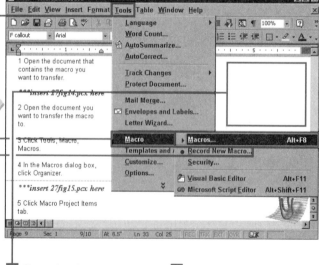

1 Open the document that contains the macro you want to transfer.

2 Open the document to which you want to transfer the macro.

3 Click Tools ⇨ Macro ⇨ Macros.

4 In the Macros dialog box, click Organizer.

TIPS

Besides transferring macros, what else can I use the Organizer for?

If you saved your macros to toolbar buttons, you can use the Organizer to transfer the toolbar from one document to another.

What else can I use the Organizer for with regard to macros?

You can use the Organizer to rename or delete your macros. Select the macro, and then click Delete to delete a macro or Rename to rename. If you click Delete, you are prompted to confirm the deletion. If you click Rename, type the new name and click OK.

Can I use the Organizer to transfer macros from one template to another?

Yes. Just select the templates you want to use in the Organizer and you can copy, rename, and delete macros just as if you were working with them in documents.

Is there anything else for which I can use the Organizer?

You can also use the Organizer to transfers style definitions from documents or templates to other documents or templates.

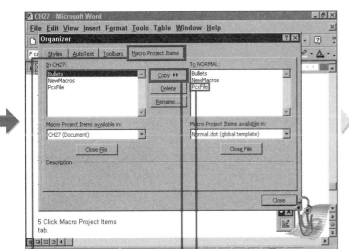

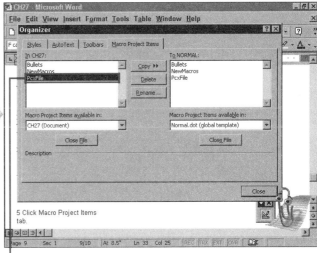

5 Click the Macro Project Items tab.

6 Highlight the macro you want to transfer from the column on the right.

7 Click Copy.

■ The macro you selected is copied to the designated document.

Troubleshooting Word Problems

FIX EDITING PROBLEMS

Problem: I can't move past a certain spot in the document.

The end of the document is marked by a short vertical line. You cannot move past this spot. If you try to click beyond this spot, nothing happens.

Problem: I deleted text by mistake.

If you delete text by mistake, click the Undo button or select Edit ⇨ Undo Clear to undo the deletion. You can also undo formatting and other editing changes.

Problem: Text started disappearing when I started typing.

Word normally is in Insert mode—that is, new text is inserted when you type. You can also use Overtype mode. In this mode, old text is overwritten as you type. You may have accidentally switched to Overtype mode by pressing the Insert key. If you see OVR in the status bar, press the Insert key on the keyboard to return to Insert mode.

Another reason is if you have scrolled to the right. The text doesn't really disappear, but it may appear to do so. Simply scroll back to the left.

Problem: The text I type is in ALL CAPS.

If you type text and it is in ALL CAPS, you most likely pressed the Caps Lock key by accident. Press this key again to turn off Caps Lock. If necessary, you can use the Format, Change Case command to change the case of selected text (or press Shift+F3).

Problem: Text wasn't inserted in the right spot when I started typing.

Remember that the insertion point indicates where text will be added, and the mouse pointer indicates the location of the mouse pointer. They

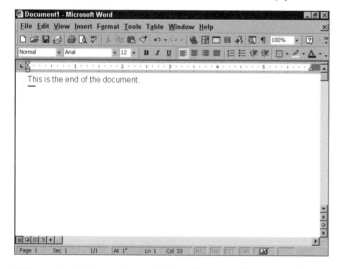

This marker indicates the end of the document. You cannot click past this point.

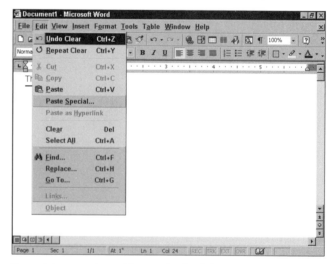

If you delete text by accident, undo the deletion by selecting Edit ⇨ Undo or by clicking the Undo button.

can be in two different spots. If you point to the spot where you want to add text, but don't click to move the insertion point, you don't move the insertion point. Be sure to point and click.

Problem: I thought I was selecting text, but somehow the text got moved.

If you select text, release the mouse button, and then try to drag the text to extend the selection, Word thinks you want to move the selected text. This feature is called drag-and-drop editing. If you see a different mouse pointer (a box with an arrow), you know that you are moving text. You can undo the move by clicking the Undo button.

If you have this same problem a lot, you may want to turn off drag-and-drop editing. To do so, open the Tools menu and select the Options command. Click the Edit tab. Uncheck the Drag-and-drop text editing checkbox.

Problem: I want to paste text, but the Paste command is grayed out.

Before you can paste text, you must first cut or copy something. If the Paste command is unavailable, it means you have not yet cut or copied something to the clipboard.

Problem: I see red squiggly lines under some words.

Word automatically checks your spelling as you type. If a word is

underlined with a red, curvy line, it means Word thinks the word is misspelled. You can see alternative spellings for such a word by right-clicking it and then selecting the correct spelling. See Chapter 5 for more help on checking spelling.

Problem: I see green squiggly lines under some words and phrases.

Word also automatically checks the grammar in your document. Word uses a green, curvy line to point out what it thinks may be grammatical errors. You can display suggested corrections by right-clicking the highlighted word or phrase. For more information on checking grammar, see Chapter 5.

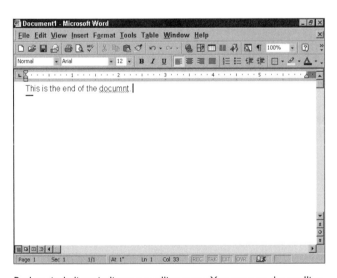

Red squiggly lines indicate a spelling error. You can run the spelling checker to check the document.

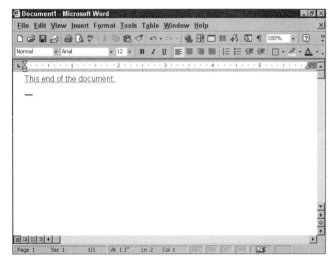

Green squiggly lines indicate a possible grammatical error. You can run the grammar checker to fix the error (or correct the mistake yourself).

FIX FORMATTING MISTAKES

Problem: My paragraph formatting changed unexpectedly.

The formatting for a paragraph is stored with the paragraph mark. Each time you press Enter, the paragraph options for that paragraph are carried down to the next paragraph. If you delete the paragraph marker, the paragraph takes on the formatting of the

following paragraph. If something bizarre happens, try undoing the change using Edit ⇨ Undo. If you have trouble visualizing where the paragraph marks appear, you can display them by clicking the Show/Hide ¶ button.

Problem: I created a bulleted list, but now I can't get rid of the bullets.

When you press Enter within a bulleted list, Word adds another list item. To turn off bullets, click the Bullets button again.

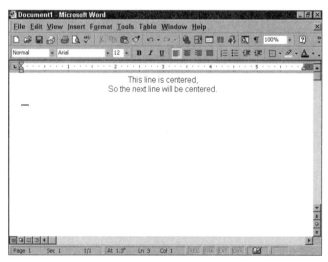

Word carries down the formatting from the paragraph above it when you press Enter.

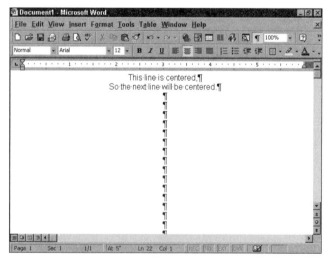

If you have trouble with the paragraph marks, display them by clicking the Show/Hide ¶ button.

Problem: I can't delete a number from the numbered list.

If you create a numbered list, Word adds the numbers automatically. You cannot delete them because they are fields. To turn off the numbers, select the paragraph(s) and then click the Numbering button.

Problem: Word starts making formatting changes without me selecting any command.

Word's AutoFormat feature makes some formatting corrections as you type. For example, if you type an asterisk and press Tab, Word creates a bulleted list. To review or change which formatting changes are made, select Tools ⇨ AutoCorrect. Click the AutoFormat As You Type tab. You see the AutoFormat changes that are made automatically as you type.

To turn off an option, uncheck its checkbox. To turn on an option, check the checkbox.

Problem: I can't see the header (or footer) I created.

In Normal view, you won't see your headers or footers. To view these items, change to Print Layout view or Print Preview.

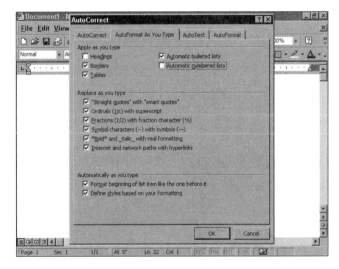

If formatting changes are made unexpectedly, review the options on the AutoFormat As You Type tab.

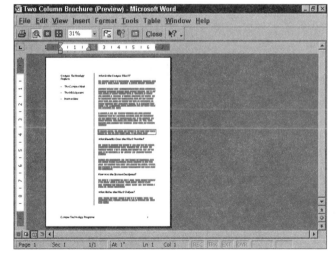

Some formatting features do not appear in Normal view. Change to Print Layout or Print Preview (shown here) to see the change.

FIX VIEWING PROBLEMS

Problem: Everything on my screen disappeared.

If everything on the screen disappears, you may have selected the Full Screen view, which hides the title bar, menu bar, toolbars, and status bar and just displays a big white area for typing text. If this happens, click the Close Full Screen button to return to Normal view.

Problem: I don't see any documents onscreen.

If you see a gray background and the menu and toolbars, it means you do not have a document open. You can choose to create a new document using File ➪ New or open an existing document using File ➪ Open.

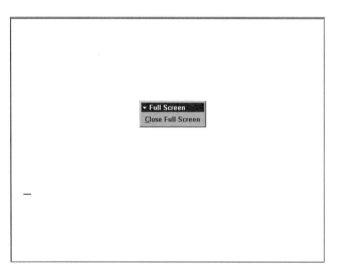

If all the toolbars have disappeared, you may be in Full Screen view. Click the Close Full Screen button.

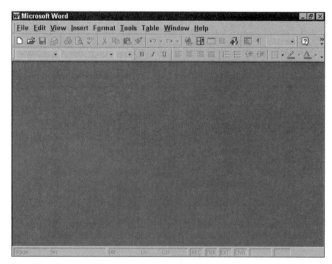

If you don't see a document, you have closed all the documents. Open a document or create a new one using the File menu.

Problem: I see arrows, dots in between each word, and some other weird mark at the end of each paragraph.

You can choose to display paragraph marks and space marks in your document. These elements do not print. To turn them on, click the Show/Hide ¶ button. To turn them off, click this button again.

Problem: My text looks really small (or really big), but I haven't changed the font.

If you have not made a change to the font size, but your text looks really big or really small, you probably have zoomed the document. Open the View menu, select the Zoom command, and check the zoom percentage. The normal zoom is 100 percent.

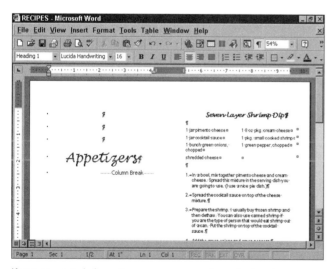

If you see weird characters onscreen, you have displayed nonprinting characters. Click the Show/Hide ¶ button to hide these characters.

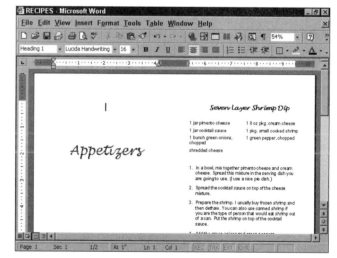

If the text size does not look right, check to be sure you have not zoomed the document.

FIX PRINTING PROBLEMS

Problem: I can't print.

If you have trouble printing, check the following things:

▶ Is the printer hooked up to your PC? Make sure the connections are tight.

▶ Is your printer plugged in? If it is plugged into a power strip, is it plugged in and turned on?

▶ Is the printer online and ready to print?

▶ Is the correct printer selected in the Print dialog box?

Problem: My printer isn't set up.

To use your printer, you must connect it to the PC and then set it up in Windows. You can use the Add Printer wizard to set up the printer. Click Start ⇨ Settings ⇨ Printers. Then double-click the Add Printer icon and follow the steps in the wizard.

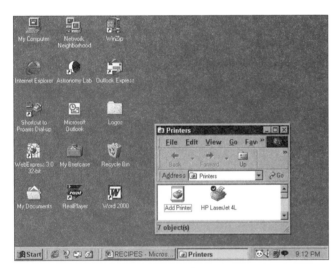

Before you can use your printer, you have to set it up in Windows. Use the Add Printer Wizard to lead you through the steps of adding a new printer.

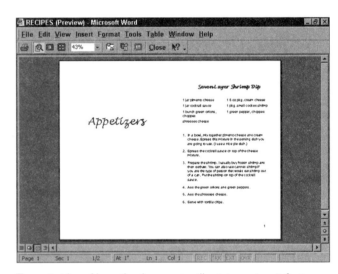

To get in idea of how the document will print, preview it first.

Problem: My document didn't print as expected.

Before printing, check the document using Print Preview. This gives you an idea of how the document will print on the page. You can get a better sense of items such as margins, headers, footers, borders, and other changes from Print Preview.

Problem: I want to cancel a print job.

You can cancel a print job by displaying the print queue. Then right-click the document you want to cancel and select Cancel Printing.

Problem: My printer is jammed or out of paper.

If your printer jams or is out of paper, you should see an error message onscreen. You can correct the problem and then resume printing.

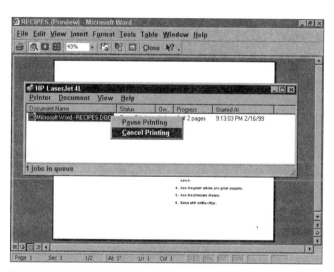

You can display the print queue and then cancel print jobs if needed.

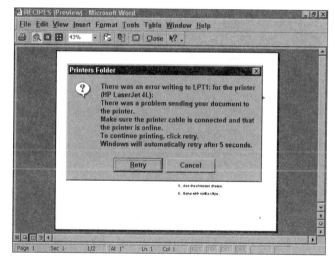

If something is wrong with the printer, you should get an error message. Correct the problem and then resume printing.

FIX TABLE, COLUMN, AND GRAPHIC PROBLEMS

Problem: I can't delete a table.

Deleting a table is tricky. You can't just drag across it and press the Delete key. Doing so deletes all the entries, but leaves the table grid. To delete the table, select Table ➪ Delete ➪ Table.

Problem: My table columns aren't the right size.

When you create a table using the Insert Table button, Word bases the column width on the size of the page margins and the number of columns you have. Each column is the same size. You can adjust the column width if necessary. Place the mouse pointer on the right border of the column you want to change. The pointer should look like two vertical lines with arrows on either side. Drag the border to resize the column width.

Problem: My table has borders, but I don't want them.

When you insert a table using the Insert Table button, Word adds a border around each cell. You may want to turn off this border. To do so, select the table using the Table ➪ Select ➪ Table command.

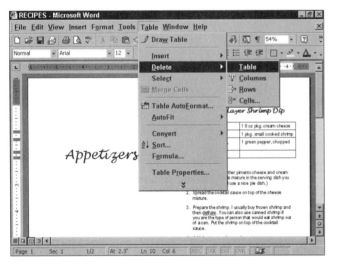

To delete a table, you have to use a special command. Use Table ➪ Delete ➪ Table.

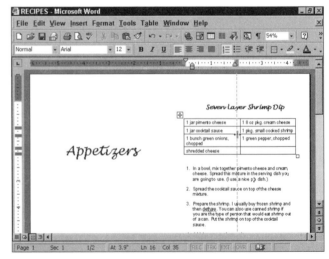

You can adjust the size of the table columns by dragging the border.

Click the down-arrow next to the Border button in the toolbar. Click the No border button. You can also use the Format ⇨ Borders and Shading command for more options.

Problem: Most of the Table commands are unavailable.

To access the Table commands, you must be within a table. Put the insertion point within the table and try again.

Problem: I don't see my columns side by side.

Columns are displayed side by side only in Print Layout view. You are probably in Normal view. To change to Print Layout view, open the View menu and select the Print Layout command.

Problem: I inserted a picture, but I can't see my text.

Sometimes the picture appears right on top of the text. (Sometimes the text flows around the picture —

usually part on top and bottom, but not on the sides of the picture.) To control how the text flows around the picture, double-click the object you want to change.

You see the Format Object (or AutoShape) dialog box. Select the Layout tab. You see the different options you can use for text wrapping. Select the wrapping style you want. The pictures of each option are pretty self-explanatory. Click the OK button. Word wraps the text accordingly.

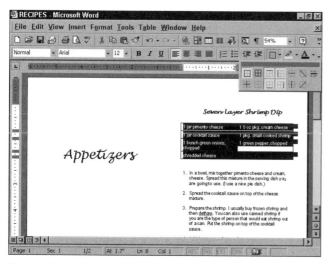

Change the borders of the table using the Borders button.

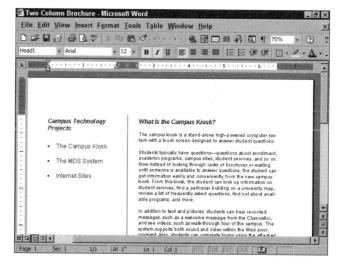

To see columns side by side, change to Print Layout view.

FIX MAIL MERGE PROBLEMS

Problem: My mail merge didn't work.

Check the following:

▶ Be sure your main document includes the appropriate merge fields to insert the data. If not, edit the main document and insert the fields. See Chapter 16 for information on editing a main document.

▶ If you need to edit the data source, display the Mail Merge Helper dialog box and click the Edit button under the Data source. Select the file name and then make any changes, as described in Chapter 16.

▶ The main document and data source must be associated. If that association is lost (for example, if you moved a document), you can

tell Word which data source to use. In the Mail Merge Helper dialog box, click the Get Data button and select Open Data Source. Select the data source file.

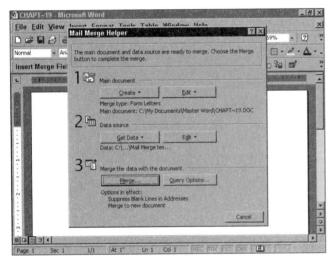

Use the Mail Merge helper to figure out which step is next, and to select to edit other files if needed.

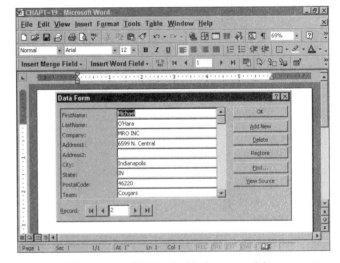

You can display the data form and add, change, or delete records.

Problem: Some features don't work as described here.

Word enables you to customize a lot of program options. For example, you can turn many of the features on and off. If something does not work as described, check the Options dialog box to see whether something has been changed. Chapter 26 covers customizing in more detail.

Problem: My macro didn't work.

If your macro did not work as expected, modify it by editing the various commands using Visual Basic. If you are not familiar with the macro commands, the easiest way is to re-record the macro and enter the same name. When prompted to replace the existing macro, select Yes. Chapter 27 covers macros in more detail.

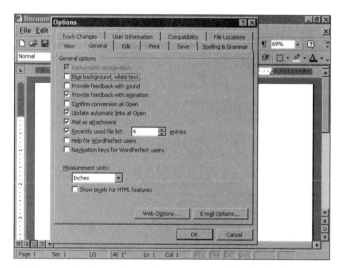

Review the Options tabs to change or reset defaults for how the program works.

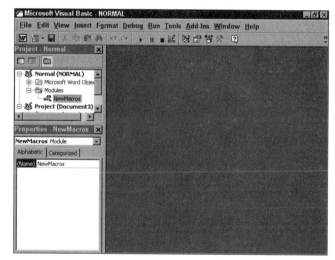

You can edit a macro you have created using the Microsoft Visual Basic Editor.

WHAT'S ON THE CD-ROM

The CD-ROM included with this book contains many useful files and programs. The disc also includes a version of the book that you can view and search using Adobe Acrobat Reader and several utility programs.

SYSTEM REQUIREMENTS

You can use this disc on any computer running Windows that has a CD-ROM drive. To get the most out of the items on the disc, you should have a 486 or Pentium computer with at least 32MB of RAM. You should have at least 200MB of free hard disk space and your system should be able to display at least 256 colors.

Use the My Computer or Windows Explorer window to display the contents of the CD-ROM.

Note: If you have trouble viewing the directory structure of the CD-ROM, or if the directory names are truncated (example: \directo~), your CD-ROM drive is currently using 16-bit drivers instead of the necessary 32-bit drivers. Please contact your CD-ROM drive vendor for information on upgrading the CD-ROM drivers.

INCLUDED SOFTWARE

The Programs folder on the CD-ROM contains 12 useful software applications. Before installing a program from this CD-ROM, you should close all other programs. To use most of the programs, you must accept the license agreement provided with the program. Make sure you read any Readme files provided with each program.

Sample Documents from the Book

You can find the sample documents used in this book in the folder named Sample Docs. Use these documents to follow the steps found in the chapters or to experiment with features. Most documents are named according to the chapter in which they are used.

PDF Version of the Book

The CD-ROM contains a version of this book that you can view and search using Adobe Acrobat Reader. You will find the PDF book files named by chapter in the folder named PDF Book. You cannot print the pages or copy text from the Acrobat files. A full and free version of Adobe Acrobat Reader 3.01 is also included on the disc. For information on how to view and search the PDF book, see the "Master Microsoft Word 2000 Visually on CD-ROM" section later in this appendix.

EarthLink Network Internet Sign-Up Offer

If you are not yet connected to the Internet, you can use the CD-ROM to set up an account and start using the EarthLink Network Internet service. You can set up your account to use Internet Explorer 4.0 or Netscape 4.5 as your Web browser.

Open the EarthLink folder on the CD-ROM. To install Microsoft Internet Explorer 4.0 and set up an Internet account, open the EarthLink MSIE4 folder. Double-click Setup.exe and then follow the instructions on your screen.

To install Netscape 4.5 and set up an Internet account, open the EarthLink Netscape folder. Double-click Setup.exe and then follow the instructions on your screen.

Adobe Acrobat Reader

Adobe Acrobat Reader enables you to view the PDF book files. To install Acrobat Reader, open the utilities folder on the CD-ROM, and then open the Acrobat Reader and Search folder. Double-click the Acrobat Reader.exe file and then follow the instructions on your screen.

Paint Shop Pro

Paint Shop Pro is a graphics program you can use to edit and create pictures. This disc contains version 5.01 of Paint Shop Pro. You may use the program free of charge for 30 days. If you wish to continue using the program, you must then purchase the licensed version.

In the Programs folder, open the Paint Shop Pro folder. To install the program, double-click Psp501ev.exe and then follow the instructions on your screen.

WinZip

WinZip compresses files to make it easier and faster to transfer information from one computer to another. This disc contains version 7.0 of WinZip. You may use the program free of charge for 21 days. If you wish to continue using the program, you must pay a registration fee.

In the Programs folder, open the WinZip folder. To install the program, double-click winzip70.exe and then follow the instructions on your screen.

Oil Change

You can have Oil Change find program updates on the Internet and install them on your computer. This disc contains a trial version of Oil Change. You must have an Internet connection to run Oil Change. During the setup process, you must register with the software manufacturer. If you do not register, you will not be able to run Oil Change.

In the Programs folder, open the Oil Change folder. To install the program, double-click ocsetup.exe and then follow the instructions on your screen.

First Aid

You can use First Aid to identify and solve problems with your computer.

This disc contains a time-limited trial version of First Aid.

In the Programs folder, open the First Aid folder. To install the program, double-click fasetup.exe and then follow the instructions on your screen.

CleanSweep

CleanSweep finds files that can be removed to free up space on your hard drive. This disc contains version 4.02 of CleanSweep. You may use the program free of charge for 15 days. If you wish to continue using the program, you must then purchase the licensed version.

In the Programs folder, open the CleanSweep folder. To install the program, double-click cs4trial.exe and then follow the instructions on your screen.

Norton Utilities

Norton Utilities includes several components to help you with computer maintenance tasks. This disc contains a trial version of Norton Utilities. If you wish to continue using the program, you must then purchase the licensed version.

In the Programs folder, open the Norton Utilities folder, double-click nu3_trybuy.exe and then follow the instructions on your screen.

TalkWorks Pro

You can use TalkWorks Pro to bring professional voice and fax messaging to your home or office.

This disc contains a trial version of TalkWorks Pro. If you wish to continue using the program, you must then purchase the licensed version.

In the Programs folder, open the TalkWorks Pro folder, double-click Twtrybuy.exe and then follow the instructions on your screen.

RealPlayer

RealPlayer speeds up the delivery of audio and video files from the Internet. This disc contains a full version of RealPlayer 5.0.

In the Programs folder, open the RealPlayer folder, double-click rp32_50.exe and then follow the instructions on your screen.

Winamp

Winamp is an audio player that enables you to play a variety of music file formats from the Internet, including the popular MP3 format. This disc contains version 2.09 of Winamp. You may use the program free of charge for 14 days. If you wish to continue using the program, you must register the software with Nullsoft Inc. and pay a registration fee.

In the Programs folder, open the Winamp folder, double-click winamp209.exe and then follow the instructions on your screen.

Master Microsoft Word 2000 Visually

You can view *Master Microsoft Word 2000 Visually* on your screen using the CD-ROM included with this book. The CD-ROM enables you to search the contents of the book for a specific word or phrase. The CD-ROM also provides a convenient way of keeping the book handy while traveling.

You must install Acrobat Reader on your computer before you can view the information on the CD-ROM.

This program is also provided on the CD-ROM. Acrobat Reader enables you to view Portable Digital Files (.pdf) files. These files can display books and magazines on your screen exactly as they appear in printed form.

To install Acrobat Reader, open the Utilities folder on the CD-ROM, and then open the Acrobat Reader with Search folder. Double-click the

rs32e301(1).exe file and then follow the instructions on your screen.

After Acrobat Reader is installed, you can view the contents of the book, found on the CD-ROM in the folder called Master Word 2000 Visually Acrobat Files. The contents are divided into six sections that correspond to the sections of the book. To view the contents of a section, double-click the section.

on CD-ROM

TIPS

Can I use an older version of Acrobat Reader to view the information on the CD-ROM?

Yes, but the latest version of Acrobat Reader offers more features, such as the ability to search all the sections at once.

How do I search all the sections on the CD-ROM at once?

You must first locate the index. While viewing the contents of the book, click the Search All button in the Acrobat Reader window. Click Indexes and then click Add. Click index.pdx, click Open, and then click OK. You only need to locate the index once. After locating the index, you can click the Search All button to search all the sections.

How can I speed up access to the information?

Copy the Master Word 2000 Visually Acrobat Files folder from the CD-ROM to your hard drive. Copying the folder to your hard drive helps speed up your searches.

Can I use Acrobat Reader for anything else?

Acrobat Reader is a popular and useful program. Many files available on the Web are designed to be viewed using Acrobat Reader. Look for files with the .pdf extension.

INDEX

INDEX

continued

INDEX

INDEX

INDEX

continued

INDEX

continued

INDEX

IDG Books Worldwide, Inc. End-User License Agreement

READ THIS. You should carefully read these terms and conditions before opening the software packet(s) included with this book ("Book"). This is a license agreement ("Agreement") between you and IDG Books Worldwide, Inc. ("IDGB"). By opening the accompanying software packet(s), you acknowledge that you have read and accept the following terms and conditions. If you do not agree and do not want to be bound by such terms and conditions, promptly return the Book and the unopened software packet(s) to the place you obtained them for a full refund.

1. **License Grant.** IDGB grants to you (either an individual or entity) a nonexclusive license to use one copy of the enclosed software program(s) (collectively, the "Software") solely for your own personal or business purposes on a single computer (whether a standard computer or a workstation component of a multiuser network). The Software is in use on a computer when it is loaded into temporary memory (RAM) or installed into permanent memory (hard disk, CD-ROM, or other storage device). IDGB reserves all rights not expressly granted herein.

2. **Ownership.** IDGB is the owner of all right, title, and interest, including copyright, in and to the compilation of the Software recorded on the disk(s) or CD-ROM ("Software Media"). Copyright to the individual programs recorded on the Software Media is owned by the author or other authorized copyright owner of each program. Ownership of the Software and all proprietary rights relating thereto remain with IDGB and its licensers.

3. Restrictions On Use and Transfer.

   (a) You may only (i) make one copy of the Software for backup or archival purposes, or (ii) transfer the Software to a single hard disk, provided that you keep the original for backup or archival purposes. You may not (i) rent or lease the Software, (ii) copy or reproduce the Software through a LAN or other network system or through any computer subscriber system or bulletin-board system, or (iii) modify, adapt, or create derivative works based on the Software.

   (b) You may not reverse engineer, decompile, or disassemble the Software. You may transfer the Software and user documentation on a permanent basis, provided that the transferee agrees to accept the terms and conditions of this Agreement and you retain no copies. If the Software is an update or has been updated, any transfer must include the most recent update and all prior versions.

4. **Restrictions On Use of Individual Programs.** You must follow the individual requirements and restrictions detailed for each individual program in Appendix B, "Master Microsoft Word 2000 Visually on CD-ROM," of this Book. These limitations are also contained in the individual license agreements recorded on the Software Media. These limitations may include a requirement that after using the program for a specified period of time, the user must pay a registration fee or discontinue use. By opening the Software packet(s), you will be agreeing to abide by the licenses and restrictions for these individual programs that are detailed in Appendix B, "Master Microsoft

Word 2000 Visually on CD-ROM," and on the Software Media. None of the material on this Software Media or listed in this Book may ever be redistributed, in original or modified form, for commercial purposes.

5. **Limited Warranty.**

(a) IDGB warrants that the Software and Software Media are free from defects in materials and workmanship under normal use for a period of sixty (60) days from the date of purchase of this Book. If IDGB receives notification within the warranty period of defects in materials or workmanship, IDGB will replace the defective Software Media.

(b) **IDGB AND THE AUTHOR OF THE BOOK DISCLAIM ALL OTHER WARRANTIES, EXPRESS OR IMPLIED, INCLUDING WITHOUT LIMITATION IMPLIED WARRANTIES OF MERCHANTABILITY AND FITNESS FOR A PARTICULAR PURPOSE, WITH RESPECT TO THE SOFTWARE, THE PROGRAMS, THE SOURCE CODE CONTAINED THEREIN, AND/OR THE TECHNIQUES DESCRIBED IN THIS BOOK. IDGB DOES NOT WARRANT THAT THE FUNCTIONS CONTAINED IN THE SOFTWARE WILL MEET YOUR REQUIREMENTS OR THAT THE OPERATION OF THE SOFTWARE WILL BE ERROR FREE.**

(c) This limited warranty gives you specific legal rights, and you may have other rights that vary from jurisdiction to jurisdiction.

6. **Remedies.**

(a) IDGB's entire liability and your exclusive remedy for defects in materials and workmanship shall be limited to replacement of the Software Media, which may be returned to IDGB with a copy of your receipt at the following address: Software Media Fulfillment Department, Attn.: *Master Microsoft Word 2000 Visually*, IDG Books Worldwide, Inc., 7260 Shadeland Station, Ste. 100, Indianapolis, IN 46256, or call 1-800-762-2974. Please allow three to four weeks for delivery. This Limited Warranty is void if failure of the Software Media has resulted from accident, abuse, or misapplication. Any replacement Software Media will be warranted for the remainder of the original warranty period or thirty (30) days, whichever is longer.

(b) In no event shall IDGB or the author be liable for any damages whatsoever (including without limitation damages for loss of business profits, business interruption, loss of business information, or any other pecuniary loss) arising from the use of or inability to use the Book or the Software, even if IDGB has been advised of the possibility of such damages.

(c) Because some jurisdictions do not allow the exclusion or limitation of liability for consequential or incidental damages, the above limitation or exclusion may not apply to you.

7. **U.S. Government Restricted Rights.** Use, duplication, or disclosure of the Software by the U.S. Government is subject to restrictions stated in paragraph (c)(1)(ii) of the Rights in Technical Data and Computer Software clause of DFARS 252.227-7013, and in subparagraphs (a) through (d) of the Commercial Computer — Restricted Rights clause at FAR 52.227-19, and in similar clauses in the NASA FAR supplement, when applicable.

8. **General.** This Agreement constitutes the entire understanding of the parties and revokes and supersedes all prior agreements, oral or written, between them and may not be modified or amended except in a writing signed by both parties hereto that specifically refers to this Agreement. This Agreement shall take precedence over any other documents that may be in conflict herewith. If any one or more provisions contained in this Agreement are held by any court or tribunal to be invalid, illegal, or otherwise unenforceable, each and every other provision shall remain in full force and effect.

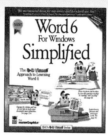

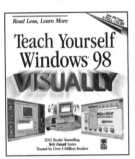

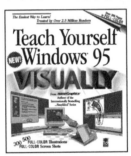

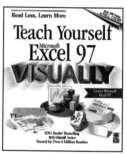

Explore your world

GET INTERNET ACCESS FROM EARTHLINK SPRINT.
WE'LL GIVE YOU TWO WEEKS FREE TO TRY IT OUT!

Get connected now to online tutorials, email and newsgroups, banking, shopping, and countless resources on the World Wide Web! EarthLink™ Sprint® delivers the world at your fingertips with the nation's #1-rated Internet access.

Check out these unbeatable member benefits:

• Unlimited Internet access at speeds up to 56K

• More local access numbers nationwide than any other ISP

• Free, reliable email

• 6MB of webspace for your own Web site

• A fully customizable Personal Start Page℠

• 24/7 toll-free customer service and tech support

• Free subscription to *bLink*™, EarthLink's member magazine

• Free new user's guide, "Getting the Most Out of the Internet"

• Free software and browsers, and much more!

Call today!
1-800-EARTHLINK
Mention Deal #4000-37102

EarthLink™

Sprint®

Take advantage of this IDG Books special offer!

CD-ROM INSTALLATION INSTRUCTIONS

The CD-ROM accompanying this book is compatible only with Windows. All of the software included on the CD-ROM is contained in separate folders listed by company name. To access the software, insert the CD-ROM into your CD-ROM drive, and then double-click the My Computer icon on your desktop (or access your CD-ROM drive through Windows Explorer). In the My Computer window, double-click the CD-ROM icon. The CD-ROM window opens on your desktop. To install and run the individual programs, open the folder of your choice, double-click the installer icon, and follow the prompts.

For more information about CD-ROM contents, please see Appendix B, "Master Microsoft Word 2000 Visually on CD-ROM."

MICROSOFT PRODUCT WARRANTY AND SUPPORT DISCLAIMER

The Microsoft program was reproduced by IDG Books Worldwide, Inc. under a special arrangement with Microsoft Corporation. For this reason, IDG Books Worldwide, Inc. is responsible for the product warranty and for support. If your CD-ROM is defective, please return it to IDG Books Worldwide, Inc., which will arrange for its replacement. PLEASE DO NOT RETURN IT TO MICROSOFT CORPORATION. Any product support will be provided, if at all, by IDG Books Worldwide, Inc. PLEASE DO NOT CONTACT MICROSOFT CORPORATION FOR PRODUCT SUPPORT. End users of this Microsoft program shall not be considered "registered owners" of a Microsoft product and therefore shall not be eligible for upgrades, promotions or other benefits available to "registered owners" of Microsoft products.